AFTER OBAMA

After Obama

African American Politics in a Post-Obama Era

Edited by
Todd C. Shaw,
Robert A. Brown, and
Joseph P. McCormick II

NEW YORK UNIVERSITY PRESS
New York

NEW YORK UNIVERSITY PRESS
New York
www.nyupress.org

References to internet websites (URLs) were accurate at the time of writing. Neither the author nor New York University Press is responsible for URLs that may have expired or changed since the manuscript was prepared.

Library of Congress Cataloging-in-Publication Data
Names: Shaw, Todd Cameron, editor. | Brown, Robert A., 1963– editor. |
McCormick, Joseph P., II, editor.
Title: After Obama : African American politics in a post-Obama era /
edited by Todd C. Shaw, Robert A. Brown, and Joseph P. McCormick II.
Description: New York : New York University Press, 2020. |
Includes bibliographical references and index.
Identifiers: LCCN 2020012642 | ISBN 9781479807277 (cloth) | ISBN 9781479818037
(paperback) | ISBN 9781479821976 (ebook) | ISBN 9781479896578 (ebook)
Subjects: LCSH: Obama, Barack. | Obama, Barack—Influence. |
African Americans—Politics and government—21st century. |
United States—Politics and government—2009–2017.
Classification: LCC E907 .A35 2020 | DDC 320.973089/96073—dc23
LC record available at https://lccn.loc.gov/2020012642

New York University Press books are printed on acid-free paper, and their binding materials are chosen for strength and durability. We strive to use environmentally responsible suppliers and materials to the greatest extent possible in publishing our books.

Manufactured in the United States of America

10 9 8 7 6 5 4 3 2 1

Also available as an ebook

To the memory of my father and aunt—
James Curtis and Annie Vivian
(Todd Shaw)

To my daughters—
Elena and Isabela
(Robert Brown)

To the three most important women in my life—
Helen, Janet, and JaiSun
(Joseph McCormick II)

CONTENTS

PART II. PUBLIC POLICIES

Introduction

There's No Such Thing as a "Black President"

TODD C. SHAW, ROBERT A. BROWN, AND
JOSEPH P. MCCORMICK II

By law I can't pass laws saying I'm just helping black folks. I am
president of the entire United States.
—President Barack Obama, *New York Times*, February 9, 2010

When we began this journey coming on ten years now, we said
this was not about us. It wasn't about me. It wasn't about Michelle. It wasn't just to be a black president, or the president of
black America. We understood the power of the symbol. We
know what it means for a generation of children, of all races, to
see folks like us in the White House. (Applause.)
—President Barack Obama, 46th Annual Congressional Black
Caucus Foundation Awards Dinner, September 18, 2016

Obama is expected to lead black America to the Promised Land
not as a voice of opposition to the government, demanding it
act on behalf of the poor and the outcast, but as the commander
in chief of the American empire.
—Fredrick Harris, *The Price of the Ticket*

What the hell do you have to lose?
—Donald Trump, Republican presidential candidate's appeal to
African American voters, August 19, 2016

With all the political turmoil that Black Americans and all Americans have endured under the very conservative and often erratic presidency of Donald Trump (including a 2020 COVID-19 pandemic and racial as well as economic unrest), many aspects of the presidency of Barack Obama feel like distant memories. We contend, however, that now, years after the Obama administration, it is very important to be sanguine about the legacy—the contributions and problems—Obama's presidency left for Black politics now and well into the future. Stated differently, this book provides a substantive accounting and examination of the many political and policy gains African Americans did and did not have to lose as Trump succeeded Obama.

Near the end of Barack Obama's presidency in 2016, Virginia McLaurin expressed an exuberance that reflected some of the joy and hope African Americans felt at the beginning of Obama's presidency in 2009. Much of this joy and hope turned into a disheartened fear and anger with the election of Donald J. Trump as Obama's successor. Still, during McLaurin's audience with Barack and Michelle Obama at the White House, though she was a 106-year-old African American woman, she literally danced as spryly as a young girl while laughing and holding the hands of the president of the United States and the First Lady.

"I tell you, I am so happy," McLaurin declared. "A black president, yay, and his black wife!"

The Obamas joined McLaurin in her gleeful dance. She had previously stated in a letter to the president, "I've never met a President. I didn't think I would live to see a Colored President. I was born in the South and didn't think it would happen."[1] For all of the understandable personal joy and racial symbolism of this moment—after all, it was Black History Month—ironically, McLaurin later had some difficulty in getting an identification card to ensure she could vote in the District of Columbia's 2016 elections. Initially, photo identification was not a requirement in the district. But due to Republican-led electoral law changes across the nation, it became a measure its critics considered the newest form of Black voter disenfranchisement in several states, including McLaurin's native South Carolina. McLaurin's struggle to ensure she could vote despite her delightful encounter story with the first "Black president" is emblematic of the ongoing barriers confronting

African American politics despite the hope and promise of the Obama era. When Barack Obama delivered his farewell address on January 10, 2017, in his adopted hometown of Chicago, there were African American members of the audience who visibly wept. They likely feared that the reforms of the Obama era would be swept away if the Trump administration and a then Republican-dominated Congress and Supreme Court were successful in implementing an extremely conservative agenda. Many of these fears have been realized.[2]

Poignant moments such as the McLaurin story offer glimpses of how African Americans invested enormous hope in and had great expectations for the Obama presidency. In his 2012 book entitled *The Price of the Ticket: Barack Obama and the Rise and the Decline of Black Politics*, Fredrick Harris argues that despite the historic nature of Obama's presidency, as the first Black person to hold that high office, Black politics and Black people invested too much racial pride in his leadership and did not give enough political scrutiny to his race-neutral, centrist policy approach.[3] From this view, the Obama administration's policies produced insufficient returns to African American communities, given that they were a constituency indispensable to Obama's 2008 and 2012 electoral victories. Harris believes deracialization—or what Charles Hamilton once saw as a limited strategy of Black candidates de-emphasizing race—became a vital feature of Obama's rise to power. "When you combine Obama's race-neutral campaign strategy," Harris states, "with his light-skin privilege and biracial heritage [white American and black Kenyan], Obama was essentially a perfect model for a 'deracialized' presidential candidate." According to Harris, an unfortunate "wink and nod" assumption emerged, whereby Black political leaders and citizens implicitly agreed that Obama's race-neutral electoral strategy was necessary if he was going to allay White voters' fears enough to be elected. But once elected, Obama was implicitly expected to address a Black agenda.[4]

The purpose of this edited volume is to give a critical, scholarly examination of the impact the eight years of the Obama presidency—2008 to 2016—had upon African American politics, mindful that this legacy and these politics were followed by a Trump era. We do this by examining various Obama constituencies and public policies so to project the course of Black politics *After Obama*. We define *African Ameri-*

can politics in two ways. We primarily define it as a *practice*. It is the collective use of political power by various African American / Black communities[5] to attain what they perceive as group empowerment, group interests, self-determination, and/or full citizenship rights, as well as equal opportunity.[6] Often, individual perceptions of race and racism compel an agreement among a majority of African Americans as to the candidates and policies they should support. However, African Americans are also widely diverse and have intersecting identities and interests shaped by differences such as gender, class, sexual orientation, and religiosity (to name a few).[7] We secondarily define Black politics as a field of research or *study*. It is a body of knowledge that directs our analytical attention to both historic and contemporary examples of varied African American efforts to challenge institutional racism, intersecting oppressions, and their vestiges. As such, this body of knowledge leads us to focus on the behavior of individuals, groups, and institutions in a wide array of political and policy-making arenas.[8] This volume will train its analytical sights mostly on the *practice* of African American politics, but we will briefly discuss the post-Obama implications for the *study* of African American politics. (See the concluding chapter.)

As implied by the opening quotes by Obama and Harris, we begin with the premise that, to date, *there is no such thing as a Black president*.[9] Obama clearly self-identified as African American, so this claim partly is a semantic device that is intended to provoke debate. But from a conceptual standpoint, we mean that neither the current American racial order nor the nature of Obama's presidency and leadership style have resulted in an American chief executive able and/or willing to freely, as well as more fully, advance the substantive political interests of African American / Black communities. First, even after eight years of an Obama presidency (and possibly in reaction to it), the conservative racial order of the United States remains one whereby actors within the dominant, governing institutions of this nation—from the presidency to the local police—are inherently influenced by systemic racism, White supremacy, and/or White nationalism despite any use of race-neutral rhetoric in public statements. We borrow from Desmond King and Rogers Smith, who explain that "racial institutional orders" can range from being "white supremacist" to "egalitarian transformative" in nature. They are "durable alliances of political actors, activist groups, and governing institutions united by their agreement on the central racial issue of their time, which their conflicts help to define." In short, they "define the range of political opportunities open to political actors."[10] Although not unitary or without strong competing claims, we presume that the current governing alliance leans more toward the White supremacist pole. Therefore, many of its actors and institutions implicitly devalue the citizenship and life opportunities of citizens and residents of color—most especially African Americans / Blacks and Latinos—at the expense of White constituencies. The election and support for the presidency of Donald Trump is the most visceral and public evidence for our claim.[11]

Second, it is true Barack Hussein Obama is a brilliant and eloquent man of Black-White biracial ancestry who ethnically self-identifies as African American. We believe he had an extraordinary presidency that ushered in a number of progressive reforms and a notable recovery of a postrecession economy. But Obama's identification with and connection to Black / African American communities were still delimited by him being president of a center-right, majority-White nation. In this introductory chapter, we argue that, as president, Obama constitutionally, juridically, and politically was not—and could not accurately be viewed as—a leader of the African American community. This is despite the enormous symbolic significance African Americans rightly attached to his being president. In fact, we outline several fundamental reasons why Obama—possibly like other Black elected officials who have juridically represented predominantly White constituencies (e.g., US senators or state governors)—was not a *Black politician* or someone who viewed himself as a spokesman of Black policy interests. He was instead a *politician who happened to be Black* or was someone who argued he was responsive to Black policy interests among many others. We agree with Harris that President Obama, like all his predecessors, should have been pressured by Black interest groups to be more accountable to the needs of African American citizens, even while it is the responsibility of others to advocate a so-called Black agenda. Even with the postrecession economic progress experienced under the Obama presidency, African Americans, in comparison to Whites, still suffered from a range of racial disparities regarding health, wealth, incarceration, and employment opportunities, among other inequalities. These remain evident today.[12] Table I.1 details a number of Black-White racial disparities that persisted amid notable

TABLE I.1. Black-White Racial Disparities

Category	2005	2009	2016
Equality Index	72.9%	71.2%	72.2%
Economics	56.8%	57.4%	56.2%
Health	76.2%	76.8%	79.4%
Education	77.2%	77.0%	77.4%
Social Justice	67.5%	57.2%	60.8%
Civic Engagement	108.1%	97.6%	100.6%

National Urban League's Equality Index, 2005–2016
Source: 2016 State of Black America—Locked Out: Education, Jobs & Justice; Black-White Equality Index.
www.stateofblackamerica.org

progress. It is taken from the National Urban League's 2016 *State of Black America*, and it is their Black-White equality index in which they create a number of parity ratios comparing Black progress relative to the progress of White counterparts. Across the dimensions of economics, health, education, social justice, and civic engagement, it reveals that the Obama presidency helped Black America to witness modest gains (despite a Great Recession between roughly 2008 and 2009). But this did not lead to fundamentally closing Black-White racial disparities.[13] In the concluding chapter, we reference Obama's argument that it is not reasonable to expect his single presidential administration to have done so.

In this chapter, we extend upon Harris's thesis in theorizing that underlying the "wink and nod" politics are concepts we call *inverted linked fate* (or *racial infatuation*) and the *inclusionary dilemma*. Unlike the standard common fate or "linked fate" concept that presumes the individual uses an assessment of the group's well-being as a proxy for her own well-being, we posit that "inverted linked fate" is the belief of many African Americans that their group well-being was tied to the individual political well-being of one leader—in this case Obama. He was admittedly the object of implicit bias and White racial vitriol—from racist caricatures of him on Tea Party signs to charges that he was a socialist and a dreaded "Muslim."[14] Thus, an inverted linked fate in such a highly racialized context muted Black calls for political accountability to Black group interests because many African Americans were protective of Obama's perceived racial legacy and infatuated with the symbolism of his leadership. Again, what further complicated this dynamic is that Obama's presidency resided within a larger racial order—a configuration of prevailing political alliances—that, in his case, colluded with a color blindness and postracial liberalism.[15] The analyses of Melanye Price, Daniel Gillion, and others have demonstrated that Obama frequently stuck to a political script that avoided discussions of race or artfully used a language of racial transcendence. But Obama was a complex political actor who, due in part to his African heritage, had his own ethnic attachments—his own linked fate—with African Americans as well as other Black people in the African diaspora. It is also likely that after his 2012 reelection, Obama felt he had greater political license to expound upon issues that implicated race and racism in ways he politically could not or did not prior to his reelection. But Price clearly indicates how Obama's unique biracial heritage and brand of pragmatism permitted him to be an effective "race whisperer" who strategically tailored his racial message, depending upon the audience in question.[16]

It was precisely because Obama's ethnic attachment to African Americans did not overcome the clear constraints of the US presidency as well as his embrace of universalist policy pragmatism that he had an *inclusionary dilemma*. Joseph McCormick describes this as the conundrum that African Americans whose election to office rests on a plurality or small majority of Black votes may want to advocate certain policy goals that meet the substantive political or economic needs of their Black constituents. However, these officials perceive a host of political and institutional barriers to such advocacy. Often, they have to seek election or reelection within moderate to conservative political contexts. Simply invoking race—no matter how well intentioned—carries the cost of being labeled as divisive. There certainly were incidents that reinforced Obama's racial reluctance or reticence, such as the incendiary assertion of former Fox News commentator Glenn Beck that President Obama "hates all white people." For several reasons, Obama was loath to directly address the racist implications of the "birther movement" led by Donald Trump, who argued Obama was a not a native-born US citizen. Later, Obama attempted to deflect the birthers' preposterous claim by presenting his birth certificate: a level of validation no other US president was compelled to provide. Another example was the ire sparked by Obama's casual but candid press conference remark that the White police officers who arrested Harvard University's African American studies professor Henry Louis Gates for trying to break into his own home were acting "stupidly." It prompted a deflation of the issue by Obama agreeing to a White House "beer garden summit" between Vice President Joe Biden, Gates, the White arresting officer, and himself.[17]

In this volume, we apply the concepts of inverted linked fate and the inclusionary dilemma to the Obama presidency. Several authors within this volume properly note that Obama and his administration employed a rhetoric and advocated policies that were framed by political respectability (e.g., Black fatherhood responsibility with a more secondary consideration of Black women) as well as neoliberalism (e.g., private investments to solve inner-city poverty). It is also true that Obama made various eloquent and admirable admissions, most especially near or in his second term, as to how race still fundamentally matters in American society. There were members of his cabinet, such as Attorney General Eric Holder, who arguably went even further in their antiracist rhetoric than did Obama, conceivably with the president's blessings.[18] We expand upon Harris's argument in that we place Obama's presidency into its larger institutional and racial-order context and thus imply the racial trajectory of his legacy in the post-Obama era.

A Preview: Our Conceptual Framework

For the purposes of clarity, we first present a conceptual framework that we unpack in this chapter. We do this to provide the reader with a set of reference points to understand our conceptions of race, the Obama presidency, and Black politics. Along the top of the figure I.1 is the current "US Racial Order." To reiterate, it is the prevailing governing configuration that determines racial power relations and the political opportunity structure. It is arranged along an ideological axis from left to right.[19] On the left side of our diagram is "Racial Liberalism," or the prospects for a racial egalitarianism that is inclusiveness of Black people and their policy interests. On the right side is "Racial Conservatism," or the threats of White supremacy that politically exclude Black people and their policy preferences or interests. Because Whites remain politically and economically dominant and lean toward racial conservatism

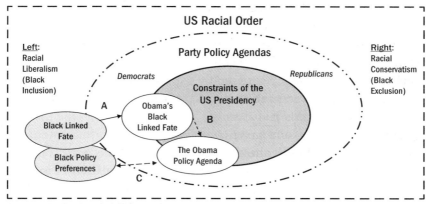

A = Inverted Linked Fate (Racial Infatuation); B = Inclusionary Dilemma;
C = Presidential Advocacy vs. Accountability Dilemma

Figure I.1. US racial order: Race, the Obama presidency, and Black politics.

(as partly evident for the 58 percent of White voters who reported voting for Trump in 2016)[20], most US political institutions, including the presidency, still lean toward racial moderation and/or conservatism and often neglect or exclude Black policy preferences or interests.[21] This racial order frames the breadth of the policy spaces and in turn the agendas of the major political parties. The median Democrat leans toward the ideological and racial left of center, and the median Republican leans toward the ideological and racial right of center. As part of a constitutional system philosophically grounded in the principle of "limited government," there are juridical and political constraints upon the US presidency that tend to serve the ends of the racial status quo—i.e., racial moderation or conservatism.[22] As the first US president to self-identify as African American, Barack Obama occupied a racially and ideologically unique space among US presidents. We reiterate that he inherently was not a Black leader, for as US head of state, commander in chief, and chief executive, he had to claim to represent all citizens and could not solely or predominantly represent African Americans. Besides, Obama was ideologically a policy pragmatist and espoused moderate, left-of-center beliefs when it came to race and race-related policies. At the same time, he had an apparent ethnic and/or racial self-identification with the Black/African American community and thus at least a limited "linked fate." On several occasions, his linked fate informed his presidential style, his rhetoric or leadership affect, as well as his cultural use of the presidency as a bully pulpit, more so in his second term than in his first term.[23] But again there were both ideological as well as juridical and political constraints upon him as president, and thus, there was a clear gap between his expressed attachments to fellow African Americans versus the policy agenda or the proposals and outputs of his administration.

African Americans as a larger community share a certain amount of common or group linked fate among each other. This is partly because they occupy a unique position in a racial regime premised on a historic discrimination against them as well as the relative exclusion of their interests and preferences from its policy arenas. However—and we cannot stress this enough—Black people in the US embraced an enormous diversity of perceived individual linked fates and policy preferences as shaped by cross-cutting cleavages, like ethnic/national origins, class, gender, region, age, religiosity, sexual orientation differences, ideology, and others. But here, we are referring to the median range for African Americans, especially voters and/or adults. We do assume that "Black Policy Preferences" are partly informed by a sense of "Black Linked Fate" and vice versa; thus, the reason why those two ovals intersect in figure I.1.[24]

Overall, our figure I.1 diagram illustrates the complicated relationships that existed between "Black Policy Preferences," "Black Linked Fate," "Obama's Black Linked Fate," and the "Obama Administration's Policy Agenda." The relationship between "Black Linked Fate" and "Obama's Linked Fate" (arrow A) is what we label "Inverted Linked Fate" or "Racial Infatuation." Obama enjoyed a very high approval rating among African Americans throughout his presidency, with an average of 89 percent in the first term and 87 percent in the second term. (See table I.2.) The same cannot be said with regards to his approval ratings among Whites, with an average of 42 percent during the first term and 36 percent during the second term. In fact, the average margin of White-to-Black job approval disagreement widened between the two terms from a 47 percent margin to a 51 percent margin. More on this later. We theorize that one way to explain his high Black approval ratings is that Blacks derived a great sense of ethnic/racial pride or symbolic satisfaction in seeing a fellow African American occupy the presidency and his

TABLE I.2. President Obama's Job Approval Ratings by Race, 2009–2017

Polling Period	Total	Overall	Whites	Black	Difference
Jan. 2–8, 2017	3563	55	44	91	−47
Dec. 5–11, 2016	3023	57	46	91	−45
Jun. 6–12, 2016	3546	53	41	90	−49
Jan. 4–10, 2016	3550	47	35	85	−50
Dec. 7–13, 2015	3554	45	33	87	−54
Jun. 8–14, 2015	3542	45	34	85	−51
Mar. 9–15, 2015	3543	47	35	88	−53
Jan. 5–11, 2015	3544	46	34	82	−48
Dec. 1–7, 2015	3042	43	32	82	−50
Jun. 2–8, 2014	3036	44	34	87	−53
Mar. 3–9, 2014	3045	43	31	88	−57
Jan. 2–5, 2014	2042	41	31	87	−56
Dec. 2–8, 2014	3050	41	30	89	−59
Jun. 3–9, 2013	3558	48	37	87	−50
Mar. 4–10, 2013	3563	49	38	87	−49
Jan. 7–13, 2013	3550	54	43	91	−48
Second Term Average		47	36	87	−51
Dec. 3–9, 2012	3637	50	39	92	−53
Jun. 4–10, 2012	3613	47	39	85	−46
Mar. 5–11, 2012	3632	48	40	90	−50
Jan. 2–8, 2012	3653	46	37	87	−50
Dec. 5–11, 2011	3665	43	34	86	−52
Jun. 6–12, 2011	3552	46	40	83	−43
Mar. 7–13, 2011	3593	47	39	90	−51
Jan. 3–9, 2011	3545	48	40	93	−53
Dec. 6–12, 2010	3089	45	36	84	−48
Jun. 7–13, 2010	3598	46	37	89	−52
Mar. 1–7, 2010	3547	49	41	91	−50
Jan. 11–17, 2010	3579	50	42	91	−49
Dec. 7–13, 2009	2577	49	41	89	−48
Jun. 1–7, 2009	3568	62	55	95	−40
Mar. 2–8, 2009	3572	62	55	96	−41
Jan. 19–25, 2009	2631	67	63	86	−23
First Term Average		50	42	89	−47

Source: Gallup Poll Selected Months, Gallup News Service. www.gallup.com

wife and family occupy the White House as First Lady and First Family. In fact, we contend African Americans inverted the linked fate relationship in defining their group well-being based upon what they perceived as the racial and political "well-being" of Obama, the individual, and/ or of his wife, Michelle, and family. Again, in figure I.1, this relationship was a strong one and thus the reason for the solid arrow.[25] As a secondary issue, Black inverted linked fate with Obama may have reinforced Obama's own sense of linked fate to the group. However, this edited volume is most concerned about the Obama presidency's impact upon Black politics as defined by Black constituencies and policy interests. At best, Obama's Black linked fate had only a small impact upon the broader policy agenda of his administration, especially as relevant to African American communities. Note that we argue both Obama's linked fate and his policy agenda partly exceeded the normal constraints of the US presidency—thus, the reason these ovals exceed the boundaries of the "Constraints of the US Presidency" oval. Some of what his administration stated it wanted to achieve and his ability to express his African American ethnic attachment was in excess of the traditional, symbolic, and juridical boundaries of the US presidency, though he may have culturally expanded the conventional boundaries of the presidential "bully pulpit," especially using the arts, music, and humor.[26] This is particularly true as framed by the "US Racial Order" and the frequent racist objections of White racial conservatives in the US Congress and elsewhere in the polity. Thus, this relationship (arrow B) is what we refer to as the "Inclusionary Dilemma" in that there is a clear gap between Obama being elected the so-called first Black president (a term we directly challenge) and his ability to expand the polity to be more inclusive of Black preferences or interests. For this reason, we use a very dotted line in between the constructs of "Obama's Black Linked Fate" and "The Obama Policy Agenda."

Lastly, the relationship between the Obama administration's policy agenda and Black policy preferences (arrow C) represents what we call the "Presidential Advocacy vs. Accountability Dilemma." We argue that all of the aforementioned constraints mean it was not reasonable to assume a so-called Black president will advocate the policy preferences of African Americans short of the willingness or ability of African American leaders, groups, and communities to hold such a president accountable. The US political system intrinsically undervalues Black concerns. So the problem is that African American advocacy must take place within the context of the US Racial Order, and this presents a unique, though not insurmountable, dilemma for Black politics. In order to push their interests, African Americans must apply political pressure to any president, especially those who are ideologically left of center / progressive and who can more readily be persuaded.[27] But the application of such pressure runs against "Inverted Linked Fate," which interprets the racial criticism of an individual African American president more broadly as an attack upon Black interests/well-being. And in the hands of racial conservatives—racists or White supremacists—such attacks are synonymous with anti-Black bias even if they vehemently deny such racial intentions. We and the contributors to this volume argue the Obama presidency has left Black politics and Black America with a complicated set of dilemmas to resolve most especially as the Trump administration has attempted to reverse much of his legacy.[28] Next, we further summarize the evidence that undergirds our conceptual framework.

Obama and the "End" of Black Politics?

Focused upon the late spring 2020 Black Lives Matter mass protests sparked by the police killing of George Floyd, the *New York Times* columnist Keeanga-Yamahtta Taylor argued these protests amplified the consistent frustration younger African Americans have had with older Black voters and Black politicians (such as Barack Obama) or White allies (such as Joe Biden). In short, Taylor stated that younger Black people demand a new Black politics that is less conciliatory and more progressive or revolutionary than that of their elders.[29] Taylor's essay "The End of Black Politics" had the exact same title as an essay written by Matt Bai also published in the *New York Times* twelve years earlier, but the two sharply diverged in what they meant. In 2008, Democratic presidential candidate Barack Obama took the advice of his expert, predominantly White campaign advisors and consistently spoke to universal themes of racial transcendence or getting beyond the divides of race. He did this in part by extolling the virtues of American exceptionalism. America was a place where a Black man with a "funny name," born of a Black father from Kenya and a White mother from Kansas, could win more delegates than US Senator Hillary Clinton to gain his party's nomination for president. "In no other country on earth," he asserted, was his story, "even possible."[30] On the August 2008 eve of Obama's historic nomination as the first African American to serve as the nominee of a major American party, Matt Bai opined whether Obama's race-neutral ascendancy represented "the end of black politics." By this, Bai was referring to what he perceived as the main currents of contemporary African American politics. The currents that emanated from the Civil Rights and Black Power eras of the 1960s and 1970s were explicitly rooted in Black group consciousness, particularistic Black grievances, and collective demands for targeted, race-specific policy solutions—e.g., affirmative action, job creation in Black communities, expanded civil rights laws, etc. Bai saw Obama as the leader of a new class of African American politicians:

> This new emerging class of black politicians . . . men (and a few women) close in age to Obama and Jesse (Jackson) Jr. seek a broader political brief [than the older generation]. Comfortable inside the establishment, bred at universities rather than seminaries, they are just as likely to see themselves as ambassadors to the black community as they to see themselves as spokesmen for it, which often means extolling middle-class values in urban neighborhoods, as Obama did on Father's Day. Their ambitions range well beyond safely black seats.[31]

Preceded by a watershed 1989 election year that first ushered in a class of "deracialized" politicians like Virginia governor L. Douglas Wilder, Andra Gillespie concludes this above class of "Phase III" new Black politicians included many examples. Among them were former Massachusetts governor Deval Patrick; former Newark, New Jersey, mayor and now US senator Corey Booker; former Congressmen Jesse Jackson Jr. and Harold Ford; and former Washington, DC, mayor Adrian Fenty. Like Obama, this class of new Black politicians attempted to run electoral campaigns where they consciously avoided any explicit appeals to Black voters and/or any direct references to the "race card." They cultivated a "crossover appeal" with White and other voters so to foment multiracial electoral coalitions. In their governing styles, many of them touted race-neutral, universalistic policy prescriptions that, in many respects, stressed neoliberal approaches of using the engine of the private market to address inequalities or maldistributions of income and wealth.[32]

However, for Bai to pose the question "Is Obama the End of Black Politics?" is to likewise beg the question, "Is Barack Obama the End of White Politics?" In Charles Henry's view, Bai's question neglected the reality that "race has remained the central divide in American politics."[33] Consistent with a decades-long pattern of racial polarization, both in 2008 and 2012, a majority of White voters (55 and 59 percent respectively) voted for the Republican candidate, while large majorities of Blacks and minorities voted for Obama, the Democratic candidate. In 2012, a whopping 92 percent of Republican candidate Mitt Romney's votes came from Whites, whereas about a third of Obama's support came from racial and ethnic minorities. From a racial and ethnic standpoint, it was only because the Obama campaign (against a backdrop of an unpopular incumbent and an economy in free fall) mobilized record numbers of Black and other minority voters to turn out to the polls that Obama garnered 53 percent of the popular vote in 2008. Later he received 51 percent in 2012.[34] During Obama's presidency, this racial polarization persisted. Again, table 1.2 illustrates how African Americans maintained very favorable views toward Obama in comparison to their White counterparts, who a clear majority most often did not approve of his job as president.

Moreover, for all of the discussions about a postracial America, we have already referenced the clear racial disparities that persist between African Americans and non-Hispanic Whites. (Refer back to table I.1.) These gaps imply a racial order persists that, in the view of Lawrence Bobo, is "somewhere between Jim Crow and Post-Racialism."[35] In the 2016 Democratic presidential race, both the campaigns of former US secretary of state Hillary Clinton and Vermont US senator Bernie Sanders were pushed by Black Lives Matter activists to more readily concede that an institutionalized or systemic racism persisted and threatened African American lives. Obama's political genius as coupled with his domestic policy moderation challenged some of the worst elements of racial discrimination, especially due to US attorney general Eric Holder's and later Attorney General Loretta Lynch's leadership of the US Justice Department. But Obama also aided and abetted a form of color-blind racism or a reluctance to fully articulate all of the African American inequalities created by the present racial order. This blindness created a political double-edge sword—a racial dilemma. As Tim Wise explains, "It was candidate Obama's use of the rhetoric of racial transcendence that made his victory possible, by assuaging White fears that we would focus on racial injustice or seek to remedy the same, were he elected president. But on the other hand, it is the same avoidance of race issue that has made it more difficult than ever to address ongoing racial bias, and has hamstrung the president's ability to push back against the opposition to his agenda, even when that opposition is framed in blatantly racist ways."[36] During his January 10, 2017, farewell address to the nation, Obama candidly stated that "race remains a potent and often divisive force in our society," and those who believed his presidency would usher in a "post-racial America" were, in fact, "never realistic." Still true to his philosophy and racial temperament, he used the language of racial transcendence in asserting the next generation's great capacity to get beyond race.[37]

When Obama has employed a form of color blindness, it has created a disjuncture within Black politics. As Fredrick Harris explains, there is a presumption among segments of the African American community that Obama and other candidates who choose deracialized strategies in order to win electoral or policy support among White voters and White politicians do so out of a form of pragmatism that slyly avoids the pitfalls of overt racial politics in order to clandestinely serve Black ends. To reiterate, Harris calls this the politics of a "wink and a nod." He explains, "An underlying assumption that permeates the discussion is that once a race-neutral candidate is elected, he or she will automatically address race-specific issues . . . this implicit arrangement is simple. Black candidates wink, and black voters nod. What is considered good campaign strategy for race-neutral black candidates is expected to be good for the interests of black communities." He goes on to reason that such assumptions lead to extremely problematic conclusions, such as some Black support for the nomination of conservative US supreme court justice Clarence Thomas because as an African American, he was presumed to eventually identify with Black concerns. But also, this assumption ignores those gains groups can only attain by explicitly demanding policy accountability from their elected leaders. Harris discusses how the Tea Party and the Christian Right consistently and successfully made demands on Republicans, just like lesbian, gay, bisexual, and transgender (LGBT) rights activists won important concessions under the Obama administration.[38] Harris concludes that more African American leaders and voters should have "instead [put] pressure on Obama to address particular policies," and thus in the game of politics, avoid functioning "more like cheerleaders than players suited up to play." While Harris acknowledges African Americans had an enormous pride in seeing one of their own and his lovely family occupy the White House, he cautions, "The very idea of an elected official as a role model for any constituency is incompatible with accountability, a central tenet of representative democracy."[39]

Harris and other Black critics of Obama's race-neutrality had strong Black critics. *Washington Post* columnist Jonathan Capehart fired back: "Harris and others appear not to care about the myriad actions Obama has undertaken that affect the lives of all Americans, yes, but also African Americans more directly. And I certainly don't advocate for Obama to burst into the East Room clad in kente cloth and brandishing a definable 'black agenda' or whatever else so many blacks seem to want from him to prove he cares."[40] Capehart stated Harris and other critics too frequently complained about "still waiting for our first black president" to address the many problems that confront Black communities. "The problem for Harris," he continues, "is they [these problems] are being addressed by the president. Not in the theatrical way Harris would like. But in the actions-speak-louder-than-words way of Obama." Capehart then listed a set of talking points with regards to administrative action on "criminal justice disparities," "the foreclosure crisis," "Black unemployment," and "the persistence of HIV/AIDS." He further argued that Harris and others did not realistically assess the institutional and ideological opposition Obama faced: "What's missing from most African American critiques of Obama," he says, is "an appreciation for Republican resistance to his agenda." He concludes, "To expect the president to introduce an explicit and definable 'black agenda' in a Congress filled with people who believe him to be a socialist destroying the country while illegitimately occupying the Oval Office is seriously naïve."[41] While we build our argument on the insights of Harris, we concede Capehart's criticism that it is very important to understand both the institutional-political dimensions *as well as* ideological dimensions of the dilemmas that shaped Obama's race-neutrality. Toward that end, we next discuss what we see as the "constitutive constraints" of the presidency, especially as Obama brought his brand of political leadership to the institution. And this has us consider how there were extant accountability and advocacy problems that confronted Black politics.

Race and the Constitutive Constraints of the Presidency

The American presidency was initially shaped under a set of racial orders—rooted in slavery—and though different today, a rightward-leaning racial order persists to this day.[42] The American presidency literature is replete with discussions about how the presidency and the executive branch, by the design of the framers of the Constitution, are one component of a limited government framework that rests upon a foundation of divided or separated powers. From one view, the framers "purposefully left the presidency imprecisely defined," due to mass fears of "monarchy" or centralized power. But with the hope "that future presidents would create a more powerful office than the framers were able to win ratification for at the time."[43] Thomas Cronin and Michael Genovese, as well as Joel Aberbach and Mark Peterson, believed these ambiguities created a series of paradoxes in which various American publics and institutions make competing and contradictory demands of the president and presidency. One example is the desire for strong leadership over the nation but a concomitant fear of centralized authority.[44] Since the days when Richard Neustadt first argued we can fundamentally understand the presidency by understanding the leadership traits of presidents, there has been a prevailing critique that too much of a focus upon the "the person of the president" and his "leadership and greatness" reifies a very complex set of political dynamics and reduces our studies to psychobabble.[45]

In Stephen Skowronek's pathbreaking work, *The Politics Presidents Make*, he argues that a more nuanced approach to understanding presidential limits and leadership is to examine the concept of "political time." It is the political opportunity structure each president confronts in exercising presidential authority relative to her or his affiliation with the preceding political regime. When considering the "political time" variables of regime strength and presidential affiliation, four typological categories emerge: *reconstructive* leaders or those who gain or are granted authoritative if not popular mandates to bring about transformative change of the preceding regime (e.g., Abraham Lincoln and Franklin D. Roosevelt), *disjunctive* leaders or those who are associated with a preceding regime that is "unpopular and dysfunctional" (e.g., James Buchanan), *articulating* leaders or those who are associated with preceding regimes that are "resilient and stable" (numerous examples), and *preemptive* leaders or those "who prematurely oppose a resilient regime"—arguably Ronald Reagan and Obama follow this type.[46] Skowronek foresaw a "waning of political time" whereby "institutional thickening" or an increasingly crowded "political universe" of institutions and interests disrupt public faith in and prompt the disequilibrium of each political regime to the point that the, "president will cease being the domineering engine of change in American politics he has historically been." The president increasingly lacks the capacity to use his authority and power to build a new political regime.

Based on Matthew Laing's work, we can conclude that Barack Obama, like Bill Clinton before him, is a preemptive leader.[47] Despite the 2008 electoral tide that swept Obama into the presidency and a Democratic majority into Congress, the persistence of various forms of racial conservatism energized a 2010 and 2014 Tea Party backlash that permitted Republicans to retake both houses of Congress and to control a majority of state governments for several years thereafter. Obama persisted with a brand of race-neutral policy universalism. So his presidency was much more of a moderate disruption *to* rather than a fundamental transformation *of* the present racial order. Again, the electoral strength of the racially conservative Tea Party and the White nationalism of Donald J. Trump's presidential candidacy both indicate that Obama's presidency did not and could not fully transform the racial order.[48] As Curt Nichols and Adam Meyers imply, we know that Obama, for all of his brilliance, likely was not a reconstructive leader with regards to race because he did not: (1) shift the "primary axis of partisan" or racial cleavage; (2) assemble "a new majority coalition" or, at least, a stable coalition around racial equality; and (3) institutionalize his "new regime into American politics," thus creating a new racial order.[49] This is not to downplay the reforms and policy victories the Obama administration won in areas such as health care, energy policy, economic recovery, as well as environmental and climate change reforms, but we do not know how well they will endure past the Trump presidency.[50] And we contend that when it comes to questions of race that impact the lives of African Americans and many others, we must be able to observe more lasting electoral and policy results several elections past 2016 to know if the "Obama coalition" is a concrete or transient political regime. The 2020 presidential election will be telling. The 2018 midterm elections, in which Democratic candidates enjoyed a resoundingly large turnout (thus retaking the US House and many state legislative seats), at least indicates the potential of a reconstituted Obama coalition to create future "blue waves."[51]

In Obama's last State of the Union Address in 2016, he directly conceded that his greatest political regret was his inability to diminish the polarization of American politics. Prior to then, Sidney Milkis and his colleagues similarly observed Obama had great difficulty creating the postpartisan regime that he frequently touted in the soaring rhetoric he used both on the campaign trail and behind presidential lecterns. Based on successive findings about the relationship between old-fashioned racism, partisanship, and opposition to Obama, we believe race fundamentally complicated Obama's attempts at postpartisanship. While he tried to transcend race, he also became a subject (if not a victim) of race. "Our core argument," Milkis and his colleagues state, "is that Obama's complex leadership approach reflects neither personal ineptitude nor confusion about political purpose, but rather a sustained effort to reconcile two competing philosophical and institutional legacies of the New American Party System that offers challenges to leadership at every turn." The first is a "transcendent form of leadership" that envisions the president as the "steward of the public welfare," and thus above the partisan fray (i.e., foreign relations, military reform, immigration reform), while the second is the "executive-centered" partisan leader who uses the presidency and the federal bureaucracy as vehicles for partisan ideals (i.e., LGBT rights, health care reform, the minimum wage debate, etc.)[52] Lawrence Jacobs and Desmond King argue that many of Obama's policy failures—from immigration reform to climate change legislation to gun control—were not simply due to a lack of presidential leadership but also a lack of "structured agency" or his inability to overcome the political opportunity barriers posed by the regime's political and economic environments. Toward the end of their article, Jacobs and King conceded that an important dimension of the present conservative regime is that it is a "racial order," whereby "Obama's election is a culmination of centuries of struggle for racial equity and, yet, his presidency is constrained by the enduring conflict of racial orders."[53]

Black Politics, Inverted Linked Fate, and the Inclusionary Dilemma

At the beginning of this chapter, we defined the *practice* of Black politics as the African American use of political power to attain group goals. But as political scientists, we are also concerned about the *study* of Black politics. One construct that students of African American politics have found to be empirically associated with a wide range of Black ideological and political behavior indicators is the aforementioned construct of "linked" or "common fate." As a component of African American racial identity as well as group centrality, linked fate is present when African Americans believe their individual well-beings are conditioned by or linked to the well-being of the group. Because there are many other social constructs—e.g., social class, gender, sexual orientation, and ethnicity—that interact or intersect with linked fate and create "cross-cutting cleavages," it is important, as Cathy Cohen noted a while ago, to think about how linked fate is often "qualified."[54] In other words, Black leaders and groups may often privilege race and racial considerations when determining how to set agendas and allocate resources so to serve group interests. However, there are a host of other considerations that matter when subsets of the community define their conceptions of group interests, which speaks to the complexity and social heterogeneity of African American communities. In fact, critics such as Adolph Reed and Cathy Cohen believe Black politics has trained so much attention upon race in determining when Black politicians and other leaders are accountable to Black group interests that intersecting forms of oppression—class, gender, sexual orientation—are neglected.[55]

Based on Harris's aforementioned "wink and nod" politics, we in turn believe that it is possible to improperly invert the relationship between the individual and her reference group, such that the group assesses its well-being based upon the well-being of an individual, or in the case of Obama, an individual leader. Again, this is "inverted linked fate" because the community uses its perceptions of the leader's political treatment by American society as one rough proxy for its own well-being. We know that African American communities, like other political communities, receive important information and take many ideological and behavioral cues from Black candidates and officeholders. Whether these candidates are like Jesse Jackson Sr. when he ran for US president or Harold Washington when he served as Chicago's first Black mayor, research has shown that such officials are often important political mobilizers of the community. Again, recall the Harris admonition against elevating elected officials to the position of role models and how this complicates democratic accountability.[56] This most certainly may be true of a Black politics that paradoxically revered Obama as an African American leader, when as US president and thus as "commander in chief of the American empire," he certainly did not see himself as *just* a Black leader.

This paradox is further complicated when, in the context of America's present racial order, Obama used what Harris calls the "politics of respectability" or a "public philosophy directed at policing the black poor." It is a practice whereby Black elites equate, "public behavior with individual self-respect and the advancement of African-Americans as a group"; thus, they believe, "'respectable' behavior in public would earn their people a measure of esteem from white America."[57] There are myriad examples of candidate and later President Obama upbraiding some segment of the African American community for not assuming the level of personal responsibility or demonstrating the type of personal conduct and deportment that Obama believed was necessary to adhere to the highest community standards. Consider the famous (and critics would argue *infamous*) Father's Day address that candidate Obama delivered at a historic Black church, the Apostolic Church of God in Chicago, Illinois, on June 15, 2008:

> Yes, we [in the Black community] need more cops on the street. Yes, we need fewer guns in the hands of people who shouldn't have them. Yes, we need more money for our schools, and more outstanding teachers in the classroom, and more after-school programs for our children. Yes, we need more jobs and more job training and more opportunity in our communities. But we also need families to raise our children. We need

fathers to realize that responsibility does not end at conception. We need them to realize that what makes you a man is not the ability to have a child—it's the courage to raise one.[58]

He also stated, "Too many fathers are MIA, too many fathers are AWOL, missing from too many lives and too many homes, they have abandoned their responsibilities, acting like boys instead of men, and the foundations of our families are weaker because of it."[59] It was this speech that infamously got Jesse Jackson Sr. into trouble when a live television microphone caught him angrily whispering that Obama should have his "nuts cut off" for "talking down to black people." But when Obama drew upon his own experiences in the Black church—most especially in Rev. Jeremiah Wright's Trinity Church of Christ with an African American inflection or a preacher's cadence in his voice—was Obama using or exploiting the unique position he occupied in the present racial order to subtly police the boundaries of a "respectable" Blackness?[60] To be sure, Obama is a masterful orator, as evidenced by his 2008 Philadelphia "race" speech, which literally saved his campaign after the Jeremiah Wright controversy. He was able to speak across disparate audiences and convey with great nuance and sensitivity a set of comments that if delivered by a less-skilled White politician could be viewed as racially insensitive by the Black community. Akin to Obama's address at the fiftieth anniversary of the historic Selma to Montgomery, Alabama, march, his "Amazing Grace" address was one of the most oratorically masterful addresses by a US president. Obama delivered the eulogy of South Carolina state senator Clementa Pinckney, who also was the pastor of "Mother" Emanuel African American Methodist Episcopal Church in Charleston and was murdered by a young White supremacist along with eight of his fellow parishioners.[61]

President Obama may have confronted what earlier in this chapter we labeled an "inclusionary dilemma" because he held the highest elected office in the land and because he was a politician who happened to be Black. In an interview with two journalists published in the *Atlantic* magazine in April 2013, President Obama's closest aide Valerie Jarrett had this to say: "He is interested . . . in describing our challenges in terms of how we are inextricably linked in mutuality. The president tries to describe our challenges in ways that are inclusive. He does not intend to polarize; he intends to unify."[62] This behavioral posture reflected his civic or political universalism. As such, the first dimension of what we call the inclusionary dilemma was more one of appearance, than perhaps an observable reality; a reality that future presidential historians will no doubt explore in greater detail. There is a second dimension of what we call the "inclusionary dilemma," which presents a dilemma for students of African American politics. Much of the available evidence indicates that President Obama, through his first term in office, was hesitant to use the formal-legal authority of his office to ameliorate the multifaceted Black predicament. Evidence from President Obama's second term indicates that his administration addressed some aspects of persistent racial inequality, especially in the area of the criminal justice system. This volume's examination of the Obama presidency gives rise to a more somber conclusion that has a major implication for African American politics as a body of knowledge: African Americans can no longer expect a Black person who is elected to office (in a predominately White political jurisdiction) to be an expressed advocate of public policies meant to address the vestiges of racial inequality. As previously noted, the election and reelection of Barack Obama as POTUS did not mean the end of African American politics.[63]

However, in the context of a polarizing American racial order, many of the above nuances were lost on segments of the White public. There was strong consensus that it is naive to assume his election heralded a new era of post-racial era politics. While it is clear that Obama's rhetoric of racial transcendence as coupled with his effective, deracialized campaigning strategies lessened degrees of implicit bias among some White moderates, across a range of indicators, racial attitudes among White elites and publics tilted toward greater intolerance— greater "old-fashioned racism." This was most especially true with regards to Obama's signature policy reform of the Affordable Care Act or so-called Obamacare. If we consider this in light of the persistent inequalities that confront Black political life—including new threats to the Voting Rights Act and persistent inequities in the criminal justice system and sentencing—this reinforces our conclusion that Obama was, according to the Skowronek typology, a preemptive leader who only slightly shifted the current trajectory of the current racial order. Therefore, it is incumbent upon Black politics (both as a practice and as a study) to locate a new metric for determining how effective and accountable Barack Obama and all Black politicians should be to various Black interests in a new period of overt racism as prompted by Trump.[64]

The Presidential Accountability versus Responsiveness Dilemma

When we combine Obama's ideological and policy commitments with the clear constraints of the presidency, we believe this highlights the problems of any president being *accountable* or *responsive* to Black policy demands. This reiterates our contention that under the current American racial order—there is no such thing as a Black president. By *accountability*, we mean a public official who answers to a constituency in order to explain her or his stances and views. While we certainly agree the persona of Obama's presidency represented a milestone of symbolic political incorporation and racial progress in America—i.e., African Americans at the highest levels of the federal government—we assert, like Harris, that Obama's race-neutrality was both often stymied by and complicit in the present racial order. For all of the ways in which the American presidency is a difficult (and frequently implausible) vehicle through which to respond to African American political needs and aspirations, Black political history is replete with examples of Black leaders and groups petitioning and pressuring the US president to recognize their full citizenship rights and equal opportunity demands.

Among the most prominent examples are Fredrick Douglass and various Black and White abolitionists in the early 1860s, demanding Lincoln shift his position on the use of presidential authority to emancipate the enslaved and enlist Black troops in Union Civil War forces; A. Philip Randolph and other civil rights leaders in the 1940s, compelling Franklin Roosevelt to issue Executive Order 8802, which tepidly barred discrimination in wartime production industries (or else they would march on Washington); or Randolph, Bayard Rustin, Martin Luther King Jr., and a host of other leaders in the 1960s, using an enormous March on Washington to demonstrate to John F. Kennedy's administration the public hue and cry for new civil rights laws as well as "Jobs and Freedom."[65] Hanes Walton Jr. and Robert Smith remind us that presidents are products of and not simply witnesses to the American racial order: "The American presidency is an office of great power and majesty, and therefore the racial attitudes of and policies of American presidents have been a crucial factor in the African American quest for universal freedom." In a typology that ranges from "White Supremacist" to "Anti-racist" they conclude that the vast majority of American presidents have either been White supremacist or racist. But they conclude that, for the most part, Barack Obama's presidency ranged from "Racially Neutral" in his first term to "Anti-racist" in his second term. They compare what they label Obama's "ethnic avoidance" of African American–targeted issues to that of Kennedy and his Catholic roots when they state, "In Obama's case, 'supererogation' would require him—more so than Kennedy—to lean over backward as not to appear to be doing anything 'for his own people.'"[66] This is why there has been such a heated, internecine debate within Black politics about whether Obama was and should have been accountable to Black interests.

On one side, figures like *New York Times* columnist Bob Herbert, political scientist Fredrick Harris, public intellectual Cornel West, and media commentator Tavis Smiley were deeply critical of Obama's lack of accountability. In fact, West and Smiley were castigated in some Black civic circles for their intense criticisms, but Smiley still wrote a book that declared the need for Obama and other politicians to be *Accountable: Making America as Good as Its Promise*.[67] On the other side, figures like civil rights leader and commentator Al Sharpton, *Washington Post* journalist Jonathan Capehart, and former MSNBC commentator and political scientist Melissa Harris-Perry often commended if not strongly defended the Obama administration and in some cases were angered by what they saw as the myopic complaints of some Black critics. Just prior to Obama's election, Wilbur Rich provided a telling comment with regards to the presidential management of Black expectations: "Presidents who ignore the black experience can count on little reaction from the media or the majority of the public. Such a strategy has guided both Democratic and Republican presidents."[68]

By *advocacy*, we mean a public official speaks on behalf of a constituency and promotes their perceived interests. It is commonly held that those persons elected to be the chief executive officer of the United States and commander in chief of its armed forces are presumed to represent (in symbolic and often mythological ways) the corporate body of the citizenry. Our opening quote from Obama stressed this. This was no less true when Obama in his first year of office received the Nobel Peace Prize. With his Stockholm address, he offered these telling words to both embrace and distance himself as US President from the presumption that he is politically beholden to the legacy of nonviolent resistance to oppression as often led by Black and other people of color:

> As someone who stands here as a direct consequence of Dr. King's life work, I am living testimony to the moral force of non-violence. I know there's nothing weak—nothing passive—nothing naïve—in the creed and lives of Gandhi and King. . . . But as a head of state sworn to protect and defend my nation, I cannot be guided by their examples alone. I face the world as it is, and cannot stand idle in the face of threats to the American people. For make no mistake: Evil does exist in the world. A non-violent movement could not have halted Hitler's armies. Negotiations cannot convince al Qaeda's leaders to lay down their arms. To say that force may sometimes be necessary is not a call to cynicism—it is a recognition of history; the imperfections of man and the limits of reason.[69]

Again, we believe Milkis and his colleagues note a fascinating contradiction or paradox of the presidency when they state, "The question remains whether the executive of a vast bureaucratic state can truly be the direct representative of the people." This matters whether she or he is trying to represent *all* of the people or supposedly *all* of the *Black* people as implied by the misleading term "Black president."[70]

Still the practice of Black politics has, at times, used seeking the office of president as a strategy to advance dependent and independent leverage strategies relative to American party system. As Ronald Walters explains in his seminal book *Black Presidential Politics in America: A Strategic Approach*, independent leverage strategies, such as the formation of Black political parties, seek to provide a "disciplined" Black electorate with an autonomous basis of political power. It should be a base that is outside a dominant party organization so to persuade or challenge that dominant party to heed to Black demands. Dependent-leverage strategies are launched from within the dominant party organization and seek to use the Black vote as a point of leverage in a "balance of power strategy."[71] Despite assertions about the "end of black politics" and the increasing social and political diversity of African American communities, the presidential candidacies of US representative Shirley Chisholm from Brooklyn, New York, and the civil rights leader Rev. Jesse Jackson Sr. attempted to lay the groundwork for the "unified" articulation of Black policy needs within Democratic primary processes. To a greater or lesser extent, they used presidential campaigns as advocacy vehicles to voice the perceived interests and needs of Black and other communities. Both Chisholm and Jackson often used race-neutral language to illustrate the universal appeal of their candidacies. But unlike Obama's 2008 campaign, they ultimately had electoral strategies that were rooted in Black politics and dependent or independent leverage strategies.

In 1972, Chisholm stated, "I am not the candidate of black America, although I am black and proud. I am not the candidate of the women's movement of this country, although I am a woman and I am equally proud of that. I am candidate of the people, and my presence before you now symbolizes a new era in American political history."[72] For her efforts, Chisholm's poorly resourced campaign only netted twenty-eight delegates from the Democratic primaries. Partly due to a sexism within the Black community, she confronted a lack of support from Black Nationalist and civil rights leaders; due to a subtle racism that was couched as political pragmatism within the women's movement, she confronted a lack of support from feminist organizations. But Chisholm demonstrated that a grassroots African American–led presidential campaign was conceivable. She broke a glass ceiling and left a legacy for Jackson and conceivably Obama to continue. Similarly, Jackson stated in his rationale for creating a "Rainbow Coalition" so to run for the 1984 Democratic nomination, "Lest there be confusion, let the word go forth from this occasion that this candidacy is not for blacks only. This is a national campaign growing out of the black experience and seen through the eyes of the black experience—which is the experience and perspective of the rejected. . . . Thus, our perspective encompasses more of the American people and their interests than does most other experiences."[73] Jackson created a grassroots campaign—supported by the Black church—and gathered a campaign staff of Black and other activists as well as policy experts who largely were unconnected with Democratic Party inner circles. Jackson's 1984 and 1988 campaigns made many historic strides that would plow a pathway for Obama's later efforts. By 1988, Jackson and his campaign scored the following victories in that they won an astounding 30 percent of all Democratic convention delegates and 29 percent of the votes in the primaries; netted some three million primary votes overall; registered and mobilized about two million new Black voters whose influences were felt in the 1986 US Senate elections, among others; demanded Democratic Party delegate allocation reforms that later would benefit Obama in his 2008 bid against Hillary Clinton; and brought a new cadre of African American leaders into the Democratic party who later went on to hold key elected and appointed posts.[74] Harris notes that Jackson's independent Black politics strategy made a level of "elite" Black political incorporation possible: "If a polarizing figure like Jesse Jackson could appeal to a significant number of white voters in 1988 emphasizing universal issues," Harris states in a somewhat tongue-in-cheek fashion, "just think what a black candidate without racial baggage could do."[75] Despite these well-known Chisholm and Jackson exemplars of Black advocacy through presidential campaigns, we contend that under the current racial order, the presidency is not a vehicle politically equipped to voice a range of Black constituent demands. Again, all of this was confounded by a Black "wink and nod" agreement—or the inverted linked fate—that had some in African American politics interpreting the well-being of Barack Obama as a proxy for the well-being of Black America.

Overview of the Chapters

To pursue the thesis we introduce in this chapter, this book is divided into two parts, with an introduction and conclusion. This introduction lays out a common conceptual framework for reading subsequent chapters written by a diverse group of political scientists who are students of Black politics, intersectional politics, and global politics.

Part 1 includes works that examine the various African American / Black constituencies that were shaped by and/or helped to shape the Obama presidency. In chapter 1, Shayla C. Nunnally examines how African American and White public opinion and political trust were shaped by race and the Obama presidency. In chapter 2, Tyson D. King-Meadows examines how elected officials and African American interest groups responded to the Obama presidency. In chapter 3, Ray Block Jr. and Angela K. Lewis-Maddox analyze the persistent racial fissures relative to race and political party identification. In chapter 4, Brian D. McKenzie discusses how African American church politics have been shaped by the Obama presidency. In chapter 5, Wendy G. Smooth introduces the use of the intersectional paradigm in this volume and examines a key Democratic Party voting block—African American women—so to critique how they and their communities fared under Obama. In chapter 6, Ravi K. Perry examines the civil rights gains and persistent challenges Black lesbian, gay, bisexual, transgendered, and queer (LGBTQ) communities confronted under Obama.

Part 2 includes works that examine various political institutions and public policies that were relevant to African American/Black constituencies and were promulgated by the Obama administration. In chapter 7, Shenita Brazelton and Dianne Pinderhughes consider the federal judiciary under Obama and his administration's enforcement of civil rights policy. In chapter 8, Khalilah L. Brown-Dean analyzes both the social justice politics and the policy dimensions of the Obama administration and criminal justice policy. In chapter 9, Julia S. Jordan-Zachery uses an intersectional, discursive analysis to interrogate how the Obama administration cast antipoverty and employment policies in ways framed by race, gender, and class. In chapter 10, Sekou Franklin, Pearl K. Ford Dowe, and Angela K. Lewis-Maddox evaluate the political and policy implications of Obama's signature domestic policy—the Affordable Care Act (ACA), or Obamacare—especially as it impacted Black communities. In chapter 11, Andra Gillespie examines an often neglected aspect of a presidential domestic policy agenda—urban policy and how African Americans and Black politics fared relative to the administration's housing policies. In chapter 12, Lorrie Frasure and Stacey Greene assess the Obama administration's immigration policy legacy, especially understanding its impact upon Black attitudes toward authorized and unauthorized immigrant communities. In chapter 13, Robert B. Packer assesses the legacy of the Obama administration's foreign policy (and to some degree military policy) as relevant to African American interests.

And the conclusion summarizes the volume's key insights and discusses our expectations regarding the Trump presidency, as well as the next African American to serve as president in light of the rapid political and demographic changes Black America is witnessing.

Conclusion: Black Interests and the Limits of Obama's Racial Legacy

In this introduction, we have offered our thoughts with regards to the racial trajectory of the Obama presidency so to indicate where Black America may stand several years after the Obama presidency. We have argued that Harris made a trenchant and accurate critique of the "wink and nod" Black politics that permitted Obama and other deracialized politicians to speak and campaign in the coded language of race neutrality so to disguise from White electorates their true intentions of targeting the Black community's needs once in office. However, we have extended upon Harris's critique by considering not only the ideological but the institutional and constitutive constraints of the American presidency and the racial order in which it resides. We assert that a Black inverted linked fate is an unwise development to the degree that it has the Black community presuming it can identify its group interests and aims according to the political fortunes of the US president—an office that supposedly serves the "entire United States" but, by design, is often removed from the people and particularly from Blacks and other people of color. The inclusionary dilemma means that politicians who happen to be Black, such as was the case with Obama, also can have fairly strong ethnic attachments to or personal linked fates with the Black community. No doubt this attachment was reinforced by Barack Obama's partnership with First Lady Michelle Obama, whose style, personal integrity, and rhetorical eloquence earned her high public regard, especially as she authentically spoke as an African American woman. But this does not mean that Barack Obama or others like him will abandon their pragmatic, universalist views that lean toward race-neutral policies. We agree with Harris's prescription when he argues that President Obama should have responded to the interests of the Black community because he was a Democratic president responding to the needs of a loyally Democratic constituency—just as the case with other constituencies. This would have been a better political formula for collective action than relying on the presumed linkages of a racialized linked fate with or the conundrums the inclusionary dilemma creates for a so-called Black presidency.

In his second term, Obama more frequently spoke out about the inequalities and injustices of race than he did in the first term. We reiterate our point that Barack Obama was a complex political figure whose political imagination and rhetorical gifts speak to how he, at times, served a political end by intentionally and repeatedly going off script. Obama's predominant political narrative of racial transcendence has, throughout the course of his political career, been tempered with his pragmatic understanding that race and racial inequality still fundamentally matter even as he has aspired for race-neutral, centrist, and universalist policies. We surmise that part of the reason for Obama going off his race-neutral script is his linked fate—his personal, ethnic, and gendered connection to the Black community and to young Black men. After all, he is an African American man who has longed for an absent father as famously captured in his autobiography.[76] During a July 2013 surprise press conference appearance, and into his second term, Obama offered a set of candid comments about the jury acquittal of George Zimmerman who shot and killed the unarmed, young Black man, Trayvon Martin, in a Florida community:

> You know, when Trayvon Martin was first shot, I said that [he] could have been my son. Another way of saying that is Trayvon Martin could have been me 35 years ago. And when you think about why, in the African American community at least, there's a lot of pain around what happened here, I think it's important to recognize that the African American community is looking at this issue through a set of experiences and a history that—that doesn't go away.[77]

The Martin case was just one of an overwhelming number of incidents in which White suspects, especially police officers and security guards, shot and/or killed unarmed Black victims. By the spring of 2020, the Martin case would be one of a dozen of the highest profile cases of police or vigilante killings of unarmed Black suspects that would prompt the mass Black Lives Matter protests.[78] Obama's 2013 commencement address to a graduating class of Morehouse College men as well as his

White House initiative aimed at amassing private, programmatic dollars to target the ills that confront young Black men and other men of color—called the "My Brother's Keeper" initiative—spoke to how he blended his own narrative of linked fate with a neoliberalist mixture of respectability politics. A White House announcement of the initiative said, in Horatio Alger terms, that its purpose was "to make sure that every young man of color who is willing to work hard and lift himself up has an opportunity to get ahead and reach his full potential." Still it is intriguing that Obama was the first sitting president to visit a federal penitentiary while his administration argued for a number of measures to disentangle the racial disparities in the criminal justice system.[79] It is hard to imagine President Donald Trump voicing such words or making even these symbolic gestures, though nascent but important federal criminal justice reform legislation was passed by Congress.[80] As Obama is clearly a strong partner to his famous spouse—Michelle Obama—and father to his daughters—Malia and Sasha—he has been projected as role model figure to many other young women and men. In the final analysis, we are not certain just how tall (metaphorically speaking) Obama's third child—Obama's legacy regarding race—will grow, given the imposed and self-imposed racial constraints of his presidency. But by the end of this volume, we call for a more imaginative African American politics that serves the ends of challenging future racial inequality and other forms of inequality by broadening our conceptions of advocacy and accountability after Obama.

NOTES

1   As references, see Garunay, Melanie. 2016. "Meet the 106-Year-Old Who Got to Dance with the President and the First Lady." White House Blog (www.white-house.gov/blog). Miller, Michelle. 2015. "'A Black President, Yay': 106-Year-Old Finally Meets the Obamas, Dances Like a Schoolgirl." *Washington Post.* DeVega, Chauncey. 2016. "Donald Trump Will 'Take Care of "the African-Americans"': Will We See a Repeat of Redemption, the Post–Civil War White Backlash?" *Salon.* Retrieved 2017 (www.salon.com).

2   Obama, Barack. 2017. "Farewell Address." Washington, DC: The White House. Tan, Avianne. 2016. "107-Year-Old Woman's Struggle to Get Photo ID Prompts Concern for Elderly People's Voting Rights." ABC News. Retrieved May 27, 2016 (http://abcnews.go.com). For a discussion of the Obama Legacy after Trump, see Eilperin, Juliet, and Darla Cameron. "How Trump Is Rolling Back Obama's Legacy." *Washington Post* (www.washingtonpost.com).

3 Harris, Fredrick C. 2012. *The Price of the Ticket: Barack Obama and the Rise and Decline of Black Politics*. Oxford: Oxford University Press.

4 Harris, *The Price of the Ticket*, 155. McCormick, Joseph and Charles E. Jones. 1993. "The Conceptualization of Deracialization: Thinking through the Dilemma." *Dilemmas of Black Politics: Issues of Leadership and Strategy*, ed. Georgia Persons, 66–84. New York: Harper Collins, 1993.

5 In this volume, we and our contributors will use the terms *Black* and *African American* interchangeably to mean all persons of African descent in the United States—whether native to the United States or foreign-born—who self-identify as "African American." We will be specific when we are referring to specific ethnic-national identities—e.g., native African, Afro-Jamaican, Black Haitian. We choose to capitalize all proper names for racial and ethnic groups/categories.

6 Walton, Hanes and Robert Charles Smith. 2012. *American Politics and the African American Quest for Universal Freedom*. New York: Pearson Longman. Walton, Hanes, Jr., ed. 1997. *African American Power and Politics: The Political Contextual Variable*. New York: Columbia University Press.

7 Among the seminal works that reminds of the cross-cutting cleavages of Black politics is Cohen, Cathy. 1999. *The Boundaries of Blackness: AIDS in the Black Community*. Chicago: University of Chicago Press. For another work that posits class as a more central line of demarcation within Black politics, see Reed, Adolph, Jr. 1999. "Sources of Demobilization in the New Black Political Regime: Incorporation, Ideological Capitulation, and Radical Failure in the Post-Segregation Era." In *Stirrings in the Jug: Black Politics in the Post-Segregation Era*, edited by Adolph Reed, Jr., 117–59. Minneapolis: University of Minnesota Press.

8 Shaw, Todd C. 2007. "The Expanding Boundaries of Black Politics." in Georgia A. Persons, ed., *National Political Science Review* 11:3.

9 Having asserted that Obama could not be a "Black President," we are fascinated by the premise of Ta-Nehisi Coates's essay that argues Donald Trump is the first "White President." See Coates, Ta-Nehisi. 2017. "The First White President." *Atlantic* 320, no. 3: 74–87. More recently, Andra Gillespie has reframed the question, "My president was black. So what?" see Gillespie, Andra. 2019. *Race and the Obama Administration: Substance, Symbol, and Hope*. Manchester, England: Manchester University Press.

10 For quotes, see King, Desmond S., and Rogers M. Smith. 2005. "Racial Orders in American Political Development." *American Political Science Review* 99: 75. See Jacobs, Lawrence R., and Desmond King. 2012. *Obama at the Crossroads: Politics, Markets, and the Battle for America's Future*. Oxford: Oxford University Press, 156.

11 For empirical evidence of the white racial psychology that undergirded the election of Trump, see Schaffner, Brian F., Matthew MacWilliams, and Tatishe Nteta. "Explaining White Polarization in the 2016 Vote for President: The Sobering Role of Racism and Sexism." Paper presented at the Conference on the US Elections of 2016. For an analysis of the broader philosophical implications of the Trump

presidency, see Giroux, Henry A. 2017. "White Nationalism, Armed Culture and State Violence in the Age of Donald Trump." *Philosophy and Social Criticism* 43, no. 9: 887–910.

12 Grunwald, Michael. 2016. "The Obama Issue: The Nation He Built. A Politico Review of Barack Obama's Domestic Policy Legacy—and the Changes He Made While Nobody Was Paying Attention." *Politico*. Bobo, Lawrence D. 2011. "Somewhere between Jim Crow and Post-Racialism: Reflections on the Racial Divide in American Today." *American Academy of Arts & Sciences* 140, no. 2: 11–36. Price, Melanye T. 2016. *The Race Whisperer: Barack Obama and the Political Uses of Race*: New York University Press. Smith, Rogers M. and Desmond King. 2009. "Barack Obama and the Future of American Racial Politics." *Du Bois Review* 6, no. 1: 25–35. Alleyne, Kenneth R. "How covid-19 is a perfect storm for black Americans." *Washington Post*, April 26, 2020. www.washingtonpost.com.

13 Each equality index calculation is a weighted parity-ratio in which the National Urban League and IHS Global Insight, the firm it contracted to produce the analysis, summarizes a wealth of data from the US census, including the most recent figures for each designated year / time period. The categories of statistics that were used for each are: *Economics*—Median Income, Poverty, Employment Issues, Housing and Wealth, Digital Divide, Transportation; *Health*—Death Rates and Life Expectancy, Physical Condition, Substance Abuse, Mental Health, Access to Care, Elderly Health Care, Pregnancy Issues, Reproduction Issues, Delivery Issues, Children's Health; Education—Teacher Quality, Course Quality, Educational Attainment, Enrollment, Student Status and Risk Factors; *Social Justice*—Equality before the Law, Victimization and Mental Anguish; *Civic Engagement*—Democratic Process, Community Participation, Collective Bargaining, Governmental Employment. Refer to League, National Urban. 2016. *2016 State of Black America: Locked Out—Education, Jobs & Justice* (www.stateofblackamerica.org).

14 Bonilla-Silva, Eduardo and David Dietrick. 2011. "The Sweet Enchantment of Color-Blind Racism in Obamerica." *Annals of American Academy of Political and Social Science* 634: 190–206. Dawson, Michael. 1994. *Behind the Mule: Race and Class in African American Politics*. Princeton, NJ: Princeton University Press. Dyson, Michael Eric. 2016. *The Black Presidency: Barack Obama and the Politics of Race in America*. Boston and New York: Hougton Mifflin Harcourt. Sugrue, Thomas J. 2009. *Not Even Past: Barack Obama and the Burden of Race*. Princeton, NJ: Princeton University Press. Tate, Katherine. 1994. *From Protest to Politics: The New Black Voters in American Elections*. Cambridge, MA: Harvard University Press. Tesler, Michael. 2013. "The Return of Old-Fashioned Racism to White Americans' Partisan Preferences in the Early Obama Era." *Journal of Politics* 75, no. 1: 110–23.

15 Smith, Rogers M. and Desmond King. 2009. "Barack Obama and the Future of American Racial Politics." *Du Bois Review* 6, no. 1: 25–35, Wise, Tim. 2010.

Color-Blind: The Rise of Post-Racial Politics and the Retreat from Racial Equity. San Francisco: City Lights Books.

16 Gillion, Daniel Q. "Obama's Discussion of Racial Policies and Citizens' Racial Resentment in the Experimental Setting." *Presidential Studies Quarterly* 47, no. 3 (2017): 517–28. Price, Melanye T. 2016. *The Race Whisperer: Barack Obama and the Political Uses of Race*. New York: New York University Press.

17 McCormick, Joseph. 2012. Paper presented at the Annual Meeting of the National Conference of Black Political Scientists. Condon, George E. and Jim O'Sullivan. 2013. "Has President Obama Done Enough for Black Americans?" *The Atlantic*. Abramson, Alana. 2016. "How Donald Trump Perpeturated the 'Birther' Movement for Years." *ABC News*. Dyson, Michael Eric. 2016. *The Black Presidency: Barack Obama and the Politics of Race in America*. Boston and New York: Hougton Mifflin Harcourt. Hughey, Matthew W. 2012. "Show Me Your Papers! Obama's Birth and the Whiteness of Belonging." *Qualitative Sociology* 35: 163–81. For the implications of the Glenn Beck quote, see Wingfield, Adia Harvey, and Joe Feagin. 2012. "The racial dialectic: President Barack Obama and the white racial frame." *Qualitative Sociology* 35, 2: 150.

18 Spence, Lester K. 2015. *Knocking the Hustle: Against the Neoliberal Turn in Black Politics*. Brooklyn, NY: Punctum Books. Dyson, Michael Eric. 2016. *The Black Presidency: Barack Obama and the Politics of Race in America*. Boston and New York: Hougton Mifflin Harcourt. "Attorney General Says U.S. a Nation of 'Cowards' when It Comes to Race." 2009. *New York Times*.

19 Language by Bobo, Lawrence D. 2011. "Somewhere between Jim Crow and Post-Racialism: Reflections on the Racial Divide in American Today." *American Academy of Arts & Sciences* 140, no. 2: 11–36. Smith, Rogers M. and Desmond King. 2009. "Barack Obama and the Future of American Racial Politics." *Du Bois Review* 6, no. 1: 25–35; Murphy, Tim. 2016. "The Clinton-Sanders Ad War Shows How Black Lives Matter Reshaped the Race." *Mother Jones*. (www.motherjones.com).

20 Based on White reactions to the May 31, 2020, police murder of the African American man George Floyd and White involvement in the larger, widespread Black Lives Matter protests, we will see if there is a durable liberalization of White attitudes on policing and systemic racism. See Parker, Kim, Juliana Menasce Horowitz, and Monica Anderson. "Amid Protests, Majorities across Racial and Ethnic Groups Express Support for the Black Lives Matter Movement: Deep Partisan Divides over Factors Underlying George Floyd Demonstrations." Pew Research Center, www.pewsocialtrends.org.

21 King, Desmond S. and Rogers M. Smith. 2014. "The Last Stand: Restricting Voting Rights and Sustaining White Power in Modern America." Tyson, Alec and Shiva Maniam. 2016. "Election 2016—Behind Trump's Victory: Divisions of Race, Gender, and Education." *FactTank: News in the Numbers*. Washington, DC: Pew Research Center. (www.pewresearch.org).

22 McNamara, Carol and Melanie M Marlowe, eds. 2012. *The Obama Presidency in the Constitutional Order*. New York: Rowman & Littlefield.

23 Cooper, Helene and Abby Goodnough. 2009. "Over Beers, No Apologies, but Plans to Have Lunch." *New York Times*. Office of the Press Secretary. 2013. "Remarks by the President on Trayvon Martin." Washington, DC: White House. Retrieved June 6, 2016 (www.whitehouse.gov). Office of the Press Secretary. 2015. "Remarks by the President in Eulogy for The Honorable Reverend Clementa Pinckney," White House: The White House. (www.whitehouse .gov).

24 Dawson, Michael. 1994. *Behind the Mule: Race and Class in African American Politics*. Princeton, NJ: Princeton University Press.

25 Newport, Frank. 2014. "Blacks' Approval of President Obama Remains Hight." Gallup. (www.gallup.com).

26 White House. 2016. "Music and Arts: Performances at the White House." (www .whitehouse.gov). Office of the Press Secretary. 2016. "Remarks by the President at the White House Correspondents' Dinner," Washington, DC: White House. (www.whitehouse.gov).

27 Foreman, Christopher H. 2010. *The African-American Predicament*: Brookings Institution Press. Washington, DC. Smiley, Tavis. 2009. *Accountable: Making America as Good as Its Promise*. New York: Simon and Schuster.

28 Remnick, David. 2016. "Obama Reckons with a Trump Presidency." *New Yorker*. (www.newyorker.com).

29 Taylor, Keeanga-Yamahtta. 2020. "The End of Black Politics." *New York Times*, June 13.

30 Wise, Tim. 2010. *Color-Blind: The Rise of Post-Racial Politics and the Retreat from Racial Equity*. San Francisco: City Lights Books.

31 Bai, Matt. 2008. "Is Obama the End of Black Politics?" *New York Times*.

32 Dawson, Michael. 2011. *Not in Our Lifetimes: The Future of Black Politics*. Chicago: University of Chicago Press. Gillespie, Andra. 2010. "Meet the New Class: Theorizing Young Black Leadership in a 'Postracial' Era." in *Whose Black Politics? Cases in Post-Racial Black Leadership*, edited by A. Gillespie, 1–44. New York and London: Routledge, Spence, Lester. 2011. *Stare in the Darkness: The Limits of Hip-Hop and Black Politics*. University of Minnesota Press: Minneapolis and London, Spence, Lester K. 2015. *Knocking the Hustle: Against the Neoliberal Turn in Black Politics*. Brooklyn, NY: Punctum Books.

33 Henry, Charles P. 2008. "Is Barack Obama the End of White Politics?" *Black Scholar* 38, no. 4: 6–10.

34 Marans, Daniel. 2016. "How Trump Is Inspiring a New Generation of White Nationalists." *Huffington Post*. (www.huffingtonpost.com). For a discussion of the long-term alliance between populist conservatism and White nationalism, see Walters, Ronald W. 2003. *White Nationalism, Black Interests: Conservative Public Policy and the Black Community*. Detroit, MI: Wayne State University Press. Shaw, Todd, Louis Desipio, Dianne Pinderhughes and Toni-Michelle Travis. 2015. *Uneven Roads: Introduction to U.S. Racial and Ethnic Politics*. Washington, DC: CQ Press.

35 Bobo, Lawrence D. 2011. "Somewhere between Jim Crow and Post-Racialism: Reflections on the Racial Divide in American Today." *American Academy of Arts and Sciences* 140: 11–36.

36 Bonilla-Silva, Eduardo and David Dietrick. 2011. "The Sweet Enchantment of Color-Blind Racism in Obamerica." *The Annals of American Academy of Political and Social Science* 634: 190–206. Wise, Tim. 2010. *Color-Blind: The Rise of Post-Racial Politics and the Retreat from Racial Equity*. San Francisco: City Lights Books.

37 Bush, Daniel. "'I Won't Stop Serving You' President Obama Tells a Crowd in Fare-well Address." PBS News Hour. (www.pbs.org).

38 Harris, Fredrick C. 2012. *The Price of the Ticket: Barack Obama and the Rise and Decline of Black Politics*. Oxford: Oxford University Press.

39 Harris. 2012. *The Price of the Ticket*.

40 Capehart, Jonathan. 2013. "Obama Can't Win with Some Black Critics." *Washington Post*.

41 Capehart, Jonathan. 2012. "Stop Waiting for and Start Paying Attention to Our First Black President." *Washington Post*. Capehart, Jonathan. 2013. "Obama Can't Win with Some Black Critics." *Washington Post*. For a "fact sheet" issued by the White House regarding its record in serving the African American community, see "Fact Sheet—Creating Opportunities for All Americans Obama Administration's Record and the African-American Community." White House. (www.whitehouse.gov). It is interesting that all of the items discussed have to do with serving the economic needs of the community. There is no mention of civil rights and racial justice/discrimination issues.

42 Smith, Rogers M. and Desmond King. 2009. "Barack Obama and the Future of American Racial Politics." *Du Bois Review* 6, no. 1: 25–35. Walton, Hanes and Robert Charles Smith. 2011. *American Politics and the African American Quest for Universal Freedom*. New York: Pearson Longman.

43 Aberbach, Joel D. and Mark A. Peterson, eds. 2005. *The Executive Branch*. Oxford: Oxford University Press. Cronin, Thomas E. and Michael A. Genovese. 2010. *The Paradoxes of the American Presidency*. Oxford: Oxford University Press. Greenstein, Fred I. 2005. "The Person of the President, Leadership, and Greatness." In *The Executive Branch: Institutions of American Democracy*, eds. J. D. Aberbach and M. A. Peterson, 218–40. Oxford: Oxford University Press. Laing, Matthew. 2012. "Towards a Pragmatic Presidency? Exploring the Waning of Political Time." *Polity* 44, no. 2: 234–59. Pika, Joseph A and John Anthony Maltese. 2010. *The Politics of the Presidency*. Washington, DC: CQ Press. For the Cronin quote see Cronin, Thomas E. and Michael A. Genovese. 2010. *The Paradoxes of the American Presidency*. Oxford: Oxford University Press.

44 Aberbach, Joel D. and Mark A. Peterson. 2005. "Control and Accountability: Dilemmas of the Executive Branch." In *The Executive Branch*, eds. J. D. Aberbach and M. A. Peterson, 525–53. Oxford: Oxford University Press, Cronin, Thomas E. and Michael A. Genovese. 2010. *The Paradoxes of the American Presidency*. Oxford: Oxford University Press.

45 Greenstein, Fred I. 2005. "The Person of the President, Leadership, and Great-ness." In *The Executive Branch: Institutions of American Democracy*, eds. J. D. Aberbach and M. A. Peterson, 218–40. Oxford: Oxford University Press. Jacobs, Lawrence R. and Desmond King. 2010. "Varieites of Obamaism: Structure, Agency, and the Obama Presidency." *Perspectives on Politics* 8, no. 3: 793–802. Laing, Matthew. 2012. "Towards a Pragmatic Presidency? Exploring the Waning of Political Time." *Polity* 44, no. 2: 234–59. Neustadt, Richard E. 1980. *Presidential Power*. New York: John Wiley & Sons.

46 Laing, Matthew. 2012. "Towards a Pragmatic Presidency? Exploring the Waning of Political Time." *Polity* 44, no. 2: 234–59. Skowronek, Stephen. 1997. *The Politics Presidents Make*. Cambridge, MA: Belknap Press.

47 Laing, Matthew. 2012. "Towards a Pragmatic Presidency? Exploring the Waning of Political Time." *Polity* 44, no. 2: 234–59.

48 Ball, Molly. 2016. "Is the Tea Party Responsible for Donald Trump?" *Atlantic* (www.theatlantic.com).

49 Nichols, Curt, and Adam Myers. 2010. "Exploiting the Opportunity for Recon-structive Leadership: Presidential Responses to Enervated Political Regimes." *American Politics Research* 38, no. 5: 806–41.

50 Michael Grunwald has argued that the Obama had a domestic policy legacy that needs to be more fundamentally understood for the shifts it prompted—Grunwald, Micahel. 2016. "The Obama Issue: The Nation He Built. A Politico Review of Barack Obama's Domestic Policy Legacy—and the Changes He Made While Nobody Was Paying Attention." *Politico*.

51 "The Democratic Blue Wave Was Real." *Guardian* (www.theguardian.com).

52 Office of the Press Secretary. 2016. "Remarks of President Barack Obama—State of the Union Address as Delivered." (www.whitehouse.gov). Tesler, Michael. 2013. "The Return of Old-Fashioned Racism to White Americans' Partisan Preferences in the Early Obama Era." *Journal of Politics* 75, no. 1: 110–23. Milkis, Sidney M., Jesse J. Rhodes and Emily J. Charnock. 2012. "What Happened to Post-Partisanship? Barack Obama and the New American Party System." *Perspectives on Politics* 10, no. 1: 57–76.

53 Jacobs, Lawrence R. and Desmond King. 2010. "Varieites of Obamaism: Structure, Agency, and the Obama Presidency." *Perspectives on Politics* 8, no. 3: 793–802.

54 For discussion of the extensive linked fate literature, refer to Cohen, Cathy. 1999. *The Boundaries of Blackness: Aids in the Black Community*. Chicago: University of Chicago Press. Dawson, Michael. 1994. *Behind the Mule: Race and Class in African American Politics*. Princeton, NJ: Princeton University Press. Gurin, Patricia, Shir-ley Hatchett and James S. Jackson. 1989. *Hope and Independence: Blacks' Response to Electoral and Party Politics*. New York: Russell Sage Foundation. Nunnally, Shayla C. 2010. "Linking Blackness or Ethnic Othering?" *Du Bois Review: Social Science Research on Race* 7, no. 2: 335–55. Simien, Evelyn M. 2005. "Race, Gender, and Linked Fate." *Journal of Black Studies* 35, no. 5: 529–50. Simien, Evelyn M. 2006. *Black Feminist Voices in Politics*. Albany, NY: SUNY Press. Tate, Katherine.

1994. *From Protest to Politics: The New Black Voters in American Elections*: Cambridge, MA: Harvard University Press.

55 Reed, Adolph, Jr. 1999. "Sources of Demobilization in the New Black Political Regime: Incorporation, Ideological Capitulation, and Radical Failure in the Post-Segregation Era." In *Stirrings in the Jug: Black Politics in the Post-Segregation Era*, ed. A. Reed Jr. 117–59. Minneapolis: University of Minnesota Press.

56 Bobo, Lawrence and Franklin D. Gilliam Jr. 1990. "Race, Sociopolitical Participation, and Black Empowerment." *American Political Science Review*: 84, no 2: 377–93. For the Harris quote, see Harris, Fredrick C. 2012. *The Price of the Ticket: Barack Obama and the Rise and Decline of Black Politics*. Oxford: Oxford University Press.

57 Harris, Fredrick C. 2012. *The Price of the Ticket: Barack Obama and the Rise and Decline of Black Politics*. Oxford: Oxford University Press. Higginbotham, Evelyn Brooks. 1993. *Righteous Discontent: The Women's Movement in the Black Baptist Church, 1880–1920*. Cambridge, MA: Harvard University Press.

58 Obama, Barack. 2008, "Text of Obama's Fatherhood Speech," Politico. Retrieved March 10. (http://politico.com).

59 Obama. 2008, "Text of Obama's Fatherhood Speech."

60 Harris, Fredrick C. 2012. *The Price of the Ticket: Barack Obama and the Rise and Decline of Black Politics*. Oxford: Oxford University Press. Price, Melanye T. 2016. *The Race Whisperer: Barack Obama and the Political Uses of Race*. New York: New York University Press.

61 Dyson. 2016. *The Black Presidency*. Ed. Jones, Angela. 2013. *The Modern African American Political Thought Reader*. New York and London: Routledge.

62 Condon, George E. and Jim O'Sullivan. 2013. "Has President Obama Done Enough for Black Americans?" *Atlantic*.

63 "53 Historians Weign in on Barack Obama's Legacy." 2015. *New York Magazine*. Retrieved May 31, 2016. (http://nymag.com). Senior, Jennifer. 2015. "The Paradox of the First Black President." *New York Magazine*. (http://nymag.com).

64 For an extensive discussion of the supporting literature and research, see Bobo, Lawrence D. 2011. "Somewhere between Jim Crow and Post-Racialism: Reflections on the Racial Divide in American Today." *American Academy of Arts and Sciences* 140, no. 2: 11–36. Burnham, Linda. 2009. "Obama's Candidacy: The Advent of Post-Racial America and the End of Black Politics?" *Black Scholar* 38, no. 4: 43–46. Craemer, Thomas, Todd C. Shaw, Courtney Edwards and Hakeem Jefferson. 2013. "'Race Still Matters, However . . .': Implicit Identification with Blacks, Pro-Black Policy Support and the Obama Candidacy." *Ethnic and Racial Studies* 36, no. 6: 1047–69, Goldman, Seth K. and Diana C. Mutz. 2014. *The Obama Effect: How the 2008 Campaign Changed White Racial Attitudes*. New York: Russell Sage. Grofman, Bernard. 2013. "Devising a Sensible Trigger for Section 5 of the Voting Rights Act." *Election Law Journal* 12, no. 3: 332–37. Holder, Eric. 2013. "Remarks at the Annual Meeting of American Bar Association's House of Delegates." *Federal Sentencing Reporter* 26, no. 2: 75–79. King, Desmond S. and Rogers M. Smith. 2014. "The Last Stand: Restricting Voting Rights and Sustaining White Power in Modern America."

Lopez, Ian F. Haney. 2010. "Post-Racial Racism: Racial Stratificationand Mass Incarceration in the Age of Obama." *California Law Review* 98: 1023–74. Marable, Manning. 2009. "Racializing Obama: The Enigma of Post-Black Politics and Leadership." *Souls* 11, no. 1: 1–15. Rachlinski, Jeffrey J. and Gregory S. Parks. 2010. "Implicit Bias, Election '08, and the Myth of a Post-Racial America." *Florida State University Law Review* 37: 659–715. Savage, Charlie. 2011. "Retroactive Reductions Sought in Crack Penalties." *New York Times*. Short, John Rennie. 2014. "The Supreme Court, the Voting Rights Act and Competing National Imaginaries of the USA." *Territory, Politics, Governance* 2, no. 1: 94–108. Sinclair-Chapman, Valeria and Melayne Price. 2008. "Black Politics, the 2008 Election, and the (Im)Possibility of Race Transcendence." *PS: Political Science and Politics*: 739–45. Tesler, Michael. 2012. "The Spillover of Racialization into Health Care: How President Obama Polarized Public Opinion by Racial Attitudes and Race." *American Journal of Political Science* 56, no. 3: 690–704. Tesler, Michael. 2013. "The Return of Old-Fashioned Racism to White Americans' Partisan Preferences in the Early Obama Era." *Journal of Politics* 75, no. 1: 110–23. Tonry, Michael. 2011. *Punishing Race: A Continuing American Dilemma*. Oxford: University of Oxford Press. Wise, Tim. 2010. *Color-Blind: The Rise of Post-Racial Politics and the Retreat from Racial Equity*. San Francisco: City Lights Books.

65 Hine, Darlene Clarke, William C. Hine and Stanley Harrold. 2006. *African Americans: A Concise History*. Upper Saddle River, NJ: Pearson.

66 Walton, Hanes and Robert Charles Smith. 2011. *American Politics and the African American Quest for Universal Freedom*. New York: Pearson Longman. Curiously, the authors typologize each president in table 12.1 and list Obama as a "Racist." But I conferred with Robert Smith, and he confirmed that this was a Freudian error.

67 Harris, Fredrick C. 2012. *The Price of the Ticket: Barack Obama and the Rise and Decline of Black Politics*. Oxford: Oxford University Press. Herbert, Bob. 2009. "Anger Has Its Place." *New York Times*. Smiley, Tavis. 2009. *Accountable: Making America as Good as Its Promise*. New York: Atria Books.

68 Capehart, Jonathan. 2012. "Stop Waiting for and Start Paying Attention to Our First Black President." *Washington Post*. Harris, Fredrick C. 2012. *The Price of the Ticket: Barack Obama and the Rise and Decline of Black Politics*. Oxford: Oxford University Press. For the Rich quote, refer to Rich, Wilbur. 2007. "Presidential Leadership and the Politics of Race: Stereotypes, Symbols, and Scholarship." In *African American Perspectives on Political Science*, ed. W. Rich, 232–50. Philadelphia: Temple University Press. Recently, Smiley expressed a great admiration for Obama—see Smiley, Tavis. 2017. "Tavis Smiley: A Letter to Obama, in Gratitude and Love." *Time*.

69 Obama, Barack. 2009. "Nobel Peace Prize Speech." *New York Times*.

70 Milkis, Sidney M., Jesse J. Rhodes and Emily J. Charnock. 2012. "What Happened to Post-Partisanship? Barack Obama and the New American Party System." *Perspectives on Politics* 10, no. 1: 57–76.

71 Walters, Ronald W. 1988. *Black Presidential Politics: A Strategic Approach*. Albany, NY: State Unversity of New York.

72 Issacs, Stephen. 1972. "Shirley Chisholm Makes It Formal: She's a Candidate." *Washington Post*.

73 Barker, Lucius. 1988. *Our Time Has Come: A Diary of Jesse Jackson's 1984 Presidential Campaign*. Urbana-Champaign: University of Illinois Press.

74 Harris, Fredrick C. 2012. *The Price of the Ticket: Barack Obama and the Rise and Decline of Black Politics*. Oxford: Oxford University Press. Morris, Lorenzo. 1990. *The Social and Political Implications of the 1984 Jesse Jackson Presidential Campaign*. Wesport, CT: Praeger.

75 Harris, Fredrick C. 2012. *The Price of the Ticket: Barack Obama and the Rise and Decline of Black Politics*. Oxford: Oxford University Press.

76 Obama, Barack. 2007. *Dreams from My Father: A Story of Race and Inheritance*. New York: Canongate Books.

77 Lanza-Kaduce, Lonn and Andrea Davis. 2013. "License to Kill: Theoretical Critique of 'Stand Your Ground' Policies." Unpublished manuscript. Office of the Press Secretary. 2013. "Remarks by the President on Trayvon Martin." Washington, DC: White House. Retrieved June 6, 2016 (www.whitehouse.gov).

78 Dungca, Nicole, Jenn Abelson, Mark Berman, and John Sullivan. 2020. "A Dozen High-Profile Fatal Encounters Have Galvanized Protests Nationwide." *Washington Post*, June 8, 2020 (www.washingtonpost.com).

79 Goldfarb, Zachary. 2014. "President Obama to Launch Major New Effort to Help Young Minority Men." *Washington Post*. Prince, Richard. 2014. "'My Brother's Keeper': Did Obama Just Become 'the Black President'?" *The Root*. Retrieved 2014 (www.theroot.com). Baker, Peter. "Obama, in Oklahoma, Takes Reform Message to the Prison Cell Block." *New York Times*.

80 Robinson, Gerard. 2019, January 6. "First Step Act's Passage Represents a Starting Point to Address Issues in the Criminal Justice System." *The Hill* (https://thehill .com).

PART I

Constituencies

1

Race, Trust, and the American Presidency

*Black-White Confidence in the Executive Branch in
the Obama Era and Beyond*

SHAYLA C. NUNNALLY

In 2008 the election of the United States' first Black president, President Barack H. Obama, marked an important historical milestone. However, without a question, the significance of this presidential election was due to the historic past of Whites refusing to support Black candidates and definitively denying the support of electing a Black president (Schuman et al. 1997). In what was perceived to be a new beginning in American politics—White Americans being more embracing of Black candidates and even one running for the highest office in the land—we have witnessed over time that President Obama's race has negatively affected White Americans' perceptions about his administration and its policies. For example, we find that Whites' support of the Affordable Care Act of 2010 decreased as they expressed more negative racial attitudes. Hence, even with respect to a nonracial issue, health policy became "racialized" through Whites' racial animus toward President Obama's race, as a Black, chief policy leader, and their attitudes "spilled over" into their health policy support (Tesler and Sears 2010; Tesler 2012). This racializing effect constitutes what Tesler (2012) refers to as the "spillover of racialization."

To explain further, in Tesler's iteration of "racialization," President Obama's race cues Whites' psyches, constantly, such that their racially resentful attitudes "spill over" into non-race-related policies because they are merely *associated* with the Black president's platform. With such implicit interpretations of the President's race, it also seems logical to think that his race has implications for Black Americans' (as shared racial group members) and other people's trust in the American presidency and the government in which he leads, as their attitudes about him "spill over" into their thoughts about the executive branch, in particular, and his administration, in general.

Depending upon constituents' perceptions of political actors' race (Gay 2002; Nunnally 2012), there is evidence elucidating racial divisions in political trust over time (Pew Research Center Report 2015; Putnam 2000; Brehm and Rahn 1997) and even trust variation. Thus, it seems within reason to turn to the Obama presidency and to submit that trust in federal government during this administration's era may not only be racially divided but also distinctive compared to other presidencies. Conversely, during the Obama presidency the "spillover of racialization" may be positive for observing Black Americans attitudes and their trust in government may be more positive than those of Whites. A longitudinal analysis of attitudes about various presidencies should reflect for both Black and White Americans a distinctive attitudinal reaction to the Obama era—an attitudinal reaction that, nevertheless, will be divided by the color line and racial schisms in political trust. Overall, expanding upon Tesler's "spillover of racialization," this chapters asks: Does having a Black president, compared to previous administrations occupied by White presidents, lead to aberrational trust in government for Blacks and Whites? I posit that the Obama presidency, indeed, had this effect.

Such nexuses between race and trust in government are the focus of this chapter. Using pooled cross-sectional time series data from the 1972–2012 General Social Survey,[1] we can determine whether there are racial differences in trust in government over time and whether the Obama presidency renders a unique "shock" to the American political system that is distinctive for Whites' (decreased) versus Blacks' (increased) trust in the executive branch of the federal government.

In the next sections, I discuss trends in political trust and the importance of the presidency in evaluations of government performance. Then, I describe the racialized nature of politics for representation and trust by individual political actors and actors as partisans in the presidency. It is important to note that, contrary to my expectation, the results of the public opinion analyses indicate that trust attitudes during the Obama presidency are more positive for Blacks than Whites; however, compared over the forty-year period, the results are not consistently aberrational. Subsequently, I examine the racial implications of these results for Americans' political trust *after* the Obama era, especially during the early years of the Donald J. Trump presidency.

Theoretical Background

Trends in Americans' Political Trust and Perceptions of US Government

Trust "is a belief about a person, institution, or context that stems from an assessment about who[m] or what can deliver an outcome with the least harmful risk and with the greatest benefit to the trustor" (Nunnally 2012: 24). Political trust translates this assessment of others to trust in political actors and institutions. In addition, political trust is important because democracy normatively works best when its citizens trust not only American political institutions but also the political actors and public servants who serve in these institutions. They help citizens feel more or less connected to government (Putnam 1993; Brehm 1998).

The all-time highest recorded trust in US federal government was in 1964, when 77 percent of Americans reported that they could trust it to "do the right thing" "always" and "most of the time" (Pew Research Center 2015). Since the 1970s, however, there has been a general decline in American political trust, falling by almost 40 percentage points. Moreover, between July 2007 and August 2015, Americans expressed the longest period of low trust since 1958 (Pew Research Center Report 2015). Scholars offer several explanations for this decline, but most notably, studies point to citizens' dissatisfaction with the performance of government (Braithwaite and Levi 1998; Bernstein 2001) its political institutions (Blendon et al. 1997; Hibbing and Theiss-Morse 2001) and its political incumbents (Feldman 1983; Citrin and Luks 2001; Cook and Gronke 2005). This especially includes those political actors associated with political scandals (Bowler and Karp 2004). In essence, *how* public servants serve in their positions affects how people think of and relate to government.

From 1972–1997, the American public's trust in the presidency and Congress also decreased; meanwhile, their trust in the US Supreme Court increased (Pew Research Center 1998). Thus, political trust in American government can vary among political institutions *and* branches of government. Feldman (1983) also finds that political trust in political institutions depends largely upon the office that political actors or incumbents hold. Political trust in the American presidency and, hence, the executive branch of government depends upon who is the sitting US president.

As criticism of political leaders serves as a major predictor of trust in government (Pew Research Center 1998), how people perceive political elites in political institutions also affects how people view and possibly trust government, in general. Therefore, it is reasonable to think about variance in people's political trust being based upon their attitudes about different branches of government and the political actors within them, who make decisions at particular points in time. As I submit, race affects how people trust in political actors and political institutions. It possibly leads to divides in political trust, especially with respect to the American presidency and the president's stances on policy issues, as chief party leaders.

The Racial Divide in Party Politics: Grounds for Racialized Political Trust in the Presidency

The president leads the executive branch. Whoever assumes the American presidency also has the ability to sway public opinion on various issues (Neustadt 1990; Kernell 1997) and set the legislative agenda for his political party's platform. Presidents, additionally, curry power and (dis)favor among the American public, such that their approval ratings indicate support or nonsupport of their administrations' policies and performances. Since the 1970s, trust in government appears correlated with the incumbent political party controlling the White House (Pew Research Center Report 2015). In addition, presidential approval ratings vary by race.

For example, Abrajano and Burnett (2012) find that Black support for the two most recent Democratic presidents, Bill Clinton and Barack Obama, on average tends to be higher than White support. Comparatively, Black Americans' support of President Obama is higher than their support of President Clinton. Even when controlling for partisanship and ideology, the difference in presidential approval ratings between Blacks and Whites remained. Thus, as Abrajano and Burnett (2012) conclude, there is some effect of racial solidarity with President Obama that appears to influence how Blacks think about President Obama compared to President Clinton. This connection lends itself to the debate about the descriptive (race) or substantive (partisanship) aspects of Americans' representation, which often exists through racialized lenses and differences in political trust.

Notably, the decline in political trust has been marked by a racial divide, wherein Blacks' political trust is less than Whites' (Putnam 1995; 2000; Brehm and Rahn 1997; Avery 2006 and 2009; Pew Research Center 2010b; Mangum 2012; Nunnally 2012). Scholars have discerned the significance of perceived racial alienation, discrimination, and distinctiveness of White political actors in decreasing Black Americans' political trust (Abramson 1977; Avery 2006 and 2009; Nunnally 2012). These racial distinctions between Whites' and Blacks' political trust over time also elucidate the complexities of race in groups relating to the political system, especially by dint of their group interests and perceived quality of representation (Nunnally 2012), and as political institutions that connect citizens to government, political parties have used the racial divide between Blacks and Whites to their advantage, thusly, racializing political trust even via the American political party system.

As race and political interests often are inextricably linked in American politics (Dawson 1994; Kinder and Sanders 1996; Mendelberg 2001), scholars have inquired whether the political interests of Blacks can be best represented equally by Blacks and non-Blacks (Whites) (Swain 1993; Tate 2003). Evidence suggests that this query depends upon the extent of trust that Blacks have in political institutions like Congress, that they may or may not perceive to host a large number of Black representatives (Tate 2003). This political trust also depends on the extent of trust that Blacks have in their representatives, who share both partisan and racial backgrounds most favorable to their political interests—hence, Black Democrats become their most entrusted political actors (Nunnally 2012). It was not until the election of President Obama that Black Americans had the opportunity to extend their political trust to the highest-level political office with a Black incumbent. It was also during this administration that Blacks' political trust surpassed that of Whites' (Pew Research Center Report 2010a). However, during the Obama presidency, trust in the overall federal government was the lowest of all presidencies, beginning with the Kennedy and Johnson administrations (Pew Research Center Report 2015).

The literature on political representation has long questioned whether descriptive representation increases the appeal political representatives and the political system have for Black Americans (Swain 1993; Tate 1993; Mansbridge 1999; Gay 2002). This is due to the historical connection between race and political interests. White political actors, most notably in the South, have blocked the full citizenship rights of Blacks until the mid-twentieth-century civil rights legislation. Black agitation for equality was in stark contrast with the status quo of the American political system, whereby federal, state, and local political institutions were complicit in the suppression of their rights prior to the civil rights movement (McAdam 1982). Most Americans trust state government more than the federal government (Pew Research Center Report 2015). Interestingly, when it comes to civil rights and trust in government, those persons who trust in federal government more than they do state government are also more likely to believe that the federal government better handles the economy and civil rights (Blendon et al. 1997). Black Americans, however, trust the federal government more than state governments, and this is likely due to the civil rights–era push toward the national government enforcing legislation to protect the rights of Black Americans that, otherwise, Southern states avoided with deliberate delay (Uslaner 2001; Nunnally 2012). Scholars often attribute Black Americans' political distrust to their historical and ongoing experiences with racial discrimination (Avery 2006 and 2009; Mangum 2012; Nunnally 2012.)

During the twentieth century, American presidents often brokered any national forum for addressing the status of African Americans. However, presidential actions regarding the civil rights of Blacks, and more broadly, antidiscrimination, varied according to partisanship (Shull 1999). For example, Democratic president Lyndon B. Johnson encouraged the passage of the Civil Rights Act of 1964, the Voting Rights Act of 1965, and the Fair Housing Act of 1968.[2] These changes in the Democratic Party's national platform precipitated a full realignment among Southern White Democrats, which drove Whites more toward the Republican Party. Meanwhile, the acts drove Black Americans overwhelmingly to support the Democratic Party (Carmines and Stimson 1989; Mendelberg 2001; Frymer 1999; Hajnal and Lee 2011). Nonetheless,

Blacks have had to navigate their relationships with the US presidents in order to pressure policies that align with their interests (Walters 1988).

This partisan realignment along the cleavage of race and civil rights has structured American two-party politics for the past five decades (Carmines and Stimson 1989). It evoked the Southern strategy by Republican presidential candidates, most especially Richard Nixon, and the implicit use of racial cuing to mobilize White voters. They now are sensitive to issues commonly "racialized" and associated with racial and ethnic minorities (e.g., welfare, immigration, crime—Mendelberg 2001). Racially provocative campaigning and promotion of policies that were implicit racial codes (e.g., welfare, law and order, crime) provoked White support. But they had the opposite effect on Blacks and detracted Black support for the Republican Party, though it was a party Blacks supported prior to the New Deal era (Weiss 1983; Frymer 1999; Mendelberg 2001; Fauntroy 2007; Rigueur 2015). These party politics contributed to racialized perceptions of the two major parties by both Blacks and Whites. Increasingly, the Republican Party's racially distancing itself from Blacks and the party's embracing conservative policies often rejected by Black Democrats meant the Republican presidencies of Ronald Reagan and George H. W. Bush were less attractive to Blacks (Shull 1999). Perceived delayed responses to natural disasters like Hurricane Katrina, which stranded many Black Americans in New Orleans without basic resources for subsistence, made President George W. Bush appear less sensitive to Blacks' well-being, thus lowering Black Americans' approval for his presidency (Pew Research Center Report 2005; Dawson 2011).

A Pew Research Center report (2012) on American partisanship found that, in 2008, about 88 percent of Black respondents indicated being "Democrats" or "Democrat-leaning," with 87 percent identifying as such in 2012. Only 6 and 7 percent, for those respective years, identified as "Republican" or "Republican-leaning." In 2008, over 40 percent of Democratic Party supporters were racial and ethnic minorities. Only 8 percent of racial and ethnic minorities identified as "Republicans" (Abrajano and Burnett 2012). Among Whites, partisanship was more evenly divided between Democrats and Republicans, with 46 percent identifying as "Republicans" or "Republican-leaning" in 2008 and 44 percent identifying as such in 2012. In 2012, among White men, the difference in Democratic (35 percent) versus Republican (57 percent) partisanship was 22 percentage points, with the greatest support being for Republicans. Increasingly, the American political party system has become divided by race.

Today, Blacks also perceive the Democratic Party as working hardest on issues of major concern to their group (Dawson 1994; Hajnal and Lee 2011). Black Americans also are more trusting of Black Democrats than they are of White Democrats (Nunnally 2012). In fact, experimental results predating the 2008 presidential primary season indicate that Black Americans trusted Democratic candidate Barack Obama more to represent Blacks' interests than Democratic candidate Hillary Clinton (Nunnally 2014). Whereas Democratic Blacks trusted candidate Obama to represent the interests of various racial (White, Black, and Latino) and race-sex (women) groups, Democratic Whites trusted candidate Obama solely to represent the interests of Blacks and Black women. Moreover, during the 2008 election, Whites trusted candidate Obama less and non-Whites trusted Obama more to address crises and be commander in chief in comparison to candidate Senator Hillary Clinton (McIlwain 2010).

Even exit poll results in both 2008 and 2012 reveal a racial divide between Blacks' and Whites' support of the Obama presidency, with Blacks offering overwhelming support in both years and Whites preferring the Republican candidate most (Senator John McCain in 2008 and Governor Mitt Romney in 2012) over Obama's candidacy (Roper Center 2008; Wilson 2012). With these interrelationships of race, trust, and partisanship, similar patterns of trust can be projected onto a Black president. During the Obama presidency, Black trust in the executive branch should be higher than White trust. In the words of Simien (2016), Obama's presidency was a "symbolic first," and shares their race (Black) and predominant partisanship (Democrat). For Whites, however, there is incongruency in race and predominant partisanship, as they tend to be more Republican (Pew Research Center 2012).

The "Spillover Effect": Race, Trust, and the Obama Presidency

No doubt, whether it is respect for the president or racialization of public policies introduced by the president, we see that Obama's race affected his presidency. Such effects also influenced Americans' political trust. As the previously mentioned research suggests, race, partisanship, and ideological leanings cue political trust. Depending upon the race of the perceiver and the race of the political actor to be entrusted, trust in government varies. Scholars have examined how a political actor's race (descriptive representation)[3] and partisanship (substantive representation) affect people's trust in government. The effects depend upon the congruency between the race and/or partisanship of the political actor and her/his constituent (Gay 2002; Nunnally 2012) as well as the perceptions of the majority race of the political actors within a political institution (Tate 2003). To this extent, even political institutions can be "racialized," as people perceive them to be dominated by or associated with people of a certain race or a political party. Thus, a Black Democratic president, like President Obama, can become associated with a political platform sensitive to non-Whites, as he is non-White and a member of the Democratic Party; a party which has become increasingly associated with non-Whites (Tesler 2013). Tesler describes how implicit cues serve as heuristics that trigger Whites' opposition to certain policies. These heuristics have the potential to decrease Whites' political trust of actors and institutions perceived as advocates for non-Whites. Non-White political elites, especially a Black Democratic president, cue negative attitudes about government and what it represents (Coates 2012).

By the same token, Americans who are non-White feel more or less trusting of political elites who do not share their partisan, ideological, and racial backgrounds, and this is evident in the distrust that Blacks feel toward White Republicans (Nunnally 2012). Turning to the theory of *inverted Black linked fate*, Black Americans, in particular, can feel a greater sense of trust in the American political system and its political institutions during the Obama presidency because, as they trust in a figurehead with a shared racial background and Democratic partisanship, government becomes a symbolic manifestation of their political desires and an amplification of the Black political presence in the highest office of the land. In this sense, Blacks' political trust should transfer, or "spill over to," President Obama and the rest of the executive branch.

Thus, for Black Americans, as a historically, politically alienated group, President Obama has the power and perceived connective will to execute government as fairly as possible because of his perceived personal interest *not* to discriminate against others who share his Black racial background. Put another way, as Blacks likely see it, Black racial sensitivity is his perceived personal, vested interest. Symbolically, this means that President Obama's administration should boost Blacks' trust in government unlike any presidency in American history. As an often "racialized" political figure, as Tesler describes, however, President Obama should have a more suppressive psychological effect on Whites' political trust, as he is perceived as more racially sensitive toward Blacks' political interests than toward Whites'.

"Symbolic racism" are White beliefs that racism no longer serves as an impediment to Blacks and thus blame is placed on Blacks for their stagnant socioeconomic status on their perceived unwillingness to work hard. Therefore, many Whites opposed policies (e.g., the Affordable Care and Patient Protection Act of 2010) proposed by President Obama's legislative agenda (Tesler and Sears 2010). These attitudes also drove increased racial conservatism, identification with the Republican Party, and the association of the Democratic Party with being the "Party of Obama" (Tesler 2013). Thus, Tesler illustrates how President Obama's race has what he calls a "spillover effect" on public policy: Whites react negatively to non-race-related policies because the policies are "racialized by association" with President Obama. It is this same "racialization by association" that effects White and Black trust in government and is most notable during the Obama years because of the novelty of a Black president.

Moreover, in other ways, Whites' and Blacks' perceived policy interests continue to be divided by racial fissures (Schuman et al. 1997; Kinder and Winter 2001). Since all previous presidents have been White, the Obama presidency was a shock to their perceived, White racial status quo. It was a political feat that heightens the "zero-sum" fears about Blacks taking over politics to the detriment to Whites perceived political interests (Nunnally 2014). Conversely, Black hope and trust in the political system should increase because of the election of the nation's first Black president, one who also shared the partisanship of almost 90 percent of Black Americans (Hajnal and Lee 2011).[4]

In this chapter, I argue President Obama has a *converse* "spillover effect" on how Blacks view political institutions at the federal level. As the nation's first Black president, Obama will have a *positivizing* effect on Blacks' trust in federal institutions, especially the executive branch of the federal government. Hence, he is a descriptive representative to fellow Black Americans (as a Black political actor) and a substantive representative to fellow Black Americans (as a Democratic partisan). For Whites, however, this "spillover effect" will be *negativizing* and decrease their trust in government. In short, *race* influences perceptions of the Obama presidency, and these perceptions will influence how people think about trust in government.

Hypotheses

I offer the following hypotheses for Blacks' and Whites' trust in government. I pay special attention to the effects of the Obama era on trust in the three branches of federal government, because of the "spillover effect" and the racialization of government:

H1: Generally, Black Americans' political trust will be less than Whites' political trust, across the forty-year survey.

H2: Black Americans should be notably more trusting than Whites in the executive branch during the presidential administrations of Clinton (2000) and Obama (2010, 2012) and less trusting during the G. W. Bush administration (2002, 2004, 2006, 2008).

H3: The "spillover" effect should indicate an increase in Blacks' political trust and a decrease in Whites' political trust, during the years of the Obama presidency (2009–2012)

H4: Compared to the years of all other presidencies over the forty-year period, Blacks' political trust should be the highest during the Obama presidency, whereas Whites' political trust should be the lowest.

Data and Methods

As my data, I use the 1972–2012 General Social Survey (GSS). It is a cumulative file that merges twenty-eight cross sections of national surveys conducted in all years (with the exception of 1992, 1997, 2001, 2003, 2005, 2007, 2009, and 2011). There is a single file for each year of the survey, and questions are repeated over a forty-year period, for a total of n = 57,061 completed interviews in the cumulative survey file. Respondents from 1972–2004 were drawn from a sample of persons age eighteen and over, who lived in noninstitutional arrangements, and as of 2006, Spanish-speakers were added to the sample. Designations for race changed over time, from "White," "Black," and "other" to include the addition of Latinos and Asian Americans (with subethnic groups) in the 2000 survey. For this analysis and the consistent measurement of persons over the forty-year period of the survey, the models are limited to the comparison of Black and White public opinion, as contextualized by the historic nature of politics, with respect to the Black-White dichotomy during this period. *Confidence in government*, or belief that political institutions will perform their ascribed duties, serves as an important proxy of political trust (Cook and Gronke 2005).

Therefore, the dependent variable for this analysis measures confidence in the executive branch of government because there is no variable that asks whether respondents "trust" specific persons or actors within the executive branch. More specifically, this question was posed to respondents: "I am going to name some institutions in this country. As far as the people running these institutions are concerned, would you say you have a great deal of confidence, only some confidence, or hardly any confidence at all in them?" The question is about the following: "*The Executive branch of the federal government* (although, not specifically referencing the 'president' or the leadership within the bureaucracy)." The questions appeared in the GSS for all years of the survey, with the exception of 1972, 1985, 1992, 2001, 2003, 2005, 2007, 2009, and 2011, for a total of nineteen cross sections of the national surveys over the forty-year period.

Due to limitations in questions being asked consistently across the forty-year period, there are a limited number of variables of interest for which the analyses can test the determinants of confidence in the American political institutions at the federal level. Nonetheless, I control for standard demographic variables: *race* (1 = Black; 0 = White,); *age* (2 = 18–24; 3 = 25–29; 4 = 30–34; 5 = 35–44; 6 = 45–54; 7 = 55–64; 8 = over 65); *gender* (female = 1); *income* (1 = under \$1,000 to 12 = \$25,000 and over—the consistent measure of income over time); *education* (years of education, 0 = no formal schooling to 20 = 8 years of college); and *region* (South = 1).

With respect to controls for people's political orientations, I account for *partisanship* (1 = Strong Democrat to 7 = Strong Republican) and *ideology* (1 = Extremely Liberal to 7 = Extremely Conservative). To compare the effects for years of a Republican versus a Democratic presidency during more recent and salient presidencies, I include dummy variables for the end of the Bill Clinton presidency (2000), the years of the survey during the George W. Bush presidency (2002, 2004, 2006, 2008), and the years of the survey during the Obama presidency (2010, 2012) to determine two things: (1) whether these years are distinct from all others in the forty-year survey and (2) whether the effect of confidence in the executive branch is more or less than it is for all other years.[5]

I employ ordinary least squares models for each of the three branches of government and their respective, federal-level institutions. Separate models test (1) a comparison of confidence between Blacks and Whites and (2) determinants of Blacks' confidence in these branches. The models comparing Blacks' and Whites' confidence in the political institutions also include interaction terms between race and year (*Black*Year*) to determine whether Blacks' attitudes are distinctly different from Whites during the years of the Bill Clinton, George W. Bush, and Barack Obama presidencies.

Previous research shows that Blacks were more trusting in government during the Clinton administration, whereas Whites were more trusting during the Reagan and George H. W. Bush administrations (Citrin and Luks 2001). Because of the post-9/11 boost in political trust among Americans (Keele 2007), we may see confidence in government wax in 2001. This may be followed by a wane in political confidence due to the unpopularity of the Iraq War and Afghanistan military involvements in 2006, and then the economic downturn in 2008.

During the Obama presidency, White attitudes trended downward, consistent with their views in 2010, wherein Whites expressed greater frustration (60 percent) and need for major reform of government (55 percent) than did Blacks (48 percent and 44 percent, respectively; Pew Research Center 2010b). Due to the notably higher level of support among Black women for the Obama presidential bids (Wilson 2012), we should see a greater level of this group's support during this presidency. Thus, I include a dummy variable for gender and year (*Female*Year*) in the Black public opinion model in order to analyze gender differences in opinions between Black women and Black men.

Results: Confidence in the Executive Branch

Figure 1.1 shows the trend in Blacks' and Whites' mean levels of confidence in the "people running the executive branch of the federal government." Notably, the two groups have a similar trend in confidence about the executive branch. Table 1.1, however, elucidates the general case, as the literature often shows, that Black Americans are generally less confident in the executive branch than are Whites, thus, confirming *Hypothesis 1*. Yet, there is an uptick in Blacks' confidence levels in 2010 and 2012, the years that coincide with the Obama presidency, and across the approximately forty-year period, we also see during these years that Blacks have higher levels of confidence in the executive branch than Whites do. As *Hypothesis 2* suggests, Black Americans, indeed, exemplify greater levels of confidence than Whites in the executive branch during the Obama presidency. Where there are slight increases in Blacks' confidence in 1994 and 1998 (years during the Clinton presidency), these increases are not as high as those noted during the Obama administration.

Consistent with the expectation in *Hypothesis 2*, table 1.1 shows that Blacks display a higher level of confidence than Whites in 2000, as noted by the statistically significant interaction term for Black Americans and the year 2000, which is a year coinciding with the end of the Clinton presidency. Given that the survey data were collected in February, March, and April of 2000, it was a year with a controversial presidential election. It witnessed allegations of Black disfranchisement in states like Florida that prolonged declaring the official winner until after the first of December of that year. Moreover, President Clinton, although embattled by the revelations of the Monica Lewinsky scandal, was still in office and substantively represented the partisanship common to almost 90 percent of Black Americans.

As expected, in the succeeding George W. Bush administration (years 2002 and 2004), Black Americans have lower levels of confidence in the executive branch. Despite the notable distinction in Black and White confidence in the executive branch, between 2002 and 2004, this

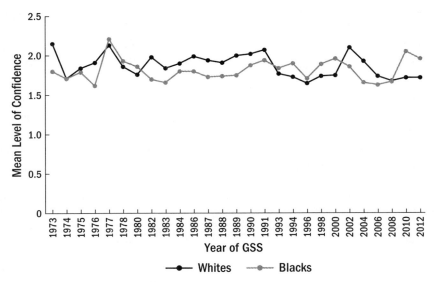

Figure 1.1. Confidence in executive branch of federal government, 1973–2012. *Source*: 1972–2012 General Social Survey (Cumulative Data File).

does not translate into glaring distinctions in Black and White views compared to the rest of the forty-year period. In 2006 and 2008, Black and White confidence in the Bush executive branch converges, with no statistically significant racial difference in their attitudes during these years. To reiterate, we see Black confidence in the executive branch outpace White confidence during the Obama presidency (refer to figure 1.1), but we also see, for the first time in the forty-year period, Black confidence in the executive branch outpace White confidence by the widest margin.

With respect to Black public opinion, table 1.2 shows that Black men and women think differently about their confidence in the executive branch. Black women generally are less confident in this branch than are Black men. However, these gender differences change during 2002, 2006, 2008, and 2010, when Black women are more trusting than Black men. Only one of these years in which Black women have higher levels of confidence is during the Obama administration. The other years interestingly are during the G. W. Bush administration. But Black women's higher level of confidence is not sustained during 2012, despite their

TABLE 1.1. Black Levels of Confidence in the Executive Branch

Covariates	Confidence in the Executive Branch	S.E.
Black	−.0601****	.0139
Age	−.0003	.0002
Female	.0171**	.0078
Income	−.0042***	.0015
Education	.0045***	.0014
South	.0309****	.0084
Partisanship (Strong Democrat to Strong Republican)	.0167****	.0022
Ideology (Extremely Liberal to Extremely Conservative)	.0062**	.0031
Year 2000	−.1234****	.0202
Year 2002	.2371****	.0271
Year 2004	.0612	.0279
Year 2006	−.1283****	.0201
Year 2008	−.1926****	.0233
Year 2010	−.1138**	.0234
Year 2012	−.1441****	.0241
Black*Year 2000	.2696****	.0542
Black*Year 2002	−.2326****	.0717
Black*Year 2004	−.2000**	.0093
Black*Year 2006	−.0344	.0509
Black*Year 2008	.0839	.0604
Black*Year 2010	.3381****	.0566
Black*Year 2012	.3304****	.0582
Constant	1.775****	.0273
R^2	0.02	
$N =$	28852	

OLS Models of Blacks' and Whites' Confidence in the Executive Branch of Government, 1973–2012

Source: 1972–2012 General Social Survey (Cumulative Data File)

Note: Models are calculated using ordinary least squares regression.

* $p \leq .10$; ** $p \leq .05$; *** $p \leq .01$; **** $p \leq .001$

TABLE 1.2. Gender Differences in Levels of Confidence

Covariates	Confidence in the Executive Branch	S.E.
Age	.0005	.0007
Female	−.0575**	.0250
Income	−.0067**	.0034
Education	−.0141****	.0040
South	.0721****	.0208
Partisanship (Strong Democrat to Strong Republican)	.0099	.0072
Ideology (Extremely Liberal to Extremely Conservative)	−.0008	.0073
Year 2000	.1507****	.0866
Year 2002	−.1243	.1026
Year 2004	−.1308	.1230
Year 2006	−.2430****	.0735
Year 2008	−.1937**	.0806
Year 2010	.1101	.0799
Year 2012	.1337	.0847
Female*Year 2000	.0346	.1050
Female*Year 2002	.2321*	.1324
Female*Year 2004	.0376	.1538
Female*Year 2006	.1730*	.0937
Female*Year 2008	.1897*	.1093
Female*Year 2010	.2373**	.1029
Female*Year 2012	.1199	.1070
Constant	1.985****	.0716
R^2	0.03	
$N =$	4020	

OLS Models of Blacks' Confidence in the Executive Branch of Government, 1973–2012
Source: 1972–2012 General Social Survey (Cumulative Data File)
Note: Models are calculated using ordinary least squares regression.
* $p \le .10$; ** $p \le .05$; *** $p \le .01$; **** $p \le .001$

higher-level support of President Obama's reelection than Black men in the same year (Wilson 2012).

Even though there is a boost in Black confidence in the executive branch by 2010, the greatest level of confidence in the executive branch is in 1977—during the Jimmy Carter presidency. Despite the uptick in Black levels of political trust, as compared to White levels of political trust, there is no notable decrease in White levels of political trust. While part of *Hypothesis 3* is confirmed, my hypothesis about Black public opinion it is not confirmed. The level of White political trust is more stable compared to previous years of the Obama presidency. Despite high levels of Black racial solidarity with President Obama, a positive "spillover effect" does not register as an anomalous condition of this presidency with extremely high levels of Black political trust for this administration; thus, I must reject *Hypothesis 4*. Nor does the Obama presidency appear to elicit an anomalous "negative" effect for Whites. However, in 2010 we see the largest gap in confidence in the executive branch (figure 1.1), with Blacks having higher levels of confidence than Whites.

Conclusion

From 1972–2012, these data analyses show Black Americans in comparison to Whites display mostly lower levels of confidence in the executive branch of government. This supports what we conventionally know about Black political trust. Although I expected there to be racial differences in political trust between Blacks and Whites for the executive branch and Blacks' political trust being greatest during the Obama administration, because of his shared race, rather, the data analyses indicate somewhat surprising results: *the Obama presidency is not an outlier*. Despite the notable increase and positivizing effects on Blacks' trust in the executive branch and its higher level than Whites' during the Obama presidency, nonetheless, Blacks' political trust is *not* discernibly higher than their political trust in the executive branch during other presidential administrations. Nor do Whites suddenly express a decrease in trust in the executive branch during the Obama administration. Contrary to expectations, there is limited discernible support for a "spillover effect" in confidence in government (whether it is among Blacks or Whites) generated by the two terms of the historic Obama presidency. However, in 2010, Black political trust clearly surpasses Whites' political trust in the executive branch. The extent of this racial divide in trust, in addition, draws attention to a notable moment in American political attitudes, when Black and White attitudes appear to be the furthest apart.

Because the pooled, cross-sectional data for this data set ends in 2012, we also are unable to account for changes in political attitudes (among Blacks or Whites) that may have occurred during the midterms in 2014 and the conclusion of the Obama presidency in 2016. Elsewhere, in the Pew Research Center Report (2015), during the Obama years, we see Blacks' trust in federal government outpacing Whites', and it is actually Whites who are the least trusting of federal government, as far as reporting trusting in it "always/most of the time." For example, only 15 percent of Whites report this, compared to 23 percent of Blacks, 28 percent of Latinos, and overall, 19 percent of Americans. The post-2012 years are critical for the cross-sectional analyses of Black public opinion because they also coincide with the advent and activism of the Black Lives Matter movement, which was initiated after the shooting death of Black teenager Trayvon Martin (on February 26, 2012) and the heightened consciousness of extralegal and law-enforcement-related deaths of Black men and women across the country since this time.

Even with respect to the Obama years, harkening the significance of Martin's death, President Obama mentioned that, if he had a son, "he'd look like Trayvon," a suggestion that he sympathized with the racialized implications of Martin's death, yet it was also the first time that the president commented on the case, weeks after the initial shooting and after criticism by many Black leaders about his silence on the incident (Tau 2012). Despite Attorney General Eric Holder's (the first Black attorney general) and Attorney General Loretta Lynch's (the nation's second, Black attorney general) leadership in the Obama administration to initiate investigations related to discrimination in police departments and police-related deaths of Black people across the country, the president has vocalized limited disdain with the loss of Black lives in police-related shootings (Diptak and Jones 2016), leaving the policy commentary on racial justice to his executive branch bureaucrats.

Nonetheless, in reference to the 2016 police-related deaths of Alton Sterling and Philando Castile, President Obama empathized in a different light with Black people, stating, "When people say 'Black lives matter,' it doesn't mean that blue lives (police lives) don't matter. But right now, the data shows that Black folks are more vulnerable to these kinds of incidents. There is a particular burden that is being placed on a group of our fellow citizens" (Diptak and Jones 2016). For him, the shootings were not a concern for Blacks, alone, but also for America, regardless of Americans' race.

Alone, the federal government's response to justice and criminal justice issues poses the biggest threat for Black Americans' confidence in government and racial divides in Black and White public opinion. For one, Blacks are more skeptical than Whites about the nation taking the steps it needs to improve racial inequality (Pew Research Center Report 2016a), and they view criminal justice as a major concern more so than Whites because of racial discrimination toward Blacks (Pew Research Center Report 2016b). Second, with the obstructionism of the Republican-led Congress, and the Senate in particular (during the latter years of the Obama presidency), as far as its delays in confirming Attorney General Loretta Lynch's nomination and outright pronouncement of denying confirmation to Merrick Garland to the US Supreme Court, in order to assure the nomination to the discretion of the nation's forty-fifth president (opening the nomination to the power of a Republican president, now Donald J. Trump), Blacks (as Democrats, especially) stood to lack confidence in a Republican-led legislative branch. In sum, such political actions on the part of the federal government leave room for Black Americans to sustain low confidence levels, if not even lower levels of confidence than currently noted, in the three branches of government. Such relationships between Black Americans and the federal government will be important for analyzing whether there is continuity and/or change in Black *and* White attitudes, "after the Obama years."

Racial divides in political perceptions feed the racialized, zero-sum trust dilemma that I have described elsewhere in Nunnally (2014), whereby Black political elites find themselves burdened by their need to navigate the uncertain terrain of representing Black people without appearing as if they are overly beholden to the interests of Black Americans in the eyes of Whites. Black political elites also have to navigate how to court an electorate that has different racial majorities within political districts depending upon the level of government, the increasing importance of race, partisanship, and turnout among racial and ethnic minorities.

This need to have a representation style that is both racially balanced and racially trustworthy in order to retain high levels of approval prior to reelection bids deepens the scope of the inclusionary dilemma. It is a matter of convincing different American racial publics that they can trust and be confident in government at the same time. This is a core element of a racial equilibrium in American politics. Moreover, the zero-sum trust dilemma (as it functions in hand with the inclusionary dilemma) is pernicious because people's racially distinctive lenses persist, despite President Obama's rhetoric of racial transcendence within the American polity. The phenomenon of building political capital across racial groups to become interracially trustworthy is part and parcel of the *inclusionary dilemma* that Shaw, McCormick, and Brown theorize in this volume.

What remains to be seen is the way in which Black Americans will navigate descriptive and substantive representations in a post-Obama political environment. Will we see the election of *another* Black president in our lifetimes, and if so, under what partisan banner? Moreover, whether this president will be responsive to needs and interests of many Black Americans remains a pertinent issue given the politics of zero-sum trust and inclusionary dilemmas. When he was a lame-duck president by 2016, President Obama evoked more symbolic and substantive measures that spoke to the concerns of Black Americans, who continue to be disproportionately affected by mass incarceration and police brutality. The Department of Justice under Obama and Attorney General Eric Holder played a critical role in raising some of the injustices Black Americans faced in the criminal justice system. However, economic disparities and localized political issues continue to affect the quality of life for many Black Americans, and targeted national policy redress of the issues specific to this group remain circumscribed—an aggressive agenda addressing disparate unemployment, wealth loss after the Great Recession due to predatory lending, concentrated mass incarceration, and police-involved killings.

After Obama, President Donald J. Trump has made it a "new normal" to question the integrity of any sector that challenges his view—i.e., government agencies, elections, and media operations. This is especially true for historically disfranchised groups like Blacks and Latinx groups as represented by persons of color. Trump speaks to and for Whites who have felt alienated by what he has framed as "political correctness" to the detriment of "truths." With the politics of immigration, citizenship, the Census, and police killings of unarmed Black Americans at the height of current discourses about race and American politics, the groups of color who have been detrimentally affected by Trump administration policies are much less likely to invest trust in the federal government. Nevertheless, after Obama, the significance of race and political trust in the American presidency and different branches of government likely will continue with disparate outcomes. Until Black or other political elites or communities resolve the zero-sum trust and inclusionary dilemmas, possibly through coalition politics, whichever racial group that stands in the political minority is likely to suffer the policy consequences.

NOTES

1 The analysis will be limited to black Americans and white Americans because the longitudinal data cover the most years for these two groups. The specific account of Latino Americans and Asian Americans in the racial and ethnic designations does not occur until the 2000 survey.

2 Johnson also appointed the nation's first black US Supreme Court justice—Thurgood Marshall—in 1967.

3 Pitkin (1967) offers three types of representation that politicians can offer. One, descriptive representation is such that the constituent and representative share the same social group (e.g., race or gender group). Two, substantive representation is such that the constituent's representative shares the same views on policies and, perhaps, shares the same partisanship. Three, symbolic representation is such that the representative supports policies that lack tangible substantive relevance for the constituent, but that address a psychological connection that a constituent has to the policies by way of issues to which the constituent relates as a member of a social group.

4 Blacks' positive attitudes about President Obama also may be influenced by his steadfast (or not) commitment to the political interests of black Americans, especially as far as promoting their socioeconomic advancement. Obama sometimes offered ambiguous policy responsiveness specific to black socioeconomic issues (e.g., black unemployment and disproportionate mortgage and home loss during the Great Recession), and despite his reluctance to discuss racial issues compared to any other Democratic president since 1961 (Gillion 2012). Nevertheless, President Obama has retained high approval ratings among black Americans, and black Americans' presidential approval ratings about him are characteristically more positive than all other Americans' have been since 2009 (Newport 2014). Similar to the findings of Abrajano and Burnett (2012), in a nutshell, racial solidarity with President Obama should have the effect of enhancing the political attitudes and relationships that blacks have with the American political system.

5 It is of special note that because the GSS also provides for panel data within the 2006 through 2012 years of the survey cross sections, we must be careful to acknowledge that persons were reinterviewed for the years subsequent to 2006. Therefore, unlike the other cross-sectional surveys, indicators of significance

for these years may point to distinct and consistent behavioral patterns of those persons reinterviewed for those years. This, however, should not detract from the qualitative statistical significance of these years, if they should be found discernibly different, because the results still indicate opinion distinctions.

REFERENCES

Abrajano, Marisa, and Craig M. Burnett. 2012. "Do Blacks and Whites See Obama through Race-Tinted Glasses? A Comparison of Obama's and Clinton's Approval Ratings." *Presidential Studies Quarterly.* 42(2): 363–375.

Abramson, Paul R. 1977. *The Political Socialization of African Americans: A Critical Evaluation of Research on Efficacy and Trust.* New York: The Free Press.

Avery, James M. 2006. "The Sources and Consequence of Political Mistrust Among African Americans." *American Politics Research* 34(5): 653–682.

Avery, James M. 2009. "Political Mistrust among African Americans and Support for the Political System." *Political Research Quarterly* 62: 132–145.

Bernstein, Jeffrey L. 2001. "Linking Presidential and Congressional Approval during Unified and Divided Governments." In *What Is It About Government that Americans Dislike?* Eds. John R. Hibbing and Elizabeth Theiss-Morse. Cambridge: Cambridge University Press, 98–117.

Blendon, Robert J., John M. Benson, Richard Morin, Drew E. Altman, Mollyann Brodie, Mario Brossard, Matt James. 1997. "Changing Attitudes in America." In *Why Americans Don't Trust Government.* Eds. Joseph S. Nye, Philip D. Zelikow, David C. King, Cambridge, MA: Harvard University Press, 205–216.

Bowler, Shaun and Jeffrey A. Karp. 2004. "Politicians, Scandals, and Trust in Government." *Political Behavior* 26(3): 271–287.

Braithwaite, Valerie and Margaret Levi, eds. 1998. *Trust and Governance.* New York: Russell Sage Foundation.

Brehm, John. 1998. "Who Do You Trust? People, Government, Both, or Neither?" Paper presented at the Duke University International Conference on Social Capital and Social Networks, 30 October–1 November, Durham, North Carolina.

Brehm, John and Wendy Rahn. 1997. "Individual-Level Evidence for the Causes and Consequences of Social Capital." *American Journal of Political Science* 41 (July): 999–1023.

Carmines, Edward G. and James A. Stimson. 1989. *Issue Evolution: Race and the Transformation of American politics.* Princeton, NJ: Princeton University Press.

Citrin, Jack and Samantha Luks. 2001. "Political Trust Revisited: Déjà Vu All Over Again." In *What Is It about Government that Americans Dislike?* eds. John R. Hibbing and Elizabeth Theiss-Morse. Cambridge: Cambridge University Press, 9–27.

Coates, Ta-Nehisi. 2012. "Fear of a Black President." *Atlantic,* September. www.theatlantic.com.

Cook, Timothy and Paul Gronke. 2005. "The Skeptical American: Revisiting the Meanings of Trust in Government and Confidence in Institutions." *Journal of Politics* 67(3): 784–803.

Dawson, Michael C. 1994. *Behind the Mule: Race and Class in African-American Politics*. Princeton: Princeton University Press.

Dawson, Michael C. 2011. *Not in Our Lifetimes: The Future of Black Politics*. Chicago: University of Chicago Press.

Diptak, Kevin and Athena Jones. 2016. "Obama on Police Shootings: This Is Not Just a Black Issue." CNN.com. July 17, 2016. www.cnn.com.

Edwards, George C. 1980. *Presidential Influence in Congress*. San Francisco: W. H. Freeman.

Edwards, George C. 2000. "Neustadt's Power Approach to the Presidency." In *Presidential Power: Forging the Presidency for the Twenty-First Century*. Eds. Robert Y. Shapiro, Martha Joynt Kumar, and Lawrence R. Jacobs. New York: Columbia University Press, 9–15.

Fauntroy, Michael K. 2007. *Republicans and the Black Vote*. Boulder, CO: Lynne Rienner.

Feldman, Stanley. 1983. The Measurement and Meaning of Political Trust. *Political Methodology* 9(3): 341–354.

Frasure, Lorrie. 2010. "The Burden of Jekyll and Hyde: Barack Obama, Racial Identity, and Black Political Behavior." In *Whose Black Politics? Cases in Post-Racial Black Leadership*. Ed. Andra Gillespie. New York: Routledge, 133–154.

Frymer, Paul. 1999. *Uneasy Alliances: Race and Party Competition in America*. Princeton: Princeton University Press.

Gay, Claudine. 2002. "Spirals of Trust? The Effect of Descriptive Representation on the Relationship between Citizens and Their Government." *American Journal of Political Science* 46(4): 717–733.

Gillespie, Andra. 2010. "Meet the New Class: Theorizing Black Leadership in a 'Postracial' Era." In *Whose Black Politics? Cases in Post-Racial Black Leadership*. Ed. Andra Gillespie. New York: Routledge, 9–42.

Gillion, Daniel Q. 2012. *Governing with Words: The Political Dialogue on Race, Public Policy, and Inequality in America*. New York: Cambridge University Press.

Hajnal, Zoltan L. and Taeku Lee. 2011. *Why Americans Don't Join the Party: Race, Immigration, and the Failure (of Political Parties) to Engage the Electorate*. Princeton, NJ: Princeton University Press.

Hibbing, John R. and Elizabeth Theiss-Morse. 2001. Introduction. In *What Is It About Government that Americans Dislike?* Eds. John R. Hibbing and Elizabeth Theiss-Morse. Cambridge: Cambridge University Press, 1–7.

Keele, Luke. 2007. "Social Capital and the Dynamics of Trust in Government." *American Journal of Political Science* 51(2): 241–254.

Kernell, Samuel. 1997. *Going Public: New Strategies of Presidential Leadership*. Washington, DC: CQ Press.

Kinder, Donald and Lynn Sanders. 1996. *Divided by Color: Racial Politics and Democratic Ideals*. Chicago: University of Chicago Press.

Kinder, Donald R. and Nicholas Winter. 2001. "Exploring the Racial Divide: Blacks, Whites, and Opinion on National Policy." *American Journal of Political Science* 45(2): 439–56.

Mangum, Maurice. 2012. "Explaining African-American Political Trust: Examining Psychological Involvement, Policy Satisfaction, and Reference Group Effects." *International Social Science Review*. 87(1/2): 3–18.

Mansbridge, Jane. 1999. "Should Blacks Represent Blacks and Women Represent Women? A Contingent 'Yes,'" *Journal of Politics* 61(3): 628–657.

Mendelberg, Tali. 2001. *The Race Card: Campaign Strategy, Implicit Messages, and the Norm of Equality*. Princeton: Princeton University Press.

McAdam, Doug. 1982. *Political Process and the Development of Black Insurgency, 1930–1970*. Chicago: The University of Chicago Press.

McCormick, Joseph P. and Charles E. Jones. 1993. "The Conceptualization of De-Racialization." In *Dilemmas of Black Politics*. Ed. Georgia Persons. New York: Harper Collins College Publishers, 66–84.

McIlwain, Charlton. 2010. "Leadership, Legitimacy, and Public Perceptions of Barack Obama." In *Whose Black Politics? Cases in Post-Racial Black Leadership*. Ed. Andra Gillespie. New York: Routledge, 133–154.

Neustadt, Richard E. 1990. *Presidential Power and the Modern Presidents*. New York: Free Press.

Nunnally, Shayla C. 2010. "Linking Blackness or Ethnic Othering? African Americans' Diasporic Linked Fate with West Indian and African Peoples in the U.S." *Du Bois Review* 7(2): 335–355.

Nunnally, Shayla C. 2012. *Trust in Black America: Race, Discrimination, and Politics*. New York: New York University Press.

Nunnally, Shayla C. 2014. "Zero-Sum Politics as a Trust Dilemma? How Race and Gender Affect Trust in Obama's and Clinton's Representation of Group Interests." *Ralph Bunche Journal of Public Affairs* 3(1): http://digitalscholarship.bjmlspa.tsu.edu.

Pew Research Center Report. 1998. "How Americans View Government: Deconstructing Distrust." March 10, 1998. www.people-press.org.

Pew Research Center Report. 2005. "Huge Racial Divide over Katrina and Its Consequences." www.people-press.org.

Pew Research Center Report. 2010a. "A Year After Obama's Election: Blacks Upbeat about Black Progress, Prospects." January 12, 2010. www.pewsocialtrends.org.

Pew Research Center Report. 2010b. "The People and Their Government: Distrust, Discontent, Anger, and Partisan Rancor." April 18, 2015. www.people-press.org.

Pew Research Center Report. 2012. "A Closer Look at the Parties in 2012: GOP Makes Big Gains among Working-Class Voters." August 23, 2012. www.people-press.org.

Pew Research Center Report. 2015. "Beyond Distrust: How Americans View Their Government." November 23, 2015. www.people-press.org.

Pew Research Center Report. 2016a. "On Views of Race and Inequality, Blacks and Whites are Worlds Apart." June 27, 2016. www.pewsocialtrends.org.

Pew Research Center Report. 2016b. "The Racial Confidence Gap in Police Performance." 29 September 29, 2016. www.pewsocialtrends.org.

Pitkin. Hannah. 1967. *The Concept of Representation*. Berkeley: University of California Press.

Price, Melanye. 2016. *The Race Whisperer: Barack Obama and the Political Uses of Race*. New York: New York University Press.

Putnam, Robert. 1993. *Making Democracy Work: Civic Traditions in Modern Italy*. Princeton: Princeton University Press.

———. 1995. Tuning In, Tuning Out: The Strange Disappearance of Social Capital in America. *PS: Political Science and Politics* 28 (4): 664–683.

———. 2000. *Bowling Alone: The Collapse and Revival of American Community*. New York: Simon and Schuster.

"Rep. Wilson Shouts, 'You Lie' to Obama during Speech." CNN.com. September 10, 2014. www.cnn.com.

Rigueur, Leah Wright. 2015. *The Loneliness of the Black Republican: Pragmatic Politics and the Pursuit of Power*. Princeton, New Jersey: Princeton University Press.

Roper Center. 2008. How Groups Voted in 2008. www.ropercenter.uconn.edu (October 24, 2015).

Schuman, Howard, Charlotte Steeh, Lawrence Bobo, Maria Krysan. 1997. *Racial Attitudes in America: Trends and Interpretations*. Cambridge, MA: Harvard University Press.

Smith, Tom W., Peter V. Marsden, and Michael Hunt. 2005. "General Social Surveys, 1972–2012." National Opinion Research Center. Chicago: University of Chicago.

Shull, Steven A. 1999. *American Civil Rights Policy: From Truman to Clinton: The Role of Presidential Leadership*. Armonk: M. E. Sharpe.

Simien, Evelyn M. 2016. *Historic Firsts: How Symbolic Politics Changes U.S. Politics*. Oxford: Oxford University Press.

Swain, Carol. 1993. *Black Faces, Black Interests: The Representation of African Americans in Congress*. Cambridge: Harvard University.

Tate, Katherine. 1993. *From Protest to Politics: The New Black Voters in American Elections*. New York: Russell Sage Foundation.

Tate, Katherine. 2003. *Black Faces in the Mirror: African Americans and Their Representatives in the U.S. Congress*. Princeton, NJ: Princeton University Press.

Tau, Byron. 2012. "Obama: If I Had a Son, He'd Look Like Trayvon." *Politico*. March 23, 2012. www.politico.com.

Tesler, Michael. 2012. "The Spillover of Racialization into Health Care: How President Obama Polarized Public Opinion by Racial Attitudes and Race." *American Journal of Political Science* 56(3): 690–704.

Tesler, Michael and David O. Sears. 2010. *Obama's Race: The 2008 Election and the Dream of a Post-Racial America*. Chicago: University of Chicago Press.

Tesler, Michael. 2013. The Return of Old-Fashioned Racism to White Americans' Partisan Preferences in the Obama Era. *Journal of Politics* 75(1): 110–123.

Uslaner, Eric. 2001. "Is Washington Really the Problem?" In *What Is It about Government That Americans Dislike?* Eds. John R. Hibbing and Elizabeth Theiss-Morse. Cambridge: Cambridge University Press, 118–133.

Walters, Ronald W. 1988. *Black Presidential Politics in America: A Strategic Approach*. New York: State University of New York Press.

Watts Smith. Candis. 2014. *Black Mosaic: The Politics of Black Pan-Ethnic Diversity*. New York: New York University Press.

Weiss, Nancy J. 1983. *Farewell to the Party of Lincoln: Black Politics in the Age of FDR*. Princeton: Princeton University Press.

Wilson, David C. 2012. "The Elephant in the Exit Poll Results: Most White Women Supported Romney." *Huffington Post*. November 8, 2012. www.huffingtonpost.com.

2

Invitations to the Dance

The Obama Administration's Complex Engagement with Black Elected Officials and Advocacy Groups

TYSON D. KING-MEADOWS

As often noted, there is great historical significance to Illinois US senator Barack Obama's victories in the 2008 and 2012 presidential elections. The image of Michelle Obama and Barack Obama, a Black First Lady and president, elegantly dancing at two inauguration balls deeply resonated with Black constituencies who never imagined they would see such a sight in their lifetimes. But in the context of his presidency, there was a much more complex dance, a more complex engagement, between the Obama presidency and Black leaders. In fact, in form and substance, there was often a turbulent relationship between President Obama, Black elected officials, and Black advocacy groups, with some leaders expressing trepidations about the president's policy agenda and political strategy. Given the structural peculiarities of American politics, Senator Obama had to be aware of elements of majority rule, party competition, and racial/ethnic identity politics to capture the nomination and to win the presidency. The 2008 presidential elections could therefore only partially satisfy the aspirations of Black civil rights leaders who championed descriptive representation and Black enfranchisement as the keys to improving the socioeconomic conditions of Black Americans. President Obama could neither overtly champion Black interests nor overtly antagonize Black champions of those interests. The risks were too great. Moreover, as the co-editors of this volume explain in the introduction, the US racial order limited Obama's capacity to execute an overtly race-conscious governance strategy, and Obama's embrace of universalism constrained his inclination to support racial particularism. Nonetheless, liberal African American leaders contended two things: first, that Obama had the administrative and legislative capacity to overtly advocate for and implement race-conscious policies and, second, that Obama had a racial and electoral obligation to take ameliorative actions. In this chapter, I unpack each contention to assert that Black critics of Obama often minimalized the capacity-inclination gap to justify their appeals for Obama to do more.[1]

Most specifically, while I agree with much of the analysis offered by Melanye T. Price in *The Race Whisperer* and by Fredrick C. Harris in *The Price of the Ticket*, I submit that both treatments oversubscribe to a vision of American "presidentialism" and underappreciate contemporary American-style "parliamentarism."[2] The former sees the executive as the predominant figure among a configuration of political actors, whereby the executive's preferences overwhelmingly (if not always) determine the content, pace, and outcomes of the policy-making process.[3] The latter, American-style "parliamentarism" creates disincentives for compromise because it encourages hyperpartisanship, ideological polarization, and tight control over legislative decision-making in Congress. Throughout this chapter, I foreground the structural differences between parliamentarism and presidentialism to excavate how each approach to governance poses unique challenges to legislators championing Black interest representation. I assert that Harris's and Price's examinations of the Obama presidency have underappreciated these structural differences and the unique challenges these differences pose to Black members of Congress and Black advocacy groups.

Briefly put, I contend that Harris and Price, albeit in different ways and to different degrees, begin with a foundational premise that President Obama was the predominant figure (or should have been the predominant figure) shaping policy outcomes. This foundational premise allowed each to set aside the ways in which parliamentarism can undermine a presidential agenda. This foundational premise also allowed each to conclude that the Obama presidency ostensibly underserved Black interests. In contrast to Harris and Price, I however begin with an alternative foundational premise, taken from Mark Peterson's work, which "view[s] the presidency and Congress as *tandem institutions* constituting the major components of the American legislative *decision-making system*" (emphasis in original). Peterson's work privileges executive-congressional negotiations (whereby no branch always holds the subordinate position) and acknowledges the interconnect-edness of actors, veto points, and multidimensional preferences.[4] By shifting to "tandem institutions," I draw conclusions decidedly differ-ent from that of Harris and Price, and I posit that Obama challenged Black spokespersons to confront the conundrum underlying "black interest representation" in an era in which the reality of parliamen-tarism both outpaces fantasies of presidentialism and threatens tan-dem institutionalism. In short, I submit that the impact of the Obama presidency is best gauged not by examining shortfalls in Obama's overt advocacy for race-conscious policies but rather by examining what Obama did to resuscitate debates about whether Black spokes-persons should be more concerned about the representation of Black interests or the enactment of legislation that advances Black progress. Consequently, I argue that Obama's "inclusionary dilemma," a theo-retical framework put forth by the co-editors in the *Introduction*, was as much about Burkean representational theory as it was about presi-dential behavior—the implications being that the Obama presidency conjoined racialized expectations with intergovernmental conflict in ways that neither branch anticipated.

To lay out the arguments in this chapter, I draw upon select pub-lic speeches by President Obama, White House documents, and press accounts detailing the Obama administration's engagement with Black elites over job creation during his first term. My policy focus is deliberate. Clashes between the administration and Black elites over employment showcased three things: Black dismay that a Black executive had not delivered tangible race-specific benefits; White fear that a Black presi-dent would practice racial favoritism; and an intergovernmental struggle between the executive and legislative branches over which representa-tive body should control employment policy. Also, these clashes over jobs best illustrate how the "inclusionary dilemma" required Obama to utilize a complex engagement strategy with Black Americans to navigate Black dismay and to outline his policy agenda. By complex engagement strategy, I refer to the following: (1) the formal and informal ways, direct and indirect, in which Obama used surrogates, meetings, and public speeches to frame his policies as both universal and race-conscious in character; and (2) the ways in which the White House framed the presi-dent's engagement by promoting certain types of engagements and not others. To begin my analysis, I outline how Black desire for "presidentialism" framed the administration's exchanges with Black elites about job creation and economic mobility. In the subsequent section, I outline the Burkean aspects of the "inclusionary dilemma." In the conclusion, I discuss how Obama used his final days in office to prepare the Obama coalition for the Trump presidency and to warn Black voters and Black elites about privileging style over substance.

The CBC versus Obama Debate over Job Creation

There is no clearer example of President Obama's difficulties in negotiating Black dismay, White fear, and intergovernmental conflict than his 2009–2011 exchanges with the Congressional Black Caucus of the 111th Congress (hereafter the Black Caucus). They debated over his reluctance to present race-based policies specifically designed to confront Black unemployment. At White House press conferences and in interviews during 2009, Obama rejected the need for specific employment policies targeting racially/ethnically identified communities and reiterated that the American Recovery and Reinvestment Act of 2009 (hereafter the Recovery Act) would provide economic relief for those communities by providing relief for all.[5] Espousing the Reagan era mantra of "lift all boats," Obama linked the Recovery Act to trickle-down economics and pitched the legislation as helping Blacks to advance into or anchor themselves within the middle class. During an April 29, 2009, press conference marking his one hundredth day in office, Obama faced a direct question from Black Entertainment Television correspondent Andre Showell about his plan. After citing statistics about double-digit Black unemployment, Showell asked, "My question tonight is, given this unique and desperate circumstance, what specific policies can you point to that will target these communities? And what's a timetable for us to see tangible results?" Obama responded by reemphasizing his general approach: "Well, keep in mind that every step we're taking is designed to help all people. But folks who are most vulnerable are most likely to be helped because they need the most help." Obama pointed out specific policies which would help Black and Latino communities (e.g., the Children's Health Insurance Program, the unemployment insurance provision of the Recovery Act, additional dollars for community health centers) before providing his "lift all boats" comment. The following Obama quote has received great scholarly attention and scrutiny:

> So my general approach is that if the economy is strong, that will lift all boats, as long as it is also supported by, for example, strategies around college affordability and job training, tax cuts for working families as opposed to the wealthiest that level the playing field and ensure bottom-up economic growth. And I'm confident that that will help the African American community live out the American Dream at the same time that it's helping communities all across the country. Okay?[6]

Consistent with the "politics of avoidance," Obama was reluctant (at this point) to offer a specific series of policy actions or recommendations which would directly link administrative action to Black needs or demands.[7]

Critics of Obama who see this early reluctance as capitulation to the racial order do so by privileging presidentialism. For example, Fredrick Harris in *The Price of the Ticket* sees capitulation when analyzing a December 2009 exchange about Black unemployment between journalist April Ryan of American Urban Radio to buttress his claim that Obama eschewed "targeted remedies to address minority unemployment." While Obama does indeed reiterate his commitment to universalism, Obama also reminds Ryan of parliamentarism. At one point during the interview, Obama states, "The only thing I can do is, you know, by law I can't pass laws saying I'm just helping Black folks. I am the president of the entire United States." Obama goes on to state, "What I can do is make sure that I am passing laws that help all people, particularly those that are most vulnerable and in need. That in turn is going to help lift up the African American community."[8] Here, Obama presents his capacity to support race-conscious policies as limited, even if he were not ideologically predisposed toward universalism. Obama also presents passage of the Recovery Act as superior to the status quo and the only viable legislative option for champions of Black interests. Harris however asserts that Obama's "comment on 'just helping Black folks' was a red herring" because what the Black Caucus "actually proposed" was quite different from racial particularism. Harris contends that the

Black Caucus's proposal "was a jobs bill that incorporated the principle of 'targeted universalism': an approach that would geographically target government-sponsored jobs projects in communities most affected by the recession and with the greatest concentrations of poverty." And, Harris continues, "[by] default, such legislation would not help everyone equally but benefit those most affected by the recession."[9]

In the above argument, Harris discounts much about the legislative process. He never unpacks the negotiations the administration had with Black congressional elites about the legislative elements contained within the Recovery Act.[10] Nor does Harris address either the enormous difficulty Obama would have faced if he publicly acknowledged targeted universalism as a governance strategy or how Republicans may have exploited the White House's public acknowledgment to further energize the Republican base for the 2010 midterm elections. Moreover, because individuals often use geographic location as a euphemism for race, it is hard to imagine that the Black Caucus and President Obama were unaware of the political risks and rewards of the group's attempt to incorporate "targeted universalism" into the legislative proposal. Put differently, Harris's "wink, nod, and vote" criticism of Obama neglects to fully unpack the complexities of the tripartite legislative "dance"— consisting of the Black community, the White House, and Congress. This trio impacted how Obama packaged, fought for, and justified his policy agenda to Blacks and non-Black Americans. Here I use "dance" as a shorthand for the performative, communicative, prospective, and communal dimensions of finding one negotiation point where each negotiator realizes the intersection of their mutual interests. Like partner-based sequence dancing, negotiation involves coordinated movements and contra movements, all governed by rules, mores, and expectations.[11] In this regard, conservatives and Republicans would have certainly countered Obama's endorsement of targeted universalism. This would have destabilized the pro-Recovery Act legislative coalition and would have further jeopardized Obama's ability to spend his postinauguration political capital. In the parlance of principal-agent theory, while Obama's public support of targeted universalism would have pleased Black principals who desired to see their Black chief executive demonstrate a race-specific commitment to policies that would benefit the group—an embrace of what Robert C. Smith might call "political blackness"[12]—this position would have also intensified suspicions among White principals that Obama could not or would not champion all interests due to racial favoritism.[13]

The consequences of this tripartite dance over jobs, and its impact on the White House's larger strategy for engaging Black America, were on full display long before December 2009. For instance, Obama gave a July 2009 speech before the NAACP Centennial Convention held at the New York Hilton (hereafter 2009 NAACP speech) in which he again used universalistic terms to outline his vision for addressing structural inequalities and Black socioeconomic despair. In this speech, Obama advanced what Harris and others *might* contend met the criteria of targeted universalism prior to the president's December 2009 exchange with journalist April Ryan of American Urban Radio. While it is consistent with the parameters of the "rhetorical presidency" and "wink and nod" politics, it is also consistent with racial particularism as well as cultural and class differentiation. Three parts of the speech are noteworthy: first, Obama reminded Blacks of his legislative and bureaucratic efforts to confront structural inequality; second, Obama asked Blacks to support his legislative efforts; and third, Obama linked his policies to Black identity and Black history.

Early in the 2009 NAACP speech, Obama remarked, "We know that even as our economic crisis batters Americans of all races, African Americans are out of work more than just about anyone else."[14] Obama next discussed racial disparities in health care and coverage, in incarceration, and in HIV/AIDS. He also differentiated these disparities from de jure segregation. Moving to the Recovery Act, Obama emphasized the reality of structural inequalities and remarked:

> That's why my administration is working so hard not only to create and save jobs in the short-term, not only to extend unemployment insurance and help for people who have lost their health care in the crisis, not just to stem the immediate economic wreckage, but to lay a new foundation for growth and prosperity that will put opportunity within the reach of not just African Americans, but all Americans. All Americans. Of every race. Of every creed. From every region of the country. We want everyone to participate in the American Dream. That's what the NAACP is all about.[15]

Midway through the speech, Obama alluded to his conflict with the Black Caucus and Black interest groups about the lack of targeted policies. He remarked, "So these are some of the laws we're passing. These are some of the policies we are enacting. We are busy in Washington. Folks in Congress are getting a little tuckered out. But I'm telling them— I'm telling them we can't rest." He continued, "The American people are counting on us. These are some of the ways we're doing our part in government to overcome the inequities, the injustices, the barriers that still exist in our country." Obama, however, concluded his NAACP Centennial Convention speech by perpetuating problematic narratives about Black youth and by continuing his hero/heroine, respectability politics depiction of the Joshua Generation. He stated, "[Black youth] might think they've got a pretty good jump shot or a pretty good flow, but our kids can't all aspire to be LeBron or Lil Wayne. I want them aspiring to be scientists and engineers—doctors and teachers—not just ballers and rappers." He continued, "I want them aspiring to be a Supreme Court Justice. I want them aspiring to be the President of the United States of America. I want their horizons to be limitless. Don't tell them they can't do something. Don't feed our children with a sense of— that somehow because of their race that they cannot achieve." Obama's next rhetorical turn addressed Black expectations: "Yes, government must be a force of opportunity. Yes, government must be a force for equality. But ultimately, if we are to be true to our past then we also have to seize our own future, each and every day. That's what the NAACP is all about." He continued, "The NAACP was not founded in search of a handout. The NAACP was not founded in search of favors. The NAACP was founded on a firm notion of justice; to cash the promissory note of America that says all of our children, all God's children, deserve a fair chance in the race of life."[16]

By framing the Recovery Act as a less appreciated version of racial particularism, if not targeted universalism, Obama may have been signaling or signifying about a trade-off within Black politics: embrace the "wink and nod" or risk further jeopardizing what Hanes Walton referred to as the "institutionalization of civil rights policy" in federal and state bureaucracies.[17] The Obama administration and its surrogates would make similar points when discussing the following policy controversies: (1) efforts to rebuild New Orleans by promoting infrastructure investment; (2) state rejection of the Affordable Care Act's provisions regarding Medicaid; (3) skepticism about the Race to the Top education policy; and (4) enactment of the Lilly Fair Pay Ledbetter Act of 2009, which amended the Civil Rights Act of 1964 and reversed a Supreme Court decision limiting when a petitioner could file an equal-pay lawsuit regarding pay discrimination.

By 2010, some Black leaders had grown increasingly frustrated with the Obama administration and the tripartite dance. Obama addressed the dance and those frustrations at the Congressional Black Caucus Foundation's Annual Phoenix Awards Dinner held in September 2009. He nodded to the Black Caucus's history in part by invoking the farewell address of North Carolina Representative George Henry White (1892 to 1901). White was the last African American elected to Congress during Reconstruction and the last African American to serve until Oscar De Priest (1929–1935). Then Obama remarked, "So we are by no means the first generation of Americans to be tested, but tested we have been." Obama continued, "Most recently we've been tested by an economic crisis unlike any that we've seen since the Great Depression. Now, I have to say that some folks seem to have forgotten just how bad things were when I took office. They seem to be exercising some selective memory. So let's just take a stroll down memory lane."[18] His stroll highlighted economic pain under the Bush administration and extolled the benefits of the Recovery Act. Obama then directed his comments to African Americans critical of his efforts, "So the next time some of these folks come up asking what the Recovery Act has done, you tell them it has prevented us going into a much worse place. That much we know. That's been confirmed. But we also know that we've got a long way to go; the progress we've made has been uneven; and that this recession has hit communities of color with a particular ferocity." Obama concluded his 2009 Phoenix Awards remarks by repeating much of what he said about Black youth at the earlier 2009 NAACP Convention and by noting what could be considered a "color-blind" approach to policy, a race-conscious approach to policy, or both. Obama stated, "A world-class education. Affordable, quality health insurance. Jobs and opportunity. All of us accepting responsibility for ourselves, and our children, and our common future. That's how we'll make life better for the African American community, and thereby make life better for the larger American community." He continued, "That is how we will build a new foundation for our economy that yields lasting, shared prosperity. That's how we'll take up the cause of freedom, and justice, and equality in our time, just as earlier generations of Americans took it up in theirs." Of course, Obama was not the first Black public figure to express a linked fate between Black citizens and their fellow Americans. Nor was he the first president to link those conjoined fates to democratic principles and to the revitalization of America. But Obama was the first Democratic president to explicitly link Black interests to a tempered version of Reagan Era trickle-down economics and to tacitly chastise Blacks for dismissing the dangers of governing on the razor's edge of Black hope and White fear.

Some scholars of Black politics have decried Obama's early actions as indicative of his "neoliberal politics" and his public retreat from negotiating with Black advocacy groups. Some scholars tacitly charged Obama with failing to protect Black constituents from the ravages of a frayed social safety net.[19] Table 2.1 is a selected compilation of Barack and Michelle Obama's engagement with Black interest groups and audiences. It suggests that Barack Obama and Michelle Obama employed a 2009–2011 strategy of engagement with the Black political class that reflected what Stephen Skowronek calls "preemptive" presidential leadership. The Recovery Act may have been the best viable proposal, since the policy options that were probable reflect prior conservative regimes.[20] Although the table is limited,[21] it is informative. It highlights the varied connections the Obamas made with the Black political class and underscores some of the spaces and venues the White House used as opportunities to lay out their policy agenda. That President Obama's remarks to the 2009 NAACP Convention come before his first formal meeting with the Black Caucus and the Hispanic Caucus is noteworthy in that regard. In sum, table 2.1 shows that members of the Black Caucus and members of Black interest groups were not as shutout from policy conversations as some observers suggested.

It took more than a calendar year after President Obama's first inauguration for the Black Caucus to command a visible space of public negotiation. On March 11, 2010, President Obama held the first publicly acknowledged formal meeting with members of the Black Caucus "to discuss the economy, job creation and the need to pass health care reform." The White House readout acknowledges that there was policy distance between the President and the Black Caucus. And, that "after remarks by

TABLE 2.1. Engagement with Black Interest Groups and Audiences

Date	Item
5/4/2009	Remarks by the First Lady at a Lamb School Hispanic Heritage event
5/8/2009	Remarks by the president to the Latino Town Hall
7/16/2009	Remarks by the president to the NAACP Centennial Convention
9/27/2009	Remarks by the president at the Congressional Black Caucus Foundation's Annual Phoenix Award Dinner
1/17/2010	Remarks by the president in remembrance of Dr. Martin Luther King Jr.
1/18/2010	Remarks by the president following intergenerational reflection on the Civil Rights movement
1/18/2010	Remarks by the president at "Let Freedom Ring!" Concert
2/10/2010	Remarks by the president at "In Performance at the White House: A Celebration of Music from the Civil Rights Movement"
3/11/2010	Readout of President Obama's meeting with the Congressional Hispanic Caucus
3/11/2010	Readout of President Obama's meeting with the Congressional Black Caucus
7/12/2010	Remarks by the First Lady to the NAACP National Convention in Kansas City, Missouri
8/6/2010	Statement by President Obama on the 45th anniversary of the Voting Rights Act
9/14-15/2010	Remarks by the First Lady and president at the Congressional Hispanic Caucus Institute's 33rd Annual Awards Gala
9/15/2010	Remarks by the First Lady at the Congressional Black Caucus Foundation Legislative Conference
9/18/2010	Remarks by the president at the Congressional Black Caucus Foundation Phoenix Awards Dinner
11/16/2010	Readout of the president's meeting with representatives of the Congressional Hispanic Caucus today
12/1/2010	Statement by President Obama on the 55th anniversary of the Montgomery bus boycott
12/26/2010	Statement by the president and First Lady on Kwanzaa
12/26/2010	Readout of the president's meeting with the Congressional Hispanic Caucus
1/17/2011	Remarks by the president on Martin Luther King Jr.'s birthday
1/17/2011	President and First Lady, Vice President Biden, cabinet secretaries, senior administration officials to honor the Martin Luther King Jr. Day of Service
2/4/2011	Obama Administration celebrates Black History by winning the future
5/3/2011	Readout of the president's meeting with the Congressional Hispanic Caucus on fixing the broken immigration system
7/21/2011	Readout of the president's meeting with the National Urban League and NAACP
7/25/2011	Background on President Obama's address at the National Council of La Raza Annual Conference Luncheon
9/14/2011	Remarks by the president to the Congressional Hispanic Caucus Institute's 34th Annual Awards Gala
9/24/2011	Remarks by the president at the Congressional Black Caucus Foundation's annual Phoenix Awards Dinner
10/5/2011	Statement by the president on the passing of Civil Rights leader Fred Shuttlesworth
10/28/2011	Statement by the president on the court approval of the settlement of the Black Farmers lawsuit
11/9/2011	Remarks by the president at the African American Policy in Action Leadership Conference
11/9/2011	White House hosts African American Policy in Action Leadership Conference
12/26/2011	Statement by the president and First Lady on Kwanzaa

Selected Items of President and First Lady Obama's Engagement with the Black Political Class, 2009–2011
Source: Author evaluation of compilations from reports and information found on www.whitehouse.gov
Note: Shawn Tang, compiler

Chairwoman Lee discussing the impact of the economy in economically distressed communities and the need for additional assistance in these areas, Members presented their concerns and solutions for broadening the impact of the recovery effort." The readout states that, "[Obama] requested that Members provide specific recommendations to the challenges concerning job creation."[22] On July 12, 2010, First Lady Michelle Obama addressed the NAACP National Convention held in Kansas City, Missouri. Though much of the speech focused on the "Let's Move" antiobesity campaign, the First Lady wove together themes of economic inequality, personal responsibility, and government action. In September 2010, First Lady Michelle Obama and President Obama presented similar themes at the Congressional Black Caucus Foundation's Legislative Conference.

Obama began his 2010 Congressional Black Caucus Foundation's Annual Phoenix Awards speech by retelling the story of the founding of the Congressional Black Caucus, hailing its founders and noting the caucus's importance to American democracy. He went on to denounce presidentialism and the notion that he would or could be the facilitator of the great change, remarking, "That's why the CBC was formed—to right wrongs; to be the conscience of the Congress. And at the very first CBC dinner, the great actor and activist, Ossie Davis, told the audience America was at a crossroad. And although his speech was magnificent and eloquent, he boiled his message down to a nice little phrase when it came to how America would move forward. He said, 'It's not the man, it's the plan.' It's not the man, it's the plan. That was true 40 years ago. It is true today." He continued, "We all understood that during my campaign. This wasn't just about electing a Black President. This was about a plan to rescue our economy and rebuild it on a new foundation."[23] In the middle of the speech, Obama continued to hammer the Ossie Davis theme and to lay out the challenges of dealing with the Republicans who wanted to "turn back the clock." He stated, "They want to do what's right politically, instead of what's right— period. They think about the next election. We're thinking about the next generation." At the end of the speech, Obama roundly rejected the Harris notion of "wink and nod politics." He stated the following:

We can't think short term when so many people are out of work, not when so many families are still hurting. We need to finish the plan you elected me to put in place. And I need you. I need you because this isn't going to be easy. And I didn't promise you easy. I said back on the campaign that change was going to be hard. Sometimes it's going to be slower than some folks would like. I said sometimes we'd be making some compromises and people would be frustrated. I said I could not do it alone. . . . It was a matter of all of us getting involved, all of us staying committed, all of us sticking with our plan for a better future until it was complete. That's how we've always moved this country forward.[24]

Obama thus put the burden on Black spokespersons and Black voters to move the policy agenda forward. The timing of this is important. Against the backdrop of the upcoming 2010 midterm elections, Obama foresaw what he would later refer to as a "shellacking" at the polls. The Republican Party picked up nearly 65 seats in the House of Representatives and the Senate. It was the largest midterm loss since the Great Depression and had been propelled by the Tea Party activists and Tea Party–aligned candidates (at both federal and state levels) who railed against the Obama administration and perceived government overreach. Many observers took the 2010 midterm elections as a repudiation to the Obama agenda and any Democratic-led attempts to deal with the economy.

However, it is the CBC-Obama exchanges *before* the 2010 midterm elections which provide the most relevant context for the 2010 CBCF speech. By midsummer 2010, it was the Democratic-led Senate and the vocal Republican Senate minority, not the Obama White House, that stalled the House Democratic agenda on job creation and the Black Caucus's hopes for securing passage of targeted universalism policies. A June 24, 2010, hand-delivered letter to the office of then Senate minority leader, Kentucky senator Mitch McConnell, by Black Caucus chairwoman Barbara Lee of California laid out the Black Caucus's frustration with Republican obstruction of legislation. "For many months the Congressional Black Caucus has been sounding the alarm about the urgent and vital need to create jobs in America, particularly in communities such as many in your state, that have disproportionately suffered the brunt of this economic crisis. These communities are in desperate need of targeted, concrete and meaningful relief." For the Black Caucus, not only had Senate Republicans held the nation's economy hostage, they had mortgaged their constituents' social mobility to score partisan points. Representative Lee pointed out that the relief everyone needed was contained in specific legislation passed by the House but ignored in the Senate, e.g., "the American Jobs and Closing Tax Loopholes Act, the Small Business and Jobs Credit Act, and [other] legislation to assist needy families." The CBC letter also highlighted the negative effect of persistent joblessness on minorities: "The weak labor market has been especially tough on youth of color, many of whom are responsible for contributing to the economic well-being of their families." And the letter continued, "While the overall unemployment rate dropped in May, the unemployment rate for African American youth age 16–19 increased to 38 percent—almost a full percentage point higher than in April 2010. Latino youth are unemployed at a rate of 28.6 percent."[25] The CBC letter to Minority Leader McConnell shined additional light on the racial dynamics of the legislative infighting and the jockeying between the White House and Congress: conflict between the Democrats and the Republicans had essentially scuttled the "CBC versus Obama" debate. The Senate was engulfed in infighting over filibuster reform. Senate Democrats were preoccupied by then majority leader, Nevada senator Harry Reid's negotiations with the Democratic National Committee over how best to minimize the likelihood of a 2010 Republican electoral sweep. The dance was forcing the White House to reconsider its 2010 message to voters. Soon after the 2010 elections, members of the Black Caucus began to publicly express their displeasure with the dance.

In 2011, President Obama once again turned to America's celebration of the Martin Luther King Jr. holiday and of Black History Month to highlight his vision for the country. Obama celebrated Black History Month by hosting a "Winning the Future" event in which "throughout the month, Cabinet Members, Administration officials, and senior staff [would] participate in events to highlight the various ways African Americans are winning the future by out-innovating, out-educating, and out-building our global competition." One of those individuals profiled on the accompanying website was Cecilia Rouse, a member of the White House Council of Economic Advisers (CEA) and a well-known labor economist and government veteran.[26] It is likely that Dr. Rouse advised Obama before he met with Ben Jealous (president of the NAACP) and Marc Morial (president of the National Urban League) on July 21, 2011, in the Oval Office. A readout of the meeting stated, "The President stressed that such an agreement [on economic growth strategies] must involve shared sacrifice and reaffirmed that we cannot afford to balance the budget on the back of the most vulnerable Americans including the middle class, low-income families, seniors, and students." Whatever "shared sacrifice" meant is unclear from the readout, but it could have been a signal to observers that Obama would not or could not seek targeted policies which could jeopardize other areas of his programmatic agenda. The readout also noted, "The President also reiterated that reducing unemployment, which disproportionately burdens the African-American community at 16.2%, remains a top priority for him and his Administration. The President also spoke with the two civil rights leaders about dramatic efforts his Administration has already made to address urban economic development [in select government programs]."[27] The meeting may have satisfied Jealous and Morial, but it did not satisfy members of the Black Caucus, who were gearing up for town hall meetings.

On August 17, 2011, FoxNews.com published a story about a town hall meeting in Detroit in which Black Caucus member and California representative Maxine Waters extolled the audience to "'unleash her' and other members of the Congressional Black Caucus on President Obama."[28] The Detroit town hall was one of many the Black Caucus would host across the country. Waters remarked, "We're getting tired y'all. . . . We want to give him every opportunity. But our people are hurting. The unemployment is unconscionable." Waters also remarked, "When you let us know it is time to let go, we'll let go."[29] A month later, Black Caucus chairman, Missouri representative Emanuel Cleaver highlighted the impatience of Black elites, particularly Democrats, who desired executive action to ameliorate double-digit Black unemployment rates. Cleaver noted, "We probably would be marching on the White House" if former Democratic president Bill Clinton had "failed to address" the problem of Black unemployment.[30] Waters and Cleaver adeptly summarized the multifaceted ways in which the Obama presidency presented the Black Caucus and Black interest groups with unchartered racial, political, institutional, and structural territory.[31] The tepid response of the Black Caucus was understandable: the caucus could neither disregard its own history (e.g., its moniker as "the conscience of the Congress" or its motto referring to Black "permanent interests"), nor could the caucus easily sidestep any fallout if they provided fodder for Obama's opponents.[32] The Black Caucus was also keenly aware of criticism that it, too, had shifted toward a more conservative policy orientation. Katherine Tate calls this shift "concordance."[33] Other scholars might call it ideological capitulation to neoliberalism and an attempt to delegitimize Black protest.[34]

For Black critics of Obama, the muffled response of Black leadership to Obama's privileging of the Recovery Act also impugned the integrity of Black representation. For example, in an August 2011 interview published in the *Nation*, Tavis Smiley criticized Obama for "putting job creation on the back burner and glossing over the plight of the poor."[35] Fellow critic Cornel West put the issue more bluntly. He remarked, "Anybody or anything that stands in the way of the empowerment of poor and working people. . . . If he's standing as an impediment, he's going to be criticized. It's just that we're not reluctant to criticize the powers that be." West went on, "We criticized congress, we criticized the mean spirited Republican Party, we criticized the spineless Democratic Party, we criticized Black leadership, the community, and so on."[36] West and Smiley saw themselves as holding Obama accountable because the Black Caucus and Black advocacy groups, like the National Urban League and the NAACP, were unwilling to do so.

On September 24, 2011, President Obama gave a speech at the Congressional Black Caucus Foundation's Annual Phoenix Awards, where he displayed frustration with the failure of Blacks to situate their expectations within the context of parliamentarism and within his capacity to overtly upend the US racial order.[37] This speech is problematic for its condescending language, but it also illustrates the larger problem Obama faced when trying to convince Black elites to buy in to his political strategy.[38] As such, I will focus here on Obama's possible motivations for the speech, as did *Washington Post* editorialist Courtland Milloy when he asked, "Why would Obama show up at a CBC dinner and take Waters and the others to task? Was this his Sista Souljah moment akin to Bill Clinton showing he had the so-called political courage to racially chide someone on the black left?"[39] I contend that Obama's motivations were to move away from "race whispering" and to talk plainly about what his success as president required Black legislators and Black voters to do in wake of the 2010 Republican wave. I will note three movements in the speech as evidence. The first movement in the speech is where Obama tries to smooth relations with the Black Caucus and tries to highlight the fallacy of presidentialism. He states, for instance, "With your help, we started fighting our way back from the brink. And at every step of the way, we've faced fierce opposition based on an old idea. . . . There has to be a different concept of what America's all about. It has to be based on the idea that I am my brother's keeper and I am my sister's keeper, and we're in this together. We are in this thing together."[40] The second moment in the 2011 CBCF speech is where Obama tries to explain the political hypocrisy of the Republican-led Congress and explain its detrimental impact on Black life. Obama states, "These Republicans in Congress like to talk about job creators. How about doing something real for job creators?" He goes on, "Pass this jobs bill, and every small business owner in America, including 100,000 black-owned businesses, will get a tax cut. You say you're the party of tax cuts. Pass this jobs bill, and every worker in America, including nearly 20 million African American workers, will get a tax cut." Obama continues, "Pass this jobs bill, and prove you'll fight just as hard for a tax cut for ordinary folks as you do for all your contributors." As I read Obama's second movement, it was not his intention to provide the economic plan with targeted universalism as the Black Caucus wanted. But he sought what Harris and other Black critics called for: policies that would have immediate and potentially long-term positive impacts on Black economic mobility. In an earlier part of the speech, Obama discussed an idea championed by the Black Caucus to provide summer jobs for low-income youth, but Obama sandwiches the idea between "We've got millions of unemployed Americans and young people looking for work but running out options" and "Tell me why we don't want the unemployed back in the workforce as soon as possible." This rhetorical intervention is important: by addressing Black "job creators" versus Black job seekers, Obama attempted to shift the grounds of the jobs debate from one in which Blackness acts like a signal of deprivation to one in which Blackness acts likes a signal of provision. The third movement is where Obama ends his 2011 speech by chastising and encouraging the crowd. These parts of the speech have garnered the most controversy, especially where Obama stated, "So I don't know about you, CBC, but the future rewards those who press on.

With patient and firm determination, I am going to press on for jobs. I'm going to press on for equality." He followed up with, "I don't have time to complain. I am going to press on. I expect all of you to march with me and press on. Take off your bedroom slippers, put on your marching shoes. Shake it off. Stop complaining, stop grumbling, stop crying. We are going to press on. We've got work to do, CBC."[41] Here is where Obama trafficked in the most stereotypical notions of grieved, anti-American, disgruntled Blacks. His rhetoric seemed to depict the Black Caucus agenda as out of touch with the wants and needs of Black hardworking Americans, if not of all Americans. Most observers, like Milloy, took Obama's words to mean that they were inadequately prepared for the fight or that they were not upholding their part of the electoral deal. In short, I see Obama's 2011 speech as a nuanced attempt to galvanize Blacks to help him confront the inclusionary dilemma rather than as a repudiation of Black interests.

By 2012, some Black leaders were more vocal in their understanding about the "inclusionary dilemma" and its impact on Obama's ability to be more forceful about racial inequality. For example, in an article in the *Crisis* (the magazine of the NAACP) evaluating President Obama's first years in office, Wade Henderson, president and CEO of the Leadership Conference on Civil Rights and Human Rights, remarked, "I think the first half of Obama's tenure has many examples of significant civil rights accomplishments that are worth noting. I don't join those who criticize him for not talking about issues of race and poverty. I think that in the current atmosphere, those statements and well-intentioned efforts would be used against him in a highly-politicized way."[42] Wade Henderson's published comments in the official organ of the oldest Black civil rights organization are particularly illustrative for two reasons. First, the Leadership Conference, a coalition of civil rights organizations, had once been criticized as myopic when the NAACP failed to support efforts in 1975 by Mexican civil rights advocates to seek passage of an amendment to the Voting Rights Act that would prohibit discrimination against language minorities.[43] Second, the Leadership Conference and its allies were carefully monitoring how Congress would respond to the Supreme Court's decision in the *Northwest Austin Municipal Utility District Number One v. Eric Holder* (2009). The court laid out a case against congressional action in 2006 that reauthorized the preclearance provision of the Voting Rights Act (VRA). Neither the Leadership Conference nor its allies could convince Congress and the public that *Northwest Austin* was a prelude to dismantling the strongest aspects of the VRA and a threat to congressional authority. The Leadership Conference's fears were realized when the Supreme Court invalidated the 2006 coverage formula in *Shelby County v. Holder* (2013) and when formerly covered states began to pass restrictive voting rights laws. One of the ironic aspects of the rhetoric coming from antipreclearance advocates in wake of *Northwest* and of *Shelby* was how the election and reelection of Barack Obama repudiated the necessity of race-conscious legislation. Henderson's words about Obama in 2012 foretold what was to come. Without judicial and legislative authority for enforcing preclearance in formerly covered states, Obama and Attorney General Eric Holder needed to leverage other VRA provisions while hoping for an electoral sweep in the 2014 elections to stymie the post-*Shelby* tide of regressive electoral reforms. Until the latter materialized, the DOJ was at the relative mercy of a Republican-led Congress.

Other Black spokespersons were less forgiving of Obama. These critics saw Obama's inaction as antithetical to the interests of Black Democrats. They saw it as decidedly relinquishing presidential authority and as capitulation to the racial order. Critics of Obama, like West and Smiley, and perhaps Harris, desired Obama to display what is tantamount to political John Henryism; whereas "John Henry" was a Black folk hero myth, "a steel-driving" railroad man who displayed superhuman abilities but worked so hard he died.[44] These critics wanted Obama to renounce color-blind universalism in favor of racial particularity. They wanted him to directly confront the "racial order" mountains of his time and to embrace what Robert C. Smith calls "political blackness" despite the political costs. In the next section, I leverage Burkean representational theory to outline the flaws of political John Henryism as it relates to the inclusionary dilemma.

Channeling Burke: Obama's Reprimand and Challenge

Viewed through the prisms of the "inclusionary dilemma" and of American-style parliamentarism, President Obama's 2011 Phoenix Awards reprimand of the Black Caucus was not unexpected. Obama's reprimand evoked the words of Edmund Burke regarding the tensions parliamentarians face when making decisions about how to behave.[45] Ostensibly an advocate for party governance in line with national interests, Edmund Burke preferred partisan politics over local clientelism. Similarly, Obama challenged the Black Caucus to confront its own Burkean Dilemma—that is, to confront the performative aspects of Black interest representation if they undermine legislative success.[46] Taken together, Obama's reprimand of and challenge to the Black Caucus are especially relevant for the practice and study of Black politics in the twenty-first century.

Obama's Reprimand

As described above, Obama chose the 2011 CBCF Phoenix Award to publicly air his frustration with the Black Caucus over job creation. The significance of Obama's reprimand rests not on him being the titular figurehead of the Democratic Party or on him identifying as African American, though both elements are important. Rather, the significance of the reprimand rests on the fact it came from an individual with a unique perspective on policy victories. No other president, save for Massachusetts senator John F. Kennedy, and certainly no other racially identified caucus member, could claim to have a policy-making perspective sharpened by election to two different branches in the federal constitutional structure *and* by racial/ethnic minority status. The political history made by Obama on January 20, 2009, held meaning for Black politics as a practice and as a field of study even in the absence of his racial self-identity. Obama became the first Democrat elected president in the twenty-first century, the first sitting federal legislator of any party to win the presidency since Kennedy won in 1960, and the first president to have previously voted on and to have helped shepherd through Congress a major piece of Black interest legislation: the 2006 reauthorized and amended Voting Rights Act of 1965. Any president with that political biography might privilege partisan unity over other considerations. President Obama's racial and political identities, White racial resentment, and Republican acrimony gave the 2008 election additional significance. Consequently, Obama could not credibly champion the expansion of executive-centered governance without seeming hypocritical or wondering about its precedential value. Nor could Obama credibly champion Congress-centered governance without weakening his institutional and bargaining position as chief executive. The reprimand was a reminder to the Black Caucus and their allies that the opportunity to secure policy victories was fleeting, especially since Obama would be evaluated through the interlocking prisms of racial, institutional, and partisan identity.[47]

Obama's Challenge

The significance of Obama's challenge to the Black Caucus stems not from the fact that it was offered but from the ways in which Obama leveraged the caucus's motto to racialize the Burkean Dilemma. Because the Black Caucus's motto reflects a commitment to advancing the "permanent interests" of Blacks wherever they reside, it was easy for Obama to use the 2011 speech to exploit "linked fate" and "inverted linked fate" to subtly raise questions about the Black Caucus's commitment to Black interests and about whether Black constituents privilege a national focus over a local focus. Both questions have implications for the "inclusionary dilemma." For instance, if most Blacks favor a legislative style that privileges the district over the nation—as Katherine Tate shows in *Black Faces in the Mirror: African Americans and their Representations in the US Congress*—their support for overt advocacy of race-conscious policies is contingent upon whether doing so will yield inclusion and substantive policy victories. However, if overt advocacy would enhance the likelihood of exclusion or noninclusion, Blacks might support universalism if doing so would yield policy victories. In other words, Blacks might support what Mary Hawkesworth calls "tactical invisibility" or allowing a White member to champion the Black policy objective and to claim credit for having pursued or achieved said objective. In doing this, Black elites would counteract the exclusionary "racing-gendering" behavior and attitudes of their White colleagues.[48] The rub, so to speak, depends on the degree to which the Black voter sees legislative style working for or against policy victories.

Likewise, the puzzle is whether the varied advocacy strategies of Black members of Congress matter to Black voters. If Black voters are indifferent or inattentive to different advocacy activities, Black legislators cannot legitimately claim credit to have advanced Black interest representation. And if Black constituents believe certain advocacy activities take away from other legislative activities, Black constituents might accuse Black legislators of shirking their ideological (and racial) duty. Even the most district-centered "homestyle" would not insulate Black legislators from being questioned about their legislative effectiveness (measured as policies proposed, passed, and signed into law). Nor would a district-centered "homestyle" dissuade challengers from characterizing Black House incumbents as inauthentic and nonresponsive to district interests.[49] Hawkesworth, Harris, and Price all presume that Black voters give equal weight to the legislative outcome and to the advocacy strategy. By this logic, tactical invisibility creates a Burkean Dilemma for Black members of Congress because racial expectations can cut both ways: being invisible could invoke the ire of Black voters who give greater weight to the *act* of representation or could invoke the praise of Black voters who give greater weight to the *outcome* of representation.[50]

My analysis of President Obama's complex engagement with the Black political class suggests that scholars may have oversold notions that Obama struck a Faustian bargain with Black voters. Despite that, I do agree with the co-editors that the "racial order" and "political time" constrained much of what Obama could have done. However, I also suggest that scholarly fascination with and popular acquiescence to presidentialism minimizes culpability for those whose formal responsibility *is* the representation of Black interests and the enactment of Black interest legislation.[51] The consequence of this fascination, as the co-editors of this volume aptly note in the introduction, was the labeling of Obama as the first "Black president." The consequence of this acquiescence, I contend, was that Black spokespersons were often unpersuaded by Obama's appeals to forego overt race-specific policy advocacy and to help him pass legislation which might meet Black needs for ameliorative action.[52]

Conclusion

While the initial relationship and the racial representation "dance" between President Barack Obama and Black spokespersons clearly had tensions, Obama was more vocal about racial inequality in his final days in office, including in his last speech (January 10, 2017), wherein he reminded Americans that their fates were inextricably linked. My analysis of Obama's engagement with the Black political class over job creation during his first years in office lead me to three conclusions about his January 2017 speech. First, Obama repudiated color-blind universalism and outlined how targeted universalism might work under the right conditions. Second, Obama acknowledged that "race whispering," "tactical invisibility," and "tandem institutionalism" could not work in an era of hyperpartisanship, extreme racialization, and voter and donor clamor for "responsible party government" at any costs. Third, Obama discredited the narratives of unfettered secularism, racial favoritism, and of government intrusion and ineptitude, which catapulted Republican Donald Trump to the White House in 2016.

That President Obama spent his final days in office both defending his record and preparing the Obama coalition for the Trump presidency illuminates the perilous search for exemplars of "political blackness" as debates in Black politics as a practice and as a field of study. For example, Obama seemed to answer his Black critics that he had not delivered on his promises to Black constituents when he did three things: (1) he issued a detailed report entitled *Progress of the African-American Community During the Obama Administration* (October 16, 2016); (2) he commanded his cabinet members to write "exit memos" for public dissemination; and (3) he categorized accomplishments in the "Administration's Record Report" using five headings ("Health Care," "Climate and Energy," "American Leadership," "Equality and Social Progress," and "Economic Progress").[53] Readers looking for Obama to claim credit by having explicit textual references to African Americans that link policy actions done specifically to benefit the group will be disappointed. Yet, by all accounts, much of the Obama administration's actions could be considered to have advanced "black interests."

That the Obama administration enjoyed policy success related to advancing Black interests but did not publicly tout much of those successes as explicitly race-conscious policies is an important point to make.[54] A study by Mendelberg and Butler examines how Obama's proposed spending on antipoverty programs was larger than that proposed by Lyndon Johnson, Jimmy Carter, and Bill Clinton, despite Obama making little to no mention of the word "poverty" and "poor" in his speeches.[55] The Mendelberg and Butler study found that "Mr. Obama made good on that commitment [to the needs of the poor and the disadvantaged] far more concretely [than his predecessors]. . . . Even after accounting for the higher numbers of poor people caught in the Great Recession, Mr. Obama's record outshines his predecessors." For instance, "Mr. Obama allocated $67,132, Mr. Clinton $39,820, Mr. Carter $20,790, and Mr. Johnson $546, again using 2014 dollars [for spending per poor family]." Citing another study, Mendelberg and Butler note that "outcomes" also matter, and "that tax and transfer policies lowered the poverty rate by only 1 percentage point in 1967, under President Lyndon B. Johnson, but by almost 13 points in 2012 [under Obama]." Mendelberg and Butler end their study this way: "While critics are right to chastise Mr. Obama for his pallid rhetoric on race, at least as president, they are wrong to say that he does not care about poor communities of color. Mr. Obama has been spending without saying. He should get at least as much credit for the former as vilification for the latter." In the volume *African American Politics and the African American Quest for Universal Freedom*, Hanes Walton Jr., Robert Smith, and Sherri Wallace echo the sentiment of Mendelberg and Butler. But they also fault Obama for not forcefully articulating his commitment to poor communities of color and for not underscoring how his proposed spending reflected that commitment. They conclude, "That Obama, a rhetorically gifted president, failed to employ this power on issues of race and poverty reflects his view of the imperative of the politics of ethnic avoidance."[56] I agree with the premise but not the conclusion. Another equally plausible conclusion, I submit, is that Obama overcame the inclusionary dilemma without the racial fanfare. Obama actualized the representation of Black interests without conveying the representation of Black interests; he avoided the downsides associated with expressing "political blackness" and engaged in "signifying without specifying."[57] Many critics of Obama wanted him to be a paragon of "political blackness." Their risk aversion made them suspicious of signification; they preferred clear messages and claiming credit. Many supporters of Obama saw signification as contrary to Black interests.

In many ways, Black voter disappointment in not being able to elect *Black politicians* to high office substantiates what former president of the American Political Science Association Jennifer L. Hochschild called "left pessimism by social scientists." Hochschild considered "left pessimism" to be a belief by contemporary social scientists on the political left that "the policy gains made by disadvantaged minority groups, or policy initiatives that have substantially diminished group-based hierarchy" have been upended. This perspective suggested that "failures to erode group-based hierarchy" reflected a faltering of core democratic institutions to address large problems in the public interest or to sustain a more egalitarian distribution of power.[58] As Hochschild notes, much of this "left pessimism by social scientists" merges with "Obama's buoyancy" and is buttressed from observations about whether Obama could alter the landscape of American racial and ethnic politics.[59] Left pessimism, as understood by Hochschild and as observed by President Obama in the 2016 *New York Times* interview from which Hochschild draws her opening epigraph, can be intellectually and civically disempowering. Obama claimed that he was "trying to inoculate [White House interns] against cynicism, which is a powerful force in our culture [because] . . . it's what passes for wisdom, being ironic and cynical."[60] In that regard, I read Obama's January 2017 speech as a warning to Americans that cynicism weakens resistance to "reconstructive" leaders (who seek to transform the political landscape by claiming an electoral mandate) and emboldens "preemptive" leaders (who seek to oppose the existing order and undue political commitments). Furthermore, the *Progress of the African-American Community During the Obama Administration* report has a reminder that Black constituents must guard against "left pessimism" and must continue to differentiate between legislative style and policy victories.

Finally, I draw two predictions about the potential future of Black politics from the 2016 election of Republican Donald Trump to the White House. First, I predict that the practice of Black politics in the Trump era will be more forceful about overt inclusion and be less tolerable of hollow victories. Obama's inclination toward parliamentarianism gave Trump the literary foil he needed to fuel his (White) America-first rhetoric. Obama's failure to subscribe to American "presidentialism" enabled Trump to present himself as the phenotypical, ideological, and cultural antithesis to tandem institutions and to Obama's cosmopolitan universalism. Where Obama negotiated with Congress, Trump has besieged Congress. Candidate Trump offered, and so far, President Trump offers Whites a president who would draw a bright line between his policy actions and their Whiteness. Candidate Trump ostensibly pledged to upend the "institutionalization of civil rights" and to alter what Richard Valley called the "parties and courts configuration."[61] President Trump has reshaped the federal judiciary and the federal bureaucracy in dramatic fashion, emboldened by a pliant Republican-led Senate. Because no Black interest policy is sacrosanct when "parties and courts configuration" shift and when the "institutionalization of civil rights" is weakened, Obama's early failures to expressly advocate for Black interests helped the racial order to reassert itself. Put differently, Obama's failure to leverage all of his legislative, administrative, and rhetorical power not only emboldened "left pessimism," but his failure left Black Democrats wholly unprepared to challenge the onslaught brought about by the Tea Party, the Republican Party's REDMAP redistricting plan, the growth in White nationalism, and the nationalization of the two midterm elections. The Trump presidency represents the earliest signs that the counter regime is gaining ground. Second, I predict that the study of Black politics in the Trump era will focus greater attention upon the innerworkings of bureaucracies and the violation of political norms. I suspect this greater attention will also lead to hypothetical counterfactuals about what the Obama presidency could have meant for Black America if not for the racial order and Obama's inclination for universalism. So far, the Trump presidency underscores the ease at which political entrepreneurs can violate political norms, can mobilize White anxiety, and can exploit hiring practices in bureaucracies for partisan (and racial) gain. The Trump presidency, at present, crowds out universalism because it traffics in prurient appeals that racialize and exclude.[62] Trump has failed to issue (and may never issue) credible invitations to any Black spokespersons likely to challenge his dance to reinforce the present racial order.

NOTES

1 See Richard Waterman, Carol L. Silva, and Hank Jenkins-Smith, *The Presidential Expectations Gap: Public Attitudes Concerning the Presidency* (Ann Arbor, Michigan: University of Michigan Press, 2016). Unlike the "double expectations gap," which assumes that presidents have equal acumen to deliver on promises and equal inclination to do so, my formulation privileges inclination and capacity (both structural and personal).

2 For a discussion on contemporary American presidentialism, see Dana D. Nelson, *Bad for Democracy: How the Presidency Undermines the Power of the People*

(Minneapolis: University of Minnesota Press, 2008). For a discussion on American parliamentarism, see Thomas E. Mann and Norman J. Ornstein, *It's Even Worse Than It Looks Was: How the American Constitutional System Collided with the New Politics of Extremism* (New York: Basic Books, 2016).

3 A presidential system (one in which a president exists) does not innately confer presidentialism—other forms of governance and distributions of power are possible (e.g., coequal power sharing, a fused system with a prime minister and a president that confers different constitutional responsibilities and legislative predominance whereby the president is more 'legislative clerk' than legislative agenda setter). Left unchecked, presidentialism undermines democratic freedoms and institutional legitimacy. Larry Diamond, *Developing Democracy: Toward Consolidation* (Baltimore, Md.: Johns Hopkins University, 1999).

4 Mark Peterson, *Legislating Together: The White House and Capitol Hill from Eisenhower to Reagan* (Cambridge: Harvard University Press, 1993), 8.

5 Harris, *Price of the Ticket*, 170–172.

6 Obama, Barack. 2011. *Public Papers of the Presidents of the United States: Barack Obama, 2009, Book 1* (Government Printing Office, 2011), 593.

7 Of course, Obama did not embrace avoidance when initiating My Brother's Keeper (though this initiative was targeted at young men of color and was largely framed as helping young men avoid pitfalls which would limit their socioeconomic mobility and educational attainment).

8 Harris, *Price of the Ticket*, 172.

9 Harris, *Price of the Ticket*, 172.

10 Harris neglects to note that Black Caucus members Charles Rangel (NY-15) and Edolphus Towns (NY-10) were early cosponsors of the legislation and at the bargaining table with the White House. (Both filed as cosponsors on January 26, 2009, the first day the legislation was submitted to the House.) Chairman Rangel of the Committee on Ways and Means was also appointed to be a member of the conference committee which would negotiate differences between the House and Senate versions. On February 10, 2009, the House voted (403–0) to instruct conferees "to not record their approval of the final conference agreement unless the text of the agreement has been available at least 48 hours." *American Recovery and Reinvestment Act of 2009: Hearings on H101, Before the House Committee of the Whole*, 111th Cong., 1st session, (2009). No Republican House member voted for the American Recovery Act and Reinvestment Act of 2009. Democrats also defeated motions to have the bill recommitted and to reject the conference report. Obama signed the bill on February 17, 2009.

11 See Alexandra Kolb, *Dance and Politics* (New York: Peter Lang, 2010).

12 Robert C. Smith, *John F. Kennedy, Barack Obama, and the Politics of Ethnic Incorporation and Avoidance* (Albany: State University of New York Press, 2013), 114.

13 Young Min Baek and Jocelyn Landau, "White Concern About Black Favoritism in a Biracial Presidential Election," *American Politics Research* 39 (2011): 291–322.

14 Barack Obama, "Remarks by the President to the NAACP Centennial Convention, July 16, 2009, Hilton New York, New York," White House, Office of the Press Secretary, July 17, 2009.

15 Barack Obama, "NAACP Centennial Convention, July 16, 2009," July 17, 2009. Applause notations omitted.

16 Barack Obama, "NAACP Centennial Convention, July 16, 2009."

17 Hanes Walton, *When the Marching Stopped: The Politics of Civil Rights Regulatory Agencies* (Albany: State University of New York Press, 1988).

18 Barack Obama, "Remarks by the President at the Congressional Black Caucus Foundations Annual Phoenix Award Dinner, Walter E. Washington Convention Center, Washington, D.C.," The White House, Office of the Press Secretary, September 27, 2009.

19 Lester K. Spence, *Knocking the Hustle: Against the Neoliberal Turn in Black Politics* (Brooklyn, New York: Punctum Book, 2015); Eddie Glaude, *Democracy in Black: How Race Still Enslaves the American Soul* (New York: Crown Publishers, 2016).

20 What should not be missed is that only days earlier, July 2, 2009, Obama released a statement on the forty-fifth anniversary of the Civil Rights Act of 1964, in which he noted, "But while the Civil Rights Act opened doors of freedom and opportunity, we know that far too many inequities and barriers remain in the African American community and across this country. And we must continue to break down these barriers in our laws, our policies, and our hearts so that we can not only fulfill the full promise of the Civil Rights Act, but perfect the union that our founders created two hundred and thirty-three years ago this week." See Obama, Barack. *Public Papers of the Presidents of the United States: Barack Obama, 2009, Book 2* (Washington, DC: Government Printing Office, 2011), 1035.

21 For example, the table does not reflect a compilation from the White House's official visitor logs, a list of the Obamas' travels or phone calls with key leaders, or the full range of ceremonial events and informal gatherings where bureaucratic, legislative, and executive staff mingled together.

22 The White House, Office of the Press Secretary, "Readout of President Obama's Meeting with the Congressional Black Caucus, March 11, 2010," www.whitehouse.gov.

23 Barack Obama, "Remarks by the President at Congressional Black Caucus Foundation Annual Phoenix Awards Dinner," September 18, 2010. https://obamawhitehouse.archives.gov.

24 Barack Obama, "Remarks by the President at Congressional Black Caucus Foundation Annual Phoenix Awards Dinner."

25 J. Taylor Rushing, "Black Caucus Hits Senate GOP for Sitting On Summer Jobs Bill," *The Hill*, June 23, 2010. See Lee letter at https://lee.house.gov.

26 Cecilia Rouse holds a PhD from Harvard University, served under Clinton on the National Economic Council (1998–1999), founded the Princeton University Education Research Section, and is a member of the National Academy of Education. She is well published and has served as a research associate of the National Bureau

of Economic Research. She is also married, a mother, served on several boards, and enjoyed deep roots in a variety of circles. In 2012, she was appointed Dean of the Princeton University School of Public and International Affairs.

27 Readout of the President's meeting with the National Urban League and NAACP, July 21, 2011. https://obamawhitehouse.archives.gov.

28 "Rep Waters to Frustrated Black Voters: 'Unleash Us' on Obama," FoxNews.com, August 17, 2011, www.foxnews.com.

29 Waters's remark is also interesting given her successful amendment (House Amendment 17) to the House version of the 2009 Recovery Act. Her amendment sought to authorize the government to "utilize job training funds [in division A of the bill] for broadband [communications] deployment and related activities [as outlined in division B]." The amendment was agreed to by voice vote. Waters presented the amendment as an opportunity to create jobs, create careers, expand job opportunities for young people, and enhance broadband to underserved areas. See *American Recovery and Reinvestment Act of 2009: Hearings on H721, Before the House Committee of the Whole*, 111th Cong., 1st session, (2009).

30 Alicia M. Cohn, "Cleaver: If Obama Wasn't President, We Would Be 'Marching on the White House,'" *The Hill*, September 18, 2011. https://thehill.com.

31 Specifically, Senator Barack Obama became the first sitting federal legislator of any party to ascend to the White House since Massachusetts Democratic senator John F. Kennedy, became the first Democratic presidential nominee to win office after the two-term presidency of Republican George W. Bush, became the first nonwhite presidential nominee of a major party to win office in the modern convention era, became the first presidential nominee of a major party to publicly claim biracial parentage, and became the first chief executive to have membership in the Black Caucus.

32 William Clay, *Just Permanent Interests: Black Americans in Congress, 1870–1991*. (New York: Amistad Press, 1993).

33 Katherine Tate, *Concordance: Black Lawmaking in the U.S. Congress from Carter to Obama* (Ann Arbor: University of Michigan Press, 2014), 5.

34 Adolph L. Reed, *Stirrings in the Jug: Black Politics in the Post-Segregation Era* (Minneapolis: University of Minnesota Press, 1999); Adolph L. Reed, *Class Notes: Posing as Politics and Other Thoughts on the American Scene* (New York: New Press, 2000); Spence, *Knocking the Hustle*, 113–147.

35 Habiba Alcindor, "Controversy Dogs Tavis Smiley and Cornel West's Poverty Tour—but Media Attention Does, Too," *Nation*, 17 August 2011.

36 Alcindor, "Controversy Dogs Tavis Smiley and Cornel West's Poverty Tour."

37 Barack Obama, "Remarks by the President at the Congressional Black Caucus Foundation's Annual Phoenix Award Dinner," September 24, 2011.

38 In full disclosure, I was at the 2011 Phoenix Award speech. The speech did sound condescending, applause notwithstanding. The speech sounded especially hurtful if one did not contextualize three things: (1) the back-and-forth between the Obama administration and black spokespersons about addressing black socioeco-

nomic concerns; (2) Obama's deep appreciation for civil rights icons Dr. Joseph Lowery and John Lewis, who were being celebrated that night; and (3) Republican stonewalling on infrastructure investment plans which were part of Obama's economic strategy. These three things do not absolve Obama of criticism, but they do reveal why this speech was perhaps more forceful and transparent than Obama or the audience realized (or wanted).

39 Michelle Singletary, "Obama's Unfortunate Remarks on People's Misfortunes," *Washington Post*, September 27, 2011; Courtland Milloy, "President Obama Courting Black People Again," *Washington Post*, September 25, 2011. Milloy was referencing the infamous 1992 moment when presidential candidate Bill Clinton criticized Sista Souljah during a Rainbow/PUSH Coalition event to celebrate the artist. For Milloy, Obama used his 2011 CBCF Speech to distance himself from black liberals in the way that Clinton used Sista Souljah's appearance at the Jackson event to distance himself from the liberal wing of the party. I do not agree with Milloy's perspective on the speech, but I do understand how he came about his perspective.

40 Milloy, "President Obama Courting Black People Again," 2011.

41 Milloy, "President Obama Courting Black People Again," 2011.

42 Kenneth Cooper, "The President's Report Card: One Year Later," *The Crisis* (Fall 2012): 6.

43 Diane Pinderhughes, "Black Interest Groups and the 1982 Extension of the Voting Rights Act," in Huey Perry and Wayne Parent, eds., *Blacks and the American Political System* (Gainesville: University Press of Florida, 1995).

44 John Henryism is a psychological construct meant to characterize how respondents (mostly black men) facing race-based obstacles engage in additional high-effort activities to overcome those obstacles. Essentially, this behavioral response to "psychosocial environmental stressors" becomes counterproductive because it often leads to poor health care outcomes. See Sherman A. James, "John Henryism and the Health of African-Americans." *Culture, Medicine, and Psychiatry* 18 (1994): 163–182; Sherman A. James, Sue A. Hartnett, and William D. Kalsbeek. "John Henryism and Blood Pressure Differences among Black Men." *Journal of Behavioral Medicine* 6 (1983): 259–278. Linda A. Jackson and Lucile L. Adams-Campbell. "John Henryism and Blood Pressure in Black College Students." *Journal of Behavioral Medicine* 17 (1994): 69–79.

45 The Burkean Dilemma posits that parliamentarians confront a conflict along two dimensions: (1) being torn between embracing a legislative style of a district delegate (where the legislator champions the preferences of the district majority) and embracing a legislative style of a trustee (where the legislator uses his/her perceptions to decide which preferences to champion), and (2) being torn between responding to national interests and responding to local interests.

46 I see no pathology inherent in wanting to see visible, authentic, black leadership. Each component is not problematic in and of itself. However, seeking all three elements at once can be problematic for securing black interest policies. Visibility

can be a detriment if it is done for largely performative purposes; political black-ness will always engender debate about what is and what is not an authentic dis-position towards black interests or black culture; leadership will always engender debate about the proper balance between organic, hierarchical, transactional, and transformative leadership. Fetishizing the "representation of black interests" can undermine appreciation for whether certain policies that advance black interests are actually proposed, passed, and enacted.

47 Tyson D. King-Meadows, *When the Letter Betrays the Spirit: Voting Rights Enforce-ment and African American Participation from Lyndon Johnson to Barack Obama* (Lanham, MD: Lexington Books, 2011), 72.

48 Mary Hawkesworth, "Congressional Enactments of Race-Gender: Toward a The-ory of Race-Gendered Institutions," *American Political Science Review* 97(2003): 529–550.

49 Richard Fenno, *Congressional Travels: Places, Connections, and Authenticity* (New York: Longman, 2006); and Richard F. Fenno Jr., *Going Home: Black Representa-tives and Their Constituents* (Chicago, 2003).

50 Kenny Whitby, *The Color of Representation: Congressional Behavior and Black Interests* (Ann Arbor, MI: University of Michigan Press, 1997); Michael D. Minta, *Oversight: Representing the Interests of Blacks and Latinos in Congress* (Princeton: Princeton University Press, 2011); Christian Grose, *Congress in Black and White: Race and Representation in Washington and at Home* (New York: Cambridge University Press, 2011).

51 Here I disagree with the co-editors as it relates to the "inclusionary dilemma." I believe that the co-editors' focus on 'expressed advocacy' is the conceptual fulcrum from which much of black concern about Obama rests. The co-editors sidestep what I find problematic—namely that expression and advocacy must be evaluated against some normative a priori baselines. Thus, because nomenclature is not neutral, the concept of expressed advocacy is replete with theoretical and practical pitfalls.

52 King-Meadows writes, "In short, President Obama would need congressional sup-port, bureaucratic cooperation, and judicial assent to give teeth to his inheritance. Without all three, Obama risked upsetting the Joshua and Moses generations. Given too much of all three, Obama risked energizing skeptics of the Johnson Framework who want judicial repudiation of all race-conscious public policies and the strongest element of the Framework, preclearance. For the liberal wing of the party, the cost of Obama's inheritance could be foot dragging, capitulation and silence on many things it wanted." King-Meadows, *When the Letter Betrays the Spirit*, 72.

53 "The Record," ObamaWhiteHouse.gov, accessed April 7, 2017, https://obamawhite-house.archives.gov/the-record.

54 Norman Ornstein, "A Very Productive Congress, Despite What the Approval Rat-ings Say," *Washington Post*, January 31, 2010.

55 Tali Mendelberg and Bennett L. Butler, "Obama Cares. Look at the Numbers." *New York Times*, August 21, 2014.

56 Hanes Walton Jr., Robert C. Smith, and Sherri L. Wallace, *American Politics and the African American Quest for Universal Freedom*, 8th edition (New York: Routledge, 2017), 271.

57 Stephanie Li, *Signifying without Specifying: Racial Discourse in the Age of Obama* (New Jersey: Rutgers University Press, 2012), 5.

58 Jennifer L. Hochschild, "Left Pessimism and Political Science," *Perspectives on Politics* 15 (2017): 6–19.

59 Hochschild cites the following: Harris, *Price of the Ticket*; Eddie Glaude, *Democracy in Black: How Race Still Enslaves the American Soul* (New York: Crown Publishers, 2016); Michael Dawson, *Not in Our Lifetimes: The Future of Black Politics* (Chicago: University of Chicago Press, 2011); Michael Tesler, *Post-Racial or Most-Racial? Race and Politics in the Obama Era* (Chicago: University of Chicago Press, 2016); Douglas Massey, *Categorically Unequal: The American Stratification System* (New York: Russell Sage Foundation, 2007).

60 Philip Galanes, "The Roles of a Lifetime," *New York Times*, May 8, 2016.

61 Hanes Walton, *When the Marching Stopped: The Politics of Civil Rights Regulator Agencies* (Albany: State University of New York Press, 1988), 1–27; Richard Valelly, *The Two Reconstructions: The Struggle for Black Enfranchisement* (Chicago: University of Chicago Press, 2004), 9–12.

62 Michael Tesler, "The Spillover of Racialization into Health Care: How President Obama Polarized Public Opinion by Racial Attitudes and Race," *American Journal of Political Science* 56 (2012): 690–704; Ismail K. White, "When Race Matters and when It Doesn't: Racial Group Differences in Response to Racial Cues," *American Political Science Review* 101 (2007): 339–354.

3

The "Obama Effect" Revisited

A Macrolevel and Longitudinal Exploration of the Influence of Barack Obama's Media Presence on Racialized Political Party Polarization

RAY BLOCK JR. AND ANGELA K. LEWIS-MADDOX

In the months leading up to his 2008 victory, many political scientists worried that America was not yet ready for a biracial president who self-identified as an African American. Some political scientists pondered whether Obama, having won once, would be re-elected to the White House, particularly since the Republican Party invested so much political energy into blocking the forty-fourth president's political accomplishments and making the 2012 campaign a referendum on Obama's shortcomings. And we are still wondering how greatly the Obama administration shaped US race relations. In many ways, Barack Obama has pushed us to reconsider (and, in some cases, rethink) what we know about Black politics.

In our attempt to make sense what Obama teaches us about race and politics after 2017 and beyond, we focus this chapter on the sociopolitical implications of Barack Obama being our former president. Specifically, there is growing literature about what has been dubbed the "Obama effect."[1] In fact, a quick scan of this literature confirms that Barack Obama's historic standing as the first POTUS (President of the United States) of color has had an impact on a wide array of political processes, attitudes, identities, and forms of participation.[2] In this chapter, we examine the influence of Obama's presence on racial divisions in partisanship. Consistent with Valdesolo and Graham (2016), we interpret these divisions as evidence of *racial polarization*. Since Obama is a Democrat, and because African Americans vote overwhelmingly for Democratic candidates in presidential elections, we define polarization as a gap in the extent to which African and Anglo Americans identify with the Democratic Party.[3] Our focus on polarization stems from the fact that partisanship has always been a racialized concept in American politics. For example, it is widely documented that African Americans' current preference for the Democratic Party stems, at least in part, from the belief that the Republican Party has been comparably less responsive to African American interests since the Realignment of 1964. More recently, Tesler and Sears (2010) have argued that anti-Black attitudes, stoked by Obama's presence, have produced a second party realignment in which racial tensions push Blacks further away from the Republican Party and entice some racially conservative Whites to join the GOP and support its candidates and policies (see also Powers 2014). While a detailed review of the Obama literature,[4] or comprehensive history of race and partisanship,[5] is beyond the scope of this chapter, we use Obama's candidacy and presidency as a test case for understanding racially polarized partisanship.

To understand racial polarization, it is necessary to take a macrolevel approach. Put differently, we are less concerned with individuals' party preference and seek instead to explore aggregate patterns across racial groups. Moreover, implied within this conceptualization is the notion of party dynamics (i.e., change, over time, in Blacks' and Whites' political affiliation). Accordingly, as the title suggests, we take a macrolevel and longitudinal approach to studying racial differences in partisanship during the Obama era. This approach requires that we apply the logic of "Obama effects" to trends in partisanship, and we explore the possibility that the relationship between the former POTUS's media presence and voters' party identification can change over time and differ by race. To begin this exploration, we ask the following questions:

1) Was there a race gap in party identification during the Obama presidency?
2) If so, did the former president's media activities influence the width of this race gap?
3) How did Obama's media presence affect the party gap? Did the former president push Whites away from the Democratic Party (while pulling African Americans into it)? Or did Obama make racial differences in partisanship disappear?

Our analysis of the effect (if any) of media presence on polarization combines methodological innovations from the macropartisanship literature in political science (MacKuen, Erikson, and Stimson 1989; Erikson, MacKuen, and Stimson 1998) with insights from the role model research in psychology (particularly, Marx, Ko, and Friedman 2009). We also adopt a research approach employed by Block and Haynes (2014); specifically, we use a "filmography" (a chronological list of Barack Obama's television appearances) obtained from the C-SPAN Video Library to develop novel measures of media presence, and we supplement that filmography with "toplines" (summary reports of polling results) from the 2008 National Annenberg Election Survey (NAES). We find that racial polarization intensifies as the frequency of Obama's media activities increases and that certain types of media appearances can actually decrease this race gap. We conclude this chapter by discussing the substantive implications of our evidence and the limitations of our research design. When discussing potential avenues for research, we focus on the fact that Obama's presidency gave race scholars the opportunity to study descriptive representation in the nation's highest political office.

Evidence of Racially Polarized Partisanship

African Americans almost unanimously support the Democratic Party. As Haynie and Watts (2010, 93) note, "Blacks are not only overwhelmingly Democratic in their partisan identification, they also consistently vote for Democratic candidates by overwhelming margins in elections at all levels." Because they were disproportionately hurt by the economic downturns of the Great Depression (and were therefore inclined to support Franklin D. Roosevelt and his New Deal politics) African Americans became a rich pool from which the Democratic Party could recruit new members. Blacks' shift away from the party of Lincoln intensified with Lyndon B. Johnson and the civil rights laws of the mid-1960s, and the alliance between African Americans and the Democratic Party has persisted into the present day.[6] Conversely, White voters—particularly those residing in the South—moved en masse to the Republican Party, thus fomenting partisan polarization along racial lines.[7] Since these racial realignments, the Democrats have cultivated a reputation for being a big-tent party that represents the interests of racial and ethnic minorities, the GOP became the preferred party for Whites, and Democratic presidential candidates have never been able to win the majority of White votes (Carmines and Stimson 1989).

Despite this racial polarization, Obama was surprisingly successful at navigating party dynamics, for he won the 2008 presidential campaign with 43 percent of the White vote, a feat that secured his place in history as the third leading Democratic White-vote getter[8] (Donovan 2010; Kinder and Dale-Riddle 2012). Obama's electoral success prompts some to believe that the race gap is closing. Blacks remained faithful Democrats, while many Whites, perhaps out of frustration with the Bush administration, swung to the Democratic Party. The logic behind this line of reasoning stems from the "hope and change" rhetoric Obama utilized during his 2008 campaign (Bligh and Kholes 2009; Plouffe 2009) and was magnified by the post-racial-America narrative that journalists and pundits attached to the idea of having the nation's first Black president (e.g., Steele 2008). Obama's racially transcendent persona,[9] combined with the oft-expressed desire to start a new chapter in American race relations, might have unified Blacks and Whites, thus consolidating support for the Democratic Party.

Others question this postracial narrative by pointing out the naiveté of believing that the political achievement of one person, no matter how significant, can atone for America's checkered racial past (see Kaplan 2011; 2009; Hunt and Wilson 2009; Parks and Rachlinski 2010). These scholars maintain that the party gap has widened, not narrowed, that Obama won the Oval Office despite rising racial tensions (Lewis-Beck and Tien 2008; Lewis-Beck, Tien, and Nadeau 2010; Lewis-Beck, Nadeau, and Tien 2012) and that group relations have actually worsened since Obama declared his candidacy in 2008 (Hutchings 2009). Put simply, there are authors claiming that Obama's candidacy may have contributed to the widening of the party gap, and there are other arguments claiming the opposite: that Obama closed this gap. Of course, we entertain the possibility that Obama had no effect on the race gap and that the Democratic Party neither gained nor lost Black and White members. This begs the first research question: Have racial differences in support for the Democratic Party increased, decreased, or remained steady since Obama stepped onto the political scene?

Using rolling cross-sectional polls from the preelection wave of the University of Pennsylvania's National Annenberg Election Survey (NAES) we offer a panoramic view of racialized party polarization during the 2008 presidential election cycle (see figure 3.1).[10] For each rolling cross section, we calculated the proportion of Blacks (dim gray solid line) and Non-Hispanic Whites (dim gray dashed line) who self-identify as Democrats. The party gap, therefore, is the arithmetic difference between these proportions. For example, if this calculation yields a positive number, then Blacks outnumber Whites when it comes to party identification (Blacks − Whites > 0). Conversely a negative value indicates that more Whites than Blacks are self-reported Democrats (Blacks − Whites < 0). A gap of zero (Blacks − Whites = 0) means that there was no racial difference on that day in party preference. Readers should note that, rather than looking at individual respondents, we are examining aggregate results across entire surveys.[11] Despite the volatility in daily trends, it is clear from the left side of the figure that the proportion of self-identified Democrats tends to be higher among Black respondents than it is among White ones, and a difference-of-means test confirms this pattern ($t = 47.10$, $p <$ .01). Moreover, a bivariate correlation analysis of party identification and survey year confirms that the proportion of Black Democrats increased slightly over the course of the 2008 election cycle ($r = .13$, $p =$ .02), while the proportion of White Democrats stayed relatively stable ($r = .03$, $p = .62$). The right side of figure 3.1 shows that this racial difference in party trends has a net effect of increasing polarization, for the actual party gap, measured here as the proportion of Black Democrats minus the proportion for White Democrats,[12] rises a little over time ($r = .12$, $p = .04$). What have we learned so far? In response to the first research question, there is clear evidence of racially polarized partisanship. In the next section, we explore the influence of Obama's media presence on this party gap.

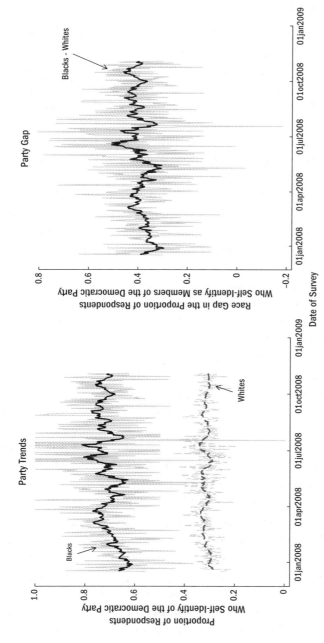

Figure 3.1. Racial polarization in political party identification—a look back at the 2008 presidential election cycle. *Source:* Created using all 316 of the "rolling cross-section" telephone polls constituting the 2008 National Annenberg Election Survey (NAES).

Notes: Data points on the left side of the figure are day-to-day reports of the fraction of NAES respondents who self-identity as Democrats (connected with gray lines), along with a seven-day moving average summarizing the overall trend (dark gray lines). The party gap (presented on the right side of the figure) represents the arithmetic difference between the fractions of Black and White Democrats.

The Impact of Media Presence

The trend curves in figure 3.1 demonstrate that overall party polarization increased to a small degree when Obama stepped onto the scene. However, while it is useful to examine temporal patterns, we are ultimately interested in any effect Obama's "media presence" had on the racial party gap. After all, there is a wealth of evidence demonstrating that Blacks and Whites tend to react differently to Obama's political prominence (see Hutchings 2009 and Parker 2016 for reviews of this research). While Blacks tended to see Obama's political ascendency as positive, Whites were much more divided about there being a "Black man in the White House" (Parker, Sawyer, and Towler 2009). We argue that this pattern of racial difference extends to the concept of party identification. In particular, we draw upon recent research that produces two conflicting predictions regarding the impact of Obama's media presence on racially polarized partisanship. On the one hand, Obama's charisma and transcendent persona might work to his advantage when it comes to party mobilization. As Block and Onwunli (2010) note, repeated interactions with Obama "habituated" voters, making them more comfortable with the possibility, and subsequent reality, of a Black president.[13] Television appearances are an ideal medium for politicians who seek to interact with constituents, and the Obama administration, more so than any other presidency, took to the airwaves to appeal to voters (see Rothman 2012). Applying this logic to our current study, habituation can assuage voters' racial concerns, and in so doing, increase Obama's popularity. The cumulative impact of such habituation is that it might have recruited more voters, regardless of race, into the Democratic Party, and by extension, decreased the race gap in party preference.

On the other hand, there is evidence suggesting that increased media exposure can backfire and intensify race-based party polarization. After all, this is the reasoning behind the criticism that Obama was too concerned with his own popularity. Numerous scholars acknowledge the former president's ability to exploit social media to appeal to voters and advance his political agenda (Harfoush 2009; Kellner 2009; McQueen and Green 2010; Rice and Sarver 2013). Tesler and Sears (2010) as well as Sugrue (2010) explore the polarizing impact of Obama's mass appeal in their work, and subsequent studies—

particularly Banks (2014a; 2014b), Parker and Barreto (2013), and Tesler (2012)—confirm that attitudes about race contributed not only to the rise of the hyperconservative Tea Party movement but also to some voters' opposition to the Patient Protection and Affordable Care Act or "Obamacare." This line of research suggests that rather than bringing voters together, Obama's media activities might have created a wedge between Blacks (many of which supported Obama enthusiastically) and Whites (some of which were worried about the implications of having a racial minority in the nation's highest political office). In short, Obama's media presence might decrease the level of party polarization in the United States, thus, narrowing the race gap in support for the Democratic Party. Alternatively, it might have widened the gap, thus increasing racially polarized partisanship.

To address our second research question—did Obama's media presence affect racial differences in partisanship?—table 3.1 presents results from a series of regression models. Our dependent variable is the aggregate measure of the race gap. It captures the difference between the proportion of Blacks and Whites in each NAES poll who identify as Democrats. As noted above, Obama's media presence is our theoretically central predictor of the party gap. The notion of "media presence" implies two things: first, Obama uses television and other media outlets to make public appeals; and second, the public is not only receiving but also responding to these appeals. Using footage obtained from the C-SPAN Video Library, we consider a host of different indicators of media presence in our examination of racialized party polarization (see table 3.3 in the Appendix for details). The control variables include a series of aggregate-level NAES items tapping into respondents' racial attitudes. To show the impact of these independent variables in fuller detail, we first add them, one by one, in separate regression models of the race gap; then, we present the result from a model containing all the variables included at the same time (see table 3.3 in the Appendix for summary information about these variables).[14]

Readers can see from the fully specified model that media presence can play an important role in explaining racial differences in respondents' identification with the Democratic Party. Media variables are the only predictors that remain statistically significant after controlling for additional factors. Holding other variables constant, a one-unit

TABLE 3.1. Media Presence and Racial Differences in Partisanship

	Baseline Model		Voter-Side Media Variables		Candidate-Side Media Variables		Aggregate Racial Attitudes		Full Model	
	Est.	(S.E.)	Est.	(S.E.)	Est.	(S.E.)	Est.	(S.E.)	Est.	(S.E.)
Forecasting Partisanship										
Race Gap at $t - 1$	0.05	(0.06)							0.04	(0.07)
Measures of Voters' Media Exposure										
Follow 2008 Presidential Campaign?			0.01	(0.02)					0.01	(0.03)
Follow Obama Specifically?			0.27+	(0.14)					0.21	(0.20)
Measures of Obama's Media Activities										
Number of Obama's TV Appearances					0.12+	(0.07)			0.11+	(0.06)
TV Appearance Type (Vignette)					−0.16*	(0.09)			−0.12	(0.08)
TV Appearance Type (Speech)					−0.12	(0.08)			−0.01	(0.07)
TV Appearance Type (Forum)					−0.21*	(0.09)			−0.18*	(0.09)
TV Appearance Type (Debate)					−0.16+	(0.09)			−0.13	(0.09)
TV Appearance Type (Rally)					−0.12	(0.08)			−0.11	(0.08)
TV Appearance Type (Roundtable)					−0.07	(0.07)			−0.05	(0.07)
TV Appearance Type (News Conference)					0.01	(0.08)			0.01	(0.08)
Control Variables										
Obama Favorability Ratings							−0.04	(0.03)	−0.04	(0.04)
Zero-Sum Perception (Jobs)							0.05	(0.31)	0.03	(0.32)
Zero-Sum Perception (Gov't. Spending)							0.07	(0.25)	−0.01	(0.26)

TABLE 3.1. (cont.)

	Baseline Model		Voter-Side Media Variables		Candidate-Side Media Variables		Aggregate Racial Attitudes		Full Model	
	Est.	(S.E.)	Est.	(S.E.)	Est.	(S.E.)	Est.	(S.E.)	Est.	(S.E.)
Zero-Sum Perception (Representation)							−0.05+	(0.03)	−0.03	(0.03)
Constant	0.37***	(0.03)	0.28*	(0.12)	0.39***	(0.01)	0.58**	(0.19)	0.49*	(0.25)
Number of Observations	310		316		315		316		309	
Adjusted R-squared	0.01		0.02		0.04		0.02		0.06	

Aggregate-Level Models of the Race Gap in Identification with the Democratic Party
Source: 2008 National Annenberg Election Survey (NAES), rolling cross section surveys
Note: Estimates are ordinary least squares (OLS) regression coefficients with robust standard errors (clustered by survey year) in parentheses.
+ $p < 0.10$, * $p < 0.05$, ** $p < 0.01$, *** $p < 0.001$, two-tailed tests

increase in the number of TV appearances that Obama makes contributes to a widening of the race gap in party preference (OLS Estimate = 0.11, S.E. = (0.06), p < 0.10). The binary measure for TV appearance type (1 = presidential candidate's forum, 0 = otherwise) is the only other independent variable that remains statistically significant in the full model, and interestingly, it has the effect of narrowing the party gap (Estimate = −0.18, S.E. = (0.09), p = < 0.05). We attribute the negative effect of political forum appearances on party polarization to the role of information on candidate preference. Presumably, low-information voters are perhaps more likely than their high-information colleagues to base their assessment of Barack Obama on extrapolitical considerations—for example, the candidate's race (see Block and Onwunli 2010 for a similar line of reasoning). Gaining information about a candidate may attenuate the degree to which voters rely on nonpolitical cues, which means that information, like habituation, can mitigate anti-Obama antagonism. Forums are venues where politicians, constituents, and journalists exchange ideas. Because they are information-rich media events, voters may learn about Obama in these political forums, and consequently, soften their views of him. Readers will notice that regression coefficients for all of the other "appearance type" predictors (which are arguably also information-providing events) are negative in sign, although their effects are nonsignificant in the full model. If information can attenuate antagonism toward Obama, then this pattern, as noted earlier, can have the net effect of lowering the party gap, particularly if Whites are being pulled into the Democratic Party.

Recall that our second research question pertains to the influence of Obama's media presence on the race gap in party identification. At this point, we have enough information to answer that question in the affirmative. Taken together, the results in table 3.1 demonstrate that racial polarization in partisanship is shaped not only by the *frequency* of Obama's media activities but also by the *type* of such activities.

Explaining the Race Gap

It is helpful to know that certain measures of media presence can affect the party gap; however, this knowledge does not tell us specifically what happens to the race gap once Obama stepped onto the political scene. Accordingly, the third set of analyses will address the third research question: If media presence affects party polarization, then how does it affect the gap between Blacks' and Whites' support for the Democratic Party? Getting at this research question requires that we create two sets of regression models. One will be a fully specified model with Blacks' Democratic Party identification as the dependent variable, and the other will be Whites' party preference as the outcome variable of interest (see table 3.2). Since proportion data has values that fall between 0 and 1, it would be ideal if we estimated predicted values that also fit within this interval. Our dependent variables are proportions rather than the party gap, which can take on both positive and negative values, and this is combined with our concern that an Ordinary Least Squares regression model would make out-of-bounds predictions. Thus, we analyze the impact of our predictors on Blacks' and Whites' partisanship using generalized linear models (GLMs) with a logit link function and the binomial family (see Agresti 2015; Baum 2008). This research approach will allow us to explore the possibility that certain predictors matter more for Whites' partisanship than for Blacks' and vice versa.

TABLE 3.2. Media Presence Effects by Race

	Black Democrats		White Democrats	
Forecasting Partisanship	Est.	(S.E.)	Est.	(S.E.)
Proportion of Democrats at $t - 1$	0.10	(0.31)	0.16	(0.28)
Measures of Voters' Media Exposure				
Follow 2008 Presidential Campaign?	0.09	(0.13)	0.03	(0.04)
Follow Obama Specifically?	0.81	(0.94)	−0.24	(0.25)
Measures of Obama's Media Activities				
Number of Obama's TV Appearances	0.54	(0.42)	−0.01	(0.11)
TV Appearance Type (Vignette)	−0.50	(0.49)	0.11	(0.14)
TV Appearance Type (Speech)	−0.54	(0.44)	−0.01	(0.11)
TV Appearance Type (Forum)	−0.84	(0.58)	0.08	(0.13)
TV Appearance Type (Debate)	−0.66	(0.50)	0.01	(0.12)
TV Appearance Type (Rally)	−0.56	(0.46)	0.04	(0.13)
TV Appearance Type (Roundtable)	−0.62	(0.44)	−0.35**	(0.11)
TV Appearance Type (News Conference)	0.02	(0.51)	−0.04	(0.12)
Control Variables				
Obama Favorability Ratings	0.04	(0.15)	0.21***	(0.04)
Zero-Sum Perception (Jobs)	0.47	(1.64)	0.31	(0.36)
Zero-Sum Perception (Gov't. Spending)	−0.25	(1.31)	−0.23	(0.28)
Zero-Sum Perception (Representation)	−0.04	(0.14)	−0.11**	(0.04)
Constant	−0.04	(1.12)	−2.16***	(0.27)
Number of Observations	309		309	
Log Pseudo Likelihood	−129.81		−128.08	

Explaining the Race Gap in Democratic Party Identification
Source: 2008 National Annenberg Election Survey (NAES), rolling cross section surveys
Note: Estimates are general linear model (GLM) coefficients with robust standard errors (clustered by survey year) in parentheses. The GLMs have a logic link within the binomial family.
+ $p < 0.10$, * $p < 0.05$, ** $p < 0.01$, *** $p < 0.001$, two-tailed tests

Table 3.2 reveals that media presence has a comparably greater effect on Whites' partisanship, even while having a minimal impact overall. Holding other variables constant, Obama's round-table media appearances tended to decrease the number of Whites who self-identified as Democrats (GLM Estimate = −0.35, S.E. = (0.11), p < 0.01). Although none of the media presence variables reach statistical significance in the model for Black respondents, several of the control variables are significant predictors of Whites' party preference. For instance, a rise in Obama's favorability coincides with an increase in the proportion of White Democrats (GLM Estimate = 0.21, S.E. = (0.04), p < 0.01), but the belief that Black elected officials favor African American constituents contributes to a decrease the proportion of White Democrats in an NAES survey (GLM Estimate = −0.11, S.E. = (0.04), p < 0.01). None of these variables predict Blacks' partisanship. This nonfinding is consistent with past research, showing that racial considerations tend to matter more for Whites than for African Americans as determinants of opinions about Obama (Block and Onwunli 2010).

Our third research question asks, How exactly does media presence shape party polarization? The more sophisticated results in table 3.2 corroborate those in displayed in figure 3.1. In both cases, the evidence suggests that media presence, along with racial considerations, can affect the race gap by pushing Whites away from the Democratic Party while having little effect on the partisan attachments of African Americans.

Conclusion

Numerous studies have examined the "Obama effect" in a variety of settings. Because partisanship is a racialized concept in American politics, we took a macrolevel approach to exploring trends over time in the race gap in party identification. We used a combination of public opinion and filmography data to examine the degree to which Obama's media presence affects this party gap. Our work confirms the existence of a party-based Obama effect. We find evidence of a media-based Obama effect. Overall, the gap between the prevalence of Black and White Democrats tended to widen as the *frequency* of the President's television appearances increased, but certain *types* of appearances (particularly, political forums) can lessen the severity of the nation's party polarization. Moreover, a deeper look at the party gap reveals that media presence, along with measures of racial attitudes, shape likelihood of White voters self-identifying as Democrats. These factors have no bearing whatsoever on the party preferences of Black voters, which is not wholly surprising when we consider that similar nonfindings comport with past Obama research, showing that it is White voters, and not African Americans, who are most sensitive to racial issues.

The candidacy and subsequent election of President Barack Obama ushered in changes for partisan politics within the Black community on several fronts. The Democratic Party finally had a candidate that seemingly had more than just an in interest in the Black community—the candidate was Black. Thus, Black Democrats believed this president would be more inclusive of African American interests. However, having a Black candidate that captured the nomination, and a Black president in the White House, may have done very little to change the dynamics of Black partisanship. It has, according to our research, affected how some self-reported White Democrats support Obama. Beyond our analysis in this chapter, there are several more questions we could ask. What impact did Barack Obama's candidacy have on Black partisanship and how will Black and White Democrats remember Obama's presidential legacy? Are Blacks who support the Democratic Party more supportive of the party as a result of Barack Obama, or are Black Democrats in the same predicament, more of the same? Moreover, how do White Democrats who supported the candidacy of Barack Obama feel about his presidency? Again, these and related questions are beyond the scope of this chapter, but we hope that the implications of our research will help to continue the conversation about the "Obama effect" on partisanship. Moreover, if we return to the notions of issue evolution and punctuated equilibria, is Obama's presidency something that destabilizes the party trends and creates a new, more polarized equilibrium? We cannot say for sure, but our results point to the idea that partisanship is still malleable. It remains to be seen whether party polarization will decrease now that Obama is no longer in office given the stark party and racial divides the Trump presidency has inspired. And in line with what other contributors to this volume, we wonder what the party gap might look like if we are fortunate enough to witness another Black presidential candidate in our lifetimes.

Moreover, the finding that the frequency and type of media presence by Obama had differing impacts on partisanship poses a dilemma to future Democratic African American presidential candidates. As Block and Haynes (2014) find in their research of former First Lady Michelle

TABLE 3.3. Descriptive Statistics for Analyses of Obama's Media Presence

Variable Description	Coding	Summary Statistic(s)
Dependent Variables		
ma01_c: Generally speaking, do you usually think of yourself as a Republican, a Democrat, an Independent, or something else? (Black respondent self-identifies as Democrat)	Measured as a proportion {0–1}	Mean = 0.709 Stand. Dev. = 0.144
ma01_c: Generally speaking, do you usually think of yourself as a Republican, a Democrat, an Independent, or something else? (White respondent self-identifies as Democrat)	Measured as a proportion {0–1}	Mean = 0.315 Stand. Dev. = 0.043
PID_Gap: Our measure of the race gap in identification with the Democratic Party	*PrDEM_Blacks—PrDEM_ Whites* {–.17–.81}	Mean = 0.394 Stand. Dev. = 0.149
Theoretically Central Independent Variables (Voter's Media Exposure)		
eb02_c: Days watched TV information about campaign in past week	{0–7}	Mean = 5.403 Stand. Dev. = 0.405
eb04rl_c: Candidate favored by TV program watched most in past week—Obama	0 = No, 1 = Yes	Mean = 0.152 Stand. Dev. = 0.067
Theoretically Central Independent Variables (Obama's Media Activities)		
Media_Freq: Number of TV appearances Obama makes on a given day	{0–3}	Mean = 0.368 Stand. Dev. = 0.539
Vignette: Did Obama make this type of TV appearance today?	0 = No, 1 = Yes	Proportion = 0.013
Speech: Did Obama make this type of TV appearance today?	0 = No, 1 = Yes	Proportion = 0.206
Forum: Did Obama make this type of TV appearance today?	0 = No, 1 = Yes	Proportion = 0.025
Debate: Did Obama make this type of TV appearance today?	0 = No, 1 = Yes	Proportion = 0.025
Rally: Did Obama make this type of TV appearance today?	0 = No, 1 = Yes	Proportion = 0.060
Roundtable: Did Obama make this type of TV appearance today?	0 = No, 1 = Yes	Proportion = 0.003
News Conference: Did Obama make this TV appearance today?	0 = No, 1 = Yes	Proportion = 0.025
Control Variables (Aggregate Racial Attitudes)		
abo01_c: Favorability of Obama	{0–10}	Mean = 5.615 Stand. Dev. = 0.326
sa01_c: Black officials more likely to favor blacks for government jobs	0 = otherwise, 1 = "strongly agree" + "somewhat agree"	Proportion = 0.229
sa02_c: Black officials more likely to support government spending for Blacks	0 = otherwise, 1 = "strongly agree" + "somewhat agree"	Proportion = 0.290
sa05_c: Good or bad if Black officials favor Blacks (Bad)	0 = otherwise, 1 = "strongly agree" + "somewhat agree"	Proportion = 0.345

Descriptive Statistics for Analyses of Obama's Media Presence

Obama, overexposure to a Black political figure may possibly weaken support among White voters. This conundrum is another aspect of what the editors of this volume have dubbed the "inclusionary dilemma." We hope that insights from this chapter will inspire Black politics scholars to continue studying the impact of media exposure on vote choice. The work of Block and Onwunli suggests that rather than lamenting the possibility of White backlash resulting from overexposure to Black candidates, African Americans who run future presidential campaigns may want to consider tailoring their media activities to minimize (if possible) the degree to which they alienate White voters. These candidates should also consider the best type of media exposure to ensure a successful candidacy. As we have shown, despite Obama's "hope and change" rhetoric and his racially transcendent persona, too much exposure, especially the wrong type of media exposure, could have a negative impact on Black candidates seeking the presidency. One of the many lessons Black politics could learn after Obama.

Appendix

The 2008 NAES includes several variables measuring voters' self-reports of their level of media exposure. One survey item asks respondents to recount the numbers of days in the past week they watched campaign programming on television, while another item asks whether the TV program respondents watched most frequently was covering Obama. To add a more direct set of variables tapping into Obama's media activities, we did a keyword search on the C-SPAN Video Library (www.c-span. org) to obtain a list of every televised campaign activity in which Obama took part during the 2008 election cycle. (Block and Haynes 2014 employ a similar approach when they examine Michelle Obama's media activities.) From this list, we created a daily tally of the number of TV appearances Obama made. Our measure ranges from 0 to 3 because, according to C-SPAN's records, the president never attended more than this number of campaign-related events on a given day. Moreover, this variable is skewed-right, for there are many days during the 2008 election when the president made no media appearances. The C-SPAN archive keeps extensive information about each media event, so we were able to include binary variables that sort the president's TV appearances by genre (campaign speech, rally, political debate, etc.). Our goal is to see if the effect of these variable is positive (i.e., that media presence widens the race gap in partisanship) or negative (i.e., media presence narrows the party gap). An effect of zero would indicate that Obama's media presence has no influence on racial differences in party identification.

NOTES

1 The Obama effect(s) to which we refer differ from the one described in Elder (2007), which is analogous to the so-called "Bradley" and "Wilder" effects and explores the degree to which Obama's race cost him support among White voters (see also Lewis-Beck and Tien 2008; Lewis-Beck, Tien, and Nadeau 2010; Tien, Nadeau, and Lewis-Beck 2012).

2 For example, scholars and journalists explore the attitudinal impact of the Obama presidency. Obama's media presence shaped both sales practices and consumer preferences. The former Illinois Senator was one of the first politicians to appeal to young voters by purchasing extensive advertisement space in video games (Sinclair 2008; Leng, Quah, and Zainuddin 2010), and the popularity of "Obamabilia"—merchandise with the former president's name or likeness on—is well documented (Korte 2012; Kramer 2013; Moody-Ramirez and Date 2014, chapter 4). Goldman and Mutz (2014), Hutchings (2009), Welch and Sigelman (2011), and Weisberg and Devine (2010) demonstrate that Obama's exploits on the campaign trail and in the Oval Office intensified the degree to which Blacks and Whites express differing opinions about race (see also Columb and Plant 2011; Effron, Cameron, and Monin 2009; Knowles, Lowrey, and Schaumberg 2009; Lybarger and Monteith 2010; Plant et al., 2009; Schmidt and Nosek 2010) and sexuality (Thompson-DeVeaux 2012) in America. Students of social identity debate whether Obama's biracial heritage and international upbringing allow him to connect more easily with non-White voters, and, equally important, to inspire these voters to identify more readily with their own racial and/or ethnic groups (Chandler, Alison, and Gold 2009; Fuller-Rowell, Burrow, and Ong 2011; Jones 2010; Thompson 2009; Williams et al. 2014; Young 2007). On a related note, Anderson-Clark and Green (2016) discovered a rise in the number of African American children with distinctly Black names. This change in naming patterns, the authors argue, is the result of African American parents appreciating the pride the former president takes in his unique—if not controversial—moniker (see Block and Onwunli 2010). Taking a more global perspective, Adem (2010) and Dragojlovic (2011) show that the forty-fourth president's media presence improved the manner in which citizens from other nations evaluate the United States government (see also Hayden 2011).

Moreover, there are widely documented links between Obama's political accomplishments and changes in behavioral consequences like agenda control (Thompson-DeVeaux 2012; Wilkinson 2009), business practices (Bligh and Kohles 2009; Marquez 2009), civic engagement (Cheney and Olsen 2010; Elder 2007; Pitts 2008; Seabrook 2009), economic outcomes (DellaVigna 2010; Halcoussis, Lowenberg, and Phillips 2009), and foreign policy decision making (Hayden 2011; Hertzberg 2009; Wilke and Sprehe 2010). Hertzberg (2009) finds that Obama's visibility sparked an overall increase in citizens' fascination with politics, and in their study of voter registration and turnout in Georgia, McKee, Hood, and Hill (2012) noticed this pattern was particularly strong among citizens of color. For an alternative conclusion, see Philpot, Shaw, and McGowan (2009), who show that Blacks' heightened turnout rates in 2008 stemmed more from race-targeted mobilization efforts than from the novelty of Obama's race. That said, the authors acknowledge that having a biracial candidate helped the Democratic Party to recruit younger, first-time, and minority voters (see also Crabtree 2009). Educational psychologists found that having Obama in office contributed to minority students getting better test scores, and, perhaps more importantly, having a positive self-image (Aronson, et al. 2009; Bedford 2009; Brown 2008; Carter 2009; Hoyt 2013; Manke 2011; Marx, Ko, and Friedman 2009; Purdie-Vaughns et al. N.D.; Purdie-Vaughns, Sumner and Cohen 2011). Finally, conversations about "Obama effect(s)" extend beyond academic and journalistic circles, for celebrities realize the POTUS's ability to set trends in music (Emdin and Lee 2012; Gosa in Carter and Yanes, eds. 2012; McLaughlin 2010), art (Cox 2009), and film (Dutton 2012; Izzo 2014; Peterson 2008).

3 Put differently, we aim to explore *inter*-race party polarization. An analysis of *intra*-race polarization, for example, an analysis of the degree to which African Americans identify with the Democratic Party compared to the GOP, is beyond the scope of this chapter.

4 See Parker's "state of the discipline" essay in the 2016 volume of the *Annual Review of Sociology*.

5 We refer readers to Carmines and Stimson (1990), Layman, Carsey, and Horowitz (2006), Philpot (2007), Fauntroy (2007), and Walton and Smith (2009) for excellent overviews.

6 We understand the racial history underlying these current patterns, for Blacks' party loyalty results just as much from the GOP being comparatively unresponsive to Blacks' interest as it does from Blacks being "captured"—to use Frymer's (2010) term—by a party that sometimes takes them for granted.

7 Aldrich (2013) and Carmines and Stimson (1990) characterize the process by which this polarization occurred as a "punctuated equilibrium" involving a pre-1960 era of party stability, followed by a brief period of sweeping change in the mid-1960s that resulted in a new baseline in party dynamics, one in which Blacks and Whites differ markedly in their party preferences.

8 Jimmy Carter leads this list, having secured 48 percent of the White vote in 1976, and Bill Clinton comes in second, with 44 percent in the 1996 contest.

9 Obama made clear his intention to fashion himself as a deracialized (if not post-racial) statesman during his speech at the 2004 Democratic National Convention

(Gillespie 2010), and he worked hard to cultivate the image of a deracialized/post-racial candidate during his campaign (Carter and Dowe 2015).

10 Employing a "rolling cross section" methodology the NAES contains a series of nationally representative telephone polls that were collected on an almost-daily basis from December 17, 2007 to November 3, 2008—the day before the 2008 presidential election. The NAES typically conducted its polls between Thursday and Sunday, and tended not to interview respondents during the midweek. There are 316 total surveys, which queried 57,967 total respondents. This gives us ample data points to examine trends over time in party preference (for examples of research using NAES data, see Kenski, Hardy, and Jamieson 2010; Romer et al. 2006). Details about the survey's design and implementation can be found at: www.annenbergpublicpolicycenter.org. Please note that the viewpoints of this this chapter are not representative of the NAES, its principal investigators, or the University of Pennsylvania.

11 Because it is difficult to predict what party identification will look like from one day to the next, we use seven-day moving averages to smooth out the substantial fluctuations in Blacks' (solid dark gray line) and Whites' (dashed dark gray line) party trends.

12 If this calculation yields a positive number, then Blacks outnumber Whites when it comes to party identification (*Blacks − Whites* > 0). Conversely a negative gap value indicates that more Whites than Blacks are self-reported Democrats (*Blacks − Whites* < 0). A gap of zero (*Blacks − Whites* = 0) means that there was no racial difference on that day in party preference.

13 For studies on habituation, particularly as it relates to candidate preference, see Gomez (2013) and Wagner and Kritzinger (2012).

14 We divide the analyses into five parts. Following Antle (2014), the baseline model includes a lagged version of the party gap variable as a predictor of the current gap so that we may determine whether current levels of the dependent variable are heavily determined by past levels. The second and third columns in table 1 model the impact of what we call "voter-side" (aggregate measures of the degree to which NAES respondents' follow the 2008 campaign in general and Obama specifically) and "candidate-side" (the items from the C-SPAN Video Library) media variables on the party gap. The fourth column controls for macrolevel trends in racial attitudes, focusing particularly on beliefs about racial policy implications of an Obama presidency. The fifth and final column adds the theoretically central predictors and control variables into a single regression model. We place details about these variables in table 3.3 in the Appendix.

REFERENCES

Aldrich, John H. 2013. "Partisan Polarization and Satisfaction with Democracy." In *Can We Talk: The Rise of Rude, Nasty, Stubborn Politics*. Eds. Daniel M. Shea and Morris P. Fiorina. New York: Pearson Education, 125–26.

Agresti, Alan. 2015. *Foundations of Linear and Generalized Linear Models*. Hoboken, NJ: John Wiley and Sons.

Anderson-Clark, Tracey N. and Raymond J. Green. 2016. "Basking in Reflected Glory: The Election of President Obama and Naming Behaviour." *Ethnic and Racial Studies* 2(May): 1–14.

Aronson, Joshua, Sheana Jannone, Matthew McGlone, and Tanisha Johnson-Campbell. 2009. "The Obama Effect: An Experimental Test." *Journal of Experimental Social Psychology* 45(July): 957–960.

Adem, Seifudein. 2010. "The Obama Effect in Japan: Some Preliminary Observations." *Black Scholar* 40(Fall): 13–21.

Antle III, W. James. 2014. "The Real Force behind America's Racial Polarization Isn't Racism. It's Politics." *The Week*, November 13, 2014, http://theweek.com.

Banks, Antoine J. 2014a. *Anger and Racial Politics The Emotional Foundation of Racial Attitudes in America*. New York: Cambridge University Press.

Banks, Antoine J. 2014b. "The Public's Anger: White Racial Attitudes and Opinions Toward Health Care Reform." *Political Behavior* 36(September): 493–514.

Baum, Christopher S. 2008. "Modeling Proportions." *Stata Journal* 8(2): 299–303.

Bedford, Megan. 2009. "The Obama Effect: Revising the Curse." Efficacy Institute, July 11, 2009, www.efficacy.org.

Bligh, Michelle and Jeffrey C. Kohles. 2009. "The Enduring Allure of Charisma: How Barack Obama Won the Historic 2008 Presidential Election." *Leadership Quarterly* 20(June): 483–492.

Block, Ray, Jr. and Chinonye Onwunli. 2010. "Managing Monikers: The Role of Name Presentation in the 2008 Presidential Election." *Presidential Studies Quarterly* 40(3): 464–481.

Block, Ray, Jr. 2011. "Backing Barack Because He's Black: Racially Motivated Voting in the 2008 Election." *Social Science Quarterly* 92(2): 423–446.

Block, Ray, Jr. and Christina S. Haynes. 2014. "Taking to the Airwaves: Using Content Analyses of Survey Toplines and Filmographies to Test the 'Michelle Obama Image Transformation' (MOIT) Hypothesis." *National Political Science Review* 16: 97–114.

Bobo, Lawrence and Franklin D. Gilliam. 1990. "Race, Sociopolitical Participation, and Black Empowerment." *American Political Science Review* 84(June): 377–393.

Boyd, Todd. 1997. "The Day the Niggaz Took Over: Basketball, Commodity Culture, and Black Masculinity." In *Out of Bounds: Sports, Media, and the Politics of Identity*, eds. Aaron Baker and Todd Boyd. Bloomington, IN: Indiana University Press, 123–141.

Bristor, Julia M. Renée Gravois Lee, and Michelle R. Hunt. 1995. "Race and Ideology: African-American Images in Television Advertising." *Journal of Public Policy and Marketing* 14(Spring): 48–59.

Brown, DaNeen L. 2008. "To Teach, They Reach for Obama: President-Elect Viewed as a Role Model for Kids." *Washington Post*, December 13, 2008.

Bryant, Alison L. and Marc A. Zimmerman. 2003. "Role Models and Psychosocial Outcomes Among African American Adolescents." *Journal of Adolescent Research* 18(January): 36–67.

Bush, Alan J., Craig A. Martin, and Paul W. Clark. 2001. "The Effect of Role Model Influence on Adolescents' Materialism and Marketplace Knowledge." *Journal of Marketing Theory and Practice* 9(Fall): 27–36.

Carmines, Edward G. and James A Stimson. 1990. *Issue Evolution: Race and the Transformation of American Politics Reprint Edition.* Princeton, NJ: Princeton University Press.

Carter, Niambi and Pearl K. Ford Dowe. 2015. "The Racial Exceptionalism of Barack Obama." *Journal of African American Studies* 19(April): 105–119.

Carter, Prudence. 2009. "Equity and Empathy: Toward Racial and Educational Achievement in the Obama Era." *Harvard Educational Review* 79(Summer): 287–297.

Chandler, Michael Alison and Maria Gold. 2009. "Multiracial Pupils to Be Counted in New Groups." *Washington Post*, March 23, 2009.

Cheney, Michael and Crystal Olsen. 2010. "Media Politics 2.0: An Obama Effect." In *The Obama Effect: Multidisciplinary Renderings of the 2008 Campaign*. Eds. Heather E. Harris, Kimberly R. Moffitt, and Catherine E. Squires. Albany, NY: State University of New York Press, 31–48.

Columb, Corey and Ashby Plant. 2011. "Revisiting the Obama Effect: Exposure to Obama Reduces Implicit Prejudice." *Journal of Experimental Social Psychology* 47(March): 499–501.

Cox, Tony. 2009. "The Obama Effect on the Arts." National Public Radio, February 27, 2009, www.npr.org.

Crabtree, James. 2009. "How Obama Won." *Renewal: A Journal of Labour Politics* 17(1): 77–82.

DellaVigna, Stefano. 2010. "The Obama Effect on Economic Outcomes: Evidence from Event Studies." Working paper.

Dillon, Sam. 2009. "Study Sees an Obama Effect Lifting Black Test-Takers." *New York Times*, January 22, 2009, www.nytimes.com.

Donovan, Todd. 2010. "Obama and the White Vote." *Political Research Quarterly* 63(4): 863–874.

Dragojlovic, Nicholas Isak. 2011. "Priming and the Obama Effect on Public Evaluations of the United States." *Political Psychology* 32(December): 989–1006.

Dutton, Charles S. 2012. *The Obama Effect.* Los Angeles, CA: Gigapix Releasing.

Effron, Daniel A., Jessica S. Cameron, and Benoit Monin. 2009. "Endorsing Obama Licenses Favoring Whites." *Journal of Experimental Social Psychology* 45(May): 590–593.

Elder, Janet. 2007. "Will There Be an 'Obama Effect?'" *New York Times*, May 16, 2007, http://thecaucus.blogs.nytimes.com/.

Emdin, Christopher and Okhee Lee. 2012. "Hip-Hop, the Obama Effect, and Urban Science Education." *Teachers College Record* 114(2): 1–24.

Erikson, Robert S., Michael B. MacKuen, and James A. Stimson. 1998. "What Moves Macropartisanship? A Response to Green, Palmquist, and Schickler." *American Political Science Review* 92(December): 901–912.

Fauntroy, Michael K. 2007. *Republicans and the Black Vote*. Ann Arbor, MI: Lynne Rienner.

Frymer, Paul. 2010. *Uneasy Alliances: Race and Party Competition in America*. Princeton, NJ: Princeton University Press.

Fuller-Rowell, Thomas E., Anthony L. Burrow, and Anthony D. Ong. 2011. "Changes in Racial Identity among African American College Students Following the Election of Barack Obama." *Developmental Psychology* 47(November): 1608–1618.

Gay, Claudine. 2001. "The Effect of Black Congressional Representation on Political Participation." *American Political Science Review* 95(September): 589–602.

Gibson, Donald E. 2004. "Role Models in Career Development: New Directions for Theory and Research." *Journal of Vocational Behavior* 65(August): 134–156.

Gillespie, Andra, ed. 2010. *Whose Black Politics? Cases in Post-Racial Black Leadership*. New York: Routledge.

Goldman, Seth and Diana C. Mutz. 2014. *The Obama Effect: How the 2008 Campaign Changed White Racial Attitudes*. New York: Russell Sage Foundation.

Gomez, Raul. 2013. "All That You Can(not) Leave Behind: Habituation and Vote Loyalty in the Netherlands." *Journal of Elections, Public Opinion and Parties* 23(March): 134–153.

Gosa, Travis. 2012. "The Audacity of Dope: Rap Music, Race, and the Obama Presidency." In *The Iconic Obama, 2007–2009: Essays on Media Representations of the Candidate and New President*. Eds. Derrais Carter and Nicholas A. Yanes. Jefferson, NC: McFarland.

Hackett, Gail and Angela M. Byars. 2011. "Social Cognitive Theory and the Career Development of African American Women." *Career Development Quarterly* 44 (December): 322–340.

Halcoussis, Dennis, Anton D. Lowenberg, G. Michael Phillips. 2009. "The Obama Effect." *Journal of Economics and Finance* 33(July): 324–329.

Harfoush, Rahaf. 2009. *Yes We Did! An Inside Look at How Social Media Built the Obama Brand*. Berkeley, CA: Newriders.

Hayden, Craig. 2011. "Beyond the 'Obama effect': Refining the Instruments of Engagement through US Public Diplomacy." *American Behavioral Scientist* 55(June): 784–802.

Haynie, Kerry L. and Candis S. Watts. 2010. "Blacks and the Democratic Party: A Resilient Coalition." In *New Directions in American Political Parties*. Ed. Jeffrey Stonecash. New York: Routledge, 93–109.

Hedström, Peter and Petri Ylikoski. 2010. "Causal Mechanisms in the Social Sciences." *Annual Review of Sociology* 36(August): 49–67.

Hertzberg, Hendrick. 2009. "The Obama Effect," May 9, 2009, www.newyorker.com.

Hoyt, Crystal. 2013. "Inspirational or Self-Deflating: The Role of Self-Efficacy in Elite Role Model Effectiveness." *Social Psychological and Personality Science* 4(May): 290–298.

Hunt, Matthew O. and David C. Wilson. 2009. "Race/Ethnicity, Perceived Discrimination, and Beliefs about the Meaning of an Obama Presidency." *Du Bois Review* 6(Spring): 173–191.

Hurd, Noelle M., Marc A. Zimmerman, and Yange Xue. 2010. "Negative Adult Influences and the Protective Effects of Role Models: A Study with Urban Adolescents." *Journal of Youth and Adolescence* 38(July): 777–789.

Hutchings, Vincent. 2009. "Change or More of the Same? Evaluating Racial Attitudes in the Obama Era." *Public Opinion Quarterly* 73(Summer): 917–942.

Iyengar, Shanto, Sean J. Westwood. 2015. "Fear and Loathing across Party Lines: New Evidence on Group Polarization." *American Journal of Political Science* 59(July): 690–707.

Izzo, David Garrett, ed. 2015. *Movies in the Age of Obama: The Era of Post-Racial and Neo-Racist Cinema*. New York and London: Rowman & Littlefield.

Jones, Suzanne. 2010. "The Obama Effect on American Discourse about Racial Identity: *Dreams from My Father* (and Mother), Barack Obama's Search for Self." In *The Obama Effect: Multidisciplinary Renderings of the 2008 Campaign*. Eds. Heather E. Harris, Kimberly R. Moffitt, and Catherine E. Squires. Albany, NY: State University of New York Press, 131–152.

Kaplan, Roy. 2011. *The Myth of Post-Racial America: Searching for Equality in the Age of Obama*. Lanham, MD: Rowan & Littlefield.

Kellner, Douglas. 2009. "Barack Obama and Celebrity Spectacle." *International Journal of Communication*, 3(2009), https://pages.gseis.ucla.edu.

Kramer, Elizabeth. 2013. "Batmobama and Obamarx: The Meanings of the Material and Visual Culture of Obama Mania." *Journal of Design History* 26: 345–61.

Kenski, Kate, Bruce W. Hardy, and Kathleen Hall Jamieson. 2010. *The Obama Victory: How Media, Money, and Messages Shaped the 2008 Election*. New York: Oxford University Press.

Kinder, Donald and Allison Dale-Riddle. 2012. *The End of Race? Obama, 2008, and Racial Politics in America*. New Haven, CT: Yale University Press.

Knowles, Eric D., Brian S. Lowery, Rebecca L. Schaumberg. 2009. "Anti-Egalitarians for Obama? Group-Dominance Motivation and the Obama Vote." *Journal of Experimental Social Psychology* 45(July): 965–969.

Korte, Gregory. 2012. "Obama Has Edge in Political Merchandise." *USA Today*, September 25, 2012, http://usatoday.com.

Layman, Geoffrey C., Thomas M. Carsey, and Menasce Horowitz. 2006. "Party Polarization in American Politics: Characteristics, Causes, and Consequences." *Annual Review of Political Science* 9(December): 83–110.

Leng, H. K., S. L. Quah, and Zainul F. Zainuddin. 2010. "The Obama Effect: An Exploratory Study on Factors Affecting Brand Recall in Online Games." *International Journal of Trade, Economics and Finance* 1(June): 1–5.

Lewis-Beck, Michael S. and Charles Tien. 2008. "The Job of President and the Jobs Model Forecast." *PS: Political Science & Politics* 41(October):687–90.

Lewis-Beck, Michael S., Charles Tien, and Richard Nadeau. 2010. "Obama's Missed Landslide: A Racial Cost?" *PS: Political Science & Politics* 43(January): 687–690.

Lewis-Beck, Michael S., Richard Nadeau, and Charles Tien. 2012. "Obama and 2012: Still A Racial Cost to Pay?" *PS: Political Science & Politics* 45(October): 591–595.

Lockwood, Penelope and Ziva Kunda. 1997. "Superstars and Me: Predicting the Impact of Role Models on the Self." *Journal of Personality and Social Psychology* 73(July): 91–103.

Lockwood, Penelope, Christina H. Jordan, and Ziva Kunda. 2002. "Motivation by Positive or Negative Role Models: Regulatory Focus Determines Who Will Best Inspire Us." *Journal of Personality and Social Psychology* 83(November): 854–864.

Lockwood, Penelope. 2006. "'Someone Like Me can be Successful': Do College Students Need Same-Gender Role Models?" *Psychology of Women Quarterly* 30(March): 36–46.

Lum, Lydia. 2009. "The Obama Era: A Post-Racial Society?" *Diverse Issues in Higher Education* 25–26(February): 14–16.

Lybarger, Jill E. and Margo J. Monteith. 2010. "The Effect of Obama Saliency on Individual-Level Racial Bias: Silver Bullet or Smokescreen?" *Journal of Experimental Political Psychology* 47(May): 647–652.

MacKuen, Michael B., Robert S. Erikson, and James A. Stimson. 1989. "Macropartisanship." *American Political Science Review* 83(December): 1125–1142.

Manke, Kody and Geoffrey L. Cohen. 2011. "More Than Inspiration: Role Models Convey Multiple and Multifaceted Messages." *Psychological Inquiry* 22(December): 275–279.

Marquez, Jessica. 2009. "Diversity: The Obama Effect." *Workforce Management* 88(4): 1.

Marx, David M. and Jasmin S. Roman. 2002. "Female Role models: Protecting Women's Math Test Performance." *Personality and Social Psychology Bulletin* 28(September): 1183–1193.

Marx, David M. and Phillip Atiba Goff. 2005. "Clearing the Air: The Effect of Experimenter Race on Targets' Test Performance and Subjective Experience." *British Journal of Social Psychology* 44(December): 645–657.

Marx, David M., Sei Jin Ko, Ray A. Friedman. 2009. "The 'Obama Effect': How A Salient Role Model Reduces Race-Based Performance Differences." *Journal of Experimental Social Psychology* 45(July): 953–956.

May, Reuben A. Buford. 2009. "The Good and Bad of It All: Professional Black Male Basketball Players as Role Models for Young Black Male Basketball Players." *Sociology of Sport Journal* 26(September): 43–461.

McKee, Seth C., M. V. Hood, and David Hill. 2012. "Achieving Validation: Barack Obama and Black Turnout in 2008." *State Politics and Policy Quarterly* 12(March): 3–22.

McLaughlin, Elliot C. 2010. "Common: 'Obama Effect' Steering Rap Away from Rims, Bling." CNN.com, September 23, 2010, www.cnn.com.

McQueen, Tammy, and Leila Green. 2010. "Obama's Election Campaign and the Integrated Use of Social Media." *Proceedings of the Eighth International Conference on Cultural Attitudes Towards Technology and Communication*: 315–330.

Moody-Ramirez, Mia and Jannette L. Dates. 2014. "Images of African Americans in Advertising, PR, and Social Media." In *The Obamas and Mass Media: Race, Gender,*

Religion, and Politics eds. Mia Moody-Ramirez and Jannette L. Dates. New York: Palgrave Macmillan, chapter 4.

Parker, Christopher S., Mark Q. Sawyer, and Christopher Towler. 2009. "A *Black* Man in the *White* House? The Role of Racism and Patriotism in the 2008 Presidential Election." *Du Bois Review* 6(Fall): 193–217.

Parker, Christopher S. and Matt A. Barreto. 2013. *Change They Can't Believe In: The Tea Party and Reactionary Politics in America*. Princeton, NJ: Princeton University Press.

Parker, Christopher S. 2016. "Race and Politics in the Age of Obama." *Annual Review of Sociology* 42(May): 17.2–17.14.

Parks, Gregory S. and Jeffrey J. Rachlinski. 2010. "Implicit Bias, Election '08, and the Myth of a Post-Racial America." *Florida State University Law Review* 37, https://ir.law.fsu.edu.

Peterson, Alan. 2008. *Hype: The Obama Effect*. Washington. DC: Citizens United Productions.

Philpot, Tasha S. 2007. *Race, Republicans, and the Return of the Party of Lincoln*. Ann Arbor, MI: University of Michigan Press.

Philpot, Tasha S., Daron A. Shaw, and Ernest B. McGowan. 2009. "Winning the Race: Black Voter Turnout in the 2008 Presidential Election." *Public Opinion Quarterly* 73(5): 995–1022.

Pitts, Bryon. 2008. CBS News, "Obama Effect Touching a New Generation," August 26, 2008, www.cbsnews.com.

Plant, E. Ashby, Patricia G. Devine, William T. L. Cox, Corey Columb, Saul L. Miller, Joanna Goplen, and B. Michelle Peruche. 2009. "The Obama Effect: Decreasing Implicit Prejudice and Stereotyping." *Journal of Experimental Social Psychology* 45(July): 961–964.

Plouffe, David. 2009. *The Audacity to Win: How Obama Won and How We Can Beat the Party of Limbaugh, Beck, and Palin*. New York: Penguin Books.

Powers, John M. 2014. "Statistical Evidence of Racially Polarized Voting in the Obama Elections, and Implications for Section 2 of the Voting Rights Act." *Georgetown Law Journal* 102(): 881–908.

Purdie-Vaughns, Valerie J., J. E. Cook, J. Garcia, Rachel Sumner, and Geoffrey L. Cohen. n.d. "Reducing Identity Threat for Minorities and Improving Performance for All Students: Longitudinal Study of the 'Obama effect' on Adolescent Achievement." Manuscript under review.

Purdie-Vaughns, Valerie J., Rachel Sumner, and Geoffrey L. Cohen. 2011. "Sasha and Malia: Re-Envisioning African-American Youth." In *The Obamas and a (Post) Racial America?* eds. Gregory Parks, Matthew Hughey, and Charles Ogletree. Oxford UK: Oxford University Press, 166–181.

Read, Barbara. 2011. "Britney, Beyoncé, and Me: Primary School Girls' Role Models and Constructions of the 'Popular' Girl." *Gender and Education* 23(October): 1–13.

Rice, Laurie L. and Andrew F. Sarver. 2013. "Change and More of the Same: New Media Communications Strategies in President Obama's First 100 Days." *Polymath: An Interdisciplinary Arts and Sciences Journal* 13(Fall): 18–37.

Romer, Daniel, Kate Kenski, Kenneth Winneg, Christopher Adasiewicz, and Kathleen Hall Jamieson. 2006. *Capturing Campaign Dynamics 2000 & 2004: The National Annenberg Election Survey.* Philadelphia: University of Pennsylvania.

Rothman, Noah. 2012. "Obama Overtakes Reagan as Most Televised President in History." MediaITE, www.mediaite.com.

Schmidt, Kathleen and Brian Nosek. 2010. "Implicit (and Explicit) Racial Attitudes Barely Changed during Barack Obama's Presidential Campaign and Early Presidency." *Journal of Experimental Social Psychology* 46(December): 308–314.

Seabrook, Nicholas R. 2009. "The Obama Effect: Patterns of Geographic Clustering in the 2004 and 2008 Presidential Elections." *Forum* 7(2 July): article 6.

Shaffner, Brian F. 2011. "Racial Salience and the Obama Vote." *Political Psychology* 32(6): 963–988.

Shoemaker, Pamela, James William Tankard Jr., and Dominic L. Lasorsa. 2004. *How to Build Social Science Theories.* Thousand Oaks, CA: Sage.

Sinclair, Brendan. 2008. "Obama's In-Game Ad Bill: $44.5K." GameSpot.com, October 30, 2008, www.gamespot.com.

Speizer, Jeanne. 1981. "Role Models, Mentors, and Sponsors: The Elusive Concepts." *Signs: Journal of Women in Culture and Society* 6(Summer): 692–712.

Steele, Shelby. 2008. "Obama's Post Racial Promise: Barack Obama Seduced Whites with A Vision of their Racial Innocence Precisely to Coerce Them into Acting Out of A Racial Motivation." *Los Angeles Times*, November 5, 2008.

Sugrue, Thomas J. 2010. *Not Even Past: Barack Obama and the Burden of Race.* Princeton, NJ: Princeton University Press.

Tate, Katherine. 1994. *From Protest to Politics: The New Black Voters in American Elections.* Cambridge, MA: Harvard University Press.

Tate, Katherine. 2003. *Black Faces in the Mirror: African Americans and Their Representatives.* Princeton, NJ: Princeton University Press.

Tesler, Michael and David O. Sears. 2010. *Obama's Race: The 2008 Election and the Dream of a Post-Racial America.* Chicago: University of Chicago Press.

Tesler, Michael. 2012. "The Spillover of Racialization into Health Care: How President Obama Polarized Public Opinion by Racial Attitudes and Race." *American Journal of Political Science* 56(July): 690–704.

Thompson, Krissah. 2009. "In Obama's Run, Finding a Long-Sought Sense of Acceptance." *Washington Post*, January 11, 2009.

Thompson-DeVeaux, Amelia. 2012. "The Obama Effect? Black Americans' Views on Same-Sex Marriage." Public Religion Research Institute, May 21, 2012, http://publicreligion.org.

Tien, Charles, Richard Nadeau, and Michael S. Lewis-Beck. 2012. "Racial Voting in 2012?" Model Politics, May 2, 2012, http://today.yougov.com.

Valdesolo, Piercarlo and Jesse Graham. 2016. *Social Psychology of Political Polarization.* New York: Routledge.

Wagner, Markus, and Sylvia Kritzinger. 2012. "Ideological Dimensions and Vote Choice: Age Group Differences in Austria." *Electoral Studies* 31(June): 285–296.

Walton, Hanes Jr. and Robert C. Smith 2009. *American Politics and the African American Quest for Universal Freedom.* 6th edition. New York: Pearson.

Welch, Susan and Lee Sigelman. 2011. "The 'Obama Effect' and White Racial Attitudes." *The Annals of the American Academy of Political and Social Science* 634(March): 207–220.

Weisberg, Herbert and Christopher J. Devine. 2010. "Racial Attitude Effects on Voting in the 2008 Presidential Election: Examining the Unconventional Factors Shaping Vote Choice in a Most Unconventional Election." *Electoral Studies* 29(December): 569–581.

Wilke, Richard and Kathleen Holzwart Sprehe. 2010. "Indonesia: The Obama Effect." Pew Global Attitudes Project, March 18, 2010, www.pewglobal.org.

Williams, Javonda, Kathleen A. Bolland, Lisa Hooper, Wesley Church, Sara Tomek, and John Bolland. 2014. "Say It Loud: The Obama Effect and Racial/Ethnic Identification of Adolescents." *Journal of Human Behavior in the Social Environment* 24(7): 858–868.

Wout, Daryl A., Margaret J. Shih, James S. Jackson, and Robert M. Sellers. 2009. "Targets as Perceivers: How People Determine when They Will Be Negatively Stereotyped." *Journal of Personality and Social Psychology* 96(February): 349–362.

Young, Gary. 2007. "The Obama Effect." *Nation*, December 13, 2007, www.thenation.com.

4

"It's Complicated"

The Obama Administration's Relationship with Black Faith Communities and Lessons for Future Presidents

BRIAN D. MCKENZIE

Since the 1980s, when conservative religious groups banded together to influence US presidential elections, scholars have closely tracked interactions between religious constituencies and national political leaders. Much of this work highlights the importance of White Evangelicals in supporting Republican presidential candidates and their social issues agenda (Green 2007; Guth, Kellstedt, Smidt, and Green 2006; Putnam and Campbell 2010). Less attention, however, has been paid to relationships between Democratic presidents and the religious voters who support their political programs. For example, Black Christians stand out as a key, highly religious, and politically cohesive segment of the Democratic Party coalition (McKenzie 2004; McKenzie and Rouse 2013; Pew Research Center 2015).[1] Yet studies that chronicle connections between Black Christians and American presidents are rare. In particular, it is instructive to consider how President Barack Obama was viewed by Black Christians in terms of policy congruence and leadership evaluations during his tenure in the White House.

In line with the inclusionary dilemma theme of this volume, I examine the Obama administrations' public and private exchanges with Black religious communities. In many ways, Barack Obama's political experiences highlight elements of the inclusionary dilemma. On one hand, Black church social networks assisted Obama in establishing a political career in Illinois politics. But this association with Black institutions, particularly Chicago's Trinity United Church of Christ, would later become a political liability for Obama as he sought support from White voters in the 2008 general election. Thus, Obama's challenge was to simultaneously appear as an advocate for African American political interests and effectively represent the nation as a whole. Since Black faith communities primarily work to advance Black interests, President Obama's team may have limited their outreach and public backing of this constituency. At the same time, Obama called for policies with broad appeal among progressives. Using the inclusionary dilemma framework as an analytic lens, this chapter explores the administration's actions and the political interests of Black Christians. To accomplish this task, the present chapter evaluates the political significance of several religious and political events that happened during Obama's presidency from 2009 to 2016. This chapter also discusses how events that occurred before 2009 influenced the trajectory of Black religious and political matters in this period. The negative publicity from the Reverend Jeremiah Wright incident in 2008, for example, along with the president's private religious life and race-neutral politics, often resulted in a disconnect between the administration and African American faith communities.

How, then, does one make sense of the president's complicated political association with religious African Americans? Although the president identifies as a Christian and periodically met with Black religious leaders for prayer, these low-profile actions often escaped public notice. In contrast, Obama's highly visible support of gay and lesbian issues placed him at odds with the political opinions of most Black Protestants. So was Obama truly working on behalf of religious Black voters? And is it possible to reconcile the president's professed religious beliefs with his strategic political agenda? A key question to explore is whether African American religious interests were helped or harmed by the nation's first Black president. The chapter addresses these issues by delving into the Obama administration's complex relationship with Black churches, their clergy, and their faith teachings. As we will see throughout the chapter, the president's political strategy regarding Black religious and political life was often motivated by personal and pragmatic considerations. The thing about being president is that you cannot please everyone. So Obama made calculated choices. I consider the consequences of these choices in detail. Furthermore, it can be argued that Obama's team may have inadequately utilized the institutional capacities of religious settings to promote the president's agenda among one of his most loyal constituencies. At the same time, this chapter posits that Black churchgoers' overwhelming support for Obama may have muted constructive dialogue about the perceived limited benefits of the president's economic initiatives for Blacks amid the Great Recession.

Finally, I comment on several developments in Black religious life since the 1980s (the vitality of Black religiosity versus increasing nonaffiliation in society, high levels of church attendance among college graduates, and growing numbers of large churches) that highlight the political significance of congregations for today's political leaders. Along these lines, I briefly reflect on the actions of the current US president, Donald Trump, as they relate to religion and politics in Black communities.

Reverend Jeremiah Wright and Obama's Race-Neutral Politics

In thinking about President Obama's links to Black churches, it is helpful to remember the political fallout from his association with African American minister, Rev. Jeremiah Wright of Trinity United Church of Christ in Chicago. In the spring of 2008, Rev. Wright, Obama's pastor of twenty years, made national headlines for his divisive remarks about racial injustice in America and suggestions that the 9/11 terrorist attacks were retaliatory acts in response to past US military actions abroad. These statements were prominently covered in the media and threatened to derail Obama's 2008 campaign (McKenzie 2011). In light of the storm caused by Wright's words, on March 18, Obama denounced the comments, stating they did not represent his own patriotic beliefs and harmonious vision for the country.

At this time, Obama's affiliation with an unpopular, Afrocentric Christian leader raised concerns among many Whites regarding the candidate's purported race-neutral political views. How could the likable, young candidate attend a church that focused on one racial group and promoted values that seemed unpatriotic? These considerations are particularly relevant for the present essay. Research on political attitudes, for instance, demonstrates that, among Whites, Obama's interactions with Black congregations tend to highlight racial tensions and cause numerous Whites to feel less favorable toward him (McKenzie 2011). At the same time, religious settings are very important to most Blacks and must be taken seriously by politicians. Thus, these opposing forces greatly influence the president's dealings with Black Christians because he must appeal to both groups. The negative impact of the Jeremiah Wright incident during the 2008 presidential campaign may have later contributed to Obama limiting his involvement with Black churches as president.

Another dimension to this story is Obama's race-neutral political strategy during his first term. As a newly elected political figure, Obama's goal was to put forward a progressive Democratic agenda for all Americans—not just Blacks. Specifically, he discussed the need for repairing the American economy and providing affordable health care in universal, rather than race-specific, language. Barack Obama was aware of the scrutiny he might encounter as the first African American president and wanted to assure non-Black voters that he represented all Americans. This was a political balancing act he negotiated throughout his term as president. So, as a matter of personal beliefs and political expediency, Obama would not engage in racial identity politics to get things done in Washington. In addition, Obama's race-neutral approach meant that he was not beholden to traditional Black institutions as a national leader (Harris 2012). Thus, the political well-being of Black Christian communities would not be prominently featured in the administration's language regarding key policy initiatives.

Obama's Personal Faith and Perceptions of His Administration

How did the former president's religious beliefs impact his governing abilities? We should point out that Barack Obama describes himself as a Christian who prays regularly and seeks religious guidance for the actions he takes as a leader and in his personal life (Miller 2008). Yet like many Americans, Obama also believes that one's religious beliefs are very personal and a private matter for citizens. The disconnect between President Obama and African American Christians, then, might be partially explained by the limited public expressions of his faith. Indeed, compared to his immediate predecessor George W. Bush, Obama's faith was not usually on display for the nation. Observers have commented, for instance, that Barack Obama rarely attends church and does not openly discuss his religious views in great detail. A number of considerations may explain this approach.

First, keep in mind that presidents are very busy and typically do not regularly attend church. Moreover, as the leading Democratic office holder, Obama is aware that many of his party's key coalition partners are not deeply religious and might disapprove of frequent, visible, religious gestures. Something else that may partially account for the president's private religious tendencies is the fact that he did not grow up in a devout Christian family where expressing one's faith was commonplace. As a late adopter of the Christian faith in adulthood, Obama's comfort level with public displays of one's religious values may be less than the typical Black Protestant.

As noted earlier in this volume, many Black voters were largely supportive of Barack Obama's leadership from 2008 to 2015. Yet this general approval trend masks important distinctions among some Black Christians. A few of the president's initiatives are worth reviewing. There is a religious element, for example, to Obama's signature piece of legislation—the Affordable Care Act. Under this health plan, individuals have access to government permitted contraceptive coverage. This provision angered many White Christian pro-life groups, while most Black Christians did not regard the issue as important compared to more pressing economic concerns. On a related note, a September 2014 Pew Research Center report documented growing perceptions among Black Protestants that the Obama administration was unfriendly toward religion. In particular, the percentage of Black Protestants expressing this sentiment increased between 2 and 9 percent from 2009 (when Obama took office) to 2014 (Pew Research Center 2014). It is possible that some religious African Americans may have reacted to the president's liberal stances regarding social and moral issues.

Note, as well, that Black congregations did not greatly benefit from social policies in terms of increased receipt of public funds for social service delivery or collaborations with government while Obama served as president (Chaves 2011). Perhaps surprisingly, the efforts of the Office of Faith-Based and Neighborhood Partnerships were not as well publicized among Black churches. Given that churches are often "points of entry" for low-income Black communities and social network links for middle-class Blacks, this neglect may have represented a "missed opportunity" for the administration to connect with the lives of Blacks.

The President's Connections with Black Faith Communities

It is critical to analyze how President Obama publicly interacted with Black faith communities, given their central role in modern African American life. However, we must consider these issues in light of the enormous challenges that Obama faced as the first Black president, governing in the midst of the Great Recession, in an extremely polarized political climate. Indeed, the administration had numerous domestic and foreign policy concerns to address, and the eyes of the world were upon the charismatic president. Religious Americans and others were eager to see how Barack Obama might tackle thorny political issues of a moral and religious nature.

Like many resourceful politicians, the Obama administration utilized Black religious leaders to promote their political agenda. To be sure, Harris (2012) notes that Obama sought aid from Black churches during his 2008 campaign when he needed additional political support. And as president, Barack Obama employed Black religious language and scriptures in public statements advancing his policies, such as the Affordable Care Act. Obama also participated in occasional teleconferences and received prayers by from prominent Black clergy, including Bishop T. D. Jakes of the Potter's House in Dallas, Rev. Kirbyjon Caldwell of Windsor Village United Methodist Church in Houston, and African Methodist Episcopal Church bishop Vashti Murphy McKenzie. These ministers and others have expressed supported for President Obama's leadership and sought to informally assist the administration when the need arose. This quasi-advisory practice is not unusual, as Rev. Billy Graham acted as "spiritual counselor" to several US presidents in the modern era (Wacker 2014). These mutually beneficial relationships afforded Obama a connection with Black faith communities that legitimized his Christian and racial identity, while clerical leaders enjoyed the ear of the president.

Obama's association with African American congregations is evident by his sporadic visits at church services as well. The president's actions in this regard displayed a type of "personal politics," and the gestures represented an acknowledgment of the importance of religious faith in the lives of Black people. The First Family, for instance, attended service at one of the nation's oldest African Methodist Episcopal churches in Washington, DC, on January 20, 2013, before the second inauguration

(Stodghill 2013). The Obama's also attended a Black Baptist church in DC the prior year around the Martin Luther King Jr. holiday. At the same time, however, some of Obama's statements before congregations have included centrist political language coupled with messages of personal responsibility and family values for Black communities (Harris 2012). Colloquially described as "talking down" to Blacks, these speeches received mixed reviews from Black political commentators.

It is also noteworthy that President Obama received regular spiritual guidance and support from other African American religious leaders. His informal faith advisor during the 2008 campaign and into his first term in office, for instance, was a young African American minister named Joshua DuBois. DuBois, a former Pentecostal associate pastor, later headed the administration's Office of Faith-Based and Neighborhood Partnerships from 2009–2013. In this role, DuBois frequently prayed with Obama and regularly sent him electronic devotional messages as the president carried out his weighty executive duties (DuBois 2013). While it is difficult to quantify the impact of such communications, the exchanges may indicate a degree of sincerity of personal religious faith on Barack Obama's part.

The President's June 2015 appearance at a memorial in Charleston further underscores the leader's acumen of Black Christian symbolism in the public sphere. A somber occasion that was widely televised, Obama gave the eulogy for his friend, Rev. Clementa Pinckney, a South Carolina state senator who was brutally murdered by a young White supremacist during the prior week. The late Rev. Pinckney's death (along with eight other parishioners who were killed) attracted national attention because of its gruesome and racially motivated nature. Shockingly, the nine Black victims were shot while attending a midweek prayer meeting at historic Emanuel African Methodist Episcopal church in Charleston. Reports noted that the church was likely targeted because of its racial composition. Obama's visible presence at the funeral service and his perceived familiarity with Black religious practices were viewed favorably by many African Americans amid this tragedy. This event highlights the overlapping themes of race, religious culture, and American politics. Obama's words at the service, thus, served three purposes, addressing a national racial tragedy, eulogizing a political ally, and further connecting with Blacks in their own institutions.

More recently, Black churches were involved in national politics as opponents of President Obama's Supreme Court nominee and supporters of symbolic political action. In March 2016, the National Black Church Initiative voiced disappointment in Obama's selection of a nominee, Circuit Court Judge Merrick Garland, who was not a Black woman (The National Black Church Initiative 2016).[2] After carefully considering several judges, Obama advanced Garland's name as a replacement for Antonin Scalia, who died in February 2016. Ultimately, Judge Garland's nomination was stalled in Congress for nearly ten months until it officially expired. Finally, in his last months of office, Obama issued several symbolic proclamations that established a few notable southern Black churches as monuments for their roles during the Reconstruction and civil rights eras ("According to Reports" 2017).

As the first Black president, religious African Americans were generally supportive of Obama. This affinity, however, meant that Black religious leaders may not have adequately communicated the political concerns of their congregations with administration officials. For example, African Americans were hard-hit financially during the Great Recession (December 2007–June 2009) and among the groups whose poverty rate remained high until the end of Obama's presidency (McKenzie 2014; US Census Bureau Current Population Survey 2012). Working through regional ministerial alliances and congregant social networks, individuals could have challenged the president's public record on race-specific economic policies. This might have encouraged administration officials to more directly address Blacks' concerns, including high unemployment rates and mortgage foreclosures.

Religious African Americans React to Obama's Endorsement of Same-Sex Marriage

Obama's public support for gay and lesbian rights in spring 2012 caused concern among many Black religious leaders. Yet others defended the move as political maneuvering in light of the evolving political climate. The mixed reactions (and sometimes silence) to President Obama's endorsement of same-sex marriage must be understood in the context of Black Protestants' general feelings about gay and lesbian behavior during this period. In 2012, Pew Research Center data show that 40 percent of

Black adults indicated they favor same-sex marriage, while only 35 percent of Black Protestants expressed similar views (Pew Center 2017a).[3] Nonetheless, Blacks' reported opinions of the president's statements on this subject are constrained by the pressures of racial group and party loyalty to the Democrats. It is well known that most African Americans are highly supportive of the Obama administration partly because of its historic significance for Black progress. Blacks' party loyalty also meant that some individuals would remain silent of this issue rather than contributing to conservative Republicans' anger over the topic.

The political opinions of religious Black Americans may further reflect a duality in group members' thinking that is evident in previous studies. Several scholars have shown, for example, that while most Black Christians view same-sex relationships unfavorably as a matter of religious teachings, their own experiences with discrimination produce general empathy toward the political plight of marginalized groups (McKenzie and Rouse 2013; Shaw and McDaniel 2007). In fact, a Pew Research Center survey (2016) demonstrates that 61 percent of all African Americans say wedding-related businesses should be required to serve same-sex couples, while Black Protestants' feelings of support/opposition to this topic are split 46 to 48 percent.

Thus, journalists' accounts of Black minister's comments on Obama's gay rights stance varied wildly, with some clergy expressing disappointment and others highlighting the politics of the decision in light of the broad Democratic agenda for fairness and equity (Cauchon 2012). In this vein, several leading Black clergy sought to focus their congregants' attention on the Obama administration's other initiatives, like health care reform and efforts to improve the economy. While ministers debated the theological merits of Obama's position on gay marriage, commentators wondered how the president's views might affect his electoral standing with African American voters (many of whom are very religious and oppose same-sex marriage) in November of 2012.

As it turns out, the importance of this issue leading up to the 2012 election seems to have diminished somewhat among Black voters. Data show that Black voter turnout actually increased from 64.7 percent in 2008 to 66.2 percent in 2012, and 93 percent of Blacks who cast a ballot selected Barack Obama as president ("President Exit Polls" 2012; File 2013: 3).[4] This extremely high level of support, nonetheless, reflects a very small decrease in votes cast for Obama (2 percent) compared to the 2008 contest. It is possible that a very small group of Black Christians may have penalized Obama in the 2012 election for supporting same-sex marriage. It is also noteworthy that although the media devotes substantial attention to the religious-bases of Americans' views toward social issue politics, this topic alone is not the most prominent concern for Blacks today.

The Political Relevance of Trends in Black Religious Life

African American churches have historically played key roles as agents of social change in Black communities, addressing the social, economic, and political concerns of their congregants (Lincoln and Mamiya 1990; Harris 1999; Billingsley 1999; McKenzie 2008; Smith 2003). As the racial and political landscape has shifted in recent times, however, scholars have raised concerns about the continued relevance of these congregations in a social-class stratified, post-civil rights America. In addition, the rise of large megachurches, particularly in the Bible Belt and Sun Belt regions, has prompted scholars to critically examine the public engagement of today's religious communities (Tucker-Worgs 2011; Harris 2010). Interestingly, Obama's relationship with Black faith communities touches upon many of these subjects.

It is worthwhile to discuss major trends in American and Black religious life that are relevant for understanding the political landscape under President Obama. A recent report from the Pew Research Center found that from 2007 to 2014, the American public overall was becoming less religious in terms of their rates of belief and practices (Chaves 2011; Pew Research Center 2015). Other studies reveal a similar decline in weekly church attendance among the population as a whole—from 42 to 38 percent. In terms of religious beliefs, Chaves (2011) notes that an important trend is the dramatic rise in the proportion of Americans who claim no religious affiliation—the so-called religious nones. By several estimates, the United States now includes a significant minority of individuals (around 23 percent) who say they have no religion at all (Pew Research Center 2015).

African Americans, however, do not display the same degree of declining religious involvement that we see in other communities. For example, numerous studies demonstrate that Blacks outpace their fellow citizens across a range of religious belief and behavior measures (Stark 2008; Putnam and Campbell 2010; McKenzie and Rouse 2013; Pew Research Center 2015). In addition, overall levels of church attendance among African Americans have been rising since the mid-1980s (Putnam and Campbell 2010). It is notable, as well, that David Briggs finds, "the percentage of white religious 'nones' rose from 15 percent in 2007 to 20 percent in 2012, while there was no significant change among Blacks" (Briggs 2015). Undeniably, Black Christian communities matter a great deal and represent fertile ground for political leaders and social reform advocates to utilize in advancing Black interests.

Among churchgoers, Black college graduates have become increasingly likely to attend religious services (Putnam and Campbell 2010). For example, 59 percent of Black Protestant college graduates say they attend church weekly, compared with 52 percent of high school graduates (Pew Research Center 2017b). These patterns demonstrate the political viability of Black faith communities. Thus, for elected officials who want to directly connect with African Americans to hear their concerns and interests, congregations provide a useful venue for exchanges. And given the growing religious involvement of middle-class Blacks, the estimated millions of married, college-educated couples that participate in churches could be useful targets for indirect political mobilization by parties, organizations, and community activists (Rosenstone and Hansen 1993). This is especially true for the South, were the majority of Blacks reside and religious participation is higher than in other parts of the country.

One can also link the political potential of Black churches to recent trends in US voting behavior. Because of Obama's candidacy, African American turnout rates were very strong in the 2008 and 2012 presidential elections. In the 2012 contest, for example, the Black voter turnout rate (66.6 percent) was higher than any other ethno-racial group in America.[5] However, "after Obama," a recent Pew Research Center report found that the voter turnout rate for African Americans dipped from a high of 66.6 percent in 2012 to 59.6 percent in 2016 (Krogstad & Lopez 2017). This decline was largely due to weak voter mobilization efforts in Black social networks and the absence of Obama as a candidate. In light of this political setback, Black political scholars and activists should formulate new strategies for harnessing Blacks' voting power in a modern era. Community institutions can play an important role in maintaining and increasing Black voting strength in future elections. For instance, today's large worship settings could be utilized as sites for collective deliberation on topics such as the Black Lives Matter movement, Voter ID laws, and financial recovery programs for families who were hurt during the Great Recession. Although there are restrictions on church-based political involvement, these spaces could provide an environment for individuals to craft group political demands and discuss possible approaches to policy changes. Indeed, for many individuals, time spent in churches may be one of few opportunities people have to meet with nonfamily members for an extended length of time.

Another politically important development in Black life is the increasing numbers of middle- and upper-middle-class suburban churchgoers. Indeed, social and economic changes in the post–civil rights era have afforded social-class mobility opportunities to a sizable number of African Americans (Davis 2012; Harris, Sinclair-Chapman, and McKenzie 2006; Wilson 1980). These positive circumstances are associated with the contemporary vibrancy of Black Christian communities and the rise of megachurches.

Black megachurches are increasingly becoming important civic institutions in Black life. It is important to note that like their smaller counterparts, megachurches vary in the levels and types of public engagement they undertake in local communities (McDaniel 2008; Tucker-Worgs 2011). The theological orientation and denominational (or independent) status of worship settings partly account for the types of civic engagement churches adopt as part of their mission. Given their huge potential, how do megachurches "measure-up" in terms of their involvement in local and national political life? Tucker-Worgs (2011, 195) notes that megachurches "have established schools and credit unions, built housing, provided recreational activities for children and adults, and engaged in the social and political issues of the day." Although their levels of community involvement may vary substantially, many of these religious behemoths provide myriad civic and social services for their churchgoers and neighboring communities. It is crucial that political elites view these contemporary institutions as useful settings for political discussions that affect African Americans.

In discussing the political relevance of Black religious communities, it is useful to examine the outreach efforts of the sitting president, Donald Trump. During the 2016 presidential campaign, for instance, a few Black evangelical church leaders expressed support for Trump's candidacy, but most Black church leaders viewed Trump's racially charged comments about impoverished inner cities and bad immigrants as offensive. Black clergy and parishioners alike wondered if Donald Trump cared about Black political interests. Attempting to make up for his limited outreach to African American voters during the presidential campaign, Trump spoke at the nondenominational Great Faith Ministries Church in Detroit on September 3, 2016 (Scott and Killough 2016). This was the first time he had addressed a predominately Black audience during his presidential bid. Although the visit was met by protesters outside the church, inside, congregants openly received Trump's message. Referring to the African American faith community as "one of God's greatest gifts to America and its people," the candidate spoke of unity and dealing with economic issues in Black communities. Overall, Trump's visit generated mixed reviews from political observers. Many skeptical analysts felt the appearance was, "scripted," awkward, or insincere (Scott and Killough 2012).

Reflecting on Obama's Complex Legacy

So, in terms of African American religious communities, What happens, after Obama? As this chapter demonstrates, the answer to this question is not quite clear. It remains to be seen if, looking back on the administration's relations with Black Christians, observers might witness evidence of symbolic deeds, rather than meaningful support for this group. Like Black politicians before him, Obama faced an inclusionary dilemma as he sought to appease religious Blacks, while representing the country as a whole. Working under these political constraints, and a sense that faith matters are deeply personal, Obama attempted to navigate the complex demands of his office. Evaluations of the former president's success or failure serving Black religious communities will, no doubt, vary among individuals. The best one can do is present an accurate account of what happened under Obama's leadership and debate the religion and politics narrative with other scholars. It is my hope that this chapter helps facilitate such conversations. And more broadly, the events described here may underscore the current political distance between recent presidents and Black Christians.

Interestingly, in recent work, Cornel West emphasizes the Black prophetic tradition's role as moral catalyst in the civil rights movement of the sixties (West 2014). The hard-fought battles that Black Christians and others endured in this era resulted in new political rights for marginalized African Americans, particularly in the South. These political accomplishments later contributed to increasing gains in Black electoral power and office-holding in the post–civil rights era. So by the time Obama sought the Democratic presidential nomination in 2008, he was the beneficiary of a long-standing, religiously influenced, Black activist tradition. In the midst of a severe economic downturn, an electoral coalition of minorities and progressive Whites elected Barack Obama as president—marking the culmination of Black political success in the modern era. But, West points out that, ironically, the Black prophetic tradition's emphasis on visible progress for marginalized Black communities has not been a major component of the Obama administration's agenda (Harris 2012). So while Black Christian protest traditions may have contributed to Obama's rise to power, many of the political concerns of this group have been neglected in favor of other concerns. Thinking through the political consequences of this conundrum may be one way of assessing the legacy of Obama's presidency on Black religious life.

Whatever conclusions one might draw regarding President Obama's relationship with Black religious groups, it is useful to compare his actions to recent presidents. In this regard, many analysts would contend that Obama's interactions with African Americans Christians were as politically meaningful or exceeded the efforts of his predecessors, George W. Bush and Bill Clinton. Recall that early in his first term, George W. Bush met with a select group of Black ministers (who might benefit from his policies) as part of his faith-based initiatives plan. But he failed to invite broad participation from leaders of the major historically Black denominations (Tucker-Worgs 2011). In addition, Bush's rhetoric and support of religious issues throughout his two terms were typically directed at political causes championed by

White evangelicals rather than Black Protestants. Secondly, Bill Clinton's notable speeches before Black religious audiences were mixed occasions for moderate policy pronouncements and symbolic gestures to Black communities (Troy 2015). The events, themselves, had little beneficial policy impact for Black Americans. By this yardstick, Obama's interactions may serve as an important benchmark for future elected leaders to consider in representing the nation's largest religious groups. We must be mindful that Black faith communities are a crucial element of the American religious scene.

As gains in Black political life are being eroded in today's polarized political climate, the Black religious sector is needed now more than ever. The period "after Obama" presents myriad opportunities for the strength and institutional resources of Black churches to benefit American society. These faith communities can serve as instruments of dissent against growing racial intolerance and rising economic inequality among Americans. Thus, public debates about religion and political life must prominently feature the concerns of Black Christians. These are important lessons to take away from the Obama administration's dealings with religious African Americans.

NOTES

1 This chapter focuses on Christians because the overwhelming majority of religious Blacks are affiliated with Christian traditions.

2 The National Black Church Initiative (www.naltblackchurch.com) is a national coalition of thirty-four thousand African-American and Latino congregations working to address social justice clauses, March 17, 2016.

3 In 2017, support for same-sex marriage increased, among Black adults overall (51 percent) and Black Protestants (44 percent).

4 Crosstabulations calculated by the author using estimates from the 2012 Current Population Survey and exit poll data from the 2012 National Election Pool.

5 Figures are from the 2012 US Census Current Population Survey November Supplement.

REFERENCES

"According to Reports." 2017. *Crisis* 124(1) (Winter):9.

Billingsley, Andrew. 1999. *Mighty Like a River: The Black Church and Social Reform.* New York: Oxford University Press.

Bonilla-Silva, Eduardo. 2014. *Racism Without Racists: Color-Blind Racism and the Persistence of Racial Inequality in America.* 4th edition. Lanham, MD: Rowman & Littlefield.

Briggs, David. 2015. "Are Black Americans the Most Religious—and Virtuous—of All?" *Huffington Post*, February 27, 2015.

Cauchon, Dennis. 2012. "Black Churches Conflicted on Obama's Gay Marriage Decision." *USA Today*, May 14, 2012.

Chaves, Mark. 2011. *American Religion: Contemporary Trends*. Princeton: Princeton University Press.

Davis, Theodore J., Jr. 2012. *Black Politics Today: The Era of Socioeconomic Transition*. New York: Routledge Press.

DuBois, Joshua. 2013. *The President's Devotional: The Daily Readings That Inspired President Obama*. New York: Harper One Publishers.

File, Thom. 2013. "The Diversifying Electorate —Voting Rates by Race and Hispanic Origin in 2012 (and Other Recent Elections)." ed. U.S. Census Bureau; Department of Commerce. Vol. P20-528, Population Characteristics: Current Population Survey. Washington, DC: U.S. Census Bureau.

Feagin, Joe, and Melvin Sikes. 1994. *Living with Racism: The Black Middle-Class Experience*. Boston: Beacon.

Green, John C. 2007. *The Faith Factor: How Religion Influences American Elections*. Westport, CT: Praeger Publishers.

Guth, James L., Lyman A. Kellstedt, Corwin E. Smidt, and John C. Green. 2006. "Religious Influences in the 2004 Presidential Election." *Presidential Studies Quarterly* 36:223–242.

Harris, Fredrick C. 1999. *Something within: Religion in African-American Political Activism*. New York: Oxford University Press.

Harris, Fredrick. 2010. "Entering the Promised Land? The Rise of Prosperity Gospel and Post–Civil Rights Black Politics." In *Religion and Democracy in the United States: Danger or Opportunity?* eds. Alan Wolfe and Ira Katznelson, 255–278. Princeton: Princeton University Press.

Harris, Fredrick. 2012. *The Price of the Ticket: Barack Obama and the Rise and Decline of Black Politics*. New York: Oxford University Press.

Harris, Fredrick C., Valeria Sinclair-Chapman, and Brian D. McKenzie. 2006. *Countervailing Forces in African-American Civic Activism, 1973–1994*. New York: Cambridge University Press.

Hochschild, Jennifer L. 1995. *Facing Up to the American Dream: Race, Class, and the Soul of the Nation*. Princeton: Princeton University Press.

Krogstad, Jens Manuel, and Mark Hugo Lopez. 2017. "Black Voter Turnout Fell in 2016, Even as a Record Number of Americans Cast Ballots." Pew Research Center Report, May 12, 2017.

Lacy, Karyn R. 2007. *Blue-Chip Black: Race, Class, and Status in the New Black Middle Class*. Berkeley: University of California Press.

Landry, Bart. 1987. *The New Black Middle Class*. Berkeley: University of California Press.

Lincoln, C. Eric, and Lawrence H. Mamiya. 1990. *The Black Church in the African American Experience*. Durham, NC: Duke University Press.

McDaniel, Eric. 2008. *Politics in the Pews: The Political Mobilization of Black Churches.* Ann Arbor: University of Michigan Press.

McKenzie, Brian D. 2014. "Political Perceptions in the Obama Era: Diverse Opinions of the Great Recession and its Aftermath among Whites, Latinos and Blacks." *Political Research Quarterly*, 67(4):823–836.

McKenzie, Brian D., and Stella M. Rouse. 2013. "Shades of Faith: Religious Foundations of Political Attitudes among African Americans, Latinos and Whites." *American Journal of Political Science*, 57(1):218–235.

McKenzie, Brian D. 2011. "Barack Obama, Jeremiah Wright and Public Opinion in the 2008 Presidential Primaries." *Political Psychology*, 32(6):943–961.

McKenzie, Brian D. 2008. "Reconsidering the Effects of Bonding Social Capital: A Closer Look at Black Civil Society Institutions in America." *Political Behavior*, 30:25–45.

McKenzie, Brian D. 2004. "Religious Social Networks, Indirect Mobilization, and African-American Political Participation." *Political Research Quarterly*, 57:621–632.

Miller, Lisa. 2008. "Q&A: What Barack Obama Prays For." *Newsweek*, July 11, 2008.

Pattillo-McCoy, Mary. 1999. *Black Picket Fences: Privilege and Peril among the Black Middle Class.* Chicago: University of Chicago Press.

Pew Research Center. 2007. "U.S. Religious Landscape Survey." Washington, DC: Pew Forum on Religion and Public Life.

Pew Research Center. 2009. "A Religious Portrait of African Americans." Washington, DC: Pew Forum on Religion and Public Life.

Pew Research Center. 2015. "U.S. Public Becoming Less Religious," Washington, DC: Pew Forum on Religion and Public Life.

Pew Research Center. 2016. "Where the Public Stands on Religious Liberty vs. Nondiscrimination," September 20, 2016.

Pew Research Center. 2017a. "Changing Attitudes on Gay Marriage." June 26, 2017.

Pew Research Center. 2017b. "In America, Does More Education Equal Less Religion?" April 26, 2017.

"President Exit Polls." 2012. *New York Times*. www.nytimes.com.

Putnam, Robert D. 2000. *Bowling Alone: The Collapse and Revival of American Community.* New York: Simon & Schuster.

Putnam, Robert D., and David E. Campbell. [2010] 2012. *American Grace: How Religion Divides and Unites Us.* New York: Simon & Schuster.

Rosenstone, Steven J., and John Mark Hansen. 1993. *Mobilization, Participation, and Democracy in America.* New York: Macmillan.

Scott, Eugene, and Ashley Killough. 2016. "Trump Brings Message of Unity to Black Church in Detroit." CNN.com, September 3, 2016.

Shaw, Todd C., and Eric L. McDaniel. 2007. "'Whosoever Will': Black Theology, Homosexuality, and the Black Political Church." *National Political Science Review* 11:137–155.

Smith, R. Drew, ed. 2003. *New Day Begun: African American Churches and Civic Culture in Post-Civil Rights America.* Durham, NC: Duke University Press.

Stark, Rodney. 2008. *What Americans Really Believe: New Findings from the Baylor Surveys of Religion*. Waco, TX: Baylor University Press.

Stodghill, Alexis Garrett. 2013. "President Obama and First Family Attend Services at Oldest Black Episcopal Church." *Grio*, January 20, 2013.

Troy, Gil. 2015. *The Age of Clinton: America in the 1990s*. New York: St. Martin's Press.

Tucker-Worgs, Tamelyn N. 2011. *The Black Mega-Church: Theology, Gender, and the Politics of Public Engagement*. Waco: Baylor University Press.

US Census Bureau Current Population Survey (CPS). 2012. Annual Social and Economic Supplement (ASEC).

Wacker, Grant. 2014. *America's Pastor: Billy Graham and the Shaping of a Nation*. Cambridge, MA: Harvard University Press.

West, Cornel, ed. 2014. *The Radical King: Martin Luther King, Jr.* Boston: Beacon Press.

Wilson, William J. 1980. *The Declining Significance of Race: Blacks and Changing American Institutions*. Revised edition. Chicago: University of Chicago Press.

5

Obama, African American Women, and the Limitations of the Politics of Recognition

WENDY G. SMOOTH

Near the end of his second term, in September of 2015, President Obama finally acknowledged the policy concerns of African American women—his most electorally loyal constituency. In his address to the Congressional Black Caucus (CBC) during their forty-fifth annual Phoenix Awards dinner, the president publicly articulated for the first time that he recognized the significant role African American women played historically in the demands for greater inclusion and equality for African Americans. By extension, he marked the centrality of African American women to building a more inclusive democracy for all Americans and helping America fulfill its promise as a modern democratic state. Obama said,

> Because all of us are beneficiaries of a long line of strong black women who helped carry this country forward. Their work to expand civil rights opened the doors of opportunity, not just for African Americans but for all women, for all of us—black and white, Latino and Asian, LGBT and straight, for our First Americans and our newest Americans. And their contributions in every field—as scientists and entrepreneurs, educators, explorers—all made us stronger. Of course, they're also a majority of my household. (Laughter and applause.) So I care deeply about how they're doing.[1]

He acknowledged that despite African American women's tremendous commitments to equality and democratic inclusion, pervasive barriers and discriminatory practices rooted in race and gender hierarchies continue to mean that they are uniquely impacted by entrenched structural inequities.[2]

However, what followed from his acknowledgments was not a rollout of a new policy proposal aimed at addressing these inequities that manifest uniquely in the lives of African American women. Women who grapple with a litany of identity markers that perpetuate racism, sexism, classism, and other systems of inequality. The speech offered no new policy solutions to address the unique conditions the president enumerated impacting African American women's lives in specific ways.

In contrast to the president's signature race policy program, My Brother's Keeper, there would be no public-private partnerships established using the power of the presidency as the motivator for participation. The president initiated no action steps directing federal departments to deploy their resources in relief of the conditions he outlined. There were no specific policy responses. Instead, President Obama offered simply the recognition that amounted to an assertion that "I see and appreciate your continued struggle." He said, "So I'm focusing on women tonight because I want them to know how much we appreciate them, how much we admire them, how much we love them. (Applause.) And I want to talk about what more we have to do to provide full opportunity and equality for our black women and girls in America today. (Applause.)" If anything, in asking for African American women's continued support in the final days of his administration, he, in actuality, requested that they cosign on a policy path that would only impact their lives to the extent that they were attached to constituency groups the administration identified as worthy of public policy attention during his presidency.

The president deployed a politics of recognition, in which he acknowledged a group of citizens; however, he did not deploy his powers as policy innovator to address or offer a targeted remediation of their condition.[3] It is very important to not overstate the centrality of what this volume frequently cites as Black linked fate of African American group consciousness, especially if they are not intersected with gender, sexuality, and other equally important identities.[4] However, President Obama appeared to offer only a tacit, ally conception of linked fate by implying his shared racial identity with African American women and his personal/familial connections to African American women—e.g., Michelle Obama and his daughters—made him a president uniquely able to identify with their needs. But in this regard, identity is not policy.

In this chapter, I examine the Obama presidency from the perspective of African American women. In both 2008 and 2012, African American women were the president's most ardent supporters, electorally providing greater support than any other demographic group. In fact, African American women provided the critical margins of victory needed in key battleground states including Florida, Michigan, Ohio, and Virginia—all of which Obama carried and each of these states African American women increased their vote share between 2008 and 2012.[5]

In this chapter, I examine how African American women benefitted from their support of the Obama presidency using traditional markers of group interests. Did they receive the attention expected as a key constituency group supporting candidate Obama? I explore the Obama presidency asking, "Did African American women receive the attention from the president that their numbers as voters and early supporters of his presidential run might suggest? If not, why?"

I explore these questions from four different perspectives. First, I center African American women as the key constituency group that accounted for Obama's electoral successes and situate what traditionally emerges when groups bear that designation in electoral politics. Second, I examine a range of policy interventions the administration pursued that we might have addressed the specific needs of African American women as a distinct group. Third, I explore African American women's descriptive representation under the Obama administration and whether the Obama administration created unique opportunities for African American women as decision makers in the administration. Finally, I argue that Obama's failures to adequately address African American women as a critical constituency is explained by two critical disconnects in his relationship to Black women.

In this chapter, I advance two key points. One, Obama failed to see African American women as an interest group, a group of voters with distinct interests and instead adopted universalist policy approaches that failed to direct concerns or interventions directly toward African American women. Second, I argue that his failure to situate African American women as an interest group worthy of attention is in part attributed to how the contract between candidate Obama and Black women first emerged. Instead of the traditional connections between a candidate and a constituency or interest group, I argue that African

American women supported the Obama administration based on their affinities for Michelle Obama, and as such, they waged a contract with the potential First Lady rather than the president himself. Ultimately, this symbolic contract hampered African American women's abilities to extract significant policy responsiveness from the administration. The treatment African American women received despite their ardent support of the president in both his elections and across his presidency is instructive for the study of Black politics overall. As I penned in a special 2012 issue of the *National Political Science Review* focused on the elections: "The 2012 election necessitates the practice and study of black politics, as if black women really mattered, because it is beyond question that they do."[6]

Examining African American women in the Obama era offers us an important opportunity to examine Black politics' present and future with a more inclusive understanding of Black women as the drivers of Black political participation who have long held this position in Black politics. What we most learn from the Obama years in relationship to African American women is that by their activism, African American women drive so much of what we regard as Black political electoral behavior. In turn, our analyses as scholars and demands as activists on behalf of the Black community must align with the realities of Black women's electoral behavior.

African American Women as Early, Critical, and Enduring Obama Supporters

Candidate Barack Obama is credited with attracting the most diverse electorate in the country's history. In fact, in 2008 Obama became the first president elected to office without a plurality of White voters. His election in 2008 marked the emergence of the "New American Electorate" that reflected the swiftly changing demographics of the country, in which minorities will make up the majority of Americans by 2050. Of all the diverse groups credited with President Obama's success in both 2008 and 2012—Blacks, Latinos, and women—it was Black women in particular who most strongly supported the president and led all other groups in the intensity of their support. African American women first showed their political heft as voters in 2008 when they made history in that election cycle with the highest voter turnout rate among all groups of eligible voters. The excitement surrounding the campaign of the nation's first Black presidential nominee on a major ticket was credited with galvanizing Black women's record mobilizing. However, these accounts offer a limited understanding of African American women's voting participation. African American women's voting in 2008 marks a continuation of a trend in their increased voter turnout that began in the 1990s.[7] Excitement over the historic nature of the election only partially accounts for their intensity.

To fully appreciate the role African American women played in Obama's rise as a virtual political unknown to his successful election, we have to take a closer look at the timetable of the 2008 election cycle. During the primaries, Black voters indeed had fewer racial suspicions than Whites of the virtually unknown Illinois senator. But ultimately, Black voters had a lower hurdle to cross than Whites to feel comfortable casting their ballots in favor of Obama and ease their skepticism regarding his electability.[8] While Black and Whites differed in their relative ease of casting a ballot for Obama in 2008, an intersectional perspective challenges us to think not only about the hurdle to cast a ballot but the motivations to support and even proselytize in support of Obama. African American women not only cast ballots in 2008, but they became an energizing force for the campaign. In 2008, African American women helped to turn the tide for then candidate Obama with their strong support in early primary states. In fact, African American women in the early primary state of South Carolina decided the trajectory of his candidacy. African Americans comprise 28 percent of the state population and, in 2008, comprised 55 percent of Democratic primary voters. This was a proving ground, and Black women became the judges. In the 2008 Democratic primary, Black women led in voter turnout in the Democratic primary, making up 35 percent of the electorate, according to exit poll data, and 78 percent supported Obama.[9]

Obama later told stories of a critical encounter with Councilwoman Edith S. Childs, a Black woman community activist, leader, National Association for the Advancement of Colored People (NAACP) cornerstone, and coincidentally, private investigator who invited him to attend a meeting in her hometown of Greenwood, South Carolina. The meeting turned out to be a small, intimate crowd of no more than twenty people. But what happened in the meeting is indicative of what Black women offered Obama in his earliest days on the campaign trail. She is credited with his signature campaign chant, "Fired Up, Ready to Go!" by offering it in the middle of his remarks that were not exciting the crowd. Obama describes how she gave energy and spirit to his campaign when, amid his remarks, she raised her fist in the air and said, "Fired up," and in a Black traditional call-and-response manner, the attendees chanted back, "Fired up!" The woman went on with "Ready to go!" and with her genius, his campaign was branded with its familiar refrain chant that carried from state to state throughout the 2008 primaries and even throughout his presidency.[10] This is only one example of the depth of energy and enthusiasm Black women offered Obama in South Carolina and other primary states. With their level of enthusiasm, they changed how Black America perceived his candidacy. Why? What did Black women see in this candidate? His authenticity as a Black candidate, capable and willing to support Black interests until that point was in constant question. Obama needed authentication among Blacks; he needed to be sanctioned as worthy of Black votes. Black women delivered that and more, but again, why?

Shayla C. Nunnally, as a scholar, captures the range of political trust dilemmas then Senator Obama faced during the early 2008 primary season, depicting the primary season as low on actual candidate information and high on predispositions and stereotypes about the candidates. Nunnally argues that such an environment exacerbated a reliance on trust factors, perceptions and cues to connect voters to the minimally known Obama. In exploring whether voters trusted either Obama or Clinton in 2008 to represent their interests, Nunnally uncovers the strong willingness of African American women above any other group studied to invest in trust of Obama. Black women forsook their gender congruence with Hillary Clinton, perceiving Obama as the most trustworthy on African American women's interests. African American women even trusted that Obama would serve as the best steward over Latina issues, more so than Clinton would.[11] Such findings underscore the significance of trust as a factor in African American women's decision-making calculus. Their high levels of trust in the unproven, virtually unknown political commodities of Obama seeks explanation for their intense support so early in 2008.

In the midst of considerable unknowns surrounding Obama, African American women saw something in him that resonated far beyond his political pedigree, his campaign message, or even his gift of oratory. African American women saw his wife, a brown girl from the South Side of Chicago. Candidate demographic characteristics can act as informational cues to voters, giving them a way to judge candidates about whom they may know very little and this was very much the case in 2008.[12] In the case of Obama in 2008, I argue that his marriage to Michelle Obama (an everyday Black woman) sent a powerful informational voting que to Black women voters that allowed them to overlook the absence of a proven record of support of Black women's issues and even the promise of supporting Black women's life circumstances, in particular. This cue allowed Black women supporters to move with ease from reluctance to overwhelming support. Black women voted on hope more than any other group. That hope was as much vested in what Michelle Obama represented and presented.[13]

Michelle Obama served as a powerful heuristic for Black women voters as many Black women saw a bit of themselves in her. As such, they concluded that Barack Obama was indeed "alright" if he chose to marry a Black woman so much like themselves. Operating as a heuristic cue, Michelle Obama provided a pathway for her husband to rise above the racial authenticity questions that mired the early days of his 2008 campaign. In addition, she provided a sense of hopefulness in his presidency.[14] On many levels, Black women connected to the ideal of an Obama presidency grounded in their beliefs that *her influence*, that *her sensibilities* would guide and inform the White House. In many ways, Black women engaged in a metaphoric political contract initially with Michelle Obama that offered transference to her husband. Therefore, through a surrogacy relationship, Barack Obama became the holder of African American women's confidence. In other words, from the onset, Black women held their confidence in Michelle Obama. With that trust, with that faith in Michelle Obama's presence and influence, Black women voters turned up their support and maintained high levels of support throughout 2008 and again in 2012. Although poll watchers and pundits predicted that voter turnout would be significantly lower in 2012, African American women actually maintained their level of mobilization in the 2012 election and consistently delivered high voter turnout rates. Again, Black women led all other groups in their support of President Obama just as they had in 2008. In keeping with traditional interest group and constituency style politics, we should understand Black women as having earned their place as constituents of the Obama administration, and as such, they were due their just reward as a constituency who had delivered their consistent support of the president.

African American Women and the Policy Responsiveness of the Obama Administration

For this very strong support of the president, Black women have received, at best, marginal policy attention. The president can be credited with some policy attentiveness to women by signing the Lilly Ledbetter Fair Pay Act as his first piece of legislation, and a later executive order further supporting gender-based pay equity in federal contracts. Despite Black women's support of the president and their critical contribution to the Democratic Party base, they have received far less in return. In this essay, I outline the Obama legacy as it relates to gender equity and, in particular, chart the president's policy attentiveness to his most ardent supporters. In broadly constructing policy responsiveness, we might read the creation of the White House Council on Women and Girls as part of the Obama accountability to African American women. Chaired by President Obama's senior advisor, Valerie Jarrett, with Tina Tchen as its executive director, this council was created by Obama's executive order on March 11, 2009. The council's mission was to coordinate the efforts of cabinet-level agencies as the advanced policies to address the interests and needs of American women, girls, and their communities. There were a range of initiatives the council undertook, and there were efforts in which it collaborated from encouraging corporate "Equal Pay" pledges to "Prioritizing School Safety: A New Curriculum for Colleges and Universities to Address Sexual Assault."[15] The council focused attention to the experiences of women of color in the US in two reports, most especially "Women and Girls of Color: Addressing Challenges and Expanding

Opportunity," published in November of 2014. This report mirrored President Obama's remarks on the plight of women and girls of color:

> As part of its efforts to address barriers and disparities that still exist for so many Americans and so many women and girls of color in particular, the Council is convening a Working Group on Challenges and Opportunities for Women and Girls of Color. This Working Group will bring together policy staff from the White House and across federal agencies—as well as experts, leaders and advocates from outside the government—to focus on issues including education, economic security, health, criminal and juvenile justice, violence, and research and data collection.[16]

Although this report provided a fairly comprehensive examination of the range of disparities women and girls of color confronted, and at moments highlighted what confronted Black women and girls, it was short on new policy prescriptions. In most instances, the report just emphasized how existing universalist programs—for example, the Earned Income Tax Credit (EITC) and the Child Tax Credit (CTC)—positively affected Black women and their families.[17] While it is important to note that the Obama administration did make important strides on behalf Black women and their families—for example, in reducing the rates of who lacked health insurance or their rates of poverty—the vast majority of these efforts were through universalist, nontargeted policies either aimed at the gender gap or at the racial gap. As Julia Jordan-Zachery notes in this volume, and as I emphasize in this chapter, the specific intersectional experiences and needs of African American women were not addressed in the policy initiatives of the Obama administration. So, as I note in the next section, African American women had to opt for descriptive representation over substantive policy responsiveness.

If Not the Policies, Perhaps the Bodies? African American Women's Descriptive Representation in the Obama Administration

The president's appointment power offers an opportunity to execute the president's campaign philosophies and assure that their appointees will promote the administration's policy agenda. The president can influence decisions by choosing leaders who closely align with the policy interests, goals, and aspirations of the administration. Anestaki and co-authors argue that appointments serve another critical purpose, which is to signal responsiveness to both loyal constituencies as well as offer responsiveness to a diverse electorate. In the modern era, diversifying the federal workforce has become a hallmark of Democratic Party politics and an explicit campaign philosophy among modern Democratic Party presidential candidates. The office of the president exerts considerable control over the demographic composition of the bureaucracy through political appointees to top-level positions, who then have responsibilities for further diversifying the federal workforce at all levels.[18]

Examining descriptive representation in Obama's appointments offers another mode of assessing his commitments to African American women. For scholars of representative democratic theory, the assumption is that a more diverse governmental workforce amounts to more representative policies that embrace the wide range of concerns articulated across groups in the country. Obama's record can be broken down between cabinet-level and top advisor appointments, appointments to the bureaucracy across agencies, and his federal judiciary appointments. It is the latter in which Obama's legacy on inclusion of Black women is strongest.

Again, Anestaki et al. offer a comparative study of three modern presidents—Clinton, Bush, and Obama—and reveal that Democratic presidents prioritize and succeed in appointing a more diverse federal workforce across all federal personnel levels. Overall, Obama fared less well in comparison to his Democratic Party predecessor Clinton in overall appointments of Blacks and, likewise, did not perform as well as Clinton in appointments of Black women. Evaluating similar points in time, Obama extended fewer political appointments to Black women than Clinton. However, to Obama's credit and despite a race neutral approach to building the federal workforce, he increased the number of Black women appointees significantly over those appointed during the Bush administration.[19] While Obama's performance in appointing Black women in large numbers lagged in relation to expectations, it is worth examining the positions of power Black women occupied during his administration and the more lasting institutional changes made during his administration by changing the demographics of the federal judiciary.

The impact of judiciary appointments extends beyond the more limited terms of political appointees. In this respect, my examination complements the chapter of Shenita Brazelton and Dianne Pinderhughes found in this volume.

African American Women and Obama Cabinet-Level and Presidential Advisory Positions

Obama's first term marked him as having the most diverse cabinet and cabinet-level appointments, with his inner cabinet including more women and men of color than his predecessors. Obama appointed a total of fourteen women and non-White men, exceeding Clinton, who made it a point to build a cabinet that "looked like America" and appointed twelve. Two of Obama's appointees were African American women at this level—one more than Clinton. The partisan divide on diversity is staggering, as both Obama and Clinton far exceeded the diversity we are seeing in the current Trump administration.[20]

However, counter to the most recent trends in which modern Democratic presidents' cabinets have become more diverse in the second term, Obama's inner circle of advisors became Whiter and more male. By the end of his second term, Bill Clinton, who had appointed nine African Americans to cabinet or cabinet-level positions in his administration by the end of his second term remained the gold standard of inclusion. Obama lagged behind this number early in his second term, sparking criticism among Black leaders and members of the Congressional Black Caucus. One congressman at the time, Charlie Rangel, lamented in a television interview that the lack of diversity in Obama's second-term cabinet was "embarrassing as hell," suggesting that in a second term, presidents have far greater latitude in their appointments to appoint people to serve who also reflect broader goals, like diversity.[21] The demographics of Obama's second-term appointees and his White House advisors drew criticisms from women and Blacks alike. Criticisms reached an all-time high following a October 2013 *New York Times* photo of Obama in the oval office with his senior advisors.[22] If a picture is worth a thousand words, the message was clear to his critics that the second-term dreams of a more radically diverse federal workforce were waning, as the optics presented in the photo drove home the message that

Obama's inner circle was a formidable group of White men with access to shape the president's ideas and positions, especially in the arena of foreign policy. My chapter begs the question, Where did this leave the representation of African American women?

By October 2015, late in the second term, the White House countered presenting its own imagery, using *Essence* magazine, a Black women's lifestyle magazine to counter the claims that Obama's White House was literally White and exclusively male. The photo spread depicted all the African American women serving on the Obama staff. With twenty-nine Black women ranging from lower-level support staff to senior advisor to the president, the photo spread communicated a White House that was at its height of inclusion. This appeal was strategic for the White House, as this was an ideal means of communicating with the base— Black women—without raising the ire of Obama critics who might not engage as readers of the Black women's lifestyle magazine. In addition, the *Essence* photo spread launched as criticisms of Obama's treatment of Black women and their concerns were mounting, regarding the My Brother's Keeper initiative and letter that circulated in June 2014.[23] Though the overall numbers of Black women political appointees did not live up to expectations for a Democratic president or the expectations imagined for the nation's first Black president, Obama did appoint a number of Black women into high-profile positions at the cabinet level and the critical role of White House advisor.

In both his first and second terms, President Obama appointed eight women to cabinet or official cabinet-level posts, which are positions that the Senate must confirm. President Obama is credited with appointing the largest number of women to such positions, exceeding the appointments of former president Bill Clinton. Across Obama's two terms in office, three African American women held appointments at this level, including Attorney General Loretta Lynch (2015–2016); Administrator Lisa Jackson, Environmental Protection Agency (2009–2013); and ambassador to the UN, Susan E. Rice (2009–2013), who also served as national security advisor (2013–2016), though that position is not considered cabinet level. All of these women are history makers as the first African American women to hold the offices they occupied. In addition to examining the number of African American women within the executive branch, we also must look to those African American women advising the president. Among them include the well-known senior advisor and friend to President Obama, Valerie Jarrett; Susan Rice, national security advisor; and several presidential assistants of directors, such as Deesha Dyer, Ashely Allison, and Ashley Etienne.[24] While pathbreaking in many ways, such appointments may speak to a deeper form of Obama's politics of recognition. Next, we turn to the Obama administration's appointment of African American women to the federal bench.

African American Women and the Judiciary

Legal scholars, pundits and the historic record overwhelmingly point out the strides the Obama administration made in diversifying the federal judiciary. Obama's nominees reflected a campaign commitment to increase the extent to which the judiciary demographically reflects the American people. At once, while the legal community celebrated the historic gains Obama made in nominating a diverse group of federal justices at all levels, there is also room to examine critical missed opportunities—namely as the Black feminist community would argue the greatest missed opportunity of all—Obama's failure to nominate an African American woman to the Supreme Court. Such an omission underscores Obama's grounding in recognition politics as ultimately in conflict with actions to make wide-scale changes on behalf of Black women. Once it became clear that Obama would indeed submit a nominee to fill the vacancy following the sudden death of Justice Antonin Scalia, advocates across the civil rights, feminist legal community, and Black women's advocacy groups began to speak out that this was indeed the moment to nominate an African American woman to the highest court. Civil rights leader and president of the Transformative Justice Coalition, Barbara R. Arnwine, organized an online petition and organized advocacy meetings with the White House, calling upon the president to act affirmatively in support of nominating the first African American woman to the court. She argued, "The appointment of an African American woman to the Supreme Court is essential to his legacy."[25] Aside from appealing to his legacy, some advocates appealed to the pure political motivations that often encourage presidents to act on nominations. Supporters of seeing an African American woman nominated couched their appeals to the White House as a matter of positive patronage politics, arguing that such a nomination could ignite the Democrat's base of African American women to mobilize on behalf of the party in the 2016 elections and invigorate women more broadly to mobilize turnout on behalf of the party. Such a strategy had proven results. The gender gap is credited with incentivizing Ronald Reagan's appointment of the first woman to the Supreme Court, Justice Sandra Day O'Connor, in large part to attend to the emerging gender gap between men and women voters that at its earliest points seemed destined to bend toward women's support of Democrats. In the 1980 election, Reagan won the presidency with 55 percent support from men and a lagging 47 percent of women voters, which gave rise to Republicans' concerns for losing women voters. Not only had women proven they could cast votes differentiating from their male counterparts, they, in turn, began showing up to the polls in higher numbers than their male counterparts did. To assure the support of politically astute women voters, Reagan signaled his party's support for women and acknowledged the growing power of women electorally and as a social movement force to influence politics. In this case, the response to women's voting patterns was beyond acknowledgment, prompting a groundbreaking shift in a significant institution, the Supreme Court of the United States of America.[26]

The Obama White House found itself caught between the demands of a critical constituency base and the wrath of Republican backlash that questioned the fundamental authority of the president to make the nomination—a truism that remained intact regardless of the nominee—and a potential backlash to the president using his appointees to reflect a commitment to identity politics. Obama's decision reflected another side of his political calculations that rang true for African American women's advancements across the two terms of his presidency. When faced with the opportunity to do more than practice a politics of recognition, the Obama administration again opted to move against traditional constituency or interest group politics, opting instead to gamble that the tightly secured African American women's vote and support would not waiver and could be regarded as assured. Of course, the election of 2016 proved this to be only partially correct. Though African American women ultimately supported the Democratic Party nominee, they did not mobilize turnout to the extent possible.[27] In some ways, Obama's calculation that

African American women did not require traditional constituency patronage politics was a misfire.

Demanding Intersectional Responsiveness: African American Women's Response to Obama's Inclusionary Dilemma

In 2013, during President Obama's second term, he announced his first signature policy program that arguably could be regarded as his first and only race-centered initiative. It was a public-private partnership that utilized, in grand form, the power of the presidency to moderate life outcomes for boys of color. His first race-based program not only failed to address African American women, it directly defined them outside the scope of impact of the initiative. "My Brother's Keeper," the president's signature program, which evolved in the wake of the Trayvon Martin killing and George Zimmerman's acquittal for the killing, became his most direct response to this "inclusionary dilemma," as noted in this volume. Though many were enthused by the president's creation of the program and marked his overt discussion of race as an important first for this second-term president, African American women offered a very different reaction. African American women found the president's first policy voice and will to act on race as insulting, in that it excluded any responsiveness to Black women's needs, his most ardent supporters. As well, the policy initiative purposefully defined them as outside the purview of need all together. Reminiscent of so many historical moments that defined the needs of the race in masculinist terms, the president's initiative drew immediate criticism from African American women activists and scholars, who were well aware of that history and its ramifications.[28] These scholars responded by first encouraging the president to recognize the fallacy of his decision and the optics it created, regarding the gendering of needs among African Americans, particularly in relation to violence. When met with defiance from the administration in the form of refusing to expand the scope beyond an emphasis on boys in order to include girls of color, groups emerged to contest the president's decisions. In June of 2014, Kimberlé Crenshaw's African American Policy Forum and others launched the #WhyWeCan'tWait social media campaign, which followed with an open letter to the White House from over one thousand activists and scholars. The open letter articulated their public outrage over the president's nonresponsiveness to a central constituency and his dismissal of their status as having exacerbated experiences with violence, which was indeed read as a presidential erasure of African American women's experiences.[29]

In that moment, Obama braved the terrain of divisive racial politics the administration so feared and confronted the perils of racial backlash for adopting a linked fate stance between the president and the plight of African Americans. Yet at the same time, the administration simultaneously defined African American women as outsiders to his race-centered policy overture. His inclusionary dilemma resulted in an exclusionary political practice deeply rooted in the African American political tradition that traces back as far as Frederick Douglass's argument for Black male suffrage only to the exclusion of Black women.

Though it began as a response to Obama's exclusionary political practice, African American women's campaign for recognition evolved beyond simply a request for inclusion of girls of color in the My Brother's Keeper initiative into a broader campaign for greater policy, research, and philanthropic attention to Black women and girls. For one, the African American Policy Forum continued with reports on Black women's experiences with violence and their erasure from state-based antiviolence campaigns. The report and the overall campaign marked the call for recognition and intervention with the apt title #SayHerName.[30] In addition, the flurry of media attention to African American women's demands and their activism received some response from the White House. The administration's White House Council on Women and Girls began to uplift more intersectional programming, including a summit on women and girls of color, the hallmark of which became the initiative known as the Collaborative to Advance Equity through Research to close the gaps in research related to women and girls of color.[31] Though far less well funded than the corollary My Brother's Keeper, many suggest that these overtures were the result of Black women's assertion of their claims and needs for responsiveness from the administration. It represented one of many forms of collective action among African American women in response to the Obama administration's politics of recognition.

Post-Obama Era Black Women's Politics—Study and Practice

There is no doubt the Obama presidency informed Black women's activism in formal politics. In spite of Obama's limited responsiveness to Black women's substantive policy needs, Black women emerged from the Obama era as a legitimate voting block that Democratic Party candidates ignore to their own certain peril. Hillary Clinton's failures to assure resources to support Black women's enthusiasm is part evidence of what happens for Democratic Party candidates that fail to recognize the power of Black women voters. In contrast, other candidates—i.e., candidates across Virginia, the Democratic US Senatorial victory of Doug Jones of Alabama, and most especially Stacy Abrams as the first African American woman Democratic candidate for Georgia governor—recognized the power of these voters.[32] While recognizing their power, the continued challenge for Black women remains, How do they have others recognize their political power to decide elections for Democrats and, perhaps most importantly, hold Democrats accountable in ways they did not with Obama that resulted in the very politics of recognition I argue in this chapter?

Aside from these challenges of maintaining accountability, we must recognize how much political regard for Black women voters has shifted "after Obama." There is significantly greater attention to Black women as voters and a genuine political curiosity regarding understanding their significance to the Democratic Party's fate for the next four years and beyond. Black women's emergence as the determinants of the Democratic Party's success has registered with pundits and Democratic Party operatives. In their own right, Black women have come to understand their own political power in new ways.[33] First, the unprecedented coverage of Black women as political actors in the wake of their voter mobilization and turnout in 2008 and again in 2012 marked them as drivers of the Democratic Party electorate. Their capabilities to change outcomes became a reality for Black women organizations and Black women voters individually. Political pundits' surprise at the impact of Black women voters resulted in an onslaught of questions designed to make sense of Black women's historic turnout in 2008 and 2012, with most resolving that it was simply their support of Obama alone, which demonstrated a shortsighted history of Black women's political organizing.[34] Black women's political participation has always presented a puzzle of sorts for social scientists and political pundits alike—what I have termed "the paradox of participation." According to every measure predicting political participation, Black women as a group perform poorly. Studies widely cited by Schulmanns find that those with higher socioeconomic status and educational achievement are expected to be more engaged in politics and vote in higher numbers. However, for Black women, they perform poorly on these measures, yet they made history as the group with the highest voter turnout in 2008 and again in 2012. Black women believing in the power of their voting prowess and the mobilization by voter participation groups in the post-Trump era pushed back against a Democratic Party that remained consistent in its usual politics of ignoring this significant constituency.[35] Black women proved that their mobilization was driven by factors beyond support of Obama's presidency, and they imagined themselves as the protectors of Obama-era policies in the Trump era. Black women proved time and again that they could enact a rescue-style politics to resuscitate the party in the wake of the Clinton loss and could provide the energy to prove the party's viability following Trump's ascension to the White House. In the slew of Trump elections, Black women proved that they were not asserting empty claims but could back up their claims as the source of the Democratic Party's recovery by their political mobilizations in the most high-profile races of the Trump era.[36]

In the wake of Black women's profound impact on Obama-era elections and their saving power in rescuing the Democratic Party in the Trump era, the study of Black women's politics is also growing. Scholars are profoundly interested in Black women's political organizing on all levels, from voting to running for public office. The challenge before scholars of Black politics, in particular, is resisting the emerging narrative that Black women's political engagement began with Obama's rise. Such a political narrative overlooks Black women's long-standing engagement with formal and informal politics that actually made their 2008, 2012, and Trump-era mobilizations possible.[37]

The challenge before a new Black politics scholarship and studying Black politics after Obama is sustaining a rigor in researching from an intersectional perspective—disaggregating Black political activism according to gender in order to project greater accuracy in what constitutes "Black politics." There are a series of questions I leave with the reader to contemplate the trajectory of Black politics after Obama: What did the Obama campaigns teach us about "the women's vote" the "Black vote"? Equally important, what did Black women "learn" as a key constituency of the Democratic Party? Did the party teach through benign neglect? Will subsequent Democratic Party campaigns learn about Black women and the internal logic of Black community support? What exactly motivated Black women, and will they ever fall for such love again? Contemporary Black politics is a politics of Black women as major voters, organizations, and civic participators. How will that redefine Black politics? How will that redefine how the Democratic Party engages the Black community? What does it look like to place Black women at the center of political outreach and engagement? How do the issues shift/change if we properly take them and their interests into account? All these questions confront us if we are to move American politics beyond a mere "politics of recognition" to one where the voices and visions of African American women truly matter.

NOTES

1 "Remarks by the President at the Congressional Black Caucus 45th Annual Phoenix Awards Dinner." White House, https://obamawhitehouse.archives.gov.

2 Ibid.

3 In this chapter, I draw on the broad critiques of the politics of recognition in which governments and other powers use recognition in lieu of redistribution of resources. This approach emerged as a popular substitute for egalitarian based redistribution policies that seek justice through deploying resources. For examples of these critiques, see Nancy Fraser (2000), "Rethinking Recognition," *New Left Review* 3: 107; and Amy Guttman, ed. (1994). *Multiculturalism and the Politics of Recognition.* Princeton, NJ: Princeton University Press.

4 Evelyn M. Simien (2005), "Race, Gender, and Linked Fate." *Journal of Black Studies* 35, no. 5: 529–50.

5 Wendy Smooth (2017), "Black Politics, as if Black Women Mattered." In *National Black Politics Review: Grassroots and Coalitions.* Routledge. 79–82.

6 Ibid.

7 Hanes Walton, Robert C. Smith, and Sherri L. Wallace (2017), *American Politics and the African American Quest for Universal Freedom.* Taylor & Francis: New York and London.

8 Ray Block Jr. (2011), "Backing Barack Because He's Black: Racially Motivated Voting in the 2008 Election," *Social Science Quarterly* 92, no. 2: 423–446.

9 "South Carolina Dem Primary Exit Poll," ABC News, https://abcnews.go.com.

10 "Remarks by the President at Rally on Health Insurance Reform," White House, September 12, 2009, https://obamawhitehouse.archives.gov.

11 Shayla Nunnally (2014), "Zero-Sum Politics as a Trust Dilemma? How Race and Gender Affect Trust in Obama's and Clinton's Representation of Group Interests," *Ralph Bunche Journal of Public Affairs* 3, no. 1: 1–29.

12 Eileen T. Walsh (2009), "Representation of Race and Gender in Mainstream Media Coverage of the 2008 Democratic Primary," *Journal of African American Studies* 13: 121–130.

13 Michelle Obama has indicated several ways the partnership of her marriage to Barack Obama benefited his early and later political aspirations. See Michelle Obama (2018), *Becoming*, New York: Penguin Random House.

14 Barbara Seals Nevergold and Peggy Brooks-Bertram (2009), *Go, Tell Michelle: African American Women Write to the New First Lady*, Albany, NY: SUNY Press.

15 "The White House Council on Women and Girls," White House, https://obamawhitehouse.archives.gov.

16 "White House Report: Women and Girls of Color: Addressing Challenges and Expanding Opportunity," White House, November 12, 2014, https://obamawhitehouse.archives.gov.

17 Ibid.

18 Aikaterini Anestaki, Meghna Sabharwal, Kenneth Connelly, and N. Joseph Cayer (2016), "Race and Gender Representation in Presidential Appointments, Ses, and Gs Levels, During Clinton, Bush, and Obama Administrations," *Administration and Society* 51, no. 2: 197–228.

19 Ibid.

20 Jasmine C. Lee (2017), "Trump's Cabinet So Far Is More White and Male Than Any First Cabinet Since Reagan's." *New York Times.* March 10, 2017.

21 Kristin Donnelly (2013), "Charlie Rangel on Obama's All-White Appointments: 'Embarrassing as Hell.'" MSNBC, January 10, 2013, www.msnbc.com.

22 Lowrey, Annie (2013), "Obama's Remade Inner Circles Has All-Male Look, So Far." *New York Times*, January 8. www.nytimes.com.

23 Taylor Lewis (2017). "29 Powerful Black Women Who Called the Shots in the Obama Administration." *Essence*, January 20. www.esscence.com.

24 Ibid. (CAWP fact sheet).

25 Jerry Markon, Sari Horwitz, and Mike DeBonis (2016), "Activists Push Obama to Nominate Black Woman to the Supreme Court." *Washington Post*, March 9, 2016, www.washingtonpost.com.

26 Daniel Wirls (1986), "Reinterpreting the Gender Gap," *Public Opinion Quarterly* 50, no. 3 (1986): 316–30.

27 Thom File (2017), "Voting in America: A Look at the 2016 Presidential Election." US Census Bureau (blogs), May 10, 2017, www.census.gov.

28 "My Brother's Keeper & the Co-Optation of Intersectionality." Crunk Feminist Collective, July 1, 2014, www.crunkfeministcollective.com.

29 Kimberle Williams Crenshaw (2014), "The Girls Obama Forgot," *New York Times*, July 30, 2014, www.nytimes.com. See "#WHYWECANTWAIT: An Overview of Our Work Surrounding the My Brother's Keeper Initiative," African American Policy Forum (AAPF), www.aapf.org.

30 "Say Her Name: Resisting Police Brutality against Black Women," (2015), African American Policy Forum, Center for Intersectionality and Social Policy Studies, Columbia School of Law, www.aapf.org.

31 See "Collaborative to Advance Equity," Anna Julia Cooper Center, https://ajccen ter.com.

32 Chandelis R. Duster and Foluké Tuakli (2017) "Why Black Women Voters Showed up for Doug Jones," NBC News, December 13, 2017, www.nbcnews.com; Vanessa Williams (2018), "For Black Women in Georgia Backing Stacey Abrams, a Chance to Break 'the Ceiling on Top of the Glass Ceiling.'" *Washington Post*, November 1, 2018, www.washingtonpost.com.

33 Andre M. Perry (2019), "Black Women Are Looking Forward to the 2020 Elections," Brookings Intuition and Higher Heights, January 10, 2019, www.brookings. edu; Andre M. Perry (2018), "Analysis of Black Women's Electoral Strength in an Era of Fractured Politics." Brookings Institution and Higher Heights, September 10, 2018, www.brookings.edu. Also see "#BlackWomenVote," http://blackwomen vote.com.

34 For an excellent discussion of Black women's political history of organizing and civic engagement, see Melissa V. Harris-Perry (2011), *Sister Citizen: Shame, Stereotypes, and Black Women in America*, Yale University Press.

35 Wendy Smooth (2018), "Black Women's Politics Pre-Dating the Age of Trump: 2019 National Conference of Black Political Scientists (NCOBPS) Annual Meeting," abstract available at SSRN, November 26, 2018, www.papers.ssrn.com.

36 Perry (2018), "Analysis of Black Women's Electoral Strength"; and see Andre M. Perry (2017), "Alabama Is a Precursor to the Black Vote's Value in 2018 and 2020," *The Avenue* (blog), Brookings, December 13, 2017, www.brookings.edu.

37 For an excellent discussion, see Julia Jordan-Zachery and Nikol Alexander-Floyd, eds. (2018), *Black Women in Politics: Demanding Citizenship, Challenging Power, and Seeking Justice*, New York: SUNY Press. See also Nikol Alexander-Floyd and Julia Jordan-Zachery, eds. (2015), "Black Women in Politics: Identity, Power and Justice in the New Millennium," *National Political Science Review*. Routledge Press: New York and London.

6

Moving the Needle?

Obama, Targeted Universalism, and the Black LGBTQ Community

RAVI K. PERRY

In this chapter, I discuss the evolution of the Obama administration's policies that affected the lives of Black Lesbian, Gay, Bisexual, Transgender, and Queer (LGBTQ) communities.[1] I discuss the dilemma—the inclusionary dilemma—that for all the ways President Obama and his administration may have moved the needle on American public opinion and the embrace of LGBTQ civil rights and marriage equality, there was less movement in terms of African American attitudes and, in turn, relatively less progress for Black LGBTQ communities. Having said this, however, I believe the targeted universalism of the administration still mattered in improving the lives of Black LGBTQ families. As I explain, targeted universalism is a policy approach whereby a policy that is crafted to appeal to and positively affect a very broad constituency—i.e., health care insurance and American uninsured families—has a positive ancillary effect upon the well-being of a specific constituency—e.g., Black LGBTQ uninsured families.

When then senator Barack Obama (D-Illinois) began his campaign for the United States presidency in early 2007, he entered the race as one of the most politically cautious candidates in history. His tenure in the United States Senate had been short—less than one term. He had purposefully stayed away from politically polarizing issues, refraining from sponsoring major bills and generally avoiding the cable talk-show circuit that many of his colleagues regularly enjoyed. He entered the Senate in 2005 with a modest amount of star power. And he was aware that his presence among the ranks of the mostly White statesmen merited a moderate amount of attention, bolstered by his keynote address during the 2004 Democratic National Convention. Obama chose to keep his head down during those first years in the Senate before announcing his intention to run for the nation's highest office.[2] Obama's lack of a substantive voting record in the Senate took many political pundits by surprise, who found themselves at a loss for ways in which to attack him politically.[3] However, a sparse Senate floor voting record did not mean a lack of a substantive policy stances. It was his strategy in favor of developing policy positions, despite varied roll call votes, that in many ways indicated both the type of campaign he would run as well as his early presidential leadership style. During that time, Obama was distinguished by a meticulous political strategy, where he was careful to stay in the center of divisive issues and opted instead to run on a message that focused on a vague, if nostalgic, concept of national unity and hope.

It comes as no surprise to those who followed Obama's political rise closely that the young Illinois senator had no clearly defined stance on same-sex marriage. Given early indications from his residency in Chicago, it could be surmised that he was generally comfortable around LGBTQ individuals and had been an LGBTQ rights advocate in his adopted hometown. His views became muddled as he ran for the presidency, as the stance of the Democratic Party was lukewarm toward LGBTQ issues. As a state senator from Chicago, he was adamant in his support of "domestic partnerships," for he considered this obscure term to be more politically palatable. Accordingly, upon his election to the presidency, his public statements supporting same-sex marriage softened. Obama took a simple, diplomatic approach by stating his belief that same-sex marriage was an issue of "state's rights," rather than a topic appropriate for federal intervention.[4] At varying times when he was questioned about his stance, he harkened back to a traditional opinion that "marriage had been a concept which he believed was between one man and one woman." He would defend his position, stating that he felt the protections that civil unions afforded to same-sex couples to be "adequate."

Two years into his presidency, Obama's views showed the first signs of change, when he admitted that he was wavering on the issue: "Attitudes evolve, including mine."[5] Obama continued to state his beliefs about same-sex marriage were in flux given the public discourse. With his reelection campaign in full swing, it was not until late in his first term that Obama openly decided to come full circle on his stance. He officially came out in support of same-sex marriage in 2012. This dramatic shift was prompted by the actions of another. Only two days before the president's announcement, Vice President Joe Biden appeared to force Obama's hand. During the Sunday talk show *Meet the Press*, Biden openly told host David Gregory that he was "completely comfortable" with the prospect of "men marrying men" and "women marrying women."[6] His comments highlighted the distance between the president's and the vice president's stance on the issue even though Biden coyly noted, "The President sets the policy."[7] But this was an admission that Obama was reluctant to affirm marriage equality.

However, the preparation for this historic announcement has been carefully contrived. The White House chose Robin Roberts of ABC News. Roberts, a Black lesbian, seemed to be the ideal choice for conveying Obama's official change in position. Though not openly lesbian at the time, she lent a credible voice to help pave the way for a very public agenda transition by the president. To be sure, President Obama's shift in his stance toward supporting same-sex marriage signaled the beginning of a new epoch for LGBTQ Americans. With the backing of the nation's highest office, long-sought-after needs of LGBTQ individuals had finally been legitimized in a way that had been sorely lacking by all previous presidential administrations. With his support for same-sex marriage, Obama acknowledged that civil marriage was not about religious beliefs, as had been propagated by prior administrations, but rather was emblematic of upholding civil rights. Hence, the president made a crucial step forward in his own evolution and for the American people. He opened the door for not only a level of social acceptance but also paved the way for future substantive policy changes at the federal level. In the next section, I discuss how, biographically, Obama may have developed a linked fate with LGBTQ Americans based on his evolving sense of identity as a biracial man from an ethnically diverse background.

Movement on LGBTQ Issues: Obama's Identity and Policy Evolution

Obama's eloquent explanation of his racial identity as a biracial man (a White American mother and Black Kenyan father) who self-identifies as Black has been documented in his memoirs. What has been less clear to the media and the public in general, is his apparent oscillation on LGBTQ issues. In retrospect, it is obvious that Obama's policy objectives and public positions, especially on the matter of LGBTQ rights, were driven exclusively by political motivations. He was accused on multiple occasions during his presidential campaigns and very often during his first term of being a "flip flopper."[8] As one key example, detractors cited his varied positions with regards to same-sex marriage, given Obama appeared to have switched opinions several times. Yet those close to him insist that Obama's positions never changed. They have gone so far as to assert that he has always been in favor of same-sex marriage. David Axelrod, the 2008 Obama campaign chief strategist, wrote in his memoir *Believer* that Obama often grew angry about the politicization of the same-sex marriage issue and detested the "compromis[ing] position" it put him in.[9] At one point, a sullen Barack Obama announced that "[he wasn't] very good at bullshitting" the people.[10]

Upon examination, Axelrod's claim that Obama softened his pro-same-sex-marriage stance for the sake of political viability seems to comport with the evidence. In 1996, when Obama first ran for the Illinois state legislature's Thirteenth District seat, he was adamant in his pro-LGBT-equality stance. On at least one instance, he put his position in writing by responding to a local newspaper questionnaire with a memo that he signed. In this nine-point memo response, he not only defines his stance on same-sex marriage but promises to actively pursue a civil-union bill for same-sex couples. What is even more telling in this memorandum is that he strongly opposed policies that marginalized such communities. He stated that he, "[Did] not favor a statewide registry . . . of people who test positive for HIV," and further advocated for "an increase in funding for state AIDS services."[11]

Yet it is exactly these types of press releases and statements that landed Obama in hot water during his first presidential campaign. After he won the state senate seat in 1996, his stances on perceived controversial issues became politically risky. He was no longer a fresh-faced newcomer but an incumbent with the potential to be ousted after one term. Just two years later, while seeking reelection in 1998, Obama filled out a handwritten response to a similar questionnaire, for the LGBT Chicago newspaper *Outlines*. In his responses, for each of the three questions relating to the candidate's stance on gay issues, Obama answered with an "undecided," thus distancing himself from divisive issues.

Years later, when Obama ran for US Senate, his position changed back to advocating same-sex marriage rights. He gave an interview to the *Windy City Times*, the cousin publication of *Outlines*, indicating his restrained support for same-sex couples. In lieu of directly coming out for same-sex marriage, he sidestepped the issue, offering his position favoring same-sex "civil unions," citing "strategic advantages." His argument was that this was the prudent choice since he believed a same-sex marriage bill would never get through both legislative bodies. Thus, he instead opted to pursue a more realistic goal. He candidly defended his choice as a political one in the interview with the *Windy City Times*, holding, "What I'm saying is that strategically, I think we can get civil unions passed."[12]

In years to come, of course, his position would change several more times. Obama was careful with his words, however, never officially contradicting himself. He asserted that he was on board with same-sex partnerships, which in his opinion would offer such couples "the same rights that we take for granted."[13] He would take the position that marriage ought not to be federalized, classifying the issue as a matter for the states to decide. He also conceded that for those who were religious, the word "marriage" held an ingrained cultural and traditional meaning.

By the time he officially announced his support for same-sex marriage in 2012, it can be safely assumed he did so out of a desire to be politically in line with his moral convictions. He won reelection in November 2012 to his second and final term, during a legislative year with a Republican-controlled Congress. His previous political constraints notwithstanding, the time was finally right for Obama to throw caution to the wind and officially change his position. His May 2012 declaration, wherein he endorsed same-sex marriage, was a historic step toward marriage equality for the LGBTQ community. It was one that was not taken lightly by the electorate at large. His public support and ramped-up policy action laid the groundwork for not only a shift in the American social dynamic, but it also led to substantive policy changes and a more inclusive liberal agenda for his second term and for the Democratic Party platform in the 2016 presidential election.

Before exploring the dramatic changes that Obama's pro-LGBTQ stance has had on Black American politics, it is first crucial to understand the broader context in which it took place. The United States has been a historically intolerant nation, discriminating against virtually every racial/ethnic or cultural minority group. Whether it was the blatant antihiring practices against Catholics, Jews, and ethnic immigrants, the internment of Japanese Americans, or the legal racial segregation of Blacks and Whites, the United States has had a long, torrid history with ethnic and racial bigotry. Perhaps the least publicized form of bigotry among these injustices, at least until recently, has been the plight of LGBTQ Americans, against whom discrimination has been both widespread and longstanding.

The Status Quo and Change: Religiosity and Americans' Views toward Same-Sex Marriage

American intolerance toward homosexuality has historically stemmed from the Protestant Christian notion of biblical marriage as a union between a man and a woman. Traditional or orthodox Christian interpretations regarding sexuality have been pervasive throughout American society and churches. While some Christian churches have taken a more liberal view, the embrace of the LGBTQ community in major American denominations has only been a recent development. According to the National Congregations Study, it was not until the twenty-first century, between 2006 and 2012, that "the share of congregations allowing an openly gay or lesbian couple to become full-fledged members grew from 37% to 48% . . . the number of congregations that allowed openly gay and lesbian members to assume any lay leadership position also increased— from 18% in 2006 to 26% in 2012."[14]

Meanwhile, Virginia has sought to legislate antisodomy laws as far back as the nation's founding, once mandating death as the only proper punishment.[15] Even in the face of the sexual revolution in 1961, every state within America had sodomy listed in its codified law as a crime. This created an environment in which it was essentially illegal to be a sexually active gay man.[16] Indeed, not only were these the laws of the states, but even as recently as 1986, the United States Supreme Court

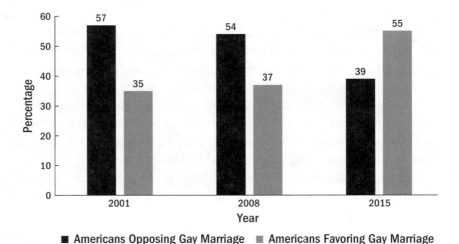

Figure 6.1. Attitudinal change toward same-sex marriage. *Source*: Pew Center, "Attitudes on Same-Sex Marriage," 2019, www.pewforum.org. Author compiled table from data.

sided with these rulings, upholding the sodomy laws of Georgia in the case of *Bowers v. Hardwick*.[17]

Not only were these antigay sentiments codified into law, they were reflected in virtually every public opinion survey. Broadly speaking, the LGBTQ civil rights movement in the United States is a contemporary phenomenon. It was not until the 1980s and 1990s, when the AIDS crisis hit, that the movement captured the collective consciousness of Americans. Hence, this attracted more scholarly, political, and journalistic attention to the problems facing gay Americans and, by extension, the LGBTQ community at large. Moreover, it was not until the 2000s when there was a consistent shift in public opinion, with each consecutive year yielding increasingly favorable views of gay Americans.

As figure 6.1 indicates, in 2001, 57 percent of Americans were explicitly opposed to legalizing "gay marriage," and only 35 percent of the nation was openly in favor of it.[18] When compared to figures eight years later, in 2009, at the end of the George W. Bush presidency, the social needle had barely moved, indicating a slight general trend in support. Individuals opposing marriage equality decreased to 54 percent and those in favor rose to a modest 37 percent.[19] Yet in the six years after Obama transitioned into the White House, the country experienced an unprecedented "liberalization" of America's views on this issue. In 2015, only 39 percent of Americans were directly opposed to gay marriage, falling by a whopping 15 percent in the immediate aftermath of the post-Bush years.[20] A July 2015 Supreme Court ruling in support of same-sex marriages witnessed 55 percent of Americans stating they were supportive of same-sex marriage.[21]

Additionally, the Pew Research Center indicates that public perception has shifted across generational and political lines. Increasing numbers of both Democrats and Republicans support equal marriage rights. As figure 6.2 illustrates, of Republicans polled in 2001, only 21 percent supported same sex marriage rights, along with a minority or 43 percent of Democrats.[22] By the sixth year of the Obama presidency in 2015, however, those numbers had leapt to an astonishing 32 percent and 66 percent, respectively.[23] These trends of larger majorities or pluralities within each political party strongly suggests that the traditional notions

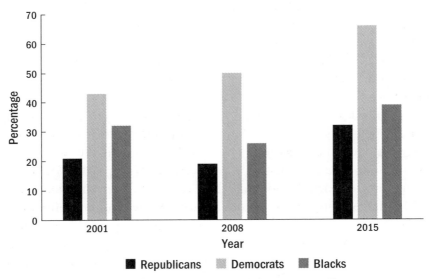

Figure 6.2. Attitudinal change toward same-sex marriage by party affiliation. *Source*: Pew Center, "Attitudes on Same-Sex Marriage," 2019, www.pewforum.org. Author compiled table from data.

of opposition to same-sex marriage are in steady decline. Next, I examine the dynamics of African American attitudes and LGBTQ civil rights, as well as same-sex marriage.

Smaller Movement: African American Attitudes on LGBTQ and Same-Sex Marriage Issues

As others have observed, one consistent feature of the LGBTQ movement in the twentieth and twenty-first centuries is the troublesome assertion that homophobia in the Black community is responsible for recent movement failures at the ballot box.[24] While elements of homophobia are known to exist in Black communities, the "Black community" simply cannot be blamed when, for example, "Black people almost certainly did not account for 10 percent of the voters on Prop 8, they accounted for seven percent."[25] Presumably as a supporter of same-sex marriage, one is less likely to practice homophobia. Thus, relative to Black Americans, attitudes on same-sex marriage may inform how many Black Americans support homophobia. Throughout the Obama presidency, Blacks increasingly expressed more favorable views on same-sex marriage. For example, while a 2015 Pew Research Center study found that a majority of Americans supported same-sex marriage, Black attitudes diverged. Only 37 percent of the Black community favored marriage equality.[26] But this is higher than was true at the conclusion of George W. Bush's final term. Then, only 29 percent of African Americans supported gay marriage.[27]

Thus, what is encouraging is the apparent impact that the Obama presidency has had on Black American attitudes, with 39 percent supporting equal marriage rights by 2015.[28] Despite the ten percentage point jump in the span of only six years, Black support for gay marriage laws still significantly trailed the rest of the non-Black and non-Hispanic majority of the nation. In 2015, Whites and non-Hispanics supported gay marriage by 58 percent. When compared by the numbers, the disparity between Blacks and non-Hispanic Whites was even more astonishing. According to the 2012 Census data, the United States is home to approximately 197.7 million White Americans, roughly 114 million of whom openly support same sex marriage.[29] The Census data from the same year identifies 41.7 million Black Americans within the

US, only about 16 million of whom support gay marriage.[30] With these figures in mind, it is hardly surprising that some African Americans feel that their racial group members are lukewarm to openly hostile toward LGBTQ individuals and the idea of same-sex marriage.

Perhaps, what is most interesting about these figures is that they seem to defy conventional wisdom with regard to the Black electorate. What has long been an established factor within the White majority is that attitudes about homosexuality and LGBTQ individuals vary according to socioeconomic status. A Perry et al. (2013) analysis of four waves of the General Social Survey (GSS) found that attitudes toward LGBT people directly relate to income levels and educational attainment. Generally, those with more money or more education are more accepting of the LGBT community than their less wealthy and less educated counterparts. In the study conducted in several waves—in 2004, 2006, 2008, and 2010—the findings for the majority of non-Hispanic White Americans (easily separated by socioeconomic status) lends credence to the conclusion that the higher one's class status, the more inclined one is to be socially liberal.[31] However, noting an inexplicable "middle-class" persistence of anti-same-sex marriage views among Blacks, Perry et al. find that the attitudes of middle-class Blacks sharply diverge with those of their White counterparts, disapproving of gay marriage at a rate of 90 percent and 60 percent, respectively.

Yet knowing this divergence exists versus understanding its broader social implications are two different animals. Obama's public support of LGBTQ equality has accelerated a preexisting trend toward social acceptance. In Black communities, however, the social stigma of an LGBTQ identity still exists, and it seemingly resides most strongly among the Black middle class. Most specifically, the coupling of the *perception* of widespread Black homophobia, and the *actual presence* of Black homophobia may be rooted in cultural differences among races. The Social Justice Sexuality Project (SJSP), which was a comprehensive study conducted in 2010, surveyed several thousand individuals at LGBTQ events. Presumably, all of these individuals identified as LGBTQ, as indicated by the survey. The respondents were a diverse population by gender, racial, and ethnic identities, religious beliefs, and socioeconomic status. The survey found that among those who identified as Christian, there was a sharp divergence in perceived discrimination.

Among the participants who identified as "Black" and those who identified as "White," the majority fell under a broad umbrella of Christianity. Yet these two racial groups split in their response to a question about racially segregated intolerance toward LGBTQ individuals. The Black respondents overwhelmingly felt that homophobia was a problem in their community.[32] The White respondents did not. Interestingly, the same Black cohort went on to indicate they believed that homophobia was a problem in *all* racial communities.[33] Conversely, the White respondents overwhelmingly disagreed with this statement, indicating that they felt homophobia was neither a problem within their racial community nor within *any* racial community.[34]

These findings indicate several important things about societal homophobia vis-à-vis both presence and perception along racial lines. First, it can be said that Blacks generally feel that homophobia is a bigger problem in the Black community than Whites feel that it is a problem in the White community. Whether this variance is due to the actual presence of homophobia or merely the perception of homophobia is actually irrelevant, and we will take the participants responses at their face value. What is interesting, however, is that the respondents' perception of homophobia in racial communities is heavily dependent upon the participant's own racial experience. In other words, the respondents to this survey tend to project the state of their own racial community into the broader racial context, assuming that everyone else's challenges are similar to their own. This is particularly problematic for LGBTQ Blacks, for marginalization of these communities often has led to increased feelings of depression and discrimination. Black LGBTQ individuals face many more problems in terms of social discrimination than do their White counterparts. Virtually every metric available indicates that LGBTQ African Americans are more concerned with and are at greater risk for homelessness, disease, joblessness, and incarceration. A 2014 African American LGBT Community Survey found that the vast majority of Black members of the LGBT community surveyed who identified as gay or bisexual men or women felt the "political and social issues" that most concerned them included racial discrimination, LGBTQ discrimination, poverty, affordable health care, unemployment, and affordable housing. All were considered more important than marriage equality.[35]

It is plausible that many may therefore conclude the Black LGBTQ persons' perceptions are in part due to the perceived homophobia within the Black community itself, combined with historic individual, systemic, and structural American racism. The findings of the Social Justice Sexuality Survey, however, cautions against a simplistic narrative, offering critical insight into potential underlying causes of Black homophobia.

For years, conventional wisdom has insisted that Black homophobia was due, in a large part, to higher levels of Protestant Christianity among Blacks. The numbers from this survey and several other recent projects refute this thinking. They show that Blacks are just as religious as Whites and indeed less religious than other racial and ethnic minorities; Hispanics, for example are overwhelmingly Catholic. Yet according to a poll conducted by Quinnipiac University, 54 percent of Catholics believe that same-sex marriage should be universally legal.[36] Clearly, according to the most recent research, religiosity in and of itself cannot bear the sole responsibility for perpetuating Black homophobia. And as Perry and Irizarry have found, even among the so-called Black Church community, attributing homophobia to "the Church" is quite the misnomer, as its parishioners are wholly less homophobic than is the largely male (older and often less educated) church leadership.[37]

Select Analysis of Key Obama Administration LGBTQ Policy Initiatives[38]

To varying degrees, the aforementioned surveys assessed the support for same-sex marriage among Black and White Americans over the last decade. As attitudes on homosexuality and same-sex marriage liberalized, the election of Barack Obama provided the opportunity for Black LGBTQ Americans to seek additional federal protections. But this process was challenging as the leaders in the LGBT movement privileged marriage equality as the cornerstone issue even though marriage was not among the top priorities of Black LGBTQ Americans. Until Obama's second term, Black leaders largely did not press him on being accountable to a "Black agenda," and even then, it largely included nothing on LGBTQ matters.

Executive Actions

While Obama did not support same-sex marriage during his first term, this administration aggressively reformed the government's various policies regarding HIV/AIDS. In October of 2009, the Department of Health and Human Services (DHHS) effectively ended the ban on HIV positive visitors and immigrants from entering the country.[39] This marked the first significant departure from the Bush-era doctrine, which had instituted several anti-LGBTQ discriminatory policies, which only served to further societal stigma. The repeal of the HIV positive ban on traveler ingress was one of the first acknowledgments from the federal medical community that HIV/AIDS should *not* be stigmatized, unlike practices in previous administrations (e.g., the Reagan administration).[40] And there were additional directives that the president put into place by virtue of his executive authority. During Obama's first year in office, he launched directives that were designed to give same-sex partners' full protection under the law, a fight that would effectively last until the *Obergefell v. Hodges* Supreme Court ruling in June 2015. The president started this new policy agenda with two presidential memos, directing all federal agencies to extend all the benefits that they legally could to same-sex couples who were federal employees.[41] This was critically important for Black LGBTQ Americans given Blacks, and Black women, make up a large share of the federal workforce. In 2014, about 18.1 percent of federal employees were Black. This is significantly higher rate than in the civilian workforce at large, where 10.4 percent of workers were Black during the same period. Of the federal employees who were Black, most of them were women. Office of Personnel Management (OPM) data indicates that the share of workers who are Black women is roughly twice as high in the federal workforce as it is among the greater civilian workforce.[42] It is important to note that during this time, most federal employees lived in states where same-sex marriage was not yet legal (e.g., Virginia and Maryland)—and states with relatively higher Black populations on average. Therefore, if someone was in a same-sex relationship, chances were that it was not recognized in any way by the state and, by extension, his/her employer. This changed the agenda to deliberately be inclusive, despite what the letter of the law said.

In January 2010, OPM extended coverage of the "equal employment opportunity" clause to encompass one's gender identity,[43] thereby making the government an employer that was decidedly friendlier toward transgender and nongender conforming individuals. Then in June 2010, the OPM gave a final policy change, allowing same-sex domestic partners to receive benefits such as long-term care insurance as well as funeral and sick leave.[44] The OPM went even further in 2012, by reclassifying the families of same-sex employees from "insurable" to those officially extended health, dental, and life insurance benefits, as well as retirement pensions and flex accounts for same-sex partners.[45] Each change in policy occurred at the direction of the president.

These extensions of benefits and reclassification of "the family" under the broad direction were relatively small victories for the then nascent Obama presidency. They were also relatively mitigated because the policies did not receive the added force of legislative support from the then Democratic-led Congress. And now, these policies are null and void under the Trump administration.

Legislation

The most substantive policy victories came in the form of major legislation changes during the Obama's first and second terms. The domino that started the ripple effect toward equality is undoubtedly Obama signing the Matthew Shepard and James Byrd Jr. Hate Crimes Prevention Act.[46] They reclassified hate crimes to protect against one's sexual identity or one's perceived sexual orientation. What is most important about this extension of the hate crimes law is it shifted the burden toward the intent of the crime, rather than the actual outcome itself. In other words, it does not matter if someone is *actually* LGBTQ or not. Rather, if he or she (or they) are the victim of a crime because the perpetrator *perceived* they were not heterosexual, the crime still qualifies as a hate crime. The demonization of LGBTQ hate crimes is incredibly important in shaping public opinion, mainly because it lumps LGBTQ hate together in the same historically reviled categories such as racism and sexism, thereby aligning the interests of the LGBTQ community with the civil rights interests of other historically marginalized persons.

The successful passage of the Affordable Care Act (ACA) is the most impactful achievement of the Obama administration. Arguably, the ACA is also Obama's most important legacy to any marginalized group, especially Black LGBTQ people. Many Black Americans have preexisting conditions, like HIV, for example. (Medicaid is the single largest source of health coverage for those who are living with HIV in the US). Moreover, the historic nondiscrimination protections of the ACA implemented major changes in our nation's health care system and ultimately served to significantly increase the number of Black and LGBTQ Americans with access to health care. According to the Kaiser Family Foundation, "Uninsurance declined and Medicaid coverage increased significantly for [the LGBTQ] population after the implementation of the ACA. . . . Under the ACA, LGB people experienced reductions in the uninsurance rate between 2013 and 2016." Section 1557 of the ACA prohibits discrimination due to "race, color, national origin, sex, age, or disability" in any program that receives federal funding. The Obama administration interpreted this clause to include gender identity and sex stereotyping. Thus, a person cannot be denied coverage due to her/his transgender identity, and any coverage must provide treatment consistent with the insured person's gender identity.

The potential repeal of the ACA, a hallmark of the Trump and the GOP agenda, would be devastating for Black LGBTQ Americans. As Julie Moreau has found, "according to Jen Kates, Vice President and Director of Global Health and HIV Policy at the Kaiser Institute, the ACA has made a [']significant difference['] for the LGBTQ community . . . : The ACA actually decreased the uninsured rate among LGBTQ folks more than other populations."

Additionally, a study by the Urban Institute found that the percentage of uninsured lesbian, gay, and bisexual adults fell from 28 percent to 11 percent between June 2013 and March 2015.[47] For Black Americans, health coverage matters.[48] According to the Center for Budget and Policy Priorities, "Health coverage is especially important for African Americans and other racial and ethnic minorities because they often have worse health status than their White counterparts. African Americans live with chronic conditions such as diabetes, heart disease, and HIV/AIDS at far greater rates than other racial groups."[49] Thus, that the ACA has led to millions more Blacks receiving insurance coverage matters tremendously to Black LGBTQ persons. The ACA, for example, helped to lower the uninsured rate for nonelderly African Americans between 2013 and 2016, from 18.9 percent to 11.7 percent. But, given that most Blacks yet reside in southern states without Medicaid expansion, it remains critical that the ACA be retained for Black LGBTQ Americans.

Equally significant for Black and other LGBTQ American is the repeal of the "Don't Ask, Don't Tell" policy within the United States Armed Forces, signed on December 22, 2010. Ironically, the Don't Ask, Don't Tell doctrine was initiated under President Bill Clinton in an effort to reduce discrimination in the military. In reality, it had the opposite effect, producing an environment which openly frowned upon LGBTQ service members. Unfortunately, this policy spelled out an obscenely discriminatory policy, which prohibited LGBTQ individuals from serving in the military under the "wisdom" that their presence would negatively impact unit cohesion. This policy spurred several well-documented military suicides, cases of depression, and an unhealthy repression of a soldier's self-identity out of a desire to serve.[50] In 2010, however, this policy changed, as Colin Powell—former secretary of state, four-star general, and former head of the Joint Chiefs of Staff—expressed his divergence from the DADT policy. On February 4, 2010, Powell gave an interview with the *Washington Post*, in which he stated that repealing the DADT rule was "the right thing to do." He justified his positions by saying that "society changes," acknowledging that "[society is] where we get our soldiers from."[51] Obama's first secretary of defense, Robert Gates, also threw his support behind the issue, calling on the military to "get it done."[52] Less than one year later, on December 22, 2010, the law was repealed, formally allowing homosexual men and women to openly serve in the military. This represented a significant departure from traditional wisdom on LGBTQ issues and opened the door to a more consistent dialogue on equal treatment. President Obama's argument supported the notion that since a soldier is asked to defend the nation, that nation should accept his or her sexuality or gender identity/expression.

Court Decisions and Laws

Perhaps bowing to pressure from White-gay-male-led lobbying groups who argued the significance of marriage rights *to them*, in February 2011, President Obama came out in support of repealing the Defense of Marriage Act (DOMA) and directed the Justice Department to no longer defend it.[53] That law defined marriage as between a man and a woman or only involving heterosexual unions. To clarify federal language, DOMA was instituted due to conservative concerns with the gay marriage issue. It nipped in the bud gay marriage as a perceived "threat to traditional marriage." This repeal represented the most significant step in Obama's shift toward officially supporting the concept of same-sex marriage altogether. While not specifically in support of same-sex marriage at the time, President Obama's support for the repeal of DOMA indicated that his views were indeed shifting.

But DOMA was not entirely repealed. In 2013, the Supreme Court struck down section 3 of DOMA, in what came to be known as the *Windsor* decision. DOMA was, in fact, largely still intact, but the high court was able to overturn the key phrasing in section 3. This clause prohibited the federal government from recognizing same-sex marriage regardless of state laws. The Supreme Court, however, stopped short of overturning the entire law, still allowing individual states to deny marriage to same-sex couples. By the time the *Windsor* decision was reached in 2013, however, President Obama had already come out in support of full marriage rights. This action paved the way for the Supreme Court's ruling in 2015. In a 5–4 vote, the court affirmed the right for all couples to marry, irrespective of sexual orientation and gender. As written by Justice Anthony Kennedy, the majority opinion stated his belief that, "no union is more profound than marriage, for it embodies the highest ideals of love."[54] The overturning of the previous ruling which relegated marriage decisions to the states is easily the most profound victory for the Obama administration on LGBTQ issues, even though the achievement was not high on the priority list of Black LGBTQ Americans. By 2015, President Obama was named "Ally of the Year" and became first sitting president to ever grace the cover of *Out*, a LGBTQ magazine.

Targeted Universalism and Obama Administration Black LGBT Support

In previous sections, I discussed President Obama's support of the LGBTQ community by referencing executive actions, policy initiatives, and court verdicts largely made possible by Obama's two Supreme Court appointments. What requires more speculation, however, is his commitment to the Black LGBTQ community. Targeted universalism is the attempt to build as much support for a policy initiative by spreading its perceived benefits as widely as possible, although clearly, its broad impact can positively impact a specific, intended constituency. While some prior research indicated Obama's use of universal language to make targeted appeals to Black communities,[55] many assumed that President Obama would pursue a domestic policy agenda that would be more overtly "pro-Black," given his history of working in the Black community in Chicago. Those who supported his 2008 presidential bid were unavoidably let down during his first term. The president sidestepped many of the issues pertaining to the Black community in particular.

And once Obama supported same-sex marriage, some Black Americans questioned publicly if their fellow community members would be less likely to vote for him in November 2012 because of Black coolness toward same-sex marriage.[56] We now know Black turnout in support of Obama's reelection was higher in 2012 than it was in 2008. In fact, political scientist Greg Lewis found that by 2012, there was not a statistically significant difference between Whites and Blacks concerning support for same-sex marriage.[57] As same-sex attitudes among Blacks changed, many of the president's policy initiatives increasingly sought to universalize both Black and LGBTQ interests, making them appeal to a new "moral majority."[58] (Refer to table 6.1) This adept political rhetoric strategy allowed Obama to address issues that primarily affected the Black LGBTQ community. By painting issues of import to Black LGBTQ Americans as though they are issues applicable to the electorate at-large, this increased the likelihood of majority-group support.

The theory of targeted/civic universalism is constructive, as it enables an analysis of Obama administration efforts beyond symbolic measures. For example, during the Obama administration, the Department of Agriculture focused on issues that helped both Black and LGBTQ persons but focused specifically and intentionally on the intersection of the two through the Rural Pride program. It was an initiative dedicated to fighting food hunger in deep southern states like Alabama and Mississippi. Other programs like First Lady Michelle Obama's "Let's Move" initiative directly addressed obesity, health, and food insecurity among African Americans but benefited Black LGBTQ persons as well. Studies show that "2.4 million (29%) LGBT adults experienced a time in [2013] when they did not have enough money to feed themselves or their family," and

TABLE 6.1. Policy Initiatives

Policy | Directive | Executive Action	Year
National HIV/AIDS Strategy	2009
Repealing "Don't Ask Don't Tell"	2010
OPM Gender Identity Provisions for Equal Opportunity	2010
Memo to HHS Allowing Visiting Access for Medicaid/Medicare Couples	2010
HHS Repealed Lifetime Ban on Gay Blood Donors 2010	2010
Prison Rape Elimination Commission (LGBT Provisions)	2011
Federal Partners in Bullying Prevention Steering Committee	2011
"It Gets Better" Video Campaign	2011
HUD LGBT Housing Equality and Crime Prevention Initiative	2012
DOJ Issue "PREA" LGBT Regulations	2012
Violence Against Women Act (Same-Sex Provisions)	2012
Affordable Care Act (LGBT Coverage Provisions)	2014
Equality Act Support Announcement	2015

Obama Policy Initiatives Impacting the Black LGBTQ Community*
Source: Compiled by author
Note: These policies address the facets of LGBT life that disproportionately affect the Black community within the United States. By allowing these policies to overlap with issues that are of particular concern to the Black community at large, the Obama administration was able to effectively universalize Black LGBT issues, under the larger LGBT umbrella. Issues such as disproportionate access to health care, fair housing, insurance, and the prevalence of orientation-based bullying have all been addressed by the Obama LGBT policy in order to mitigate their effects on the Black community.

that "LGBT people experience disproportionate levels of food insecurity and higher participation rates in the SNAP program, especially those raising children."[59]

In 2015, the White House added the first ever gender-neutral bathroom in a step that *Politico* described as "an example of how the administration has been advancing the discussion by raising the profile of transgender issues, an area of debate that is especially hotly contested right now."[60] The White House went even further by hosting the first ever Briefing on Trans Women of Color to mark the Trans Day of Visibility.[61] The briefing included over fifty women of color—including Black trans persons—and focused on the "uptick in murders of transgender women over the past several years . . . within a national political climate intent on legislating away transgender people's right to use the restroom or engage in school sports."[62]

Other initiatives established by the Obama administration also indicated how a universal policy or position can have a targeted benefit for Black LGBTQ persons. For example, the DHHS reversal on their HIV positive travel ban. In fact, during his time in office, President Obama aggressively advocated for HIV/AIDS funding increases, research grants, and HIV inclusive policy. In 2009, he rolled out his national strategy to address HIV/AIDS, which reauthorized uninsured and underinsured people who were living with HIV to receive proper health care.[63] Additionally, he provided a funding increase of $50 million for the AIDS Drug Assistance Program (ADAP) and another $31 million for HIV prevention services, such as educational programs and contraception access.[64] In 2012, President Obama continued his support for the ADAP program by announcing an additional $35 million for treatment and $15 million for preventative care.[65] His willingness to openly address and combat AIDS significantly distinguished him from past presidents and allowed him to simultaneously address the overlapping needs of the Black and LGBTQ communities. According to the DHHS, in 2010, the Black population represented a staggering 44 percent of individuals with *new* HIV infections.[66] In 2011, Blacks constituted 41 percent of the US population living with HIV.[67] These numbers are most problematic when we consider Blacks only made up 12 percent of the US population in 2010[68] and 13.2 percent of the population in 2014.[69] The disproportionate number of Black men with HIV demonstrates that the Black community faces the gravest burden when dealing with HIV- and AIDS-related health concerns. Inversely, in 2014, Whites comprised 77 percent of the national population but accounted for less than half of HIV-positive individuals.[70] On HIV/AIDS, the Black LGBTQ community is still in dire need of federal support.

In November 2015, The White House endorsed the Equality Act, indicating it would "advance the cause of equality for millions of Americans."[71] As another example of a universal bill with targeted implications, the Equality Act would amend the 1964 Civil Rights Act to ban discrimination on the basis of sexual orientation or gender identity; thus, it directly linked the historic civil rights bill with the fight for LGBTQ equality. This linkage perhaps was not lost on Black civil rights organizations, whose support for the Equality Act was less than enthusiastic. Some in the Black community expressed support for the act that banned

LGBTQ discrimination while also wishing such protections were not tied to the Civil Rights Act. According to the *Washington Post*, Wade Henderson, former president of the Leadership Conference on Civil and Human Rights, said at the time, "[The civil rights community has] 'supported the concept of the Equality Act from its very inception.' . . . It recognizes, however, there are questions that could benefit from further analysis."[72] Meanwhile, the nation's largest Latino advocacy group, the National Council of La Raza, declared support for the Equality Act on the day of its introduction, making an announcement via Twitter.[73] Civil rights activist and member of Congress John Lewis has also supported the legislation since its inception. On May 2, 2015, the Equality Act was reintroduced in the House of Representatives by Rep. David Cicilline (D-RI) and in the Senate by Sens. Jeff Merkley (D-OR), Tammy Baldwin (D-WI), and Cory Booker (D-NJ). According to the Human Rights Campaign, "the bill was introduced with 241 original cosponsors—the most congressional support that any piece of pro-LGBTQ legislation has received upon introduction."[74]

Even with its advocacy of LGBTQ and Black LGBTQ civil rights, the Obama administration made fewer strides regarding the appointment of LGBTQ persons to federal positions. By the end of his administration, he appointed more than 250 LGBTQ persons. In fact, of the top policy employment positions, President Obama filled 53.5 percent[75] of the positions with women or other minorities, including racial and orientation-specific minorities. While the appointment of LGBTQ persons was higher than any prior administration, most of the appointees were White, and of the non-White appointees, an even smaller number were Black. What is perhaps most problematic with these appointments is that, for the most part, Black LGBTQ appointees were limited to the few positions that served Black LGBTQ communities. Gay Black men, such as Greg Millett, who was the senior policy advisor to the Office of National AIDS policy, served a purpose that was both constructive and delimiting for Black LGBTQ people. It can be argued that since HIV/AIDS is a problem that disproportionately affects Black gay men, it is only reasonable that at least several people deciding AIDS policy should themselves be both Black and gay. Yet this kind of thinking inherently perpetuates the idea that Black LGBTQ persons should only be appointed to leadership over policy areas specific to Black people—e.g.,

AIDS, poverty, or incarceration. Cornelius Baker and Douglas Brooks were two other Black gay men who served on the now-defunct Presidential Advisory Council on HIV/AIDS (PACHA). In June 2017, PACHA experienced mass resignations, only to be followed by a collective firing in December 2017.[76] Of the Black lesbian women who were presidential appointees, the most powerful was Monique Dorsainvil, who was the deputy director of Advance and Special Events. While this was assuredly an important position, especially for the day-to-day life of any presidential administration, it surely cannot be classified as a senior leadership position with any significant influence on policy. No Black openly trans person was appointed by Obama, but Raffi Freedman-Gurspan, a Jewish trans woman of color adopted from Honduras, was appointed as senior associate director for Public Engagement. The president did quietly support greater diversity among the Black LGBTQ community through his federal judgeship nominations, including the confirmations of Florida judge Darrin Gayles to the district court for the southern district of Florida and Staci Michelle Yandle as a justice to the district court for the southern district of Illinois. However, they were but two of fifteen openly LGBT federal judicial appointees. Among ambassadors, none of Obama's openly LGBTQ nominations were Black Americans—not even for positions with predominantly Black populations, such as Haiti, South Africa, or the Dominican Republic.[77]

After Obama: Beyond the Rhetoric

President Obama's mostly unilateral and noncongressional routes for federal reform have spoken louder than his words. His administration garnered the most important legal victories and policy changes of any prior president to date. It is also important to note that the work is not done and yet has been substantively hindered by actions of the Trump administration, such as the mass firing of PACHA members. With no replacements, it can be reasonably assumed that the Trump administration is not interested in the issue. Surely, on many other matters identified by Black LGBTQ persons as priority issues, the Trump administration has yet to act.

While Obama moved the needle significantly on LGBTQ issues and even provided several new protections for LGBTQ individuals, these communities still confront an enormous number of societal and legal hurdles. I coded President Obama's four most important speeches that deliberately addressed the needs of LGBTQ Americans. This reveals the need for greater inclusivity with the president's official rhetoric. My analysis of the remarks he made at the Pride Month celebrations of 2011, 2013, and 2014, and the 2011 Human Rights Campaign dinner reveals the word "gay" being used a total of thirty-six times.[78] Contrasted with the complete lack of the words "race" or "Black" in any of these speeches, it is evident that President Obama's rhetorical priorities may have been *too universal* and should have had greater particularity. The words "lesbian" and "transgender" were only used seven times and ten times, respectively.[79] This may indicate a trend that conflates the word "gay" to refer to LGBTQ people as a monolithic whole. In this case, however, words matter. The content of Obama's speeches gives credence to the idea that despite this enormous progress, there is still plenty of work to be done. It is worth noting that Obama's 2011 World AIDS Day Speech included perhaps the only reference where Obama specifically acknowledged Black LGBTQ policy needs: "When new infections among young black gay men increase by nearly 50 percent in 3 years, we need to do more to show them that their lives matter."[80] This statement is a great example of targeted universalism, in that Obama is speaking about the impact of HIV/AIDS on all persons and yet specifically highlights the Black LGBTQ experiences as a targeted population.

It can hardly be expected that the first Black President of the United States and the first US President to aggressively pursue pro-LGBTQ policy initiatives could address all the problems facing varied LGBTQ citizens. This may be a variance of what the editors of this volume call the "inclusionary dilemma." Within the civil rights and larger policy arenas, Obama had political constraints as to the LGBTQ policy reforms he could make, and within the LGBTQ policy arena, his use of targeted universalism in policy and language limited his ability to directly address Black LGBTQ needs. Despite overwhelming odds, the Obama administration made significant contributions to improving the life chances of Black LGBTQ Americans through executive orders, federal directives, judicial decisions, and legislation. But the nation after Obama still has much further to go when it comes to addressing Black LGBTQ rights. The top priorities of Black LGBTQ people—housing, employment, education—remain largely unaddressed by federal elected officials. Sadly, many of the gains Black LGBTQ Americans achieved under the Obama administration have been rescinded by the Trump administration, thereby suggesting the need for congressional legislation to permanently enshrine protections for Black LGBTQ Americans. Meanwhile, Congress throughout much of the Obama administration, and especially during his second term, failed to pass several proposed laws supported by groups, such as the National LGBTQ Task Force, that would positively impact Black and Black LGBTQ Americans, including but not limited to: the Voting Rights Advancement Act (H.R. 2867; S. 1659), End Racial Profiling Act (H.R. 1933; S. 1056), HEAL for Immigrant Women and Families Act (H.R. 1974), Raise the Wage Act (H.R. 2150; S. 1150), Comprehensive LGBT Nondiscrimination Bill (H.R. 3185; S. 1858), and the Runaway and Homeless Youth Act (H.R. 1779; S. 262). There are many issues beyond same-sex marriage that directly impact the lives of Black LGBTQ Americans given the intersections of racism, homophobia/heterosexism, and poverty. For example, 40 percent of American youth experiencing homelessness are LGBTQ, and most of them are Black; Black lesbians have the highest rates of poverty among same-sex couples; and at least twelve Black transgender women were murdered during Obama's second term. Meanwhile, state lawmakers have introduced over a hundred anti-LGBTQ legislative efforts in one-third of the states. And the Human Rights Campaign fund has documented the Trump administration's multiple instances of open hostility toward LGBT rights and representation.[81] To be sure, millions of Black LGBTQ Americans wait in earnest for more progress—or to regain lost ground—after Obama.

NOTES

1 I wish to acknowledge the able research assistance of Isaiah R. Wilson and X. Loudon Manley for their significant collaboration.

2 Zeleny, Jeff, Kate Zernike. "Obama in Senate: Star Power, Minor Role." *New York Times*, March 9, 2008.

3 Fund, John. "President 'Present.'" *National Review*. September 3, 2013. www.nytimes.com.

4 Bowers, Becky. "President Barack Obama's shifting stance on gay marriage." *PolitiFact*. May 11, 2012. www.politifact.com.

5 Leibovich, Mark. "You and I Change Our Minds. Politicians 'Evolve.'" *New York Times Magazine*. March 15, 2015. www.nytimes.com.

6   Somnez, Felicia. "Biden 'Comfortable' with Same-Sex Marriage." *Washington Post.* May 7, 2012. www.washingtonpost.com.

7   Ibid.

8   Schwarz, Hunter. "Obama and Clinton Love to Celebrate Gay Marriage Now. Here's How Late They Were to the Party." *Washington Post.* June 26, 2015. www. washingtonpost.com.

9   Axelrod, David. *Believer: My Forty Years in Politics.* New York: Penguin Press, 2015.

10 Ibid.

11 Baim, Tracy. "Obama Changed Views on Gay Marriage." *Windy City Times.* January 14, 2009. www.windycitymediagroup.com.

12 Ibid.

13 Gabbatt, Adam, Ewan MacAskill. "Barack Obama Speaks Out and Declares Support for Same Sex Marriage." *Guardian.* May 9, 2012. www.theguardian.com.

14 Masci, David. 2014. "National Congregations Study Finds More Church Acceptance of Gays and Lesbians." Pew Fact Tank. www.pewresearch.org.

15 Virginia resident and "founding father" Thomas Jefferson, in proposing content for Amendment 8 to the US Constitution, titled "A Bill for Proportioning Crimes and Punishments," wrote, "Whosoever shall be guilty of Rape, Polygamy, or Sodomy with man or woman shall be punished, if a man, by castration, if a woman, by cutting thro' the cartilage of her nose a hole of one half inch diameter at the least:" http://press-pubs.uchicago.edu. And just in 2014, did the Virginia House of Delegates vote to eliminate an unconstitutional sodomy ban than made oral and anal sex a felony: http://thinkprogress.org.

16 Associated Press. "Supreme Court Strikes Down Texas Law Banning Sodomy." *New York Times.* June 26, 2003. www.nytimes.com.

17 Bazelon, Emily. "Why Advancing Gay Rights Is All About Good Timing." *Salon Magazine.* October 19, 2012. www.slate.com.

18 Center, Pew Research. "Changing Attitudes on Gay Marriage." Pew Research Center. July 29, 2015. www.pewforum.org.

19 Ibid.

20 Ibid.

21 Ibid.

22 Ibid.

23 Ibid.

24 See for example, Coates, Ta-Nehisi. 2009. "Prop 8 and Blaming the Blacks." *Atlantic.* January 7, 2009. www.theatlantic.com; and Williams, Joseph. 2012. "Black voters divided on gay marriage." *Politico.* May 9, 2012. www.politico.com.

25 See Coates. 2009. "Prop 8 and Blaming the Blacks."

26 Ibid.

27 Ibid.

28 Ibid.

29 US Census Bureau. Statistical Abstract of the United States: 2012. 131st edition. Washington, DC. 2011. www.census.gov.

30 Ibid.

31 Within the four-wave sample, the weighted distribution of the frequency of Blacks responding to the first question of whether or not "same-sex relations" "were wrong" was 654 respondents. Correspondingly, there were 714 Black respondents who responded to the second analyzed GSS query on whether or not there is a "right" for "same-sex marriage." More information on the study can be found here: Perry, Ravi K,Yasmiyn Irizarry, and Timothy J Fair. 2013. "Money Changes Everything? African American Class-Based Attitudes toward LGBT Issues." In *Living with Class: Philosophical Reflections on Identity and Material Culture*, eds. Ron Scapp and Brian Seitz. New York: Palgrave Macmillan.

32 Battle, Juan, Antonio Jay Pastrana, and Jessie Daniels. 2013. Social Justice Sexuality Project: 2010 National Survey, including Puerto Rico. ICPSR34363-v1. Ann Arbor, MI: Inter-university Consortium for Political and Social Research (distributor). http://doi.org/10.3886/ICPSR34363.v1.

33 Ibid.

34 Ibid.

35 See "African American LGBT Community Survey," Center for Black Equity. http://centerforblackequity.org. Survey Question Response Distribution: Gay and Bisexual Men, n = 1,165; Lesbians and Bisexual Women, n = 670; Under 35, n = 838; 45 and Over, n = 749.

36 Human Rights Campaign Staff. "Quinnipiac Poll: 54 Percent of American Catholics Support Same-Sex Marriage." *Human Rights Campaign Online*. March 8, 2013. www.hrc.org.

37 Irizarry, Yasmiyn A, and Ravi K. Perry. 2018. "Challenging the Black Church Narrative: Race, Class, and Homosexual Attitudes." *Journal of Homosexuality* 65(7): 884–911.

38 The Human Rights Campaign monitors an evolving compilation summary of data that compiles the "accomplishments" of the Obama administration in regard to LGBT equality. Accordingly, we do not examine every HRC identified "accomplishment." For brevity, we excise the major efforts, as defined by media attention, impact, timing, and those determined to be of significant benefit to Black members of the LGBTQ+ communities. For the complete list announced via press releases, see https://www.hrc.org.

39 United States Executive Office. "Obama Record for the LGBT Community." White House. www.whitehouse.gov.

40 Furthermore, they coupled the diagnoses of HIV and AIDS together, making the fallacious assumption that one went hand in hand with the other. Research has long indicated that HIV is only spread through bodily fluids, which are most concerning for those engaging in unprotected sex or exchanging intravenous drugs. AIDS is an acquired syndrome of HIV and is not coupled with the virus in many cases.

41 Ibid.

42 See Jamieson, Dave. "The GOP War with the Federal Workforce Will Hurt Black Workers the Most." *Huffington Post*, January 5, 2017. www.huffingtonpost.com.

43 Ibid.
44 Ibid.
45 Ibid.
46 Ibid.
47 See Karpman, Michael, Laura Skopec, and Sharon K. Long. 2015 "QuickTake: Uninsurance Rate Nearly Halved for Lesbian, Gay, and Bisexual Adults since Mid-2013." Urban Institute Health Policy Center, April 16, 2015. http://hrms.urban.org. Also see Moreau, Julie. 2017. "How Repeal of Affordable Care Act Could Impact LGBTQ Community" NBC News, January 21, 2017. www.nbcnews.com.
48 See Artiga, Samantha et al., *Key Facts on Health and Health Care by Race and Ethnicity*. Kaiser Family Foundation, June 2016. http://files.kff.org.
49 See Baily, Peggy et al. "African American Uninsured Rate Dropped by More Than a Third Under Affordable Care Act: Repealing ACA and Cutting Medicaid Would Undercut Progress." Center on Budget and Policy Priorities, June 1, 2017. www.cbpp.org.
50 Braswell, Harold, and Howard I. Kushner. 2012. "Suicide, Social Integration, and Masculinity in the US Military." *Social Science and Medicine* 74(4): 530–536.
51 DeYoung, Karen. "Colin Powell Now Says Gays Should Be Able to Serve Openly in the Military." *Washington Post*. February 4, 2010. www.washingtonpost.com.
52 Ibid.
53 See Associated Press. 2011. "Obama: DOMA Unconstitutional, DOJ Should Stop Defending in Court." *Huffington Post*, February 23, 2011. www.huffingtonpost.com.
54 Kerr, Orin. "What's in the Same-Sex Marriage Ruling." *Washington Post*. June 26, 2015. www.washingtonpost.com.
55 See Perry, Ravi K. 2011. "Kindred Political Rhetoric: Black Mayors, President Obama and the Universalizing of Black Interests." *Journal of Urban Affairs* 33(5) (December):567–590.
56 See Toure. 2012. "Will Black Voters Punish Obama for His Support of Gay Rights? The President Might Be on the Right Side of History, but He's on the Wrong Side of a Crucial Voting Bloc." Time, May 9, 2012. http://ideas.time.com.
57 See Demby, Gene. 2013. "Crunching the Numbers on Blacks' Views on Gays." *Code Switch*. National Public Radio, May 2, 2013. www.npr.org .
58 Stephanie Coontz argues that new coalitions of Americans who embrace LGBT issues have become the moral majority with influence: Coontz, Stephanie. 2015. "Now who's the moral majority." CNN.com, April 6, 2015. www.cnn.com.
59 Gates, Gary. "L.G.B.T. People Are Disproportionately Food Insecure." 2014. Unpublished manuscript. www.semantic scholar.org.
60 Wheaton, Sarah. "Latest White House Feature: Gender-neutral Restroom." *Politico*. April 8, 2015. www.politico.com.
61 "Historic White House Briefing on Trans Women of Color Marks Trans Day of Visibility." National Center for Transgender Equality (blog). March 31, 2015. www.transequality.org.

62 Ibid.

63 United States Executive Office. "Obama Record for the LGBT Community." White House. www.whitehouse.gov.

64 Ibid.

65 Ibid.

66 Centers for Disease Control. "HIV in the United States: At a Glance." March 2015. https://stacks.cdc.gov.

67 Ibid.

68 Ibid.

69 Department of Housing and Urban Development. "Census Quick Stats." Accessed September 25, 2015. http://quickfacts.census.gov.

70 Ibid.

71 Eilperin, Juliet. 2015. "Obama Supports Altering Civil Rights Act to Ban LGBT Discrimination." *Washington Post*. November 10, 2015. www.washingtonpost.com.

72 Ibid.

73 Johnson, Chris. 2015. "Will Civil Rights Groups Support Equality Act?" *Washington Blade*, July 29, 2015. www.washingtonblade.com.

74 See "The Equality Act." Human Rights Campaign. www.hrc.org.

75 Eilperin, Juliet. "Obama Has Vastly Changed the Face of the Federal Bureaucracy." *Washington Post*, September 20, 2015. www.washingtonpost.com.

76 See Guarino, Ben. 2017. "Trump Administration Fires All Members of HIV/AIDS Advisory Council." *Washington Post*, December 29, 2017. www.washingtonpost .com.

77 Refer to various sources: "Presidential Appointments Initiative." 2013. Victory Institute, www.victoryinstitute.org. "White House Hires Its First Openly Transgender Staffer." 2015. PBS News Hour, www.pbs.org, August 15. Halloran, Liz. 2014 "Black Openly Gay Judge Would Be Federal Bench's First." NPR, www.npr. org, February 5. Johnson, Chris. 2014 "Lesbian Judicial Nominee Sails through Hearing." *Washington Blade*, March 12. www.washingtonblade.com. Itkowitz, Colby. "The Six Openly Gay U.S. Ambassadors Were Together in One Room." *Washington Post*, March 25, 2015.

78 United States Executive Office. "President Obama and the LGBT Community." Accessed Sep. 20, 2015. White House. www.whitehouse.gov.

79 Ibid.

80 See Obama, Barack. 2011. "Remarks by the President on World AIDS Day." White House, December 1, 2011. https://obamawhitehouse.archives.gov.

81 Acosta, Lucas. 2020. "The Real List of Trump's 'Unprecedented Steps' for the LGBTQ Community." In Human Rights Campaign Fund: Human Rights Campaign Fund, June 11. www.hrc/blog.org.

PART II

Public Policies

7

Black Federal Judges and Civil Rights in the Age of Obama

SHENITA BRAZELTON WITH DIANNE M. PINDERHUGHES

One of the most important components of a presidential legacy is the appointments to the federal judiciary. Because federal judicial appointments are for lifetime tenure, the impact is longstanding. John Marshall's decree declaring the role of the judicial branch to "say what the law is" confers broad authority to the third branch of government. The power of the judiciary is expansive because the US Supreme Court is the final arbiter of the Constitution. Through judicial appointments, a president can appoint ideologically congruent judges, thus having a powerful influence on the way the Constitution is interpreted. Not only does the judiciary define the constitutional powers of the president and Congress, it delineates the rights and liberties of individuals. When the political branches of government have failed to act, the judiciary has served as the counter majoritarian institution protecting civil rights. Particularly, minorities have turned to the courts to seek redress from grievances of civil rights violations. Because of the historical role the judiciary has in the area of civil rights, we explore the impact of judicial appointments by President Barack Obama as the first African American president.

Specifically, we examine the demographics of the federal judiciary and the impact President Obama had on diversifying the federal bench. We discuss the record-breaking number of women and minorities Obama appointed to federal courts at all levels. Considering the historic and current struggles of African Americans in attaining civil rights, we focus our discussion on the appointment of Black federal judges. We highlight the historic firsts for African American appointees and the continuing need for Black federal judges, particularly in the South. We also discuss the inclusionary dilemma in the context of President Obama's selections for staffing the federal judiciary. We discuss Obama's decision not to

TABLE 7.1. Judicial Appointments by President

President	Total Minority Judges[1]	Black Judges (Total)	Black Judges District Courts	Black Judges Circuit Courts	Minority Justices US Supreme Court
Roosevelt	0	0	0	0	0
Truman	2	2	1	1	0
Eisenhower	1	1	1[2]	0	0
Kennedy	4	3	2	1	0
Johnson	13	10	7	2	1 (Marshall—1967)
Nixon	11	6	6	0	0
Ford	6	3	3	0	0
Carter	58	37	28	9	0
Reagan	23	7	6	1	0
GHW Bush	19	11[3]	10	2	1 (Thomas—1991)
Clinton	90	61[4]	53	9	0
GW Bush	58	24	18	6	0
Obama (2009)	120	61[5]	53	9	1 (Sotomayor)

1. Minorities identified are African Americans, Latinos, Asian Americans, and Native Americans.
2. Appointment to the US Court of Customs, which is presently organized as the US Court of International Trade.
3. The total is 11, considering President Bush appointed Timothy Lewis to the District Court and to the Third Circuit. Bush also appointed Clarence Thomas to the DC Circuit Court and to the Supreme Court.
4. The total is 61, considering President Clinton appointed Johnnie Rawlinson to the District Court and to the Ninth Circuit.
5. The total is 61, considering President Obama appointed Andre Davis to the District Court and to the Fourth Circuit.
Source: The Federal Judicial Center, www.fjc.gov

appoint a third African American justice to the Supreme Court, and we examine his record-breaking number of African American appointments to the lower federal courts. Despite these historic appointments, President Obama's appointment power was not unfettered. Recall from the introductory chapter of this volume that there are constitutional, political, and juridical constraints to the powers of all presidents, including Obama. His judicial appointment power was subject to the advice and consent of the Senate. We discuss the historic delays and challenges President Obama faced in nominating judges in view of a Republican Senate. The confirmation of federal judges, particularly Supreme Court nominees, has grown increasingly ideological, especially since the failed confirmation of Robert Bork in 1987.[1] We then examine the gains, or lack thereof, in nominating African Americans to the federal bench. We also assess the impact of President Obama's appointments given the record number of vacancies that were remaining at the end of his presidency, leaving an opportunity for President Donald Trump to fill these remaining positions. Finally, we assess the impact of Obama's appointees in view of voting rights litigation. Voting rights are particularly pertinent for racial minorities who have been historically denied these rights but have made gains in electing minorities to public office. To provide an accurate assessment of Obama's judicial appointments, we first examine diversity in the federal judiciary from a historical perspective.

A Historical Perspective of Diversity in the Federal Judiciary

The legacy of Obama's appointments to the federal judiciary is best assessed in view of the long struggle of appointing minority judges. In 1937, William H. Hastie was the first African American appointed to a federal judgeship. Although his appointment was a significant first, it was not a lifetime appointment; his appointment was for a fixed term to a federal district court in the Virgin Islands.[2] Hastie later ascended to one of the highest and most prestigious positions with an appointment to Third Circuit in 1950. At the time of his circuit court appointment, he was only one of two African Americans on the federal bench. In 1945, Irvin C. Mollison was the first African American to attain a lifetime federal judgeship with an appointment by President Franklin D. Roosevelt to the US Customs Court. President Dwight D. Eisenhower followed Roosevelt's steps by nominating Scovel Richardson to the US Customs Court in 1957. Richardson's appointment made him the third Black judge sitting on the federal bench.

African Americans gained some momentum when President John F. Kennedy appointed three Black judges, including the appointment of the first Black judge to sit on a federal district court. It was President Lyndon Johnson who appointed significantly more African Americans, having ten appointed to the federal bench. Most notable was Johnson's historic appointment of Thurgood Marshall to the US Supreme Court in 1967. However, the Nixon and Ford administrations appointed fewer minority judges than Johnson, creating a dearth of such judges on the federal bench. African Americans did not realize substantial gains in judicial appointments until the administration of President Jimmy Carter.

Before the Carter administration, there had been an overwhelming lack of diversity at all levels of the federal bench. At the beginning of Carter's term, there were 20 African American judges (3.5 percent of the judiciary) and 5 Latino judges (0.9 percent) out of a total of 521 federal judgeships.[3] President Carter was the first president who to sought to affirmatively identify and appoint a significant number of women and minorities to the federal bench. To increase diversity, President Carter created the US Circuit Judge Nominating Commission to affirmatively seek women and minority candidates for federal judgeships. With the utilization of the commission, the Carter administration increased the number of African American judges to 37 and Latino judges to 16.[4]

Carter's efforts began a trend among his Democratic successors in affirmatively seeking to appoint diverse candidates to the federal judiciary. However, appointments of his Republican successors lacked racial diversity. President Ronald Reagan only appointed 24 minority judges, while George H. W. Bush appointed 21. Both Republican presidents lacked a significant number of appointments of African American judges with Reagan and H. W. Bush appointing 7 and 13 Black judges, respectively. Of the Republican presidents, George W. Bush appointed more minorities than Reagan and H. W. Bush combined. President G. W. Bush appointed a total number of 58 minority judges, with 24 African American appointees. President Bill Clinton appointed 91 minorities, including 61 African Americans. The trend for Democratic presidents is the appointment of significantly more minority candidates than Republican presidents.

President Obama's Appointments of Minority Judges to the Bench

President Obama continued the pattern of his Democratic predecessors in appointing a larger number of women and minority judges. Most notably, Obama made history by appointing Sonia Sotomayor, the first Latina, as well as the third woman, to sit on the Supreme Court. He continued to make history by appointing the fourth woman with the nomination of Elena Kagan. In sum, Obama appointed a total of 136 women (41.9 percent of all appointees), 61 African Americans (19.1 percent), 36 Latino (11.3 percent), 21 Asian Americans (6.3 percent), and 1 Native American (0.3 percent). These appointments surpass the number of prior presidential appointments for women and every racial minority group. In this chapter, we focus on Obama's appointments of African Americans to the federal judiciary. We explore the impact of the presence of Obama's Black appointees to the federal district and circuit courts, as well as the historic appointment of Justice Sotomayor and the impact of Obama's inclusionary dilemma insofar as his choice to not nominate an African American to the US Supreme Court.

Historically, federal district courts—the trial courts of the federal system—have been the primary institution enforcing civil rights to protect minorities. Particularly, African Americans have utilized the federal district court as the predominant vehicle for retaining redress of civil rights grievances.[5] The power of federal district courts goes beyond declaring discriminatory laws unconstitutional. District courts have power to oversee school desegregation plans, issue injunctions preventing the enactment of discriminatory voting laws, and redraw legislative district lines to protect and ensure the power of minority voters.

Because of the broad remedial powers of the federal district courts, appointments to these courts present an expansive opportunity for a president to influence jurisprudence to further his policy preferences. Additionally, the president can make the greatest number of appointments to federal district courts because of the sheer number of judgeships. There are 94 district courts with 663 judgeships authorized by Congress. Since the presidency of Ronald Reagan, presidents have appointed more than 250 judges to the federal district courts, comprising more than 35 percent of all district court judgeships. Therefore, appointments to the federal district courts present an opportunity for presidents to further their policy agenda by appointing ideologically congruent judges.[6] To achieve a federal bench that is reflective of the president's priorities, some presidents (namely Democratic presidents) seek to appoint diverse racial minority appointees.

Prior to the presidency of Obama, racial minorities comprised 19.8 percent of all judges sitting on federal district courts. Recognizing the importance of these appointments, 36 percent of President Obama's district court nominees belong to a racial minority, which is the greatest percentage of any president.[7] Obama nominated the largest percentage of African Americans of any prior president. He nominated 76 African Americans to federal district courts, representing 19.1 percent of all nominees.[8] Of those 76 African Americans who were nominated, he successfully confirmed 61 nominees. Additionally, he nominated 36 Latinos, 24 Asian Americans, 2 Native Americans, and 1 Pacific Islander.[9] Of these racial minorities, all Latino nominees were confirmed, while three Asian Americans and one Native American failed confirmation. Considering all of the nominees who were racial minorities, African Americans were the largest minority group that was confirmed. However, they were also among the largest minority group that were not confirmed by the Senate.

We discuss a few of the noteworthy African American Obama appointees and their impact on the federal bench. President Obama appointed Judge Debra Brown to the Northern District of Mississippi in 2013. She is the first African American woman appointed in Mississippi and sits as the only African American judge in that district. Judge Brown presided over *Cowan v. Bolivar County Board of Education*, a school desegregation case originating from a 1965 lawsuit. In 2016, Judge Brown rendered a decision requiring the consolidation of underfunded majority African American schools with majority White schools. The case was a historic victory for African Americans living in the Mississippi Delta, ending decades-long segregation and inadequate public school funding. President Obama also appointed Judge Carlton Reeves, who is the second African American federal judge in the history of Mississippi. Judge Reeves first became renowned[10] for giving a speech addressing racism, bigotry, and privilege during the sentencing phrase of a trial of three White men who were convicted of murdering an African American man. Judge Reeves also rendered a historic decision by ruling Mississippi's law prohibiting same-sex marriage unconstitutional. Other firsts include the appointment of Irene Berger of West Virginia and Wilhelmina Wright of Minnesota, who are the first Black women appointed in their respective states. Of the African Americans sitting on federal district courts, President Obama elevated four African American district court judges to a circuit court of appeals.

An appointment to the federal circuit court is among the most prestigious positions in the legal profession. Because the US Supreme Court grants certiorari in only 1 percent of appeals, federal circuit courts practically serve as the court of last resort for the vast majority of litigants. Due to the low rate of granting certiorari, federal circuit courts render the overwhelming number of decisions affecting states within their circuit. Among Obama's circuit court nominees is the appointment of Ojetta Thompson, the first African American appointed to the First Circuit. That court's jurisdiction encompasses Maine, Massachusetts, New Hampshire, and Rhode Island, as well as the US territory of Puerto Rico. Also of note is Obama's appointment of Raymond Lohier, the only active African American judge sitting on the Second Circuit, a position vacated by Justice Sonia Sotomayor.[11]

Of the three Supreme Court vacancies that arose during his term, Obama nominated one Latina (Sotomayor), one White woman (Kagan) and one White man (Merrick Garland). Obama successfully appointed two of these three nominees: one replacing a White woman, Sandra Day O'Connor, and the other replacing a White man, David Souter. Given Clarence Thomas's lack of support for policies benefiting the African American community, Obama could have appointed another African American to the court with stronger linkages to the Black community.

Obama may have viewed these Supreme Court vacancies as his inclusionary *judicial* dilemma based on the perception that the nomination of an African American was based on his Black racial identity and pressure from Black interest groups and legislators. Given the significant amount of attention Supreme Court nominees receive, Obama may have perceived the nomination of an African American as a constraint presented by the inclusionary dilemma. Due to less media coverage of appointments to the lower federal courts, Obama had significantly less political and institutional barriers to overcome in choosing to appoint a greater number of Black lower federal court judges, thus less likely presenting an inclusionary dilemma. Furthermore, Obama's approach to inclusion and diversity significantly benefited African Americans with his historic number of appointments of not only Black judges but members of all racial and ethnic minorities. Even though there may have been more barriers in nominating an African American to the Supreme Court in comparison to the lower federal courts, there yet remains a significant lack of diversity in states that have very few to no African Americans who sit on federal trial and appellate courts.

Persistent Disparities in African American
Judicial Appointments

Although the increased number of racial minority appointments is historic, racial diversity on the federal bench remains low, particularly in districts having high African American populations. There are 94 district courts, ranging from 2 to 28 sitting judges per district. New York's Southern District has the largest number of African American district court judges, totaling 7 of 28, four of whom are Obama appointees. However, African American judges remain underrepresented in key districts. There are no active Black judges in federal district courts in Savannah, Georgia or Shreveport, Louisiana. In fact, the district in which Savannah and Shreveport are situated have never seated an African American federal judge.

There is also a great need for minority representation on the federal circuit courts. Before the Obama administration, 14 African Americans judges sat on the federal circuit courts, comprising only 8.3 percent of circuit court judges. Obama appointed and the Senate confirmed 9 African American judges, including 4 women, to the federal circuit court, increasing the proportion to 12.6 percent. However, these statistics must be disaggregated to obtain an accurate assessment of the number of Obama's Black appointees to the federal bench. The Ninth Circuit is the largest circuit, having jurisdiction over California, Arizona, New Mexico, Oregon, Washington, Idaho, and Montana. Of the 29 authorized judgeships for the Ninth Circuit, there are only 2 African Americans, one of whom is an Obama appointee.

The lack of African American circuit court judges is particularly noteworthy in circuits in southern states. The Eleventh Circuit has jurisdiction over Alabama, Georgia, and Florida, with an average African American population of 22.5 percent. However, that circuit has only 1 African American judge of the 12 authorized judgeships for the court, therefore comprising only 8 percent of authorized judgeships. This statistic is even more troubling, considering that Alabama and Georgia have African American populations of 26.8 and 31.7 percent, respectively. The Fifth Circuit is another court that has a disproportionately low number of African American judges, seating 2 of 17 judgeships, or 12 percent of authorized judgeships. The Fifth Circuit governs federal law for Texas, Louisiana, and Mississippi—states that have the highest African American populations in the United States. Although the African American population of 12.5 percent in Texas is closer to the national average, the population in Louisiana and Mississippi of 32.5 and 37.6 percent is more than twice the national average. The lack of minority candidates on the federal bench is due in part to the Senate's delay and failure to confirm Obama's nominees, particularly minority candidates.

Historic Delays in the Senate

A significant component of the Obama legacy regarding appointments to the federal bench is the Senate's historic delays in confirming judicial nominees. The amount of time nominees waited until a Senate hearing and/or confirmation was unprecedented. This was due in substantial part to the unparalleled obstructionism of the Republican Congress. Although President Obama had nominated more than three hundred judges, he was unable to successfully appoint seventy-five judges, most notably Judge Merrick Garland to the US Supreme Court. We explore the extent of obstructionism of these delays as well as the impact the delays have had on the judiciary and particularly on African American nominees. We also discuss the extent racialized politics played a contributing factor in the obstructionism in judicial appointments for President Obama as the first African American president.

To accurately assess the extent of obstructionism, we first discuss the nomination process and the powerful role of the Senate. Pursuant to Article II, the president's power to appoint federal judges is subject to the Senate's "advice and consent." The Senate has employed this power by subjecting virtually all judicial nominees to the Senate's confirmation. Because of the impact and importance of nominees to the US Supreme Court, the president extends a substantial amount of time and energy choosing his nominees. In contrast, nominees to the lower federal courts are not typically "hand chosen" by the president. Rather, senators play a larger role by recommending potential candidates to the president when there is a vacancy in that senator's home state. Senators suggest potential candidates even when they are not of the president's party, although the president tends to nominate candidates closer to

his preferences. The president often consults with the home-state senator because of the norm of senatorial courtesy. That is, fellow senators
will support or oppose a nominee based on the recommendation of
the home-state senators. Senatorial courtesy is most often employed
through the process of the "blue slip." Once the president formally
nominates a candidate, the chair of the Senate Judiciary Committee will
send the home-state senators a blue slip of paper that asks whether they
support the president's nominee. If the senator fails to return the "blue
slip," the chair may not schedule a hearing to consider the nominee, let
alone schedule a confirmation vote on the Senate floor.

The norm of senatorial courtesy is strongest when the vacancy is in
the district court of the senator's state.[12] Since district courts are the trial
courts of the federal system, the court sits at the base of the judicial hierarchy, having minimal power to influence policy on a national scale. Thus,
presidents are less concerned of the impact of these courts on policy. For
senators, a district court vacancy affords them the opportunity not only to
make a recommendation based on patronage but also to seat a more ideologically congruent candidate that has power to impact the jurisprudence
in that senator's state. The influence of the president is more prominent for
circuit court vacancies since its jurisdiction spans several states.

Considering judicial nominations dating back to the Carter presidency, Obama had unparalleled challenges in the Senate. Most notably
was the failed confirmation of Judge Merrick Garland to the US Supreme Court. On March 16, 2016, President Obama nominated Judge
Garland of the DC Circuit Court to the US Supreme Court. President
Obama's prior appointments of Justices Elena Kagan and Sonia Sotomayor replaced two liberal justices, thereby maintaining the ideological
balance of the court. Justice Antonin Scalia's death in February 2016 presented President Obama with a third Supreme Court vacancy, which has
not occurred since the presidency of Ronald Reagan. This appointment
was particularly important, as Justice Scalia comprised a four-justice
conservative voting bloc, with Justice Anthony Kennedy serving as the
fifth "swing justice." President Obama's appointment would have shifted
the ideological composition of the Supreme Court toward a five-justice
liberal voting bloc.

Anticipating a difficult confirmation in the Senate, Obama chose
Garland, who was not only respected by Democrats but had been lauded

by Republicans. In addition to the considerations based on our discussion regarding the inclusionary dilemma, Obama's choice in Garland arguably was the least controversial. Despite Garland's bipartisan respect, Senator Mitch McConnell, chair of the Senate Judiciary Committee, not only refused to schedule a hearing on Garland's nomination but also refused to meet with the nominee. Garland's failed nomination holds the record for the longest Senate delay of a Supreme Court nominee of 310 days, which is more than twice as long as the prior record.

Senate Republicans' obstruction of Judge Garland reflects the obstruction Obama faced for his lower federal court nominees. Though Democrats gained a majority in the Senate in 2009, Republican senators insisted that President Obama consult with them for judicial nominees.[13] Although 83 percent of President Obama's nominees were confirmed, the time for scheduling and holding hearings on those nominees is unprecedented. Based on Goldman et al.'s (2013) and Slotnick et al.'s (2017) indexes of obstructionism, which was measured by examining the number of failed confirmations and delays of more than 180 days, the obstruction rate in 2009–2010 for Obama's district court nominees was 50.8 percent and 65 percent for circuit court nominees.[14] These rates are comparable to the rate of obstructionism under George W. Bush's administration. However, the obstruction rate skyrocketed in 2011 and 2012. The obstruction rates for Obama's district court nominees were 87.2 percent and 95.2 percent for his circuit court nominees. For the last two years of Obama's presidency, the Senate had completely obstructed Obama's nominees, having an obstruction rate for district and circuit court nominees of 98.3 percent and 100 percent, respectively. These rates far exceed that of any modern president. Because Senate Democrats lacked a filibuster-proof majority, they changed the rules in 2013 to only requiring a simple majority to invoke cloture for lower federal court nominees. Although Obama had more success after the Senate rules changed, delays and vacancies remained. Judicial vacancies not only impaired the functionality of the US Supreme Court, but numerous vacancies in lower courts significantly impaired the entire third branch of government. According to the Administrative Office of the US Courts, there were 29 vacancies categorized as a "judicial emergency," which was measured by the length of delays and number of case filings. For district courts, the number of cases pending for two to three years doubled from

2013 to 2015. These "judicial emergencies" were carried forward to the administration of Donald Trump. Most of these courts categorized as a "judicial emergency" are located in the South. District courts located in Texas had the greatest number of "judicial emergencies" with ten. The Eleventh Circuit—whose jurisdiction covers Alabama, Georgia, and Florida—has nine emergency vacancies.

The Senate's obstruction of Obama's lower court nominees had a significant effect on those who were African American. The Senate failed to confirm 69 of Obama's nominees, 16 of whom were African American. We highlight a few of these failed nominees. Among those is the failed nomination of US Attorney Jennifer May-Parker to the Eastern District of North Carolina. In 2013, President Obama nominated May-Parker given North Carolina Senator Richard Burr's previous recommendation of her to the position. However, Senator Burr withdrew his support for May-Parker by failing to return his blue slip to the Senate Judiciary Committee. After a delay without a hearing, President Obama renominated May-Parker in January 2014. But again, Burr failed to return his blue slip, thus ending May-Parker's candidacy to the federal bench. When questioned, Burr stated that he submitted a slate of names to the White House for district court vacancies but that a disagreement between his and the administration's preferred nominees resulted in a "stalemate."[15] Then in April 2016, President Obama nominated Patricia Timmons-Goodson, North Carolina's first African American female state supreme court justice. Despite an American Bar Association's unanimous rating of "well-qualified," Burr stated that he blocked Timmons-Goodson's nomination because the White House failed to consult him.[16] The confirmation of May-Parker or Timmons-Goodson would have filled a ten-year vacancy for the Eastern District, which holds the record for the longest judicial emergency in the nation. Moreover, either candidate would have been the first African American judge seated in that district in a state with an African American population of more than 20 percent.

We also highlight the failed nominations of two African American nominees for the Northern District of Georgia. In January 2011, President Obama nominated federal magistrate Judge Linda Walker, upon Georgia senators Johnny Isakson's and Saxby Chambliss's recommendation. Obama also nominated federal public defender Natasha Silas, a nominee not favored by the Georgia senators. The White House sought to confirm the two nominees as a slate. Isakson and Chambliss returned their "blue slips" for Walker but failed to do so for Silas. Although the Georgia senators did not state their reasons for their failure to support Silas, some believe is was due in part to her lower American Bar Association (ABA) rating. A substantial majority of the ABA Judiciary Committee rated Judge Walker as "well-qualified" but rated Ms. Silas as "qualified," along with a minority of the committee rating her as "not qualified."[17] However, scholars have presented evidence that ABA ratings are biased against African Americans and women.[18] In fact, African Americans who have similar professional credentials are 42 percent less likely than Whites to receive a high rating from the ABA. This highlights the subtle but significant persistence of race in shaping the judicial selection process. Women are likewise 19 percent less likely than men to receive a higher rating.[19] We also note the impact of delay on circuit court nominees. The Senate failed to confirm three African Americans to the circuit courts, including the nomination of Judge Abdul Kallon to the Eleventh Circuit. The confirmation of Judge Kallon would have seated the second Black active status judge on that court. The need of a second judge is imperative for a circuit whose jurisdiction governs a large minority population of Alabama, Georgia, and Florida.

The low rates of confirmation during the Obama administration can be explained by the utilization of racialized politics. Although evidence of racialized politics is well documented regarding the level of public support for and perception of President Obama's policies,[20] there is similar albeit anecdotal evidence of racialized politics from Republican members of Congress in appointments to the judiciary. The infamous shout of "You lie" from Rep. Joe Wilson during President Obama's 2009 congressional address is a vivid example of the racism and racialized politics that plagued the Obama presidency. This racialization was evident in Obama's appointments to the federal bench. Particularly, members of the Congressional Black Caucus (CBC) opined that some of the obstructionism of Obama's judicial nominations were because of the president's race.[21] In fact, Rep. James Clyburn stated that the obstructionism was reminiscent of the obstructionism during the passage of civil rights legislation in the 1950s and 1960s.[22] Also, CBC members expressed concern regarding obstructionism of African American judicial nominees.[23] This obstructionism perpetuated a number of vacancies on the federal bench. The obstructionism and resulting vacancies allowed President Trump to not only appoint a conservative justice in Neil Gorsuch but also provided Trump with the opportunity to fill numerous vacancies for positions that Republicans had blocked during Obama's presidency.

Federal Judges and Voting Rights

Similar to scholarship examining descriptive representation for minority members of legislative bodies,[24] scholarship has demonstrated the impact of judicial outcomes when minority judges are appointed to the bench. This scholarship tends to show that Black judges render decisions favorable to Black litigants and policies. Scholarship has demonstrated that African American district court judges are three times more likely to rule in favor of a plaintiff asserting an employment racial discrimination claim, and African American circuit court judges are more likely to uphold the constitutionality of race-based affirmative action programs.[25] Moreover, the presence of an African American judge on a circuit court panel increases the likelihood that their non-Black colleagues would vote to uphold the constitutionality of affirmative action. These studies highlight the importance of appointing Black judges to all levels of the federal judiciary. These appointments are particularly important given the current legal challenges to civil rights and, particularly, voting rights.

The lack of African American judges sitting on federal courts, particularly in southern states, has important consequences for adjudicating both civil and voting rights claims. The landmark Voting Rights Act of 1965 (VRA) afforded African Americans expansive protections from discriminatory voting practices in the South. Particularly, Section 4 of the VRA provided federal oversight for states that either had less than 50 percent of its voting age population registered to vote or did not vote as of the 1964 presidential election. Section 5 of the VRA required states that met these criteria to obtain permission, denoted as preclearance, from the Department of Justice or the DC Federal District Court to enact any change in a voting law. The federal government would grant preclearance if it determined that the proposed law would not deny or abridge any voting right on the basis of race or color. The role of the Department of Justice was particularly noteworthy given Eric Holder was appointed and served as its first African American attorney general.

In a 5–4 decision, the US Supreme Court in *Shelby County v. Holder* (2013) severely weakened the VRA by holding unconstitutional Section 4's formula for determining the states required to obtain preclearance. The court's majority, comprising of its conservative justices, determined that the formula set forth in Section 4 was outdated but, nonetheless, stated that Congress could pass legislation to update the formula to determine the states that would be covered under Section 5.[26] Most likely, the conservatives of the court acted strategically in rendering their decision, cognizant that it was unlikely to invite a congressional override given a Republican Congress.[27] Now, states are no longer required to seek preclearance from the federal government. Shortly after the Supreme Court's decision in *Shelby County*, states that were subject to preclearance immediately began enacting voter ID laws. States having significantly large minority populations, such as Texas, North Carolina, Arkansas, and Virginia, enacted voter ID laws.

Therefore, the protections afforded minority voters under Section 5 are no longer effective. Preclearance under the VRA had placed the burden on states to establish that a proposed change in a voting law was not enacted with a discriminatory intent or had a discriminatory effect. Previously, if the state failed to obtain preclearance before the law took effect, the state law was unenforceable. After *Shelby County*, a VRA remedy is now limited to plaintiffs and the federal government filing suit to seek an injunction or to challenge the law after its enactment. Now, plaintiffs must prove that a law has a discriminatory intent or effect. Therefore, the burden has shifted from states requiring them to establish the absence of a discriminatory intent or effect to plaintiffs and the federal government being required to prove any discriminatory intent or effect. Moreover, the primary duty of determining compliance with the VRA has now shifted from DOJ's and DC District Court's preclearance oversight to lower federal courts across the nation. Obama's appointments to the lower federal courts are particularly important in view of the role they now play in adjudicating voting rights claims. We now explore the impact of Obama's appointees and African American jurists regarding voting rights.

Since *Shelby County*, the Fourth, Fifth, and Eleventh Circuits now have a vital role in adjudicating VRA claims. These circuits have jurisdiction over states that had been required to seek preclearance, which were

Alabama, Georgia, Mississippi, South Carolina, Virginia, Louisiana, and Texas. After the swift enactment of voter ID laws, which have been found to disenfranchise minority voters,[28] the Obama administration's DOJ sued states that enacted onerous voter ID laws. Particularly, we examine litigation regarding North Carolina's and Texas's voter ID laws.

Two months after the Supreme Court's decision in *Shelby County*, North Carolina passed a voter ID law. Although the 1965 Voting Rights Act had not required the state of North Carolina to obtain preclearance, forty of its counties were required to do so. North Carolina's 2013 voter ID law not only required voters to present a government-issued photo ID but also restricted the number of days for early voting, eliminated same-day registration and preregistration for sixteen- and seventeen-year-old youths. The NAACP and DOJ filed lawsuits on the grounds that the new law discriminated against minority voters. Although a district court upheld the law, the Fourth Circuit struck down the law as a violation of the VRA. A three-judge panel held that the state legislature enacted the law with the intent to discriminate against African American voters.[29] Key to the court's decision was its Democratic-appointed judges, two of whom are Obama appointees. This decision did not come as a surprise as the circuit's ten Democratic appointees dominated the fifteen-member court. The Fourth Circuit's decision was particularly important given that the US Supreme Court declined to review the decision in denying certiorari. The President had much success in appointments to the Fourth Circuit, confirming six judges. Since circuit court panels are chosen randomly, these appointments raise the probability of empaneling liberal judges who are more likely to strike down discriminatory voting laws. Nevertheless, more conservative circuits have also struck down voter ID laws.

A district court in Texas and the Fifth Circuit both held that Texas's voter ID law was a violation of the VRA in *Veasey v. Abbott*. Deemed as one of the most restrictive voter ID laws in the nation, Texas had required its voters to present a limited list of government-issued identification. Although a gun license was an approved form of identification, a state college or university ID was insufficient. Obama appointees in the Fifth Circuit played a significant role in striking down the law. District Court Judge Nelva Ramos, a Latina Obama appointee, not only held that the voter ID law had a discriminatory effect but also held that the state legislature enacted the law with the discriminatory purpose of disenfranchising African American and Latino voters.[30]

On appeal to the Fifth Circuit, a three-judge panel upheld the decision on the grounds that the effect of the law discriminated against minority voters because those voters are less likely to possess the approved forms of identification.[31] What is even more noteworthy are the judges who sat on this panel. The Fifth Circuit is one of the more conservative circuits in the US, comprised of ten Republican appointees of its fifteen active judges. This circuit only has one Latino and two African American judges despite having high minority populations in the states under its jurisdiction. However, the panel that decided *Veasey v. Abbott* was not only comprised of two Democratic appointees but also two African American judges. Chief Judge Carl Stewart, a Clinton appointee, and district court Judge Nannette Brown, an Obama appointee, sat on *Veasey v. Abbott*'s panel. Chief Judge Stewart's appointment of Judge Brown to sit by designation may have been strategic. Typically, circuit court judges are randomly assigned to convene in a three-judge panel. Due to judicial vacancies, a circuit's chief judge has power to appoint district court judges within their circuit to fulfill the demands of the circuit's caseload. Because of the Fifth Circuit's two remaining vacancies, Chief Judge Stewart retains this appointment power. Of the seventy district court judges sitting within the Fifth Circuit, appointing one of the nine African American judges to sit on *Veasey v. Abbott*'s panel may have been a mechanism to increase the probability of striking down a voter ID law strongly championed by conservatives in a conservative circuit. A similar mechanism was used during the Civil Rights Era by Fifth Circuit's former Chief Judge Elbert Tuttle, who assigned liberal district court judges to sit on its circuit panels when adjudicating civil rights cases.[32] The third panelist, Judge Catharina Haynes, a George W. Bush appointee and author of the court's opinion, may also have been a strategic opinion assignment. Having a Republican-appointed judge author the court's opinion may have been a mechanism to help sway her fellow Republican-appointed judges upon the court's rehearing en banc.

In July 2016, the Fifth Circuit heard *Veasey v. Abbott* en banc, seating all fifteen of its active judges.[33] A majority of the court held that the voter ID law violated the VRA because it had a discriminatory effect for minority voters who disproportionately found it more difficult to obtain the requisite identification. The court's division en banc had a strong ideological tenor. Although one Reagan and three Bush appointees struck down the voter ID law, all of the five Democratic appointed judges joined the majority, and the remaining six conservatives dissented. Three of the five Democratic appointees are President Obama's nominees that replaced two George H. W. Bush appointees. Although the Texas legislature amended its voter ID laws in June 2017 in response to court orders that found the law discriminatory, Judge Ramos again held that the amended law disproportionately affected minority voters. The Fifth Circuit subsequently upheld the constitutionality of the voter ID law.

Conclusion

African American representation on the federal bench is consequential for jurisprudence, as its presence influences law in areas that directly affect minorities' civil rights, especially in voting rights. Justice Sotomayor was criticized for stating that she "would hope that a wise Latina woman with the richness of her experiences would more often than not reach a better conclusion than a white male who hasn't lived that life."[34] However, her comments allude to the notion that minority judges view litigants and their claims based on their varied life experiences. As previously discussed, empirical scholarship supports this claim. Our discussion demonstrates the significant effect African American jurists have on voting rights cases, particularly cases challenging voter ID laws. Clearly, the presence of African American judges has substantial and influential impact. As a group that has experienced discrimination, African American judges are arguably more cognizant of claims of discrimination; they are likely to share a degree of racial group consciousness and linked fate with other African Americans.

In view of the importance and influence of minority jurists, President Obama's appointments of diverse judges will have a lasting legacy on the federal bench. Obama nominated a historic number of African Americans to the federal judiciary. He also appointed a greater number of women and minorities of all races and ethnicities than his Democratic predecessors. Considering the historic number of minority appointments, the inclusionary dilemma was evident in selecting his nominees to the US Supreme Court evident in his choice not to nominate an African American to the court. Despite this choice, the policy positions of his two appointees, Elena Kagan and Sonia Sotomayor, tend to support the Black community. Obama's historic appointment of Sotomayor as the first Latina justice can be viewed as his desire to circumvent the inclusionary dilemma by fostering diversity and multiculturalism without being perceived as favoring the Black community. Alternatively, Obama may have perceived greater leeway in nominating more African Americans to the lower federal courts because these nominations were of a lower profile than the Supreme Court. These judges were able to fulfill some of Obama's policy objectives of protecting civil rights for racial and ethnic minorities. Particularly, Obama judicial appointments to the lower federal courts were key in several voting rights cases. Obama appointees sitting on courts of appeals often cast a critical vote, striking down discriminatory voting laws. However, Obama's ability to confirm all of his judicial nominees were stymied because he faced a Republican Senate for the majority of his presidency. Most notably was the failure to confirm Merrick Garland to the US Supreme Court. But Obama's inability to confirm Garland was also reflective of the opposition he faced in confirming many African American nominees to the bench.

Furthermore, the presidency of Donald Trump will likely limit the influence of President Obama's appointments, considering the individuals that President Trump has nominated during his first term in office. These jurists have been extremely conservative and overwhelmingly racially and ethnically homogenous. Considering the number of vacancies and conservative tenor of these nominees, President Trump's appointees are likely to stymie the impact of an Obama judiciary. However, these minority jurists will most likely serve as a check against Trump's conservative nominees.

NOTES

1 Epstein, Lee, René Lindstädt, Jeffrey A. Segal, and Chad Westerland, "The Changing Dynamics of Senate Voting on Supreme Court Nominees," *Journal of Politics* 68 (2006): 296.

2 Goldman, Sheldon, *Picking Federal Judges: Lower Court Selection from Roosevelt through Reagan*, New Haven: Yale University Press, 1997.

3 Scherer, Nancy, "Diversifying the Federal Bench: Is Universal Legitimacy for the US Justice System Possible?" *Northwestern University Law Review* 105 (2011): 587; "Biographical Directory of Federal Judges," Federal Judicial Center, accessed July 15, 2016, www.fjc.gov.

4 Scherer, "Diversifying the Federal Bench." "Biographical Directory of Federal Judges."

5 Scheingold, Stuart A., *The Politics of Rights: Lawyers, Public Policy, and Political Change*, Ann Arbor: University of Michigan Press, 2010.

6 Epstein, Lee, and Jeffrey A. Segal, *Advice and Consent: The Politics of Judicial Appointments*, New York: Oxford University Press, 2005.

7 "Demographic Diversity of President Obama's Judicial Nominees," Alliance for Justice, accessed July 7, 2016, www.afj.org.

8 Ibid.

9 President Obama also nominated four judges who identify as biracial. Two judges identify as African American and Hispanic, and two identify as Asian American and Hispanic.

10 Badger, Emily. "A Stunning Reckoning with Mississippi's Past, from a Black Judge Sentencing 3 White Men for a Lynching," *Washington Post*, February 18, 2015, www.washingtonpost.com.

11 While Judge Lohier is the only active Black judge sitting on the Second Circuit, there are also two Black judges with senior status sitting on the court. A federal judge can assume senior status when he or she attains the age of sixty-five and has at least ten years of service. A senior-status judge has a reduced caseload but retains his or her current active-status salary. Also, a senior-status judge has authority to conduct almost all of the duties of an active status judge but, among other things, serves as a chief judge or justice of a court. See Block, Frederic, "Senior Status: An Active Senior Judge Corrects Some Common Misunderstandings," *Cornell Law Review* 92 (2006): 533.

12 Epstein et al., "The Changing Dynamics of Senate Voting on Supreme Court Nominees." Steigerwalt, Amy, *Battle over the Bench: Senators, Interest Groups, and Lower Court Confirmations*, Charlottesville: University of Virginia Press, 2010.

13 Letter from Senator Richard Burr to President Barack Obama, July 21, 2009.

14 Goldman, Sheldon, Elliot Slotnick, and Sara Schiavoni, "Obama's First Term Judiciary: Picking Judges in the Minefield of Obstructionism," *Judicature* 97 (2013): 7; Slotnick, Elliot, Sara Schiavoni, and Sheldon Goldman, "Obama's Judicial Legacy: The Final Chapter," *Journal of Law and Courts* 5(2017): 363–422.

15 "Q&A: Burr Talks Gun Rights, Sequester, Same-Sex Marriage," *WRAL.com*, March 27, 2013, www.wral.com.

16 Press Release of Senator Richard Burr on April 29, 2016, www.burr.senate.gov.

17 "Ratings of Article III Judicial Nominees, 112th Congress," American Bar Association Standing Committee on the Federal Judiciary, April 21, 2011, www.americanbar.org.

18 Sen, Maya, "How Judicial Qualification Ratings May Disadvantage Minority and Female Candidates," *Journal of Law and Courts* 2, no. 1 (2014): 33–65.

19 Maya, "How Judicial Qualification Ratings May Disadvantage Minority and Female Candidates," 46.

20 Tesler, Michael, "The Spillover of Racialization into Health Care: How President Obama Polarized Public Opinion by Racial Attitudes and Race," *American Journal of Political Science* 56 (2012): 690; Piston, Spencer, "How Explicit Racial Prejudice Hurt Obama in the 2008 Election," *Political Behavior* 32 (2010): 431.

21 Domain, Emma, "Black Caucus Sees Race as Factor in Filibusters, Eyes Rules Change." November 19, 2013, Roll Call, https://cbc-butterfield.house.gov.

22 Ibid.

23 Ibid.

24 Preuhs, Robert R., "The Conditional Effects of Minority Descriptive Representation: Black Legislators and Policy Influence in the American States," *Journal of Politics* 68 (2006): 585–599.

25 See Chew, Pat K., and Robert E. Kelley, "The Realism of Race in Judicial Decision Making: An Empirical Analysis of Plaintiffs' Race and Judges' Race," *Harvard Journal on Racial and Ethnic Justice* 28 (2012): 91; Kastellec, Jonathan P., "Racial Diversity and Judicial Influence on Appellate Courts," *American Journal of Political Science* 57, no. 1 (2013): 167–183.

26 *Shelby County v. Holder*, 133 S. Ct. 594 (2013).

27 See Howard, Robert M., and Amy Steigerwalt, *Judging Law and Policy: Courts and Policymaking in the American Political System*, Abingdon: Routledge, 2012.

28 See Barreto, Matt A., Stephen A. Nuno, and Gabriel R. Sanchez, "The Disproportionate Impact of Voter-ID Requirements on the Electorate—New Evidence from Indiana," *PS: Political Science and Politics* 42 (2009): 111–116; Cobb, Rachael V., D. James Greiner, and Kevin M. Quinn, "Can Voter ID Laws be Administered in a Race-Neutral Manner? Evidence from the City of Boston in 2008," *Quarterly Journal of Political Science* 7(2012): 1–33; and Vercellotti, Timothy, and David Andersen, "Voter-Identification Requirements and the Learning Curve," *PS: Political Science and Politics* 42(2009): 117–120.

29 *NAACP v. McCrory*, 2016 US App. LEXIS 13797 (4th Cir. 2016).

30 *Veasey v. Perry*, 71 F. Supp. 3d 627 (S.D. Tex. 2014) (case name later changed to *Veasey v. Abbott*, substituting Texas's former Governor Rick Perry as the defendant for its current governor, Greg Abbott).

31 *Veasey v. Abbott*, 796 F.3d 487, 493 (5th Cir. 2015).

32 Barrow, Deborah J., and Thomas G. Walker, *A Court Divided: The Fifth Circuit Court of Appeals and the Politics of Judicial Reform*, New Haven: Yale University Press, 1988.

33 *Veasey v. Abbott*, 796 F.3d 487, 493 (5th Cir. 2015), reh'g en banc granted, 815 F.3d 958 (5th Cir. 2016).

34 "Sotomayor Explains 'Wise Latina' Comment," CBS News, July 14, 2009, www.cbsnews.com.

8

Monumental Promises, Incremental Gains

Criminal Justice Reform in the Obama Era

KHALILAH L. BROWN-DEAN

Today, I want to focus on some aspect of American life that remains particularly skewed by race and by wealth, a source of inequity that has ripple effects on families and on communities and ultimately our nation—and that is our criminal justice system. . . . Justice is not only the absence of oppression, it is the presence of opportunity. Justice is giving every child a shot at a great education no matter what zip code they're born into. Justice is giving everyone willing to work hard the chance at a good job with good wages, no matter what their name is, what their skin color is, where they live.
—President Barack H. Obama, 2015.

Thousands crowded into the Philadelphia Convention Center, eager to hear President Barack H. Obama address the country's oldest civil rights organization, the National Association for the Advancement of Colored People (NAACP), at its 2015 annual convention. Media outlets from around the world jockeyed for position in the press pit to analyze the text of the president's remarks. It wasn't the president's first speech before the assembled body of activists, community leaders, business executives, elected officials, and concerned citizens. Many of those delegates sat just a mile away from the convention site in 2008 when then-Senator Barack Obama outlined how the country's failure to reconcile issues of race undermined progress and eroded the public's trust (Obama 2008). A year later, President Obama delivered an inspiring speech at the organization's centennial celebration. This time, however, those who were able to secure a coveted ticket to the NAACP address weren't there to hear a well-crafted oration. The timing and context of this speech signaled a greater imperative.

Criminal Justice Reform as Inclusionary Dilemma

Much has been made of the significance of Barack Obama's role as the nation's first Black president. Scholars such as Harris (2013) and Price (2016) have previously addressed whether the myopic focus on Obama as "Racial Healer-in-Chief" undermines efforts to substantively improve Blacks' political and socioeconomic fate. Similarly, Jeffries (2013), Spence (2016), and Glaude (2016) examine how government's retreat from addressing public problems combined with the rhetoric of a post-racial America challenges efforts to achieve meaningful reform. This tension between Obama's racial identity and his substantive policy priorities has been at issue since he first emerged on the national stage. Scholars and pundits question whether candidate Obama's message of hope was incongruent with the contemporary realities of American life. Take for instance an oft-cited passage from his 2004 address to the Democratic National Convention:

> I stand here today grateful for the diversity of my heritage, aware that my parents' dreams live on in my two precious daughters. . . . I stand here knowing that my story is part of the larger American story, that I owe a debt to all of those who came before me, and that in no other country on Earth is my story even possible. . . . There's not a black America and white America and Latino America and Asian America; there's the United States of America. (Obama 2004)

Joseph McCormick defines an *inclusionary dilemma* as "the conundrum that African Americans who are elected to office by a plurality or small majority of Black votes may want to advocate certain policy goals that meet the substantive political or economic needs of their Black constituents, but . . . perceive a host of political and institutional barriers to such advocacy."[1] Amid growing public demands to address ongoing tensions over biased policing, excessive sentencing, and the often lethal consequences of disproportionate minority contact, Obama's professed commitment to comprehensive reform was constrained by institutional norms, federalism, and a skepticism about individual responsibility that most frequently came from Republican detractors.

Almost immediately, the transition from candidate to president demanded a response to the complicated and dangerous intersection of race and justice. Two weeks before the United States inaugurated its first African American president, an unarmed civilian named Oscar Grant III was shot in the back while handcuffed by an Oakland transit officer (McKinley 2009). Yet it was the arrest of noted Harvard Professor Henry Louis Gates while attempting to enter his home in an affluent Cambridge, Massachusetts, neighborhood that commandeered the president's and, indeed, the nation's attention. President Obama responded to the arrest by hosting a "beer summit" at the White House. The guests included Vice President Joe Biden, Professor Gates, and the White arresting officer. Although President Obama saw the meeting as an opportunity to break down racial barriers and achieve understanding, some critics argued that the president missed a meaningful opportunity to address the insidious and pervasive nature of racial profiling.[2] The kumbaya summit ended with Professor Gates giving Sergeant Crowley a copy of his memoir and a mutual promise to meet for beers in Cambridge. Was this enough? Almost a year to the date of the summit, the US Department of Justice, headed by President Obama's appointee Eric Holder, opened a federal investigation into the murder of Oscar Grant III, but Attorney General Holder declined to pursue charges (Kambon 2015). The officer involved, Johannes Mehserle, served less than a year for an involuntary manslaughter conviction.

The July 2015 address to the NAACP came a year after the murder of eighteen-year-old Michael Brown sparked a massive uprising in Ferguson, Missouri. Brown's death and the subsequent decision not to prosecute Officer Darren Wilson was viewed by many as a systemic failure to protect the most basic civil rights of communities of color. Two years prior, President Obama famously suggested that seventeen-year-old Trayvon Martin could have been his son after a jury failed to convict his killer, George Zimmerman. This sentiment of shared pain permeated the president's speech in Chicago after the murder of Hadiya Pendleton, a young woman who was gunned down in a park just weeks after performing at his inauguration. Yet the NAACP speech was markedly different from the president's prior statements about violence, policing, and incarceration. This speech outlined an ambitious strategy to transform justice with measured, incremental steps designed to reduce the racially disparate impact of a decades-long approach to punishment. This approach offered monumental promises with only incremental results.

Taken together, these events highlight the need to address the most pervasive institution structuring the meaning of Black life in America: the criminal justice system. Without question, comprehensive criminal justice reform has been one of the most visible priorities on President Obama's policy agenda. Yet, what progress has resulted from this priority? And to what extent has that progress been effectively reversed under his successor's administration? I argue that in spite of the monumental promise to transform America's approach to punishment, institutional constraints such as federalism and partisan politics have limited the substantive results.

Concentrated Punishment

Hyperincarceration in the United States has garnered substantial attention from scholars, activists, and analysts (Hartney 2006; Vasiliades 2005; Alexander 2009; Burch 2013; Lehrman and Weaver 2014; Coates 2015; Stevenson 2015). Yet beyond crime rates, the racially disparate consequences of this autonomous system hold significant implications for institutionalizing Black political power. African Americans are disproportionately represented in every realm of punitive control, from surveillance to arrest to conviction to incarceration to postrelease supervision. Crime control policies, then, shape individual access and communal representation.

In this chapter, I interrogate President Obama's record through the lens of what I term "concentrated punishment." Concentrated punishment refers to the disproportionate rates of surveillance, incarceration, and disenfranchisement that constrain a community's political presence. The urban concentration of these communities, coupled with their distinct racial/ethnic diversity, provide an ideal case for evaluating the consequences of President Obama's record on criminal justice reform. To be sure, President Obama inherited a ballooning criminal justice system set in motion by decades of "tough on crime" public policies and zero-tolerance policies marked by racial disparities. Indeed, it seemed, being tough on crime was one of the few areas of agreement between Democrats and Republicans. Yet President Obama also entered office after his predecessor, George W. Bush, signed into law the Second Chance Act of 2007, which brought federal attention to the dearth of meaningful opportunities for the formerly incarcerated. In his pioneering theory of the "political process model," Doug McAdam (1982) argues that the changing structure of political opportunities, combined with organized grassroots efforts, can help produce social change. In the context of criminal justice reform, a growing bipartisan emphasis on the inefficiencies and ineffectiveness of punishment have helped to open up political opportunities for change. In one of his last major acts of office, President George W. Bush introduced the Second Chance Act of 2007 by saying:

> The United States was built on the belief that each human being has limitless potential and worth. Everybody matters. We believe that even those who have struggled with a dark past can find brighter days ahead. One way we act on that belief is by helping former prisoners who've paid for their crimes—we help them build new lives as productive members of our society. The work of redemption reflects our values. . . . Our government has a responsibility to help prisoners to return as contributing members of their community. (Bush 2007)

Despite President Bush's reentry initiative and President Obama's bold critique of the criminal justice system, a collection of institutional constraints and contemporary events have both limited and invigorated the Obama administration's ability to fundamentally reform punishment policies in the US.[3] The Obama-Biden transition website outlined five policy priorities to enhance civil rights by reforming the criminal justice system. Those plans included expanding drug courts, reinforcing hate crime statutes, ending racial profiling by federal agencies, creating a prison-to-work incentive program, and most notably, *completely* eliminating the sentencing disparity between crack and powder cocaine (Change.gov 2008). Only two of those policy priorities were prominent on the Obama administration's governing agenda. I address this claim by examining the Obama administration's efforts in two key areas: (1) sentencing reform, and (2) public safety. The key thread underlying both of these priorities has been the forty-year war on drugs that sharply increased the number of people serving long sentences for nonviolent offenses. The passage of key legislative reforms such as the 1994 Violent Crime Control and Enforcement Act helped expand the autonomy of and resources allocated to law enforcement agencies while significantly extending the reach of the criminal justice system.[4] I begin by highlighting the behemoth growth of the criminal justice system that set the tone for the challenges President Obama attempted to address. From there I analyze key policy reforms within these two domains to characterize President Obama's legacy of criminal justice reform. Finally, I outline a reform path for President Obama's successor.

Scope of the Problem

The transition from massive acts of insurgency to formalized participation in the electoral process has been well documented and debated within the established literature (Tate 1994; Walters 2005; Kousser 1999; Vallely 2004; Hajnal 2010; Walton et al. 2011; Brown-Dean et al. 2015). Indeed, a central goal of the civil rights movement was the removal of institutional barriers to full political incorporation. The passage of the Civil Rights Act of 1964 and the Voting Rights Act of 1965 helped open up American society and ushered in an impressive cadre of new voters and elected officials. Over the last forty years, Americans have elected minority governors in nine states, mayors in cities as diverse as Newark and Denver, seated our first Latina Supreme Court justice, and even an African American president.

All of these changes suggest that minority communities have worked extremely hard to overcome their past exclusion. However, the expanded reach of the criminal justice system, coupled with the increased adoption of civil penalties, threaten to undermine many of those gains. On any given day, there are more than 2.5 million Americans behind bars with over 7 million under some form of criminal supervision (Ghandnoosh 2016; Wagner and Rabuy 2016). Punishing roughly 2 percent of the total US population may not register much concern among many Americans, but punishment in the United States stretches far beyond the walls of the nearly eight thousand correctional facilities scattered across the country.[5] From shaping access to housing, to defining opportunities for employment, the collateral consequences of a conviction challenge the standing of individuals while generating new demands for monitoring and implementing these punishments.

Although Blacks make up just 12 percent of the total US population, they comprise 60 percent of all Americans behind bars. If current trends persist, one in three young Black men will enter prison at some point in his lifetime (Mauer 2006). Blacks are significantly *overrepresented* in America's correctional institutions with an 800 percent increase in Black incarceration over the last sixty years (Sawyer and Wagner 2020). Latinos' incarceration rates have also risen steadily since the 1970s.[6] Together, African Americans and Latinos comprise nearly 60 percent of all Americans who are behind bars.

Changes in crime control policy, such as the adoption of mandatory minimum sentences, have increased the number of people going into prison while simultaneously extending the length and depth of their involvement with the state. Each year, over 650,000 people are released from prison and often return to communities already grappling with the effects of crime, poverty, violence, and inferior education (Wacquant 2001; Clear 2007). Community members struggle to secure access to housing, education, and employment. This struggle is intensified for those leaving prisons and attempting to return to their families. These civil penalties limit opportunities for the formerly incarcerated to support their families and make positive contributions to their communities. In turn, the expanded reach of the criminal justice system has a disproportionate impact on groups already struggling to define their place in American society. For example, over 25 percent of African Americans and about 20 percent of Latinos live below the federally established poverty line. The bulk of these communities, and the bulk of the communities to which the formerly incarcerated return, are concentrated in urban areas. These areas face the challenge of reconciling high demands for social service with limited resources. These figures also speak to the degree to which social standing is stratified along the lines of race, gender, and social class.

Beyond prison, a criminal conviction in the United States is accompanied by an array of civil penalties and restrictions that define every aspect of one's daily life. From jobs to housing to accessing the voting process, the collateral consequences of a conviction impose stringent restrictions on social, economic, and political standing. In states like

Ohio, Connecticut, Missouri, and Virginia, for example, residents are required to pass a state licensing exam in order to work as a cosmetologist or barber. Though these fields represent some of the most popular trades offered within prisons, individuals with a felony offense cannot be bonded to hold these types of jobs. These penalties are administered at the local and state level yet often arise in response to policy-making at the federal level. As a result, the US criminal justice system has emerged as one of the most influential and powerful institutions in the United States in shaping the economic opportunities of its citizens.[7]

The development of mass incarceration in the United States stretched across presidential administrations and political parties. In the late 1960s, Richard Nixon launched a "law and order" campaign in response to riots that erupted in cities like Los Angeles, Detroit, and Chicago. Black leaders argued that these riots emerged from a growing sense of frustration that the policy victories of the civil rights movement had not been realized. Yet, to supporters of the "law and order" strategies, the riots resulted from a blatant disrespect for the law that permeated Black communities. President Nixon's law-and-order approach helped ensure his victory in the 1968 presidential election. It also shifted the criminal justice system from an emphasis on rehabilitation to incapacitation. This law-and-order focus permanently changed the face of law enforcement while drawing greater public support for harsher punishment.

President Nixon's strategy provided a framework for the Reagan administration's War on Drugs, a movement that permeated both national and state-level action (Fortner 2015). The most prominent features of this policy initiative included the adoption of mandatory minimum sentences and the abolishment of parole. In turn, these policies significantly increased the number of individuals behind bars for nonviolent offenses while also lengthening their period of incarceration. These drug-control policies have led to a sharp increase in the arrest, prosecution, and imprisonment of many Americans. It's fitting, then, that sentencing reform emerged as a major plank in President Obama's reform platform.

Crack Is Whack . . . but Powder Ain't so Bad

As the junior senator from Illinois seeking the Democratic nomination, Barack Obama called for a new criminal justice system based on greater transparency, fairness, justice, and equity. Central to that push was adopting policies to make the US criminal justice system smarter and not just harder on crime. The Obama administration's appointment of Eric Holder as attorney general (AG) signaled to the activist community that President Obama was serious about carrying out the criminal justice improvement promises of his presidential campaign. Before becoming AG, Holder built a distinguished career prosecuting high-profile corruption cases and advocating for hate-crime legislation following the brutal murder of James Byrd Jr. in Jasper, Texas, and Matthew Shepard in Wyoming. The choice to have Holder lead the influential Department of Justice (DOJ) was a sharp departure from the DOJ's leadership over the previous eight years. Holder had the respect of both Democratic and Republican congressional leaders and was viewed as someone whose respect for the law could help overcome a widening partisan divide.

In 1986, President Reagan signed the Anti-Drug Abuse Act of 1986, which authorized $97 million to build new prisons, $200 million for drug education, and $241 million for treatment programs. The bill also created mandatory minimum penalties for drug offenses. The bill included a provision that harshly punished those convicted of selling crack cocaine versus those convicted of selling powder cocaine. The law created a 1:100 disparity such that the sale of 5 grams of crack cocaine or 500 grams of powder cocaine led to a mandatory five-year sentence. Over the years, mandatory minimums were criticized for creating racial disparities in sentencing and incarceration, with research showing that although Blacks and Whites use drugs at fairly comparable rates, there are sharp racial and class differences in relation to which form of cocaine is used (Hart 2014). Advocacy groups such as the NAACP Legal Defense and Education Fund, the American Civil Liberties Union, and Families Against Mandatory Minimums targeted this disparity and its discriminatory impact to no avail. Even the bipartisan US Sentencing Commission urged Congress to equalize the punishment for the crack-powder disparity.

With the president's backing, US senator Dick Durbin (D-IL) introduced the Fair Sentencing Act (S.1789) in 2010 to completely eliminate the 1:100 disparities under *federal* law. Although the original bill unanimously passed the Senate, it encountered some opposition from Republicans and some Democrats in the House, who erroneously believed crack was more addictive than powdered cocaine and thus more likely to induce violence and addiction. In spite of a strong bipartisan commitment to addressing the disparity, a complete elimination did not seem likely. Although African Americans and Latinos were most affected by the disparity, some community leaders worried that eliminating the disparity might reignite the crack epidemic that plagued urban communities decades before (Stanberry and Montague 2011). Party leaders in both the House and Senate brokered a compromise to reduce the sentencing disparity from 1:100 to 18:1. President Obama signed the legislation into law in August 2010, marking his first and most significant step toward sentencing reform.

The bipartisan consensus that backed the Fair Sentencing Act quickly dissipated after the emergence of the Tea Party movement during the 2010 midterm elections. Forty-five Tea Party–backed candidates (32 percent of those who ran) won election to Congress and effectively convinced Republican Party leaders that supporting any Obama-backed initiatives would be detrimental to the conservative movement. Given Congress's constitutional authority to set legislative decisions, the Tea Party ascendancy in Congress signaled a death knell for coordinated justice reform.

In 2015, a bipartisan congressional effort emerged to revisit criminal justice reform. The Sentencing Reforms and Corrections Act (S. 2123) was an attempt to reduce federal mandatory minimum sentences for certain drug and gun crimes. It went a step beyond previous proposals by making those reductions retroactive for some offenders and promoted studies of effective mechanisms to reduce recidivism and improve reentry. A similar bipartisan bill was introduced in the House yet failed in the Senate due to strong opposition from Senator Jeff Sessions, who would later become attorney general in charge of overseeing the country's vast system of justice. At the close of 2018, President Trump signed the First Step Act into law, marking the first comprehensive federal attempt at reform in years. The act was narrower in scope than original reform bills and only applies to federal prisoners who comprise less than 10 percent of the total incarcerated population.

To counter Congress's inaction and, at times, outright hostility in his second term, President Obama exercised his authority to issue pardons and certificates of clemency. By the end of his second term, President

TABLE 8.1. Presidential Pardons

President	Number	% of Total
Obama	348	63.6
G. W. Bush	11	2.0
Clinton	61	11.2
G. H. W. Bush	3	0.6
Reagan	13	2.4
Carter	29	5.3
Ford	22	4.0
Nixon	60	11.0
Total	547	

Commutations by President—From Nixon to Obama
Source: Department of Justice, table compiled by author from data, www.justice.gov

Obama had commuted the sentences of 348 people and granted clemency to many serving life sentences for nonviolent offenses. As table 8.1 illustrates, that number is significantly higher than his seven predecessors combined. In fact, Obama granted more than 60 percent of all of the presidential commutations granted since Richard Nixon.

Although much attention has been placed on the need to dismantle mandatory minimum sentences and grant prosecutors more discretion, data from the United States Sentencing Commission suggests that mandatory minimums were authorized in about 24 percent of eligible cases.[8] For all of the public pronouncements and heart-wrenching stories of redemption, none of President Obama's sentencing reforms have significantly reduced the number of people behind bars. Much of this can be attributed to legal restrictions that limit executive action to those serving time for *federal* convictions. According to the Federal Bureau of Prisons (2016), fewer than two hundred thousand of the 2.3 million inmates in the US are serving time in federal facilities. This number includes about thirty-five thousand people held in privately managed and/or immigration detention facilities ("Statistics" n.d.) Indeed, the most rapid prison growth has occurred in the maze of two thousand state and local prisons scattered across the country. To be sure, policy reform—or the lack thereof—at the federal level serves a signaling effect for lower levels of government. For example, executive efforts to protect minors and children from deportation prompted state-level action on immigration in a number of states such as Texas, Connecticut, and Arizona.[9] Similarly, the inability of the federal government to address gun violence prompted several states to adopt comprehensive reforms. Some states, like Connecticut and New Jersey, added new restrictions on weapon types, while Wyoming, Alaska, and Tennessee have passed legislation to reinforce the rights of gun owners (McDaniel, Korth, and Boehn 2014). In January 2016, President Obama announced that his administration would end solitary confinement for juvenile offenders incarcerated within the federal prison system, citing decades of research on the adverse psychological effects of solitary confinement. While it was an impressive statement, it was limited in its scope and had minimal impact. According to the Bureau of Prisons there were only twenty-six inmates under the age of eighteen who were federally adjudicated at the time of President Obama's announcement. None of those inmates were serving their sentence in federal prisons.[10] President Obama outlined his hope for greater state-level attention in an op-ed to the *Washington Post*:

> The Justice Department has completed its review, and I am adopting its recommendations to reform the federal prison system. These [recommendations] include banning solitary confinement for juveniles and as a response to low-level infractions, expanding treatment for the mentally ill and increasing the amount of time inmates in solitary can spend outside of their cells. These steps will affect some 10,000 federal prisoners held in solitary confinement—and hopefully serve as a model for state and local corrections systems. And I will direct all relevant federal agencies to review these principles and report back to me with a plan to address their use of solitary confinement.
>
> States that have led the way are already seeing positive results. Colorado cut the number of people in solitary confinement, and assaults against staff are the lowest they've been since 2006. New Mexico implemented reforms and has seen a drop in solitary confinement, with more prisoners engaging in promising rehabilitation programs. And since 2012, federal prisons have cut the use of solitary confinement by 25 percent and significantly reduced assaults on staff. (Obama 2016)

Federalism as a Constraint

The limited outcomes of President Obama's sentencing plans highlight a *structural barrier* to contemporary criminal justice reform efforts: *federalism*. States have traditionally played an important role in shaping the meaning of citizenship. From historical efforts to block the integration of public schools to current attempts to address immigration, power sharing allows states to play a pivotal role in shaping access to democracy *and* in determining which citizens can be excluded from its benefits. The tremendous variation in the scope of state law is matched by the variation in the procedures and eligibility standards for reviewing individual cases. As Lisa Miller (2008) convincingly illustrates in her book *The Perils of Federalism*, power sharing in the domain of crime-control policy can often create additional barriers to effectively redefining the relationship between politics and punishment.

The policies set by state institutions reflect the presence of a diverse set of actors with differing levels of influence and, often, competing interests. The Tenth Amendment provides states with the authority to make laws regarding the health, safety, and well-being of its residents. As a result, state policing powers are executed within an intricate context of federal oversight and internal discretion. Freund (1904) affirms the importance of understanding state power in this observation: "The maxim of this power is that every individual must submit to such restraints to remove or reduce the danger of the abuse of these rights on the part of those who are unskillful, careless, or unscrupulous." It is this state power that limits the gains achieved by President Obama's promise to reform sentencing.

Over the last thirty years, the level of state influence has increased in response to federal mandates and growing internal pressure caused by changing migration patterns, partisan political shifts, and public outcry. States have assumed greater responsibility for various functions of the criminal justice system such as law enforcement, prisons, and the administration of civil penalties. Further, states determine how resources will be allocated to address a host of policy concerns. As a result of these changes, state institutions have expanded their policing powers as well as their authority to set the boundaries of punishment. To date, the most significant efforts to reform sentencing have occurred at the state level, with major changes in areas such as felon voting rights, death penalty abolition, the reclassification of certain drug offenses, and juvenile justice reform.[11] All of these functions point to the need to evaluate the governing environment of these institutions and their relationship to the struggle for citizen inclusion and justice.

Hard and Incremental

Public institutions, particularly those at the state level, play an important role in shaping limits on citizenship. However, the exclusive focus on these formal mechanisms yields an incomplete picture. America's pursuit of equality and inclusion is facilitated by its democratic processes yet given meaning by the actors who govern and are governed by them. Therefore, a proper analysis of the limits on President Obama's criminal justice reforms must also account for the dialectical exchange that occurs between the public and various elite forces. From massive protests to hashtag activism, citizen engagement around issues of public safety and law enforcement were a consistent source of pressure during the Obama administration. Sparked by the murders of young people like Tamir Rice and Michael Brown and emboldened by the torturous conditions suffered by Kalief Browder, the relationship between communities of color and those sworn to protect them elevated perceived policing abuses in a national conversation. A groundswell of mass action challenged President Obama to directly address police abuses of their authority. Most notably, the emergence of loosely connected organizations around the country united under the mantra "Black Lives Matter" have expressed outrage at such abuse. The movement's most visible leaders often found themselves at odds with traditional political and community leaders who they accused of accepting glacial paced incrementalism as an acceptable strategy for meaningful reform. These young leaders have demanded *immediate not incremental action* and have asserted their demands during campaign events, national conferences of so-called progressive organizations, freeways during rush hour, NBA basketball games, and anywhere they could draw attention to their demand that *Black bodies be valued.* This in-your-face approach to activism, coupled with their refusal to compromise, prompted a sharp critique from President Obama. During a meeting with young activists in London, Obama sharply criticized Black Lives Matter activists by saying:

> Once you've highlighted an issue and brought it to people's attention and shined a spotlight, and elected officials or people who are in a position to start bringing about change [who] are ready to sit down with you, then you can't just keep on yelling at them. . . . And you can't refuse to meet because that might compromise the purity of your position. The value of social movements and activism is to get you at the table, get you in the room, and then to start trying to figure out how is this problem going to be solved. . . . You then have a responsibility to prepare an agenda that is achievable, that can institutionalize the changes you seek, and to engage the other side, and occasionally to take half a loaf that will advance the gains that you seek, understanding that there's going to be more work to do, but this is what is achievable at this moment. (Obama 2015)

The choice to make these remarks during an address to British youth struck some as odd. To others, it was reminiscent of racial code speak that peppered his previous critiques of absentee Black fathers and negligent Black mothers (Price 2016; Spence 2016). President Obama convened a meeting of hip-hop artists in April 2016 to help bridge this generational divide and also drum up support for his male mentoring initiative, My Brother's Keeper. The gathering included rappers Kendrick Lamar, Talib Kweli, Wale, Ludacris, and J. Cole, who address themes to such issues as community pride, economic challenges, mass incarceration, and the collateral consequences in their music (Bonnette 2015). These meetings seem to confirm the view that the Obama administration opened the White House to a diverse set of activists and public voices. However, the novelty of these gatherings was often overshadowed by the inundation of allegations of police abuse of power.

In December 2014, two NYPD officers were ambushed and gunned down while on patrol. Their deaths in the midst of a federal review of New York's stop-and-frisk practices and just months after massive uprisings in Ferguson, Missouri, sparked outrage from law enforcement officers across the country, who blamed President Obama and activists for inducing what they named "the Ferguson effect." The Ferguson effect suggests that protests against police-involved shootings have stoked the flames of antipolice rhetoric and behavior. In turn, police officers are reluctant to enforce the law, and criminals are emboldened to defy it. This view stands in sharp contrast to Black Lives Matter activists who accused President Obama of being too sympathetic to law-enforcement demands and failing to speak out against abuses of power with the same vigor he has chastised activists (Bergner 2014).

President Obama's most significant action in the realm of police reform was the creation of the Task Force on 21st Century Policing that was created by executive order in December 2014. The task force was formed in direct response to the murder of Michael Brown and the concern that community relations had deteriorated across the country. The task force was comprised of a law enforcement officials, scholars, and community leaders, whose mission was to outline best practices to prevent future civil unrest. It was not intended to be a fact-mining effort that would charge offending police departments. The task force's final report was released in 2015 and suggested that community stake-holders work together to reduce disproportionate minority contact by emphasizing community policing. The goal, according to the group's chair, was to work on building strong relationships *before* bad situations happened.

A month prior to the report's release, the nation's attention focused once again on civil unrest in an American city over excessive use of force allegations. This time it was the death of an unarmed Black man named Freddie Gray, who died in Baltimore police custody. Gray died from severe spinal cord injuries suffered during transport in a police van. As word quickly spread of his death, riots broke out across the city, stranding thousands of school-age children on the way home and causing significant damage to Baltimore's most fragile neighborhoods. President Obama's response to the death of Freddie Gray and the resulting unrest drew sharp criticism from both conservatives and community activists alike. In a statement given from the Rose Garden, he said:

> I think there are police departments that have to do some soul searching. I think there are some communities that have to do some soul searching but I think we as a country have to do some soul searching. This is not new. There is no excuse for the riots and violence. It is not a protest. It is

not a statement. It's a handful of people taking advantage of the situation for their own purposes, and they need to be treated as criminals. (Obama 2015)

To date, six officers have been charged in Gray's death, and there have been no convictions. In May 2015, the US Justice Department, led by Obama appointee Attorney General Loretta Lynch, announced that it would provide $75 million over three years to help outfit local police departments with body cameras. The hope was that these new cameras would both protect the public from abuse and shield officers from illegitimate critique. While some, such as Baltimore mayor Stephanie Rawlings-Blake, applauded the use of technology to enhance public confidence, others feared it was simply a Band-Aid solution to a much deeper wound of unchecked police authority. Questions over privacy rights, the costs of technology upgrades, and the ability of police officers to turn off cameras have all been leveled against President Obama's most significant act of police reform.

Conclusion

In spite of his bold intention to fundamentally reform America's approach to punishment, President Barack Obama was limited by institutional constraints, such as federalism. However, massive insurgency at the grassroots level has elevated public concerns over criminal justice reform and has provided a political imperative to act, even if that action has involved incremental measures and compromise. Most notably, the formation of the Black Lives Matter movement by Patrisse Khan-Cullors, Opal Tometti, and Alicia Garza was borne out of the frustration that the continued acquittals of police officers accused of killing unarmed Black citizens has reinforced the perception among many that the lives of people of color are systematically deemed less valuable than others. The movement and its massive acts of grassroots insurgency directly exacerbated the inclusionary dilemma faced by Obama and other members of his administration. The deaths of Trayvon Martin, Michael Brown, Rekia Boyd, Akai Gurley, Walter Scott, and other Black folk encouraged activists to build a collective effort that would address *systemic* challenges and not just individual experiences.

Meaningful reform, then, must be pursued by a both-and strategy that consolidates electoral participation, governance, and grassroots organizing. Nelson (1996) articulates this need in the following way:

> Future racial progress in American will depend in large measure on the implementation of community mobilization strategies from the bottom up. This process must begin with the formation of independent community organizations dedicated to the goal of citizen education. In this regard, the point should be underscored that the goal of political education is just as important as the goal of electoral mobilization. Black leaders must make Black citizens aware of the fact that the process of politics is multi-dimensional. They must also emphasize the fact that collective consciousness must precede collective action. Thus when Black citizens vote they must vote instrumentally. Black instrumental politics must express itself in the arena of school politics, and around issues of health, safety, the environment, parks and recreation, zoning, and legislative redistricting. . . .
>
> Furthermore, the Black community must take the responsibility of building for itself a systematic network for the expression of oppositional politics. Under present circumstances, it is unrealistic to expect that the answers to social and economic needs of urban Black communities will come from city administrations wedded to strategies of corporate-centered development. Black leaders and organizations must build bridges of cooperation and forge intelligence networks essential to the promotion of effective oppositional strategies in the political process. Until the imperative of oppositional politics is met, the American political process will remain an unresponsive and hostile domain for the pursuit of the basic goals of Black liberation politics. (Nelson 1996, 12–13)

This need to pursue both an electoral and grassroots-activist strategy is buttressed by the realization that many of the gains made during Barack Obama's tenure as the United States' first Black president have been threatened and undermined by his successor. Since the 2016 presidential election, stocks in private prison corporations like the GEO Group and Correction Corporation of America have soared, adding over $1 billion to market values (Sarhan 2017). Seventeen states, including

Connecticut and Vermont, have moved to decriminalize small amounts of nonmedical marijuana, opting for substance abuse treatment over expensive incarceration (Berke and Gould 2019). In spite of the movement toward legalization at the state level, medical and recreational usage of marijuana remain illegal at the federal level. The Drug Enforcement Administration (DEA) contends that marijuana is a dangerous drug with "no currently accepted medical use and high potential for abuse" ("Drug Scheduling" n.d.). The effectiveness of states' marijuana laws rests solely on enforcement and implementation. According to a report issued by the American Civil Liberties Union (ACLU), marijuana accounted for over 52 percent of all drug arrests, with enforcement costs reaching nearly $4 billion per year (Hayes 2017).

Although Blacks and Whites use marijuana at relatively comparable rates, Blacks are four times more likely to be arrested for marijuana-related offenses. This racial disparity is even greater in states like Minnesota and Iowa, where Blacks are eight times more likely to be arrested (Nellis 2016). At present, racially disparate arrest rates sharply limit the number of African Americans legally allowed to operate or work in dispensaries, while expanding the pattern of hyperincarceration. Together, these patterns reflect an ongoing resistance, particularly at the state level, to institutionalizing the criminal justice reform legacy of America's first Black president.

NOTES

1 Shaw, Brown, and McCormick outline the inclusionary dilemma concept in the introduction of this volume.

2 For a detailed statistical discussion of racial profiling at the national and state level, see "Restoring a National Consensus" (2011).

3 It should be noted that my focus in this chapter is not on crime rates, but on crime control policies.

4 The 1994 Violent Crime Control and Law Enforcement Act became a major source of debate during the 2016 Democratic Presidential Primaries. Critics argued that former Secretary of State Hillary Clinton inherited the legacy of her husband's endorsement of the bill. Her chief opponent, Senator Bernie Sanders, made the racially disparate impact of the act's policies a chief focus of his campaign outreach to communities of color. See Williams (2016).

5 This figure includes state, federal, and Native American jails and prisons. It does not include prisons in US territories, military prisons, or immigration detention facilities. See Wagner and Rabuy (2016).

6   Hispanics were first accounted for in the US Census beginning in 1970. Before that time, the Census, along with the Bureau of Justice Statistics, simply "assigned" members of this ethnic group to one of the traditional racial groups. For more information on the historical use of race/ethnicity in the US Census see Nobles (2000).

7   My focus here is on the penalties associated with a criminal conviction. However, in some jurisdictions, these penalties can be imposed based on mere suspicion or arrest. For example, Americans arrested for certain drug-related crimes can be denied employment in a number of fields (e.g., nursing and home health aides) and denied access to public housing.

8   See the 2015 US Sentencing Commission report, *Quick Facts on Mandatory Minimum Penalties*. According to this report, only 14 percent of offenders remained subject to a mandatory minimum penalty at the time of sentencing.

9   One of President Obama's chief immigration efforts was the 2012 Deferred Action for Childhood Arrivals (DACA) program that would have protected young people who arrived in the United States before their sixteenth birthday from deportation. It included provisions requiring that applicants earn a high school diploma, GED, or complete military service, and not be convicted of a serious misdemeanor or felony. In June 2016, the US Supreme Court upheld a lower court ruling that deemed the president's plan overstepped the scope of executive authority. The original lawsuit was filed by twenty-six states including immigrant-heavy states Texas, Arizona, and Florida. See Park and Parlapiano (2016).

10 The federal prison system does not have juvenile facilities. As a result, juvenile inmates convicted on federal charges serve their time in local or state correctional facilities. The new rule only applies to those local/state facilities under federal contract.

11 For a comprehensive overview of major state-level sentencing reforms see Parker (2016).

REFERENCES

Alexander, Michelle. 2009. *The New Jim Crow: Mass Incarceration in the Age of Colorblindness*. New York: New Press.

Bergner, Daniel. 2014. "Is Stop and Frisk Worth It?" *Atlantic*, April 2014.

Berke, Jeremy and Skye Gould. 2019. "This Map Shows Every U.S. State Where Pot Is Legal." *Business Insider*, January 26, 2018, www.businessinsider.com.

Blumstein, Alfred. 1982. "On the Racial Disproportionality of United States' Prison Populations." *Journal of Criminal Law and Criminology* 73:1259–81.

Bonnette, Lakeyta. 2015. *Pulse of the People: Political Rap Music and Black Politics*. Philadelphia: University of Pennsylvania Press.

Brown-Dean, Khalilah L., Zoltan Hajnal, Christina Rivers, and Ismail White. 2015. "Fifty Years of the Voting Rights Act: The State of Race in Politics." Joint Center for Political and Economic Studies. Washington, DC.

Burch, Traci. 2013. *Trading Democracy for Justice: Criminal Convictions and the Decline of Neighborhood Political Participation*. Chicago: University of Chicago Press.

Bush, George W. 2007. "Remarks on H.R. 1593, the Second Chance Act of 2007." White House, April 9, 2008, https://georgewbush-whitehouse archives.gov.

Change.gov, Office of the President-Elect. United States, 2008. Archived Web Site. www.loc.gov.

Clear, Todd C. 2007. *Imprisoning Communities: How Mass Incarceration Makes Communities Worse*. Oxford, UK: Oxford University Press.

Coates, Ta-Nehisi. 2015. *Between the World and Me*. New York: Spiegel and Grau.

Daly, Kathleen and Michael Tonry. 1997. "Gender, Race, and Sentencing." *Crime and Justice* 22:201–252.

"Drug Scheduling." n.d. US Drug Enforcement Agency. www.dea.gov.

Dyson, Michael Eric. 2016. *The Black Presidency: Barack Obama and the Politics of Race in America*. New York: Houghton Mifflin.

Fortner, Michael. 2015. *Black Silent Majority: The Rockefeller Drug Laws and the Politics of Punishment*. Cambridge, MA: Harvard University Press.

Freund, Ernst. 1904. *The Police Power, Public Policy, and Constitutional Rights*. Chicago: University of Chicago Press.

Ghandnoosh, Nazgol. 2016. "U.S. Prison Population Trends 1999–2014: Broad Variation Among States in Recent Years." The Sentencing Project.

Glaude, Eddie. 2016. *Democracy in Black: How Race Still Enslaves the American Soul*. New York: Crown Publishing.

Gottschalk, Marie. 2006. *The Prison and the Gallows: The Politics of Mass Incarceration in America*. Cambridge: Cambridge University Press.

Gottschalk, Marie. 2009. "The Long Reach of the Carceral State: The Politics of Crime, Mass Imprisonment, and Penal Reform in the United States and Abroad." *Law and Social Inquiry* 34:2.

Hajnal, Zoltan. 2010. *America's Uneven Democracy: Turnout, Race and Representation in City Politics*. Cambridge: Cambridge University Press.

Harris, Fredrick. 2012. *The Price of the Ticket: Barack Obama and the Rise and Decline of Black Politics*. Oxford: Oxford University Press.

Hart, Carl. 2014. *High Price: A Neuroscientist's Journey of Self-Discovery that Challenges Everything You Know about Drugs and Society*. New York: Harper Perennial.

Hartney, Christopher. 2006. "US Rates of Incarceration: A Global Perspective" (fact sheet). National Council on Crime and Delinquency. www.nccdglobal.org.

Hayes, Christal. 2017. "Marijuana Arrests Were up Last Year and You're Paying Billions For It." *Newsweek*, www.newsweek.com.

Jeffries, Michael. 2013. *Paint the White House Black: Barack Obama and the Meaning of Race in America*. Palo Alto, CA: Stanford University Press.

Kambon, Malaika. 2015. "Centuries of Rage: The Murder of Oscar Grant III." *San Francisco Bay View National Black Newspaper*, February 25, 2015, http://sfbayview.com.

Kennedy, Randall. 1997. *Race, Crime, and Law*. New York: Pantheon Books.

Key, V. O. 1949. *Southern Politics in State and Nation*. New York: Knopf.

Kousser, J. Morgan. 2000. *Colorblind Injustice: Minority Voting Rights and the Undoing of the Second Reconstruction*. Durham, NC: University of North Carolina Press.

"Restoring a National Consensus: The Need to End Racial Profiling in America." 2011. Washington, DC: Leadership Conference on Civil Rights. https://failuretolisten .files.wordpress.com.

Lehrman, Amy and Vesla Weaver. 2014. *Arresting Citizenship: The Democratic Consequences of Crime Control*. Chicago: University of Chicago Press.

Mauer, Mark, 2006. *Race to Incarcerate: A Graphic Retelling*. (Revised Edition). New York: The New Press.

McAdam, Doug. 1982. *Political Process and the Development of Black Insurgency, 1930–1970*. Chicago: University of Chicago Press.

McDaniel, Justin, Robby Korth, and Jessica Boehn. 2014. "In States, a Legislative Rush to Nullify Federal Gun Laws." *Washington Post*, August 29, 2014, www.washington-post.com.

McKinley, Jesse. 2009. "In California, Protests After Man Dies at Hands of Transit Police." *New York Times*, January 9, 2009, www.nytimes.com.

Mettler, Suzanne B. and Joe Soss. 2004. "The Consequences of Public Policy for Democratic Citizenship." *Perspectives on Politics* 2, no. 1 (March): 55–73.

Nellis, Ashley. 2016. "The Color of Justice: Racial and Ethnic Disparity in State Prisons." Washington, DC: The Sentencing Project.

Nelson, William E. Jr. 1996. "Race and Political Empowerment: The Crisis of Black Leadership." William Monroe Trotter Institute. Boston: University of Massachusetts.

Nobles, Melissa. 2000. *Shades of Citizenship: Race and the Census in Modern Politics*. Palo Alto, CA: Stanford University Press.

Obama, Barack H. 2004. "Barack Obama's Keynote Address at the 2004 Democratic National Convention." PBS News Hour, July 27, 2004. www/pbs.org/NewsHour.

Obama, Barack H. 2008. "Transcript of Obama Speech." Politico, March 18, 2008, www.politico.com.

Obama, Barack H. 2015. "Remarks at the 2015 NAACP National Convention." White House, July 14, 2015, www.whitehouse.gov.

Park, Haeyoun and Alicia Parlapiano. 2016. "Supreme Court's Decision on Immigration Case Affects Millions of Unauthorized Immigrants." *New York Times* June 23, 2016.

Parker, Nicole. 2016. "The State of Sentencing 2016: Developments in Policy and Practice." Sentencing Project, February 10, 2016, www.sentencingproject.org.

Price, Melanye. 2016. *The Race Whisperer: Barack Obama and the Political Uses of Race*. New York: New York University Press.

Sarhan, Adam. 2017. "Prison Stocks Soar Under Trump as Sessions Okays Private Jails." *Forbes*, February 4, 2017, www.forbes.com.

Sawyer, Wendy, and Pete Wagner. 2020. "Mass Incarceration: The Whole Pie 2020." Prison Policy Initiative. www.prisonpolicy.org.

Spence, Lester. 2016. *Knocking the Hustle: Against the Neoliberal Turn in Black Politics.* Galeta, CA: Punctum Books.

Stanberry, Artemesia, and David Montague. 2011. *Travesty of Justice: The Politics of Crack Cocaine and the Dilemma of the Congressional Black Caucus.* Dubuque, IA: Kendall Hunt.

"Statistics." n.d. Federal Bureau of Prisons, updated January 9, 2020, www.bop.gov.

Stevenson, Bryan. 2015. *Just Mercy: A Story of Justice and Redemption.* New York: Spiegel and Grau.

Tate, Katherine. 1994. *From Protest to Politics: The New Black Voters in American Elections.* Cambridge, MA: Harvard University Press.

US Sentencing Commission. 2015. *Quick Facts on Mandatory Minimum Penalties.* www.ussc.gov.

Valelly, Richard M. 2004. *The Two Reconstructions: The Struggle for Black Enfranchisement.* Chicago: University of Chicago Press.

Vasiliades, Elizabeth. 2005. "Solitary Confinement and International Human Rights: Why the US Prison System Fails Global Standards." *American University International Law Review* 21:71–99.

Wacquant, Loic. 2001. "Deadly Symbiosis: When Ghetto and Prison Meet and Mesh," *Punishment Society* (3)(1): 95–153.

Wagner, Peter and Bernadette Rabuy. 2016. "Mass Incarceration: The Whole Pie." Prison Policy Initiative, March 14, 2016, www.prisonpolicy.org.

Walton, Hanes, Josephine Allen, Sherman Puckett, and Donald Deskins. 2011. "Dead Certain: The Election of Barack Obama and Its Implications for Racial Politics." In *The Obama Phenomenon: Implications for a Multiracial Democracy.* Chicago: University of Illinois Press.

Williams, Vanessa. 2016. "1994 Crime Bill Haunts Clinton and Sanders as Criminal Justice Reform Rises to Top in Democratic Contest." *Washington Post*, February 12, 2016, www.washingtonpost.com.

9

What about Black Women?

How Economic Policies Targeting Urban Americans Disappear Black Women

JULIA S. JORDAN-ZACHERY

We are true to our creed when a little girl born into the bleakest poverty knows that she has the same chance to succeed as anybody else, because she is an American; she is free, and she is equal, not just in the eyes of God but also in our own.
—President Barack Obama, inaugural address, January 21, 2013

Upon assuming the presidency of the United States of America, Barack Obama signaled that policy decision-making had to take into account the functioning of gender in society. To this end, the first law he signed was the Lilly Ledbetter Fair Pay Act (January 29, 2009). As stated by President Obama, the law honored his grandmother, "who worked in a bank all her life, and even after she hit that glass ceiling, kept getting up again," and his young daughters, "because I want them to grow up in a nation that values their contributions, where there are no limits to their dreams" (quoted in Stolberg 2009). As signaled by President Obama, this law honored women regardless of their social location—it was universalistic in nature. As my colleague and I have argued, President Obama invoked rhetorical devices of sameness among and between women. The employment of such rhetorical devices of sameness, as it relates to gender and some would say also race, we argue, fails to account for the lived realities of women of color and their experiences with pay equity and other forms of workforce discrimination (Jordan-Zachery and Wilson 2017). In this chapter, using the Urban and Economic Mobility initiative undertaken by President Obama, I explore how and if race-gender is recognized in the framing of what I generally refer to as urban policy. There is a distinctive race-gender dimension to urban policy. "Poverty remains highest in urban areas, at 20 percent in both 2011 and 2012, up from 19.8 percent in 2010 and 18.7 percent in 2009" (Nichols 2013). Among this population, data suggest that poverty is both raced and gendered. A closer look at how race-gender and space shape experiences with poverty shows that single-headed households, which tend to be headed by women, are disproportionately Black (Eichner and Gallagher Robins 2015). Given this reality, it is important, from both an academic and practical perspective, to engage in an analysis of the relationship between race-gender and space in relation to urban policy-making. This is the purpose of this chapter. This analysis specifically looks at how Black women are treated in the urban policy-making process of the Obama administration. However, it also serves as an analysis of how Black women are understood in Black politics more specifically as it grapples with the larger question of how ideologies of gender, which often engage a rather masculinist approach, influence the quest for freedom and equality. An analysis of the Obama administration is somewhat of a proxy for an analysis of how gender, particularly Black womanhood, is treated in Black politics. As I argue, the ideologies of gender that influence urban policy, resulting in the invisibility of Black womanhood, are also prevalent in Black politics. Thus, to unpack these ideologies through a critical analysis of urban policy is informative for answering the question: What should Black politics look like beyond Obama?

Black feminists have long called for analyses to critically assess how gender ideologies operate within a multiplicity of political practices and processes (see Alexander-Floyd 2007; James 1999; among others). Alexander-Floyd indicts Black politics in her assertion that the reliance on Black cultural pathology and the narrative of the emasculated Black male (which are prevalent in the urban policies proposed by the Obama administration) produces a politics whereby "the plight of Black people is seen as co-extensive with that of males of the race" (2007, p. 144). Consequently, the inequalities faced by Black women are too often disregarded. While some have written critiques of Obama's racial politics and the implication for Black politics (see Harris 2012), there has been relative silence on his race-gender politics and responses to public policy issues—particularly those targeting poor Black women. So, as we contemplate the nature and meaning of Black politics after Obama, we are left with the same question that predated Obama: What about Black women?

Although not always explicitly stated, gender is an important variable in the policy-making process and in politics (Apple 1994). In this chapter, I focus specifically on race and gender and their intersection in the framing of President Barak Obama's urban policy proposals. Data suggest that, regarding many of the issues targeted by the urban policy proposals, social location, in terms of race and gender and space, matters (this is in the next section). I employ a Black feminist critical policy analysis framework to analyze and explain how President Obama and his administration address the challenges of urban dwellers across gender and its intersection with other oppressive structures. As explained, Black feminist critical policy analysis diverges from a more positivist approach that tends to inform more traditional policy analyses. A Black feminist framework integrated with frame analysis provides a useful approach for assessing political artifacts for evidence of race-gender ideology and, conversely, cultural race-gender beliefs and/or stereotypes (Alexander-Floyd 2007; Berger 2004; Collins 2000; Crenshaw 1989; King 1973). This analysis is not necessarily concerned with analyzing or explaining the conditions under which women, particularly women of color, are marginalized in the policy process. Additionally, this analysis is not concerned with the epistemology, intentionality, or rationalization of President Obama's decision to employ particular frames in his discourses on urban policy. Rather, my focus is on the frames themselves and how power dynamics and hierarchies are deployed.

President Obama has put forward a comprehensive and integrated urban policy that focuses on creating economic opportunity and community revitalization. This approach brings together multiple agencies under the auspices of the Urban Affairs Office and is designed to address issues from inequality and crime to transportation and housing. Under the general umbrella of creating economic opportunity, the administration's policies focus on rewarding hard work by raising the minimum wage, providing high-quality early childhood education, creating pathways to jobs, supporting strong families, increasing access to healthy food and increasing financial literacy. Another general policy, community revitalization, includes building promise zones, ending homelessness, bringing healthy foods to communities, and creating sustainable communities. Combined, these policies seek to create economic opportunity and promote community revitalization in "distressed" and "under-resourced" urban communities.

This analysis first offers data on why we need to think about women, and Black women specifically, in the formulation of urban policy. From there, I present an overview of Black feminist critical policy analysis. I place Black feminist critical policy analysis in conversation with more traditional approaches to policy analysis to offer a rationale for why this framework is particularly well suited for an analysis of policy targeting urban economic growth and development and why it is useful for uncovering gender ideologies in policy-making and Black politics generally. Specifically, I rely on Black feminist critical policy analysis to examine President Obama's urban policy discourses. Following this, I present the Black feminist frame analysis. The analysis is of five reports issued by the White House or on behalf of the White House and include *Creating Pathways to Opportunity, Promoting Responsible Fatherhood, Neighborhood Revitalization Initiative, Federal Strategic Plan to Prevent and End Homelessness*, and *Economic Importance of Nutrition Assistance*. Finally, the analysis focuses on the potential impact of the policy approach on the lived experiences of those in urban America. By utilizing a Black feminist critical policy analysis, I hope to offer an example of the ways in which this particular analytical tool can be used to analyze and examine policy targeting directly and indirectly minoritized and often marginalized bodies. I also seek to show why it is important for a post-2016 Black politics to move beyond the traditional boundaries of study—such as voting behaviors—to explore the stages of policy formation and the implications for the diversity of Black folk, particularly along identity markers such as gender and class. The failure to critically analyze differences within Black politics and in assessing the Obama administration is that "this single-axis approach generates discursive framings for political agitation that not only fail to address how racism and sexism impact black women, but also distort our understanding of racism and sexism" (Alexander-Floyd 2012, p. 8). Expanding Black politics to include analyses of in-group differences and deploying a multiaxis approach, as done in this analysis, is apropos for bringing to the forefront the intended and unintended effects of public policies on race-gendered bodies.

Race-Gender and Space Matters: A Case for Black Women

At times, the policy-making process can ignore the lived experiences of racially marginalized and minoritized women (Black, Latina, Asian American, and First American). This often occurs when women are treated as a homogeneous category and/or when race is treated as a homogenous category. The universalistic approach to speaking about race-gender fails to address how race-gender inequalities are experienced both between groups and within groups. The result is that Black women, and all women of color, are left out of the policy logic that undergird urban policy. Across the various issue areas addressed in the holistic urban policy proposals, unemployment, family stability and well-being, and homelessness, among others, Black women are disproportionately represented. This suggests that race-gender and place matter.

Data inform us that Black women experience inequality differently from White women and Black men. For example, "Earnings growth has been sharpest for White women, outpacing that of their Black and Hispanic counterparts" (US Bureau of Labor Statistics 2012). Furthermore, within groups of women, there continues to be a downward trend in Black women's economic position. Black women's greater work efforts have not been enough to lessen the disproportionately high poverty rates experienced by these women (*Black Women in the United States* 2015). As reported by the Institute for Women's Policy Research (IWPR) "Women of all major racial and ethnic groups earn less than men of the same group, and also earn less than white men" (Hegewisch, Ellis, and Hartmann 2015). In 2014 the median weekly earnings of Black women were $611, only 68.1 percent of White men's earnings as opposed to the $734 earned by White women, which was 81.8 percent. Earnings for a full-time week of work resulted in Hispanic women well below, and Hispanic men and Black women not much above, the qualifying income threshold for receipt of food stamps of $596 per week for a family of four.

A study by the National Women's Law Center (2011) indicates that Black women have lost more jobs during the most recent economic recovery (258,000) than they did during the recession (233,000). Additionally, "Poverty rates for women were once again higher than for men, and were especially high for many groups of women of color, women who head families, foreign-born women, and women 65 and older living alone" (National Women's Law Center 2011, p. 1).

The family is a cornerstone of the urban policy proposals. These proposals seem to relegate women to more of a supportive role as opposed to primary targets of policy. However, from existing data, we are informed that there is a relationship between family formation, gender, race, and poverty. Recent and historical data suggest that not only are families headed by a single adult more likely to be headed by women, but in relation to men solo-headed families, women-centered families experience more poverty—31 percent for women and 16.4 percent for men (Nichols 2013). Within the group of women, Black-women- and Latina-headed families experience poverty at a greater rate (Single Mother Statistics 2020). Contributing to this problem is their experiences with the labor market. "Out of more than 10 million low-income working families with children, 39% were headed by single working mothers or about 4.1 million. The proportion is much higher among African Americans (65%), compared with whites (36%)" (Single Mother Statistics n.d.). As a result of economic insecurity, many female-headed households also experience higher rates of housing instability and insecurity and, consequently, homelessness. Consider that among all homeless families nationwide, 71 percent are headed by single women with children, and African Americans, in general, accounted for 43 percent (National Center on Family Homelessness 2011). A study on evictions in Milwaukee shows that Black women account for 30 percent of all evictions, although they account for only 9.6 percent of the population (Desmond, 2014). In comparison to other groups, Black women experienced higher rates of evictions. Consider that in Black neighborhoods with high rates of poverty, one woman in seventeen faced eviction in comparison to one male in thirty-three. In White neighborhoods of similar economic standing, the ratio of the women who experienced evictions was 1:150 as compared to 1:134 for men (Desmond 2014).

According to the Department of Defense's recent study, Black female veterans are disproportionately facing a number of challenges, including homelessness. It is estimated that Black women account for 45 percent of homeless veterans, in comparison to 41 percent White, 7.6 percent Latina, and 1.3 percent Asian (quoted in National Coalition for Homeless

Veterans 2014). Furthermore, Black women, who are more likely to be sexually assaulted in the military, are among the fastest growing segments of the homeless population (National Coalition for Homeless Veterans 2013).

What is made evident by these data is the persistent and multifaceted race-gender inequalities between Black and White women. These inequalities demonstrate the value of taking an intersectional approach to policy-making—one that recognizes how social location influences lived realities of the policy-targeted group(s). When policy logics fail to account for different lived realities that result from the intersection of gender, race, and class differences—both between and within groups—then the effectiveness of public policies are compromised.

Black Feminist Policy Analysis: It Too Has a Place in Black Politics

Traditional policy analysis is grounded in a narrow, falsely objective, overly instrumental view of rationality that masks its latent biases and allows policy elites and technocrats to present analyses and plans as neutral and objective when they are actually tied to prevailing relations of power (Marshall 1997, p. 3). The question then becomes, What approach is suitable for a policy analysis that unveils these power structures? Critical policy analysis, in collaboration with Black feminist theory, provides an analytic lens for exploring and explaining the ways in which the interests of women of color (and their multiple and intersecting identities) and the interests of the state (particularly a raced-gendered neoliberal state) intersect and, more often, in a contradictory nature.

In this analysis, I pay particular attention to the policy logic process. Using an intersectional approach to the analysis, I integrate Black feminist standpoint theory and frame analysis to thematically identify and analyze President Obama's construction of urban policy. Intersectionality considers how multiple forms of oppression, race, class, gender, and sexuality inform the lived realities of Black women and women of color (Collins 2000; Berger 2004; Harris-Perry 2011; Jordan-Zachery 2009, 2017).

While feminists have long advocated for a different form of policy analysis—specifically a feminist critical policy analysis—there remains a dearth of research that utilizes Black feminist thought for policy analysis. Black politics, in general, has failed to offer a systematic analytic approach to the study of policy analysis, although there has been much written on the impacts of some policies, such as affirmative action, on the lived realities of Black folk. Black feminists and critical scholars such as K. Sue Jewell (1992), Dorothy Roberts (1997), and Zenzele Isoke (2013) have employed Black feminism in their analyses of public policies. And Barnett (1976) has offered a theoretical analysis of racial public policy. However, little work exists in terms of explicitly detailing the central components of a Black feminist critical policy analysis. Black feminism, as argued by Patricia Hill Collins (2000, p. 13) is "subjugated knowledge" birthed from and grounded in an African worldview and the multiple and interlocking oppressions of race, class, and gender that Black women in the US confront. Epistemologically, Black feminist thought calls into question how to understand the lived realties of Black women and apprehend meaning(s) of such realities. To this end, Black feminists have challenged the often negative social construction of Black womanhood. In the context of public policy, Black feminists argue that gender, race and class influence the effects of public policies. In terms of methodology, Black feminists such as Collins (2000), hooks (1994), Jordan-Zachery (2009), and others suggest approaches grounded in the lived experiences of Black women and also approaches, such as discourse analysis, that are designed to uncover values and often hidden power relations. This approach is well aligned with Bacchi's (1999) suggestion on the use and value of discourse analysis as a means of uncovering power dynamics and relations. Finally, a Black feminist approach is action-oriented (Collins 2000). Actions are designed to challenge the often negative social construction of Black womanhood and often the omission of Black women from policy agendas with the goal of achieving a more just and equitable society.

A central assumption of this study, growing out of Black feminist thought, is that public policies are value-laden (nonneutral) and reflect hegemonic race-gender-class beliefs and assumptions. When applied to policy-making, a Black feminist lens:

a. Centers the intersectionality of race, class, and gender (among other oppressive structures) in the analysis of the policy-making process from the definition stage to the implementation stage. This is not to suggest that all Black women, for example, experience the effects of public policy in the same manner.

b. Interrogates policy-making as a political process that is influenced by (and that does influence) divergent and, at times, contradictory material and discursive power configurations. As such, it seeks to uncover the "norms" (race, gender, and class) embedded in the framing of not only the policies themselves but also the logic of the policies.

c. Offers critical responses to public policy that seek to address systematic and institutional structures of oppression. In that sense, it is an approach to policy analysis that seeks to transform state-centered policies for a more just and equitable outcome.

Approach to the Study

The approach to the study merges intersectionality with frame analysis, a form of discourse analysis that is concerned with analyzing how an issue is defined and, ultimately, how the issue is addressed (or not). Gitlin (1980) suggests that there are two general functions of frames that prove useful for unpacking the core ideology/ideologies and embedded meaning/meanings. The first is the function of presentation—"selecting emphasis and exclusion"—and the second is the function of interpretation—"persistent patterns of cognition, interpretation, and presentation. Symbol handlers routinely organize discourse, whether verbal or visual" (Gitlin 1980, p. 7). These two functions of frames are well suited for analyzing race-gender structures of President Obama's response to the economic decline (and resulting issues) of urban areas. This understanding of framing, integrated with Black feminist thought, allows me to describe and interpret the structure and power of a communicating text (Entman 1993; Gitlin 1980; Tuchman 1978).

Through the analysis of the frames, I am able to determine which identities and ideologies become salient in the framing of the various elements of the larger urban policy agenda. As argued by Reese (2001, p. 11), "frames are organizing principles that are socially shared and persistent over time, that work symbolically to meaningfully structure the social world." Frames, according to Goffman (1974), offer a basic cognitive structure that provides a guide for understanding and constructing our reality. There is some debate as to whether frames are consciously or unconsciously manufactured and used (see Entman 1993). In this analysis, frames are thought to be simultaneously consciously and unconsciously produced. As argued by Goffman (1974, p. 24), "We tend to perceive events in terms of primary frameworks, and the type of framework we employ provides a way of describing the event to which it is applied." These primary frameworks—"the natural" and "the social"—inform how members of society understand daily living (Goffman 1974, p. 26). Natural frameworks "identify occurrences seen as undirected, unoriented, unanimated, unguided, 'purely physical.'" Social frameworks "provide background understanding for events that incorporate the will, aim, and controlling effort of intelligence, a live agency, the chief one being the human being" (Goffman 1974, p. 22). Frame analysis is a tool for ordering information about how people perceive political problems. We can use frame analysis to listen and grasp the fears and pains of a class, a community, or a nation, and then to crystallize their understanding of a problem (Ryan 1991, p. 73).

I focus on the discursive structures and rhetorical devices used in the various reports, as they are an integral part of understanding how race-gender structures influence and shape policy logics. Frames are manifested "by the presence or absence of certain keywords, stock phrases, stereotyped images, sources of information, and sentences that provide thematically reinforcing clusters of facts or judgments" (Entman 1993, p. 52). To this end, the analysis of the data asks the following questions:

1. Do the frames employ an intersectional approach? More specifically, I ask, How do policy makers and shapers recognize constituting systems of race and gender that produce marginal experiences and identities among urban dwellers? Additionally, I ask, How are these systems integrated into the understanding of these social issues?
2. Who and what is excluded in the policy suggestions and understanding of the issues?

The analysis involved multiple steps. My approach to understanding the framing of urban policy first involved a simple reading of the texts to get a sense of the issues they were discussing. My second and third readings determined what frames were employed in the talk. In general, Black feminist theory was employed to understand the broad themes used in the various reports on urban policy. The first stage of the analysis involved the use of open coding to identify, name, and categorize issues prevalent in the reports. Open coding allowed me to uncover broad themes in the data (see Patton 2002). A more systematic process designed to uncover and group subthemes followed this step. This stage involved the use of a constant comparison technique, which involves comparing and contrasting themes and concepts that emerged from the reports (Strauss and Corbin 1990). The following questions helped to guide this process: How are the issues of poverty and unemployment talked about in reference to specific groups, such as African Americans and women? How is the concept of family understood? After the identification and grouping of frames, done through axial coding, the final stage of the analysis involved examining data, via inductive and deductive reasoning, that did not fit into the metaframe and subframe categories (Glaser and Strauss 1967; Strauss and Corbin 1990).

My research assistants and I coded five reports issued by the White House. We first used the following key words (and their derivatives): urban, women, race, African American / Black, revitalization, unemployment, poverty, poor, and family. Once these key words were identified, we then used the individual paragraphs, within which the word was located, as the primary unit of analysis. The paragraphs were then coded for how they discussed these particular populations and/or issues. These broad themes that dominated the five reports (thought of as metaframes) include universalism, neoliberalism, individualism, personal responsibility, and race-gender neutrality.

Frame analysis, like other forms of qualitative analysis, is not without concern. For one, there is the concern of subjectivity (that such studies lack scientific rigor). I rely on theoretical grounding, Black feminist thought, to address this concern. A theoretically grounded approach suggests that a study may be subjective, as there is no such thing as one universal truth and as such objectivity. By making the study as transparent as possible—providing a detailed approach to how the themes are identified and offering detailed quotes also help to address the concern of subjectivity. A transparent approach to the study helps the reader to trace and follow the logic of the analysis. Regarding the applicability of such qualitative studies, I argue that applicability comes from the approach Black feminist critical policy analysis to the study as opposed to the text analyzed.

As I argue, the discourse used in the reports portend to a type of race-gender neutrality while obscuring the very race-gender effects of the urban policy initiatives. Employing a Black, critical feminist policy analysis proves useful for uncovering the manner by which seemingly neutral dominant policy discourses hide race-gender policy effects.

Discursive Structures and Rhetorical Devices: The Logic of Urban Policies

This analysis is concerned with how the intersection of the race and gender is integrated into the logic of the urban policy-making process. Accordingly, the analysis is not concerned so much with what the reports say and the claims they make as with what they fail to say. As exemplified across the five reports, there was a type of passiveness that rendered some groups, such as Black women, and issues, such as race-based inequality, invisible. Consequently, the reports left absent government's responsibility in ongoing race-gender inequality, discrimination, and racism.

Across the five reports, *race* was the least used term (appearing only three times in the five reports) followed by *Black / African American*, which was deployed a total of nine times (see table 9.1). The term *woman/women* were used twenty times, and *poor* was mentioned fifteen times. The most widely used terms were *family* (402 times), *poverty* (109 times), and *unemployment* (102 times).

The actual usage of the various terms tells a story, but this story is further complicated by further analysis. Using Black feminist theory, I analyze how the terms were used. The deployment of some key words in conjunction with the context within which they were used suggests a type of neutrality, at best, and omission, at worst. So while the Obama administration implies that gender is an important factor in the design of policy, the policy logic of urban policies (as reflected in these five

TABLE 9.1. Usage of Terms

Report	Urban	Women	Race	Black	Revitalization	Unemployment	Poverty	Poor	Family
Pathways	3	4	0	4	12	41	50	9	107
Homelessness	4	0	0	0	0	8	40	3	42
Opening Doors	4	15	3	3	0	4	8	2	155
Opportunity	0	0	0	0	50	2	11	1	11
Fatherhood	0	1	0	2	0	6	0	0	87
Total	11	20	3	9	62	102	109	15	402

Occurrences of Key Terms

Source: Compiled by the author from documents: *Creating Pathways to Opportunity* (2011); *Building Neighborhoods of Opportunity* (2011); US Interagency Council of Homelessness (2011); *Promoting Responsible Fatherhood* (2012); *Supporting Families, Strengthening Communities* (2013)

reports) shows that gender is not necessarily centered. Black women are missing in the Obama administration's attempts to economically and morally revitalize urban America.

Universalism and the American Dream: Race, Gender, and Social Positions

The inequitable conditions faced by African Americans, and African American women specifically, were rarely mentioned in the policy logic for revitalizing urban America. In the five reports, Black / African American women were not mentioned. When the reports spoke of the social position of Blacks (and other racially minoritized groups) it was done in a universalistic manner. Consider the following:

- "A new initiative to expand infrastructure employment opportunities for minorities, women, and socially and economically disadvantaged individuals will provide pathways into the construction industry for otherwise historically marginalized groups" (*Creating Pathways to Opportunity* 2011, p. 45).

- "We must fight to ensure that all Americans, regardless of the family or neighborhood they grow up in, can see their hard work realize the American dream. That promise is a cornerstone of American society, a tenet central to the prosperity of our nation" (*Creating Pathways to Opportunity* 2011, p. 31).
- "The Department of Labor's $40 million competitive grant program supports local efforts to prepare unemployed noncustodial parents, and other individuals with significant barriers to unemployment, for work through transitional employment, while assisting them to gain unsubsidized employment intended to promote family engagement and long term self-sufficiency" (*Promoting Responsible Fatherhood* 2012, p. 6).
- "Although a top notch education and a good, stable job are two of the cornerstones to success and factors for self-sufficiency, for many low income families, upward mobility cannot happen without addressing other key ingredients to opportunity like access to affordable health care and supports to keep families stable and strong" (*Creating Pathways to Opportunity* 2011, p. 37).
- "The Administration is working to help these families work hard and earn self-sufficiency by raising minimum wage, directly boosting wages for 15 million workers, and cutting taxes for low-income working families" (*Supporting Families, Strengthening Communities* 2013, p. 7).

The ideology of universalism suggests that all would benefit from policies and that there is no need for policy to respond to differentials resulting from race, gender, and class. Furthermore, this policy logic approach relies on the notion of equal opportunity. This policy logic does not speak to historical and contemporary structures and their continued impact in the inequitable distribution of resources. Finally, the policy logic of universalism is couched in the ideology of the "American dream," which serves to anchor the policy in a previously established rhetoric of equality. The use of the rhetoric of the American dream is used to justify the policy by suggesting that this ideal is available to all regardless of social location. Such rhetorical devices are part of the neoliberal approach to addressing difference while not speaking of race-gender differences. Working in tangent with the "American dream" and the neoliberal approach, often implicitly and explicitly stated, is the ideal of individualism. The rhetorical devices and discursive structures are used to suggest that government will do its part by offering some policies, but it is up to the individual to overcome barriers once they are offered said opportunity. An underlying assumption is that the free market, and individual participation in this structure, is the means to achieving equality. Another underlying assumption of this frame argues that race-gender hierarchies and structures do not influence the free market. The result is that government is absolved from addressing its role in perpetuating and maintaining race-gender hierarchies.

Some Families Need Fixing: Family, Race, and Poverty

The frames used in the policy logic concerning the family (promotion and stability) and the revitalization of urban America include: (a) pathology and fixing, as well as (b) economic and personal responsibility. As examples of these frames, I offer the following:

- "These numbers are especially stark for minority communities: over 30 percent of Hispanic, African American, American Indian and Alaska Native children today live in poverty. Too many of our children live in neighborhoods of concentrated poverty, marked by high unemployment rates, rampant crime, health disparities, inadequate early care and education, struggling schools, and capital disinvestment" (*Creating Pathways to Opportunity* 2011, p. 2).
- "Black boys in poor families have the worst employment outcomes in young adulthood of any sub-group and poor black children are more likely than their peers to be poor in adulthood" (*Creating Pathways to Opportunity* 2011, p. 23).
- "Not only do unplanned pregnancies present significant challenges to young mothers and fathers, research shows that children born outside of two-parent married families are more likely to be poor, drop out of high school, have lower grade-point averages, and poorer school attendance records—factors that can help continue the cycle of poverty. For those Americans that do have children, the President believes in personal responsibility and being able to support one's family financially as well as emotionally" (*Creating Pathways to Opportunity* 2011, p. 40).
- "And data show that low-income men from communities of color are significantly more likely to be nonresident fathers than resident fathers.

Roughly one out of every three Hispanic children and more than half of African-American children grow up in homes without their fathers present" (*Promoting Responsible Fatherhood* 2012, p. 2).

- "Encouraging financial literacy. The Building Assets for Fathers and Families Initiative provides asset building services and financial education that encourages non-custodial parents to establish savings accounts and access other services to in-crease financial stability" (*Promoting Responsible Fatherhood* 2012, p. 6).

Fathering and the Economic Model

One consistently used narrative related to the family ethic made a connection between parenting, particularly fathering, and economy. The documents lay bare the dominant role of economic self-sufficiency as a means for achieving family well-being. Economic stability and self-sufficiency are seen as proxies for care. This frame suggests that good economic (male) providers do so in order to care for their families (Christiansen and Palkovitz 2001). The policy logic seeks to allow men to achieve autonomy and control over their private lives. Prior research implies that this normalizing project of Black manhood fails to take into account how previous practices and policies often limit Black men's access to the resources necessary for such a normalizing project to occur (see Edin and Nelson 2001; Jordan-Zachery 2008; Staples 1982; Young 2006).

In promoting the economic model of fathering, there was some recognition that fathers face external barriers. Thus, it was recognized that

the choice to be an active, engaged parent is influenced by factors in the family and the community. For example, it can be especially hard for fathers who are trying to do the right thing to maintain their dignity and motivation in the face of unemployment or underemployment. (*Promoting Responsible Fatherhood* 2012, p. 2)

Ignored in the above frame are references to the impact of structures and the government that make it relatively difficult for men of this social location to function in the normalized understanding of manhood and fatherhood.

Motherhood and the Ethic of Family Well-Being

The role of women in the support of the family was rarely mentioned in the various reports. The frames of the role of mothers in the family were presented as follows:

- "The goals are to impact rates of father absence, support fathers who are there for their families, affirm the roles of mothers and other caretakers, and ensure that every child has a caring adult in their life" (*Creating Pathways of Opportunity* 2011, p. 40).
- "As a mother, neighbor, or a friend you can contribute to a culture of high parental involvement. This requires purposeful and consistent messages and actions that reinforce responsible fatherhood" (*Promoting Responsible Fatherhood* 2012, p. 28).

These quotes suggest two frames: individualism vis-à-vis the government and that the role of women in the family is to support fathers. As reflected in the second quote, taken from the report *Promoting Responsible Fatherhood*, the woman's role is to support men in their goals of being better parents. There was little to no framing of women and economic stability and/or literacy education as a means of escaping poverty and, consequently, improving the well-being of their families. Mothers are to principally support the nurturing of parentally involved fathers. This policy logic seems to suggest a particular hegemonic form of masculinity (Connell 1995). Such a discursive structure works in tangent with the frame that suggest that the absence of fathers results in social problems ranging from crime and delinquency to poor school achievement and poverty. Thus, if men are allowed to serve in their proper place and women assume the role of supporters, all will be right with the family.

The framing of parenting, race, and urban revitalization (economic and moral) advances normative expectations of mothers and fathers. Successful manhood and fatherhood is understood in terms of financial support (and implied the disciplinarian role). Again, ignored in this logic is that many of these men (and women) targeted by this policy logic reside in communities with limited resources. However, this approach seeks to institutionalize a particular understanding of family formation and functioning. The policies promote what Abramovitz (1988) refers to as the "family ethic" or the "Standard North American Family" described by Smith (1999) for structuring social welfare policy. This model privileges a particular type of family formation—a two-parent, male-breadwinner, and female-caretaker model. As Dorothy Smith argues, the "Standard North American Family" (SNAF) serves as an ideological frame that is employed in public and policy discourses "to coordinate multiple sites of representation" (Smith 1999, p. 160). The use of SNAF fails to address race-gender inequalities and the race-gender impacts of previously existing policies and how they shape urban dwellers' experiences with inequality—of which economic inequality is one element.

Conclusion

The focus of this work, Black feminist policy analysis, is on how the structure of the discourses in reports on urban policy represent the philosophy of the Obama administration and how such a philosophy may continue race-gender inequity—a cornerstone for those of us who study Black feminist politics. This, I argue, extends the notion of the inclusionary dilemma faced by President Obama as it moves us beyond how he grappled with race to an analysis of how he grappled with the intersection of race, gender, and class in his policy decision-making. Urban social policy has been relatively nonexistent since the 1970s (see Kantor 2013; Mettler 2007). President Obama has sought to systematically address the lack of attention paid to urban communities. In his speech at the United States Conference of Mayors, June 2008, Barack Obama stated,

> We need to stop seeing our cities as the problem and start seeing them as the solution. Because strong cities are the building blocks of strong regions, and strong regions are essential for a strong America. That is the new metropolitan reality and we need a new strategy that reflects it. (quoted in Border 2008)

His efforts included the creation of a White House Office of Urban Affairs. However, it leaves out gender.

President Obama's approach to urban policy may be summarized as universalistic and race-gender neutral. In the report *Creating Pathways*, it is stated,

The interconnected challenges in high-poverty neighborhoods require interconnected solutions to address the compounding effects of the multiple barriers facing children and families who live in these neighborhoods. . . . The Neighborhood Revitalization Initiative will help break the cycle of intergenerational poverty, improve the educational outcomes of low-income children, and empower individuals and community organizations to transform their neighborhoods into places of opportunity. (2011, p. 32)

The approach to revitalizing urban communities seeks to address the various and interlocking issues faced by many who reside in these communities. However, it is devoid of addressing race and gender (and their interlocking nature) as part of the context within which many of the challenges faced by some urban dwellers occur. And Black politics today has also failed to systematically address this omission. (I speculate as to why this might be the case below.)

Black poverty and inequality (and the gendering of such) remain a serious problem in major urban areas (Berger 2015; Musterd and Ostendorf 2013; Ovadia 2003; National Women's Law Center 2011; Semyonor et al. 2000). However, across the five documents that inform this analysis, there is a failure to offer a critical examination of how those, particularly those that are race-gendered, living in these distressed communities are connected to a wider race-gendered system within the US. Instead, policy seems to be engaged in a normalizing project that appears to be more concerned with ensuring that men participate in the labor force in a particular manner, as opposed to addressing racism and sexism.

What happens when Blackness is couched primarily in terms of manhood, and womanhood (when mentioned) is framed in a race-neutral manner? A Black feminist policy analysis reveals how seemingly benign universal policies can have a less than positive impact when some groups are left out of the policy logic. What this analysis reveals is that Black women (and women in general) are simply absent from the policy logic of urban revitalization. Often framed in a neoliberal race-gender neutral discourse, urban policies promote an individualistic approach to addressing the various and intersecting problems faced by those residing in urban communities. Ignored are the race-gender systemic and structured processes and practices that are designed to advantage one group over another. Also ignored in the policy logic are the implications for de facto and de jure segregation—the legislative activities of the past that resulted in racial (and economic) segregation. According to Massey and Dentón (1998) African Americans experience levels of sociospatial segregation exceeding the maximum degree ever experienced by any other ethnic group in the US.

Urban policy rests on the assumption that poverty and resulting challenges are "the product of market dynamics, naturally occurring phenomena, and . . . cultural limitations" (Bonilla-Silva 2010, p. 2). Furthermore, the policy logic suggests that individuals and communities shoulder the responsibility for achieving equality and justice (Sweet and McCue-Enser 2010). Following from this logic is the belief, stated and unstated, that government's role is to provide opportunities only and not to address the impact of race-gender hierarchies. As Robinson (2009, p. 221) argues, "The concerns of urban Black communities require race-aware [and gender-aware] advocacy because the processes by which they come into existence and are sustained are fundamentally racialized [and gendered]."

This ideology of race-gender neutrality coupled with the ideology of neoliberalism results in a homogeneity project that masks a plethora of historical, socioeconomic, and ideological differences among different groups of women and between genders. As a result, the reality of women's heterogeneity is often obscured and neglected in policy deliberations and the study of such. Employing a race-general, neoliberal urban policy logic will prove less than effective in addressing the systemic problems faced by urban dwellers, particularly Black women. It is for this reason that an intersectional approach (grounded in Black feminist politics) to policy formation is advocated. An intersectional approach centers the lived realities and experiences of race-gendered individuals regardless of social location and, as such, would account for and recognize differences between and among groups of women and men.

An intersectional approach is relevant for all aspects of the policy-making process but is particularly fruitful for the policy logic stage. This is the case because the

identification of different socially-situated perspectives will not only provide more precise information but also yield greater insights into systems of marginalization and oppression. This will assist policy makers and service providers alike to deliver more effective and efficient programs and services to better meet the needs of those individuals and groups most disadvantaged by social inequities. (Rummens 2003, p. 25)

The Obama administration is to be commended for addressing the challenges faced by urban dwellers via a multipronged pluralistic policy approach. What it failed to do was to deploy an intersectional strategy. Such an approach recognizes the race-gender composition of jobs and housing segregation, thereby, allowing the policy approach to move beyond neutrality and individualism. An intersectional approach to urban policy would begin to challenge the systemic and institutional approach to the reproduction of inequality. Such an approach is needed because place and its intersection with race/ethnicity, gender, and family structure are important determinants of economic and social well-being.

So, what are the implications of this study for Black politics after Obama has left office? For one, it suggest that Black politics can no longer be gender blind. Gender, like other markers of difference must be included in our analyses. Second, the silence of Black politics in general suggests, like Obama, that Black politics is engaging in a type of politics that rest on the prototypical "citizen," this prototypical citizen tends to see race and not gender. Consequently, Black women, transwomen, and others deemed outside of the "good" Black society tend to be ignored in scholarship. Cathy Cohen (2014) asserts,

The politics of those most marginal in Black communities are usually discussed when they conform to traditional understandings of what constitutes legitimate politics, ranging from engagement with formal political institutions to the traditional, extra-systemic politics of riots, boycotts, and protests, to the adherence to dominant norms and expectations regarding behavior. (32)

Black politics can no longer be complicit in the politics of Black respectability—which creates the perfect storm for the dilemma in which Obama found himself. Finally, Black politics must be open to analyzing more than just institutions, mobilization, political figures, and voting behaviors. If nothing else, the Obama administration showed us why it is important to consider the impacts of public policies across a range of differences. Thus, in the post-Obama era, Black politics must expand its boundaries in terms of what and who is studied and also the approaches for the study of politics.

BIBLIOGRAPHY

Abramovitz, M. 1988. *Regulating the lives of women: Social welfare policy from colonial times to the present.* Boston: South End Press.

Alexander-Floyd, N. 2007. *Gender, race, and nationalism in contemporary Black politics.* New York: Palgrave Macmillan.

Alexander-Floyd, N. 2012. "Disappearing acts: Reclaiming intersectionality in the social science in a post-Black feminist era." *Feminist Formations* 24 (1): 1–25.

Apple, M. W. 1994. "Texts and contexts: The state and gender in educational policy." *Curriculum Inquiry*, 24(3): 349–359.

Bacchi, C. 1999. *Women, politics, and policies. The construction of policy problems.* London: Sage.

Barnett, M. R. 1976. "A theoretical perspective on American racial public policy." In M. R. Barnett and J. A. Hefner (eds.), *Public Policies for the Black Community: Strategies and perspectives* (pp. 1–53). Port Washington, NY: Alfred Publishing.

Berger, M. 2004. "Workable sisterhood." Princeton, NJ: Princeton University Press.

Black women in the United States. 2015. National Coalition on Black Civic Participation. March 30, 2015. http://ncbcp.org.

Bonilla-Silva, Eduardo. 2010. *Racism without Racists: Color-Blind Racism and the Persistence of Racial Inequality in the United States.* Rowman & Littlefield Publishers.

Border, J. M. 2008. "Obama urges mayors to focus on urban growth, but not to expect increased federal aid." *New York Times.* June 22, 2008. www.nytimes.com.

Building Neighborhoods of Opportunity: Neighborhood Revitalization Report. 2011. White House. July 2011. https://obamawhitehouse.archives.gov.

Christiansen, S., and Palkovitz, R. 2001. "Why the good provider role still matters." *Journal of Family Issues* 22: 84–106.

Cohen, Cathy. 2014. "Deviance as resistance: A new research agenda for the study of Black politics." *Du Bois Review* 1, no. 1: 27–45.

Collins, P. H. 2000. *Black feminist thought: Knowledge, consciousness and the politics of empowerment.* 10th anniversary edition. New York: Routledge.

Connell, R. W. 1995. *Masculinities.* Cambridge, MA: Polity Press.

Creating pathways to opportunity. 2011. White House. October 14, 2011. https://obamawhitehouse.archives.gov.

Crenshaw, K. 1989. "Demarginalizing the intersection of race and sex: A Black feminist critique of antidiscrimination doctrine, feminist theory, and antiracist politics." In K. Maschke, *Feminist legal theories* (pp. 23–52). New York: Taylor & Francis.

Desmond, M. 2014. "Poor Black women are evicted at alarming rates, settting off a chain of hardship." How Housing Matters. MacAuthor Foundation, March 2014, www.macfound.org.

Edin, K., and Nelson, T. 2001. "Working steady: Race, low-wage work, and family involvement among noncustodial fathers in Philadelphia." In E. Anderson, and M Denton (eds.), *Problem of the century: Racial stratification in the United States* (pp. 375–404). New York: Russell Sage Foundation.

Eichner, Alana, and Katherine Gallagher Robbins. 2015. "National Snapshot: Poverty among Women & Families, 2014." National Women's Law Center. www.nwlc.org.

Entmacher, J., Gallagher Robbins, K., Vogtman, J., and Morrison, A. 2014. "Insecure and unequal: Poverty and Income among women and families 2000–2013." National Women's Law Center. www.nwlc.org.

Entman, R. 1993. "Framing: Towards clarification of a fractured paradigm." *Journal of Communication* 43, no. 4: 51–58.

Gitlin, T. 1980. *The whole world is watching: Mass media in the making and unmaking of the new left*. Berkeley, Los Angeles, and London: University of California Press.

Glaser, B., and Strauss, A. 1967. *The discovery of grounded theory*. Hawthorne, NY: Aldine.

Goffman, E. C. 1974. *Frame analysis: An essay on the organization of experience*. Cambridge, MA: Harvard University Press.

Harris, Fred. 2012. *The price of the ticket: Barack Obama and the rise and decline of Black politics*. New York: Oxford University Press.

Harris-Perry, M. 2011. *Sister citizen: Shame, stereotypes, and Black women in America*. New Haven, CT: Yale University Press.

Hegewisch, A., Ellis, E., and Hartmann, H. 2015, March. "The Gender Wage Gap: 2014 Earnings Differences by Race and Ethnicity." Institute for Women's Policy Research. March 6, 2015. www.iwpr.org.

hooks, b. 1994. *Outlaw culture: Resisting representation*. New York: Routledge.

Isoke, Z. 2013. *Urban Black women and the politics of resistance*. New York: Palgrave Macmillan.

James, Joy. 1999. *Shadowboxing: Representations of Black feminist politics*. New York: St. Martin Press.

Jewell, K. S. 1992. *From mammy to Miss America and beyond*. New York: Routledge.

Jordan-Zachery, J. S. 2008. "Policy interaction: The mixing of fatherhood, crime and urban policies." *Journal of Social Policy* 37, no. 1, 81–102.

Jordan-Zachery, J. S. 2009. *Black women cultural images and social policy*. New York: Routledge.

Jordan-Zachery, J. S. 2017. *Shadow bodies: Black women, ideology, representation and politics*. New Jersey: Rutgers University Press.

Jordan-Zachery, J., and Wilson, S. 2017. "'Talking' about gender while ignoring race and class: A discourse analysis of pay equity debates." In *Black women in politics: Identity, power and justice in the new millennium*. Eds. N. Alexander-Floyd and J. Jordan-Zachery. Special issue. *National Political Science Review* 16: 49–65.

Kantor, P. 2013. "The Two faces of American urban policy." *Urban Affairs Review* 49, no. 6: 821–850.

King, M. C. 1973. "The politis of sexual stereotypes." *Black Scholar* 4: 12–23.

Marshall, C. 1997. "Dismantling and reconstructing policy analysis." In C. Marshall (ed.), *Feminist critical policy analysis: A perspective from primary and secondary schooling* (pp. 1–38). London: Falmer.

Massey, D., and Dentón, N. A. 1998. *American apartheid: Segregation and the making of the underclass.* Cambridge, MA: Harvard University Press.

Mettler, S. 2007. "The transformed welfare state and the redistribution of political voice." In P. Pierson and T. Skocpol (eds.), *The transformation of American politics* (pp. 191–222). Princeton: Princeton University Press.

Musterd, S., and Ostendorf, W. eds. 2013. *Urban segregation and the welfare state: Inequality and exclusion in western cities.* New York: Routledge.

National Center on Family Homelessness. 2011. "The characteristics and needs of families experiencing homelessness." Needham, MA. www.files.eric.ed.gov.

National Coalition for Homeless Veterans. 2014. "'Bridging the gap': Emerging unmet needs—African Amerian populations: Needs and services." 2014 National Coalition for Homeless Veterans Annual Conference. May 28, 2014. www.nchv.org.

National Coalition for Homeless Veterans. 2013. "Halfway home: Progress in the plan to end veterans homelessness." 2013 National Coalition for Homeless Veterans Annual Conference. May 29, 2013. www.nchv.org.

National Women's Law Center. 2011. "Employment crisis worsens for black women during the recovery." August 3, 2011. www.nwlc.org.

Nichols, A. 2013. "Poverty in the United States." Urban Institute. September 17, 2013. www.urban.org.

Ovadia, S. 2003. "The dimensions of racial inequality and occupational and residential segregation across metropolitian areas in the United States." *City and Community* 2, no. 4: 313–333.

Patton, M. 2002. *Qualitative research and evaluation methods.* Thousand Oaks, CA: Sage.

Promoting Responsible Fatherhood. 2012. White House. June 2012. https://obamawhite house.archives.gov.

Reese, S. 2001. "Framing public life: A bridging model for media research." In S. Reese, O. Gandy, and A. Grant (eds.), *Framing Public Life* (pp. 7–31). Mahwah, NJ: Erlbaum.

Roberts, D. 1997. *Killing the Black body: Race, reproduction, and the meaning of liberty.* New York: Random House.

Robinson, J., III. 2009. "Coloring the blind spot: The urban Black community as an object of racial discourse in the age of Obama." *Western Journal of Black Studies* 33, no. 3: 212–223.

Rummens, J. A. 2003. "Ethnic ancestry, culture, identity, and health: Using ethnic origin data from the 2001 Canadian Census." *Canadian Ethnic Studies* 35, no. 1: 10–25.

Ryan, C. 1991. *Prime time activism: Media strategies for grassroots organizing*. Boston, MA: South End Press.

Semyonor, M., Y. Haberfeld, Y. Cohen, N. Lewin-Epstein. 2000. "Racial composition and occupational segregation and inequality across American cities." *Social Science Research* 29: 175–187.

"Single Mother Statistics." 2020. https://singlemotherguide.com/single-mother-statistics/#:~:text=Out%20of%20more%20than%2010,compared%20with%20whites%20(36%25).

Smith, D. E. 1999. *Writing the social: Critique, theory and investigations*. Toronto: University of Toronto Press.

Staples, R. 1982. *Black masculinity: The Black male's role in American society*. San Francisco: Black Scholar Press.

Stolberg, S. G. 2009, January 29. "Obama Signs Equal-Pay Legislation." *New York Times*. January 30, 2009. www.nytimes.com.

Strauss, A., and Corbin, J. 1990. *Basics of qualitative research: Grounded theory procedures and techniques*. Newbury Park: Sage.

Supporting Families, Strengthening Communities: The Economic Importance of Nutrition Assistance. 2013. Executive Office of the President: Washington, DC. www.obamawhitehouse.archives.gov.

Sweet, D., and McCue-Enser, M. 2010. "Constituting 'the people' as rhetorical interruption: Barack Obama and the unfinished hopes of an imperfect people." *Communication Studies* 61, no. 5: 602–622.

Tuchman, G. 1978. "The news net." *Social Research* 45: 253–276.

US Bureau of Labor Statistics. 2012. "Highlights of women's earnings in 2011, Report 1038." Accessed January, 15, 2015 from: www.bls.gov.

United States Interagency Council of Homelessness. 2010. "Opening doors: Federal strategic plan to prevent and end homelessness." http://usich.gov.

Young, A. 2006. *The minds of marginalized Black men: Making sense of mobility, opportunity, and future life chances*. Princeton, NJ: Princeton University Press.

10

Barack Obama and the Racial Politics of the Affordable Care Act

SEKOU FRANKLIN, PEARL K. FORD DOWE, AND
ANGELA K. LEWIS-MADDOX

The Affordable Care Act was a monumental accomplishment
for our country and the African American community.
—US Representative Emmanuel Cleaver (D-MO), January 19, 2011

Barack Hussein Obama's election as president of the United States in
2008 was one of the momentous events in the nation's history. His
electoral coalition was the most racially and ethnically diverse in the
history of presidential elections, as non-Whites comprised nearly one-
third of the general electorate vote.[1] African Americans were central to
his electoral coalition. Over 65 percent (or 15.9 million people) voted in
the election compared to 66.1 percent of Whites.[2] Obama's repeat performance in 2012 further underscored the racial mosaic of voters who
made up his electoral and governing coalitions.

Health care reform was a major source of tension in the 2008 presidential election. Other candidates in the 2008 Democratic Party primary, such as Senators Hillary Clinton and John Edwards, called for an
individual mandate to purchase health insurance. Obama, on the other
hand, rejected this proposal even though it would later become a central
component of his health care reform law in 2010. He eventually settled
for a private-public insurance program similar to the universal insurance program that was implemented by his 2012 rival in the presidential
election, Mitt Romney, when he was the governor of Massachusetts in
2006.[3]

These policy debates ensured that health care reform, principally
a program that universalized insurance, would be a priority during
Obama's first term. On February 17, 2009, Congress passed Obama's

stimulus legislation called the American Recovery and Reinvestment Act. Part of the stimulus package invested funds on expanding the health care workforce in underserved communities.[4] A week later, Obama explained the merits of universal health care to a joint session of Congress. Referencing the legacy of President Theodore Roosevelt's support of public health insurance, he said that "health care has weighed down our economy and the conscience of our nation long enough. . . . Health care reform cannot wait, it must not wait, and will not wait another year."[5] A year after the speech, the Patient Protection and Affordable Care Act (also referred to as the Affordable Care Act, ACA, and Obamacare) of 2010 was passed after a contentious, partisan debate in Congress.

The ACA is Obama's signature domestic policy achievement. As Jacobs indicated, the ACA "enacted the largest change in social welfare policy since the Great Society and perhaps the New Deal, impacting one-seventh of the country's gross domestic product and restructuring the business models of the country's largest industries."[6] It extended health insurance to an estimated twenty million Americans by 2016 through federal and state health exchanges and Medicaid expansion, mandated that individuals purchase health insurance, and provided subsidies to help low-income Americans with their health care costs.[7]

As part of the ACA, Obama announced a "national strategy" to reduce the HIV/AIDS population by 25 percent in five years, and he initially set aside $30 million to implement this strategy. The plan was propelled by Black lawmakers and the 250-member National Working Group on Health Disparities and Health Reform that mobilized grass-roots support for the ACA.[8] The ACA expanded mental health coverage to millions of previously uninsured Americans and boosted funding for community health centers.[9] Expanded coverage for wellness programs to preempt chronic illnesses was further included in the legislation. Coverage for home visitation programs (Section 2951 of the statute) to assist with maternal and prenatal care was also embedded in the ACA.[10] Furthermore, the law removed coinsurance and deductibles in Medicare Part B in order to assist senior citizens with a dozen "early detection and prevention" services.[11]

The ACA was especially significant for African Americans. A year before the passage of the Affordable Care Act, 23.4 percent of Blacks had no health insurance compared to 15.2 percent of Whites.[12] Racial disparities existed in access to good medical care, treatment, and services even when controlling for socioeconomic status. Similar racial disparities existed for premature death rates, infant mortality rates, the quality of medical care, and chronic illnesses, such as heart disease and cancer.[13] These disparities added over dollars to the overall costs of medical care in the United States.[14] After the implementation of ACA, Blacks experienced the sharpest decline of nonelderly uninsured populations. Their uninsured rate dropped by 5.4 percent compared to 2.3 percent among Whites and 5.1 percent among Latinos as of 2013–2014.[15]

This chapter examines the Obama presidency, the politics of race and health care, and the role that African Americans played in shaping the ACA. The essay argues that race—and specifically the elimination of racial and health disparities—was very much part of the ACA's development. From the perspective of Black lawmakers and health equity advocates who worked hand-in-glove with the Obama administration, the ACA was not race neutral or indifferent to Blacks and the working poor. As indicated in the opening commentary by Congressman Emmanuel Cleaver (D-MO), the law had special significance for African Americans even though Obama publicly discussed its impact in deracialized terms. Daniel Dawes, a leading advocate for health equity and author of the groundbreaking book *150 Years of Obamacare*, called ACA the "most comprehensive minority health law" and the "most inclusive [health] law" in the history of the United States. He identified sixty-two provisions that "directly address inequities in health care" that are embedded in the ACA.[16] This essay thus argues that Obama's ACA was substantively accountable to the coalition of Black lawmakers and activists— what we refer to as a policy ecosystem—who were purposeful about incorporating provisions in the bill designed to reduce racial disparities and income-based inequities in health care.

The first part of our chapter provides a broad overview of the debates surrounding deracialized campaign strategies and their relationship to policy ecosystems. We then look more closely at the political wrangling over the bill at both the national and state level. This is followed by a closer examination of how African Americans and health equity advocates—in consultation with the Obama administration— incorporated racial equity and civil rights protections in the ACA framework. Afterward, we draw from the National Public Radio/Robert Wood Johnson/Harvard School of Public Health (NPR/RWJ/HSPH) poll of one thousand African Americans to assess the status of African Americans in the era of the Affordable Care Act.

Deracialization, Obama, and the Affordable Care Act Ecosystem

Deracialization is an electoral strategy that purportedly allows Black officials to ease racial tensions by focusing on issues that appeal to *all* voters, such as education, quality-of-life issues, and transportation.[17] Jeffries states that deracialized candidates "defuse[d] the effects of race by avoiding references to ethnic or racially-construed issues, while at the same time emphasizing those issues that appear to a wide community."[18] In some cases, Black candidates will assume conservative positions on crime and fiscal issues that appeal to moderates and non-Blacks.

Some officials will use deracialized strategies to champion social and economic justice policies, which if implemented, can potentially reduce racial inequities. Yet, they will promote these policies as universalistic or race neutral. Charles Hamilton, an early supporter of deracialized strategies, argued that the Democratic Party should develop a platform that augmented universal, progressive policies in order to thwart attempts by Republicans to use race as a wedge issue.[19] Issues such as health care, environmental policies, and consumer protections are universal policies that have been historically supported by Black progressives, which presumably can appeal to moderates and even some conservatives.

There is no consensus among scholars about the value of deracialized strategies. McCormick and Jones contend that if Black elected officials ignore policy issues that are widely embraced by African Americans, then a deracialized strategy neglects Black political expression.[20] Others argue that if Black candidates make overt appeals to African Americans, then they should expect an "anti-Black" backlash from White voters.[21] Summers and Klinker further imply that the concept of deracialization oversimplifies how Black candidates win and govern in biracial jurisdictions.[22] They believe that Black elected officials' charisma, fund-raising abilities, and campaign organizations are more influential to their electoral and governing successes than the use of a deracialized strategy.

Despite the attempts by some Black officials to deemphasize race, some scholars believe deracialized candidates and politicians can still advance substantive policies important to Black constituencies.[23] For example, Douglas Wilder's deracialized campaign successfully won him the 1992 gubernatorial race in Virginia. Despite a looming budget crisis in the state, he appointed more Blacks to state offices than any governor in Virginia's history. He also reduced racial disparities in education, increased assistance to the Aid to Families with Dependent Children (AFDC) program, expedited the delivery of food stamps, expanded eligibility for Medicaid to pregnant women and children, and removed the state sales tax on prescription drug medication.[24]

On the other hand, some critics believe deracialization fails to reduce racial animus. The mere presence of a Black candidate in a high-profile election can indirectly and unintentionally racialize a campaign.[25] A deracialized strategy in a biracial election may encourage the opposing (White) candidate to rely upon racial priming to mobilize Whites and moderate voters.[26] The media can also inject race into a deracialized campaign, even when media organizations are merely celebrating the importance of having a viable Black candidate in the race.

The election of Donald Trump as the forty-fifth president of the United States offers some insight into the functionality of deracialization in a racially charged political climate. During the campaign, Trump frequently used racial and ethnic appeals to mobilize White voters. This included the employment of anti-immigration rhetoric that attacked undocumented residents and attempted to criminalize Mexican immigrants.[27] His repeated calls for Muslim ban were viewed as Islamophobic and anti–Middle Eastern.[28] He also portrayed Black communities as pathological and so rife with crime that only zero-tolerance policing measures could ameliorate their predicament.[29] Accordingly, the 2016 presidential election and Trump's subsequent victory underscores the salience of racial priming as an electoral strategy and perhaps the diminishing influence of deracialization.

Returning back to the 2008 election, Obama navigated long-standing racial divisions by advocating for quality-of-life issues, access to comprehensive health care, and expanding educational opportunities. These issues were critically important to median voters and moderate Whites but also appealed to African Americans and the broader civil rights community. His public advocacy for universal health care and other redistributive measures, as Price writes, further evoked "the narrative of patriotic whiteness" in order to convince Whites that the enactment of universal health care and other redistributive measures "was part of a national lineage."[30] In general, Obama's electoral framework and approach to governance deemphasized race-specific policies.

Some political observers have been particularly critical of Obama's brand of deracialization. While scholar-activist Cornel West labeled Obama a "Rockefeller Republican in Blackface,"[31] Harris believed that Obama's strategy of race-neutral universalism offered diminishing returns for working and low-income African Americans. Harris contended that the president should have enacted redistributive programs that addressed racialized poverty. Reed further stated that ACA was "built around placating insurance and pharmaceutical industries," similar to Clinton's failed health care initiative.[32] He argued that Obama's principal failure is not advocating for a Black agenda or race-specific policies but his acquiescence to capital at the expense of poor and working-class people. George also reprimanded Obama as an "adherent of the neoliberal doctrine of colorblind racism."[33] He believed Obama's capitulation on the public health insurance option (also referred to as the public option) during the ACA debate exposed his true allegiance to neoliberalism's prioritization of market-based initiatives.

The public option was a central tenet of Obama's "Healthy America" plan during the 2008 campaign. It would have created a universal health insurance program similar to federal employees' health insurance. The broader health care initiative also proposed to protect chronically ill consumers from being denied coverage and proposed guaranteed insurance for children. The ACA, however, excluded the public option but included modified versions of insurance coverage for children and the chronically ill.

Political scientist Cathy Cohen provides a useful explanation undergirding these criticisms of Black progressives. Obama's other identity-based constituency groups can identify substantive policies that address their interests. Women's rights groups celebrated the passage of the Fair Equity Pay Act of 2009. LGBTQ activists pressured Obama to repeal the Don't Ask, Don't Tell policy in the military. The Latino community, which despite facing a record number of deportations, applauded the president when he gave citizenship protections to undocumented youth with the Deferred Action for Childhood Arrivals (DACA) executive order. On the other hand, the absence of similar interventions for African Americans (or the perception that no substantive policies were implemented) has created the impression that Obama had no political will to use the weight of the federal government to ameliorate systemic racism.[34]

Despite the merits or shortcomings of deracialization, most analyses of this approach privilege actor-centered (candidate/politician) frameworks. They undervalue how institutional gridlock in the legislature (e.g., city council, state legislature, congress, etc.) and bureaucracy restricts equity-based policies. Deracialization studies also give less attention to the interactions between Black candidates/politicians and other political actors involved in policy development. Policies such as the ACA, the Fair Pay Equity Act, and the DREAM Act are coproduced by the executive branch, congressional allies, and advocacy groups regardless of whether the president uses race or identity-specific appeals to mobilize support for the law. We refer to this constellation of actors as a policy ecosystem. These actors coproduce the policy along with the president and embed their ideological preferences into the framework of the law.[35] At times, some political actors who are part of this policy ecosystem can inhibit the full implementation of the policy.

In the case of the ACA, there was a preexisting policy ecosystem of advocates and members of Congress who were deeply engaged in health equity debates for decades. When health care reform was introduced in Congress in the spring 2009, this group logically shifted their focus to ensuring that the interests of Blacks and other racial minorities would be addressed in the bill. Health equity was just as much of a priority for this group as the public option. These advocates and lawmakers made a concerted effort to communicate these concerns to Obama.

At the other end of the policy ecosystem were conservative Republicans and activists who waged a campaign against the ACA. After the 2010 congressional midterm elections, when Republicans captured control of the House of Representatives, the lower chamber took more than fifty votes from 2011–2016 seeking to repeal Obamacare. The more vigorous repeal efforts occurred at the state level. The Tea Party and Republican Party's ascendance in the 2010 and 2012 elections allowed them to capture the majority of the statehouses, some of which erected roadblocks to the ACA. As this book approaches publication, the future of the ACA is unclear, as the Trump administration continued to undermine it by legal challenge.

Moreover, the repeal efforts were and are influenced by racial animus despite Obama's best efforts to position the ACA as a race-neutral policy. Tesler and his colleagues found that racial polarization toward the ACA in 2009 and 2010 was significantly starker than the Black-White divide over First Lady Hillary Clinton's advocacy for universal health care (also known as HillaryCare) in 1993.[36] Other studies also uncovered sharp racial divisions toward the health care bill, with Blacks expressing greater enthusiasm for the law compared to Whites and Latinos.[37]

The national Health Tracking Poll sponsored by the Henry J. Kaiser Family Foundation provides insight into the racial polarization toward the health care legislation.[38] Blacks and Latinos had the highest favorability for the ACA in the two years after its passage. From 2013–2015, the highest support was among Blacks, with 67 percent compared to 34 percent of Whites expressing support for the ACA. On average, 62 percent of Blacks, 54 percent of Latinos, and 33 percent of Whites supported the ACA from 2011–2015 (figure 10.1).

Overall, the political environment surrounding ACA was racially charged. At a Congressional Black Caucus (CBC) reception in November 2009, Representative Jesse Jackson Jr. (D-IL) said, "You can't vote against healthcare and call yourself a Black man."[39] His comments were directed toward congressman Artur Davis (D-AL), the only CBC member to vote against the House bill. Senate Majority Leader Harry Reid twice referred to the Republican Party's intransigence to health care reform as similar to those who fought against the abolition of slavery. The reference was condemned by the Black conservative group Project 21, as well as Michael Steele, the head of the Republican National Committee.[40] The *Atlantic* columnist and author Ta-Nehisi Coates wrote about a "pattern of racial paranoia" toward the ACA that was fueled by anti-Black sentiment in the Obama era. To illustrate this point, he pointed to conservative commentator Glenn Beck's reference of Obamacare as a "reparations" policy.[41]

The pro-ACA and anti-ACA forces—the policy ecosystem orbiting the ACA—underscore why it is important to move beyond actor-

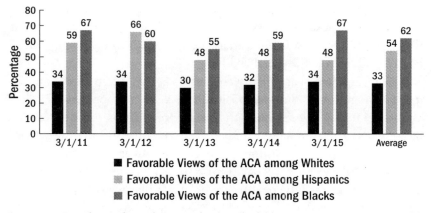

Figure 10.1. Racial attitudes and support for the affordable care act. *Source*: Kaiser Health Tracking Poll: The Public's Views on the ACA, www.kff.org.

centered approaches that investigate the effectiveness of deracialization. Obama may have publicly championed the ACA as racially transcendent, but the development of the policy was heavily influenced by political actors who were explicit about the racial implications of the law. As a policy instrument that restructured the political economy, the Obama administration interpreted the ACA as responsive to the overt demands of leading health equity activists, Black lawmakers, and liberal allies. Likewise, some opponents to the ACA used racially primed messages to stigmatize the law. Hostilities toward the legislators in support of the ACA reached such a heightened level of anger that several members of Congress reported being spat upon and berated with racial and gay slurs.[42]

In the next section, we examine the legislative debate over ACA and the challenge with adopting the public option, the centerpiece of the progressives' interests in universal health care. We then look at how the politics of race shaped the debate and implementation of the statute.

Barack Obama and the Affordable Care Act (ACA)

The ACA was signed into law on March 23, 2010. Although Obama was criticized for abandoning the public option, his strategic approach to getting health care reform was influenced by the experiences of

Democratic Party lawmakers in 1993 who worked with President Bill Clinton. At the time, the president and First Lady Hillary Clinton were accused of forcing a universal health care proposal through Congress without consideration of what kind of bill was acceptable to members of their own party. As Hacker indicates, Clinton's muscular approach failed to account for intraparty divisions between liberal, moderate, and conservative Democrats, all of whom had different policy proposals for health care reform. The lessons of "HillaryCare," along with the fact that Democrats were more unified behind health care reform in 2009, may have convinced the Obama administration to give Congress authorship of the ACA.[43] Once Obama delegated power to Congress, Democrats in the Senate moderated the bill in order to bridge intraparty divisions and potentially win support from moderate Republicans.

The ACA's omission of the public option disappointed many progressives, but steering it through Congress was a long shot from the very beginning. The proposal won approval in the House; however, it faced stiff opposition in the Senate and had to be approved by a bipartisan group of lawmakers—the "Gang of Six"—that was initially tasked with shepherding the entire bill through the upper chamber. Incorporating the public option was a distinct possibility, but congressional gridlock, the filibuster, and a polarizing political climate made approval of the measure a "challenge of monumental proportions."[44] In the end, because the ACA was adopted without the public option, it incentivized insurance providers to implement the law.[45] It also relied on state governments to expand Medicaid and establish health exchanges in some cases, as well as expand mental health, maternal, and other services.

Shortly after the ACA was signed into law, Republican governors and state attorneys filed a challenge in federal court to the constitutionality of the individual mandate and Medicaid expansion part of the statute. The Supreme Court reviewed the statute in the case *National Federation of Independent Business (NFIB) v. Sebelius* after twenty-five states joined the lawsuit.[46] On the opposite side were thirteen governors and various groups such as the NAACP Legal Defense Fund (LDF) that filed amicus briefs supporting the ACA. The LDF argued that the minimum coverage provision of the law gave marginalized groups access to health care and would ameliorate health disparities.

On June 28, 2012, the Supreme Court upheld the individual mandate, the most important provision of the ACA, thus guaranteeing the long-term existence of the law. The second part of the ruling, however, allowed states to reject Medicaid expansion. The expansion intended to allow states to extend coverage beyond their traditional Medicaid populations. In most states, eligibility for Medicaid was restricted to residents who fell at or below the federal poverty line. Working-poor residents whose incomes were higher than the federal poverty guidelines, those with chronic health conditions, seniors with excessive prescription drug costs, and adults with no children were not eligible for Medicaid in many states. These individuals fell into the "coverage gap" in which they were too poor or sick to afford private insurance, yet their incomes were higher than the eligibility guidelines for traditional Medicaid.[47]

Under the ACA, the federal government promised to pay 100 percent of the costs of Medicaid for those in the "gap" during the initial three years and 90 percent of the coverage until 2020. Presumably, the Medicaid dollars could boost state and local economies by defraying costs of emergency care and other medical services.[48] States that rejected Medicaid expansion were expected to lose out on hundreds of millions of dollars. Twenty-six states expanded Medicaid as of May 2016. The majority of southern states rejected expansion proposals.

Most governorships and state legislatures controlled by Republicans resisted Medicaid expansion. They claimed that it would destabilize state budgets and that its inflexibility would lead to the poor delivery of medical care.[49] For example, Georgia governor Nathan Deal adamantly opposed the initiative. Governor Bill Haslam of Tennessee also opposed Medicaid expansion. However, after his reelection in 2014 and due to pressure from grassroots organizations, he proposed an alternative to Medicaid, a hybrid insurance program called Insure Tennessee that would have insured 250,000 people who fell into the coverage gap. The program was crafted in consultation with Health and Human Services' (HHS) Center for Medicare and Medicaid Services. In both states (Georgia and Tennessee), state lawmakers adopted a measure that preempted the governors from expanding health care or creating a hybrid program through executive action. Arkansas also implemented a hybrid program supported by Republican governor Asa Hutchinson but opposed by the state legislature.

The ACA and the Politics of Race

The ACA departs from conventional narratives about deracialization due to the policy ecosystem that emerged around and in response to the law. On the one hand, racial equity and civil rights protections were pushed to the forefront by health equity advocates and members of Congress who were in regular communication with the White House, and in some respects, they prioritized this issue above the public option. At the other end of the spectrum were anti-ACA activists, state lawmakers, and Republican members of Congress.

Although Obama championed health care reform as a universal program that helped all uninsured Americans, race influenced how Americans interpreted the law. The Obama administration, his congressional allies, and advocacy groups interpreted the ACA as uniquely addressing the needs of working-poor Blacks. On the other hand, racial conservatives and leading Republicans interpreted the statute as an entitlement for Blacks and other people of color as "more free stuff" for special interests, according to Mitt Romney, the 2012 Republican nominee for president. Romney made these comments after he was booed at the national NAACP convention for threatening to repeal the ACA if elected.[50]

In the previous section, we indicated that Obama delegated much of the authority for crafting the bill to Congress in the early stages of the ACA. This allowed congressional allies to bridge ideological divisions in the Democratic Party. However, it also gave members of Congress the power to remove some provisions from the final bill, such as the public option that was endorsed by progressives.

CBC members had some influence in shaping the bill as well. Their involvement in health equity policies predated Obama's rise in politics by two decades. In 1984, Louis Stokes (D-OH) worked closely with HHS Secretary Margaret Heckler to establish the Task Force on Black and Minority Health. HHS released a report a year later under the same name, which was the "first federal government report comprehensively examining the issue and calling for action."[51] Dawes states that Heckler's advocacy was a "brave act" that "put her job at risk," considering that other members of the Reagan administration resisted this effort.[52] This advocacy eventually led to the passage of the Disadvantaged Minority Health Improvement Act of 1990.

During the year-long battle over ACA, CBC members sharpened their focus on health disparities. Congress members Jesse Jackson Jr. (D-IL) and Elijah Cummings (D-MD) introduced the Health Equity and Accountability through Research Act a year before the ACA's passage. Based on these deliberations, the ACA included an amendment that elevated the National Center on Minority Health and Health Disparities to the status of an institute. The institute currently has more administrative capacity over minority and health disparities–related research and budgets.[53]

In March 2009, James Clyburn (D-SC) sponsored the Access for All America Act that proposed to expand community health centers and the National Health Service Corps. The Nurse and Health Care Worker Protection Act of 2009 introduced by John Conyers (D-MI) intended to update safety standards for health care professionals.[54] Congressman Edolphus "Ed" Towns of New York encouraged lawmakers to strengthen consumer protections for senior citizens in ACA.

In addition, Delegate Donna Christensen (D-VI) sponsored the Health Equity and Accountability Act of 2009 to create targeted strategies for eliminating racial disparities in health care.[55] As a leading figure in the CBC Health Braintrust, she and other health equity advocates lobbied the White House at a special summit in March 2009 to make racial and health disparities elimination a top priority in the ACA.[56] After the bill was adopted, she established the Health Equity Leadership Commission to ensure "the provisions that serve to eliminate health disparities and foster health equity are implemented to the fullest extent."[57] Bills seeking to expand resources and health coverage to people suffering from diabetes, HIV, and Alzheimer's diseases were sponsored by Maxine Waters (D-CA) during the ACA debate.[58]

Most of the CBC bills failed to pass as standalone legislative items. Still, strategically, CBC members and liberal allies used the bill sponsorship during the ACA debate as an agenda-setting process for health equity and civil rights groups. Some of their policy recommendations were then embedded into the ACA's framework with Obama's consent, or they were implemented by administrative agencies after the law was adopted. The CBC also joined forces with the Congressional Hispanic Caucus and Congressional Asian Pacific American Caucus—collectively called the Congressional TriCaucus—to highlight how repealing the ACA would exacerbate racial disparities in health care.[59]

Liberal allies joined the CBC's call for the inclusion of health equity provisions in the ACA. Senator Benjamin Cardin stated that health disparities would be addressed by the law, especially pertaining to African Americans, whose "life expectancy is 5.3 years lower than whites." Cardin called for a "national strategy to reach out to minority communities to define and address their special needs."[60]

The National Working Group on Health Disparities and Health Reform mobilized grassroots support for the ACA. The group worked with the Congressional Tri-Caucus leading up to the White House summit in March 2009. During the year-long negotiations, organizations such as the National Black Nurses Association, National Urban League, NAACP, and other groups collaborated with the National Working Group on a health equity agenda.[61] This ecosystem of actors (members of congress, civil rights groups, and the National Working Group) lobbied the Obama administration to announce the national strategy to reduce HIV/AIDS discussed earlier in the chapter.

The National Working Group's efforts further led to the development of a "National Action Plan to Reduce Racial and Ethnic Disparities in Health." Early discussions for an action plan actually began in 2006 when two thousand health care professionals and activists convened for the National Leadership Summit for Eliminating Racial and Ethnic Disparities. This meeting evolved into the National Partnership for Action, which, jointly with the HHS's Office of Minority Health, coordinated strategy sessions and Regional Health Equity Councils intended to reduce disparities.[62]

One of the more significant parts of the ACA is Section 1557, the nondiscrimination clause that prohibits the exclusion from health insurance coverage on the basis of race, gender, medical history, and condition, genetic condition, and other related characteristics. This rule was amended in 2016 after civil rights groups such as the Leadership Conference on Civil Rights lobbied HHS to extend nondiscrimination coverage to more groups.[63] In addition to clarifying protections for the LGBTQ, disabled, and limited-English-proficient consumers, Section 1557 extended protections to consumers using wellness programs for preventative services.

The fight over Medicaid expansion was particularly important to African Americans. Medicaid expansion intended to cover individuals at or below 138 percent of the federal poverty level ($27,000 for a family of three).[64] This eligibility guideline combined with premium tax cuts in the federal and health exchanges could provide partial or full coverage to as much as 90 percent of Blacks. Thus, African Americans had the most to lose when SCOTUS gave states the power to opt out of Medicaid expansion in *NFIB v. Sebelius*.

The failure to expand Medicaid in half of the states excluded a projected 4.5 million uninsured adults, including 42 percent of the Black uninsured adult population.[65] About 60 percent of uninsured Blacks resided in states that rejected Medicaid expansion, including Florida, Texas, Georgia, and Mississippi.[66] While many conservatives believed Medicaid expansion would destabilize state economies, at the mass level, much of this opposition was undergirded by racial resentment.[67] With the possibility of repeal during the Trump administration, the efforts to address disparities in access to health care will face additional roadblocks.

The National Conference of Black State Legislatures (NCBSL) countered Medicaid expansion opponents when it adopted "Resolution HHS-14–20" at their 2013 annual meeting. The resolution highlighted the Congressional Budget Office's projection that the ACA would reduce budget deficits. It recognized that "the majority of states that have chosen not to expand coverage under the ACA are in the southern geographic region of the country where African Americans are concentrated most heavily."[68] The most vigorous fight by Black lawmakers and advocates occurred in Louisiana, where there resided one of the country's highest uninsured Black populations. At the time, the state's Republican governor Bobby Jindal "was perhaps the nation's foremost opponent to Medicaid expansion."[69] After his departure, however, the newly elected Democratic governor John Bel Edwards issued executive order JBE 16–01 on January 12, 2016, to expand Medicaid coverage. Similar battles involving Black lawmakers occurred across the country. In the last section of this chapter, we give close attention to how these debates at the subnational level influenced concerns about health care among African Americans in the ACA era. The next section further looks at the impact of racism on attitudes toward health care.

African Americans, the ACA, and Subnational Political Actors

To gauge Black attitudes toward health care in the era of ACA, we draw from a national survey of one thousand Blacks. The survey, administered by National Public Radio/Robert Wood Johnson/Harvard School of Public Health (NPR/RWJ/HSPH) from January 10 to February 7, 2013, was delivered nearly three years after the ACA was signed into law.[70]

Ordinary least squares (OLS) regressions are used to evaluate responses to two sets of questions that are important for this study. The first dependent variable was created from an additive index that ranks the respondents' sentiments from low to high satisfaction with their health care based on responses to the following questions: (a) "Overall, how do you feel about the health care services that you and your family have used in the last few years? Would you say you are very satisfied, somewhat satisfied, somewhat dissatisfied, or very dissatisfied?"; and (b) "How confident are you that you would have enough money or health insurance to pay for a major illness? Are you very confident, somewhat confident, not too confident, or not at all confident?" A second dependent variable was produced from an additive index in response to four questions about the respondents health care status (a higher score on the index indicates that the respondents have severe health problems): "In the past 12 months, have you or a family member had a serious problem with: (a) having enough money to pay doctor and hospital bills; (b) paying for prescription medicines that were needed; (c) getting health care that was needed; and (d) getting mental health care that was needed."

We included two variables in the NPR/RWJ/HSPH survey to examine subnational political actors that were coded as dummy variables: whether the individuals resided in one of the twenty-six states where the attorney generals joined with the NFIB in opposing Obamacare, and if the respondents live in one of the thirteen states where the governor filed an amicus brief in favor of health care reform. Included in the regression models is a variable created from an additive index that ranks the respondents' experiences with discrimination from low to high. We then control for region, urbanicity, marital status, gender, social class (income, education, status of personal finances, employment), religion, and whether the respondents had health insurance.

Findings

After the ACA was signed into law, states and localities were left to debate and implement critical parts of the statute (Medicaid expansion, federal versus state exchange, expansion of community health centers) at a time when an anti-Obama and racial resentment wave swept the nation. This meant that Obama could not escape the racial animus toward the ACA even though he universalized the messaging about the law. State lawmakers were instrumental in shaping the full implementation of the ACA. The findings in the NPR/RWJ/HSPH poll provide some insight into the influence of the ACA ecosystem at the state level.

As indicated in table 10.1, satisfaction with health coverage is associated with Blacks' social class. African Americans whose personal finances have improved, as well as those with higher education, steady employment, and higher incomes, are more satisfied with their health coverage. Not surprisingly, those without health coverage experience greater dissatisfaction with their health coverage. Religiosity is also slightly associated with Black satisfaction with health care. Those experiencing higher levels of discrimination are further dissatisfied with their health coverage. Policy alliances with Obama are also associated with satisfaction. Blacks residing in a state where a governor filed an amicus brief in support of the law were slightly more likely (p < .10) to be happy with their health status.

There were also interesting findings among those Black respondents whose health status was precarious. The respondents who are doing financially well were less likely to have health problems. Education has a minor, though noticeable, effect on improved health status. On the other hand, health problems persisted among the uninsured and rural respondents. Those who experienced more racial discrimination reported having more severe challenges with their health. Those living in states where the governor filed amicus briefs supporting the ACA were less likely to have problems.

Overall, the national poll suggests that the three most important factors shaping Black attitudes toward health care are social class (no health coverage is part of this phenomenon), experiences with discrimination, and the influence of state-level officials. To the last point, a policy ecosystem emerged in response to the ACA. For many African Americans

TABLE 10.1. Satisfaction with Health Coverage

	Improved Health Status	Bad Health Problems
Male	−.06 (.10)	.09 (.08)
Personal Finances	.91 (.11)***	−.57 (.09)***
Religiosity	.10 (.05)*	.04 (.04)
Married / Living with Partner	−.11 (.11)	.07 (.09)
Employment	.31 (.11)***	−.08 (.09)
Uninsured	−.34 (.14)**	.51 (.12)***
Education	.01 (.05)	−.07 (.04)*
Household Income	.08 (.03)***	−.03 (.02)
Region (South)	.07 (.11)	.001 (.09)
Metro Center (Urban)	.17 (.11)	−.16 (.08)*
Racism	−.06 (.01)***	.04 (.01)***
Attorney General	.20 (.12)	−.16 (.10)
Governor (Amicus Brief)	.28 (.15)*	−.30 (.12)**
Constant	4.24*** (.35)	1.97 (.28)
R-Square	.20	.17
N =	750	752

* $p < .10$, ** $p < .05$, *** $p < .01$
African Americans and Health Status in the Era of the Affordable Care Act
Source: National Public Radio / Robert Wood Johnson / Harvard School of Public Health
N = 1,081

who resided in states where governors opposed the ACA, especially for those in the southern region, their health status was unstable. Black lawmakers interpreted the attack on Obamacare by state officials as an attack on African Americans. Congressmembers Sheila Jackson Lee (D-TX) and Al Green (D-TX) likened the *NFIB v. Sebelius* lawsuit to the legal challenges to the 1964 Civil Rights Act and the Voting Rights Act of 1965.[71] Yet for African Americans who lived in states where governors were allied with the president, their health status seemed to be improving from 2010 to 2013.

Conclusion

Obama's presidency operated within the context of an inclusionary dilemma, as stated at the beginning of this volume. If he articulated an explicit race-specific agenda, it would have angered Whites. Even when he embraced universal policies such as universal health care, racial polarization was stark. On the other hand, by not explicitly embracing race-specific policies, he angered some Black activists and intellectuals for ignoring so-called Black interests.

Our chapter makes several arguments regarding Obama and the ACA. We acknowledge that Obama used a deracialized/race-neutral strategy to publicly advocate for the ACA by framing it as a racially transcendent policy that reflected the best of American exceptionalism. Despite this strategy, the ACA included equity-based measures—as much as sixty-two provisions—that were long-championed by health care justice advocates and Black lawmakers. For Black advocates and lawmakers who were part of the ACA ecosystem, the law reinforced their preexisting commitments to health equity.

Thus, the ACA was not divorced from a so-called Black agenda, but it reinforced Black policy interests and racial equity concerns in health care. The public rhetoric of universalism was less important than the actual policy itself and how the bureaucratic agencies (e.g., HHS, CDC, etc.) implemented the law in order to reach uninsured populations and low-income African Americans. The health care bill underscores that Black candidates, such as Barack Obama, who run deracialized campaigns are unable to eliminate or avoid racial animus during their election contests and their tenure in office. The ACA, in fact, exaggerated levels of racial polarization despite the fact that the bill was mostly articulated in race-neutral terms. The resentment was partially fueled by state lawmakers, especially in the South, who vigorously fought against Obamacare. The resentment to the ACA and other ameliorative policies helped to get Trump elected in 2016.

The Trump candidacy brought to the forefront of American political discourse an undercurrent of racial animus that permeated American society. During the 2016 presidential election, Trump expressed a particular distaste toward the ACA, which reflected his long-standing resentment of Obama. Before his inauguration, he nominated Republican congressman Tom Price, an opponent of Obamacare, as his secretary of Health and Human Services. The nomination, and later confirmation, signaled that repealing and replacing Obamacare would be his top domestic priority.[72] In his first two years in office, Trump used executive action (e.g., executive orders, administrative rule changes, noncooperation with funding requirements, etc.) to weaken the ACA. For instance, his administration froze payments to health insurers receiving risk adjustment payments, it cut $26 million to ACA-related outreach programs, and it reduced cost-sharing payments to health insurers.[73] Other administrative measures, along with Congress's repeal of the individual mandate as part of the Republican-backed $1.5 trillion tax cut in December 2017, also weakened Obamacare.

Congress made several attempts to repeal the ACA in its entirety during Trump's first year. In fact, the Senate came within one vote of ending Obamacare. After the House voted to repeal the health insurance program, the Senate rejected it in a late night session on July 28, 2017. Three Republicans (Lisa Murkowski, Susan Collins, John McCain) joined Democrats in saving the program.

Certainly, Obamacare's survivability amid racial and party polarization has been due to pressures from interest groups and health justice advocates. Since the 2016 election, more Americans have expressed support for the ACA than opposed it.[74] Hacker and Pierson also state that efforts to repeal Obamacare have failed because of the slim Republican majority in the Senate during Trump's initial two years and because the program has grown in popularity. They describe it as "a new ecosystem in which efforts at retrenchment that could not have survived in the past now have some prospect of success."[75] In other words, it is difficult to end a socially beneficial program such as the ACA once it is entrenched in the framework of American policy-making and is widely embraced by a large segment of the electorate.

As it stands, Obamacare is here to stay, but it will continue to be used as cannon fodder for polarizing Americans along racial and party lines. Opponents will seek to weaken the ACA through administrative measures to minimize its impact or convince Americans that it is ineffective. Proponents such as health justice advocates, the CBC, and liberals will push to strengthen the ACA in the next decade, including the expansion of Medicaid. Yet the long-term survivability of Obamacare may eventually depend on how persistent African American voters are in maintaining a policy ecosystem that protects it.

NOTES

1 Pew Research Center Hispanic Trends, "Dissecting the 2008 Electorate," April 30, 2009, www.pewhispanic.org.

2 Tasha S. Philpot, Daron R. Shaw and Ernest B. McGowen, "Winning the Race, Black Voter Turnout in the 2008 Presidential Election," *Public Opinion Quarterly* 73, no. 5 (2009): 995–1022.

3 Andrew Cline, "How Obama Broke His Promise on Individual Mandates," *Atlantic*, June 29, 2012, www.theatlantic.com; Sara R. Collins, et al., "The 2008 Presidential Candidates' Health Reform Proposals: Choices for America," Commonwealth Fund, October 1, 2008, www.commonwealthfund.org.

4 Kathleen Sebelius, "Remarks by Health and Human Services Secretary Kathleen Sebelius at a National Urban League Guilds Luncheon," Washington Newsmaker Transcript Database (Infotrac Newsstand app), July 30, 2010.

5 "Remarks of President Barack Obama—As Prepared for Delivery Address to Joint Session of Congress," White House, February 24, 2009, https://obamawhitehouse. archives.gov.

6 Lawrence R. Jacobs, "What Health Reform Teaches Us about American Politics," *PS: Political Science and Politics* 43, no. 4 (October 2010): 619–623.

7 Jill Quadagno, "Right Wing Conspiracy? Socialist Plot? The Origins of the Patient Protection and Affordable Care Act," *Journal of Health Politics, Policy and Law* 39 (1): 35–56.

8 Bob O'Keefe, "CDC Crucial in HIV/AIDS Plan: Obama Aims to Cut Spread of Disease by 25% in 5 Years," *Atlanta Journal-Constitution* (Infotrac Newsstand app), July 14, 2010; "HHS Announces $30 Million in New Resources to Support the National HIV/AIDS Strategy," *States News Service* (Infotrac Newsstand app), September 24, 2010; Sebelius, "Remarks by Health and Human Services Secretary."

9 Shoshannah A. Pearlman, "The Patient Protection and Affordable Care Act: Impact on Mental Health Services Demand and Availability," *Journal of American Psychiatric Nurses Association* 19, no. 6 (2013): 327–334.

10 Regina A. Galer-Unti, "The Patient Protection and Affordable Care Act: Opportunities for Prevention and Advocacy," *Health Promotion Practice* 13, no. 3 (May 2012): 308–312; Denise K. Thompson et al., "The Patient Protection and Affordable Care Act of 2010 (PL 111–148): An Analysis of Maternal-Child Health Home Visitation," *Policy, Politics, and Nursing Practice* 12, no. 3 (2011): 175–185.

11 "Rep. Towns Applauds New Preventative Health Services for Seniors through the Affordable Care Act," *States News Service* (Infotrac Newsstand app), June 22, 2011.

12 R. A. Cohen, B. W. Ward and J. S. Schiller, *Health Insurance Coverage: Early Release of Estimates from the National Health Interview Survey, 2010*. Atlanta, GA: National Center for Health Statistics, June 2011.

13 Brian D. Smedley et al., eds., *Unequal Treatment: Confronting Racial and Ethnic Disparities in Health Care* (Washington, DC: National Academies Press, 2003), 29–79; California Pan-Ethnic Health Network, "Fact Sheet: Benefits for African

American of New Affordable Care Act Rules on Expanding Prevention Coverage," http://cpehn.org, retrieved August 5, 2016; Coleen McMurray, "Do Blacks Receive Second-Class Healthcare?" Gallup, July 20, 2004, www.news.gallup.com; Magali Rheault, "Healthcare Costs Challenge US Minorities, Gallup Organization," Gallup, July 16, 2007, www.news.gallup.com; American College of Physicians, "Racial and Ethnic Disparities in Health Care." March 31, 2003. Philadelphia: American College of Physicians, 2003. www.acponline.org.

14 Kelly Brewington, "Cost of Racial Disparities in Health Care Put at $229 Billion between 2003, 2006: Hopkins-Maryland Report 'Stunning, Shocking,' Sebelius Says," *Baltimore Sun* (Infotrac Newsstand app), September 18, 2009.

15 The Kaiser Commission on Medicaid and the Uninsured, "Key Facts about the Uninsured Population," Henry J. Kaiser Family Foundation, October 2015, p. 3.

16 "Daniel E. Dawes Interviewed on News One Now, Thursday May 26 2016, Pt. 1," Johns Hopkins University Press, YouTube video, 6:44, https://youtu.be/_0-1ciLc Wek.

17 Georgia Persons, ed., *Dilemmas of Black Politics* (New York: Harper Collins, 1993); Huey L. Perry, *Race, Politics, and Governance in the United States* (Gainesville: University Press of Florida, 1996); Charles Jones and Michael Clemons, "A Model of Racial Crossover Voting: An Assessment of the Wilder Victory," in *Dilemmas of Black Politics*, ed. Georgia Persons (New York: Harper Collins, 1993), 128–14; Robert B. Albritton, George Amede, Keenan Grenell, and Don-Terry Veal, "Deracialization and the New Black Politics," in *Race, politics, and Governance in the United States*, ed. Huey L. Perry (Gainesville: University Press of Florida, 1996), 183; Raphael J. Soneshein, "Can Black Candidates Win Statewide Elections?" *Public Opinion Quarterly* 105 (1995): 219–241; Judson L. Jeffries and Charles E. Jones, "Blacks Who Run for Governor and the U.S. Senate: An Examination of Their Candidacies," *Negro Educational Review* 57 (2006): 243–261.

18 Judson Jeffries, "Blacks and High Profile Statewide Office: 1966–1996," *Western Journal of Black Studies* 22 (1998): 167.

19 Charles V. Hamilton, "Deracialization: Examination of a Political Strategy," *First World* 1 (March/April): 3–5.

20 . McCormick, Joseph and Charles E. Jones, "The Conceptualization of Deracialization: Thinking through the Dilemma," in *Dilemmas of Black Politics: Issues of Leadership and Strategy*, ed. Georgia Persons (New York: Harper Collins, 1993), 66–84.

21 Andra Gillespie, *Whose Black Politics? Cases in Post-Racial Black Leadership* (New York: Routledge, 2009); Byron D'Andra Orey and Boris Ricks, "A Systematic Analysis of the Deracialization Concept," *National Political Science Review* 11 (January 2007):325–334; and Robert C. Smith, *We Have No Leaders* (Albany: State University of New York Press, 2006).

22 Mary Summers and Philip A. Klinkner, "The Election and Governance of John Daniels as Mayor of New Haven," in *Race, Politics, and Governance in the United States*, ed. Huey L. Perry.

23 Perry, *Race, Politics, and Governance in the United States.*

24 Judson Jeffries, "Blacks and High Profile Statewide Office: 1966–1996."

25 Alvin J. Schneider, "Analyzing the Wilder Administration through the Construct of Deracialization Politics," in *Race, Politics, and Governance in the United States,* ed. Huey L. Perry (Gainesville: University Press of Florida, 1996), 15–28.

26 McCormick and Jones, "The Conceptualization of Deracialization"; Nicholas A. Valentino, Vincent L. Hutchings and Ismail K. White, "Cues that Matter: How Political Ads Prime Racial Attitudes During Campaigns" *American Political Science Review* 96 (March 2002): 75–88. Racial Priming was evident during the 2008 campaign when Geraldine Ferraro suggested that Obama's success was directly related his race. See Joyce Purnick, "Ferraro is Unapologetic for Remarks and Ends Her Role in Clinton Campaign," *New York Times*, March 13, 2008, www.nytimes.com.

27 Kevin R. Johnson, "Doubling Down on Racial Discrimination: The Racially-Disparate Impact of Crime-Based Removals," *Case Western Reserve Law Review* 66, no. 4 (2016): 995, 999, 1021.

28 Ronald F. Ingelhart and Pippa Norris, "Trump, Brexit, and the Rise of Populism: Economic Have-Nots and Cultural Backlash," paper for the Roundtable on "Rage Against the Machine: Populist Politics in the U.S., Europe and Latin America," Annual Meeting of the American Political Science Association, Philadelphia, Pennsylvania, September 2, 2016, p. 5.

29 Michael Barbaro, et al., "Trump Backs Stop-and-Frisk Across the U.S.," New York Times, September 22, 2016, www.nytimes.com.

30 Melanye T. Price, *The Race Whisperer: Barack Obama and the Political Uses of Race* (New York: New York University Press, 2016), 88–89.

31 L. Z. Granderson, "What's Motivating Some of Obama's Black Critics?" *CNN Wire* (Infotrac Newsstand app), July 26, 2013; Cornel West, *60 Minutes* (Infotrac Newsstand app), March 20, 2016.

32 Adolph Reed Jr., "Nothing Left: The Long, Slow Surrender of American Liberals," *Harper Magazine*, March 2014, http://harpers.org .

33 Herman George, "Neoliberalism in Blackface: Barack Obama and Deracialization, 2007–2012," *Journal of Pan-African Studies* 6, no. 6 (December 2013): 235.

34 Cathy Cohen, "Obama, Neoliberalism, and the 2012 Election: Why We Want More than Same-Sex Marriage," *SOULS: A Critical Journal of Black Politics, Culture, and Society* 14, nos. 1–2 (November 2012): 19–27.

35 There is scant research about policy ecosystems. Yet for a brief discussion of this conception see Christopher J. Manganiello, *Southern Water, Southern Power: How the Politics of Cheap Energy and Water Scarcity Shaped a Region* (Chapel Hill, NC: University of North Carolina Press, 2015), 71; Ted Piccone, *Five Rising Democracies: And the Fate of the International Labor Order* (Washington, DC: Brookings Institution Press, 2016), 90.

36 Michael Tesler and David O. Sears, *Obama's Race: The 2008 Election and Dream of a Post-Racial America* (Chicago: University of Chicago Press, 2010), 156; Michael

Tesler, "The Spillover of Racialization of Health Care: How President Obama Polarized Public Opinion by Racial Attitudes and Race," *American Journal of Political Science* 56, no. 3 (July 2012): 690–704.

37 Michael Henderson and D. Sunshine Hillygus, "The Dynamics of Health Care Opinion, 2008–2010: Partisanship, Self-Interest, and Racial Resentment," *Journal of Health Politics, Policy and Law* 36 (December 2011): 953; Eric D. Knowles, Brian S. Lowery, Rebecca L. Schaumberg, "Racial Prejudice Predicts Opposition to Obama and His Health Care Reform Plan," *Journal of Experimental Social Psychology* 46 (2010): 420–423; Angela K. Lewis, Pearl K. Ford Dowe, Sekou Franklin, "African Americans and Obama's Domestic Policy Agenda: A Closer Look at Deracialization, the Federal Stimulus Bill, and the Affordable Health Care Act," *Polity* (2013) 45, 1: 1–26.

38 "Kaiser Health Tracking Poll: The Public's Views on the ACA," Henry J. Kaiser Family Foundation, kff.org/tag/tracking-poll, retrieved June 30, 2016.

39 Mike Soraghan, "Jesse Jackson: `You Can't Vote Against Health Care and Call Yourself a Black Man'," *The Hill*, November 18, 2009, http://thehill.com.

40 J. Taylor Rushing, "Reid Doubles Down on Slavery Analogy," *The Hill*, December 8, 2009, http://thehill.com.

41 Ta-Nehisi Coates, "Fear of a Black President," *Atlantic*, September 2012, www.theatlantic.com.

42 Paul Kane, "Tea Party Protesters Accused of Spitting on Lawmaker, Using Slurs," *Washington Post*, March 20, 2010, www.washingtonpost.com.

43 Jacob S. Hacker, "The Road to Somewhere: Why Health Reform Happened: Or Why Political Scientists Who Write about Public Policy Shouldn't Assume They Know How to Shape It," *Perspectives on Politics* 8, no. 3 (September 2010): 866.

44 Hacker, "The Road to Somewhere," 869.

45 Simon F. Haeder and David L. Weimer, "You Can't Make Me Do It, but I Could Be Persuaded: A Federalism Perspective on the Affordable Care Act," *Journal of Health Politics, Policy and Law* 40, no. 2 (April 2015); Kevin Young and Michael Schwartz, "Healthy, Wealthy, and Wise: How Corporate Power Shaped the Affordable Care Act," *New Labor Forum* 23, no. 2 (2014): 34.

46 This case was merged with *Florida v. Department of Health and Human Services.*

47 Rachel Garfield and Anthony Damico, "The Coverage Gap: Uninsured Poor Adults in States That Do Not Expand Medicaid—An Update 2016," issue brief, Kaiser Commission on Medicaid and the Uninsured, January 21, 2016, Menlo Park, CA: Henry J. Kaiser Family Foundation; Benjamin Sommers and Arnold Epstein, "U.S. Governors and the Medicaid Expansion—No Quick Resolution in Sight," *New England Journal of Medicine* 368, no. 6 (February 7, 2013): 496–499; Carter C. Price and Christine Eibner, "For States That Opt Out of Medicaid Expansion: 3.6 Million Fewer Insured And $8.4 Billion Less in Federal Payments," *Health Affairs* 32, no. 6 (June 2013): 1030–1036.

48 Maggie Fox, "States Losing Billions in Refusing to Expand Medicaid, Report Finds," *NBC News*, December 5, 2013, www.nbcnews.com.

49 Sommers and Epstein, "U.S. Governors and the Medicaid Expansion."

50 Yvette Carnell, "Romney Says NAACP Booed Him Because They Wanted More 'Free Stuff,'" *Your Black World*, July 12, 2012, http://yourBlackworld.net.

51 Daniel E. Dawes, *150 Years of Obamacare* (Baltimore, MD: John Hopkins University Press, 2016), 35.

52 Dawes, *150 Years of Obamacare*, 35.

53 "Cummings Welcomes Elevation of Minority Health Center," *State News Service* (Infotrac Newsstand app), March 21, 2010.

54 James Clyburn, Health Equity and Accountability Act of 2009, 111 Bill Profile H.R. 3090 (2009–2010), http://congressional.proquest.com; John Conyers, Nurse and Health Care Worker Protection Act of 2009, 111 Bill Profile H.R. 2381 (2009–2010), http://congressional.proquest.com.

55 Donna Christensen, Access for All America Act, 111 Bill Profile H.R. 1296 (2009–2010), http://congressional.proquest.com.

56 Dawes, *150 Years of Obamacare*, 98.

57 "Congresswoman Christensen Convenes Health Equity Leadership Commission," *States News Service* (Infotrac Newsstand app), August 16, 2010.

58 Maxine Waters, Minority Diabetes Initiative Act, 111 Bill Profile H.R. 4404 (2009–2010), http://congressional.proquest.com; Maxine Waters, Alzheimer's Treatment and Caregiver Support Act, 111 Bill Profile H.R. 4123 (2009–2010), http://congressional.proquest.com; Maxine Waters, Routine HIV Screening Coverage Act of 2009, 111 Bill Profile H.R. 2137 (2009–2010), http://congressional.proquest.com.

59 "Tricaucus Stands Up for Minority Health," *States News Service* (Infotrac Newsstand app), January 19, 2011.

60 "Cardin Says We Will Provide Universal Health Coverage and Affordable Care for All Americans," *States News Service* (Infotrac Newsstand app), December 23, 2009.

61 Dawes, *150 Years of Obamacare*, 102.

62 National Partnership for Action to End Health Disparities, *National Stakeholder Strategy for Achieving Health Equity* (Rockville, MD: US Department of Health and Human Services, Office of Minority Health, April 2011).

63 The Leadership Conference on Civil Rights et al., letter to Secretary Sylvia Matthews Burwell (HHS) and Director Jocelyn Samuels (HHS Office of Civil Rights) regarding "Nondiscrimination in Health Programs and Activities, Proposed Rule," November 9, 2015; Office of Civil Rights and Office of the Secretary (HHS), "Nondiscrimination in Health Programs and Activities" (45 CFR Part 92, RIN 0945-AA02), *Federal Register* 81, no. 96 (May 18, 2016): 31376–31473.

64 The Kaiser Commission on Medicaid and the Uninsured, "Health Coverage for the Black Population Today and Under the Affordable Care Act," Henry J. Kaiser Family Foundation, July 2013, 4.

65 Ida Hellander, "The U.S. Health Care Crisis Five Years after Passage of the Affordable Care Act: A Data Snapshot," *International Journal of Health Services* 45, no. 4 (October 2015): 713.

66 The Kaiser Commission on Medicaid and the Uninsured, "Health Coverage for the Black Population Today and under the Affordable Care Act," 4–5.

67 Daniel Lanford and Jill Quadagno, "Implementing ObamaCare: The Politics of Medicaid Expansion under the Affordable Care Act of 2010," *Sociological Perspectives* (July 2015): 12–13.

68 National Conference of Black State Legislatures, "Resolution HHS 14–20: Calling for Medicaid Expansion across the Country," 37th Annual Legislative Conference, 2014 Ratified Policy Resolutions (Ratified December 13, 2013), December 11–13, Memphis, Tennessee, 38.

69 Drew Altman, "n La. and Ky. Shifts on Medicaid Expansion, a Reminder of Governors' Power in Health Care," *Wall Street Journal*, August 3, 2016, http://blogs.wsj.com.

70 A stratified sampling design was employed that oversampled areas with high concentrations of African Americans. A dual-frame landline / cell phone telephone design was then used to survey 1,081 African Americans (662 on landline and 419 on cell phones).

71 "Press Conference with Representative Sheila Jackson Lee (D-TX) and Representative Al Green (D-TX)," part 2 (Infotrac Newsstand app), March 25, 2010.

72 Michael McCarthy, "Trump Chooses Obamacare Opponent to Lead Health and Human Services," *British Medical Journal* (November 30, 2016): 1.

73 "Trump Administration Freezes Billions in Obamacare Payments, Outraging Advocates," Politico, July 8, 2018, www.politico.com; Ken Alltucker, "Trump Administration Slashes Funding for Obamacare Outreach," *USA Today*, July 10, 2018, www.usatoday.com; Mitchell Hartman and David Brancaccio, "Trump to Cut off Federal Subsidies to Health Insurers under Obamacare," *Marketplace*, October 13, 2017, www.marketplace.org.

74 See "Kaiser Health Tracking Poll: The Public's Views on the ACA," Kaiser Family Foundation, July 25, 2018 www.kff.org.

75 Jacob Hacker and Paul Pierson, "The Dog That Almost Barked: What the ACA Repeal Fight Says about the Resilience of the American Welfare State," *Journal of Health Politics, Policy, Law* 43, no. 4 (August 2018): 574.

11

Race, Real Estate, and Responsiveness

The Obama Administration's Legacy on Housing Policy and Outcomes

ANDRA GILLESPIE

Housing is a basic necessity, and for many, buying a house represents the fulfillment of the American Dream (Caliendo 2015, 65–67). In turn, housing statistics and housing policies are important gauges by which to measure the progress of racial equality and by which to assess a presidential administration's responsiveness to race-related issues. Barack Obama's responsiveness to housing issues is particularly important because of the housing and economic context in which he took office. The collapse of the housing market was a key factor in the 2008–2009 Great Recession. He had to address housing to help stabilize the US economy. The question is, were African Americans helped or harmed disproportionately by his efforts to stabilize the housing market? In this chapter, I empirically trace the state of African American homeownership over the course of the Obama presidency in comparison to other groups. I look at homeownership, foreclosure, and mortgage refinancing rates by race in addition to residential segregation patterns. I also discuss policies that the Obama administration initiated to help struggling homeowners and to reduce residential segregation.

Studying homeownership and residential segregation reduction policies in the Obama administration is, especially after that administration has left office, important for two reasons. First, such an examination contributes to the larger debate about what President Obama did for Blacks while in office. Currently, scholars are grappling with the question of whether President Obama's decision to present himself as a deracialized politician was a signal that Blacks could only expect to win symbolic political gains in his presidency (See Harris 2011; Price 2016;

Gillespie 2018). As stated earlier in this volume, Fred Harris raised the possibility that Obama would present himself as racially transcendent in public while quietly advocating for Black interests behind the scenes (Harris calls this "wink and nod" politics), though he questioned why Blacks would find this to be acceptable (Harris 2011, 139). By examining housing policy, among other things, we can see if President Obama was quietly advocating for Black interests out of the public eye. This may be his effort at avoiding what the editors of this volume call the "inclusionary dilemma" of Black politicians attempting to include Black interests within often racially hostile American policy regimes. Second, now that President Obama's successor, Donald Trump, has had enough time to put his own stamp on housing policy, we have the advantage of being able to compare the different approaches to and motivations behind particular housing policies. Toward being able to frame current politics, this chapter will end with a brief discussion of how President Obama's housing policies—the Obama Housing legacy—have fared in the Trump administration.

Why Home Ownership Is Important

The role of homeownership in wealth accumulation for Americans cannot be understated. Many scholars have noted that the value of a home is the primary source of wealth for the people who own them (Caliendo 2015, 65). The political economy of race in the United States has simultaneously amplified the importance of homeownership for Blacks and limited their ability to benefit financially from homeownership. In their classic treatise on wealth inequality in the United States, Melvin Oliver and Thomas Shapiro (2006) note that the vast majority of Black wealth is tied to home equity. To be sure, home equity represents the largest asset that most people (of any race) have; for African Americans, though, home equity represents the majority of their assets. For instance, in their initial study using the 1987 Survey of Income Program Participation, Oliver and Shapiro found that home equity comprised 43 percent of the wealth of Whites and 63 percent of the wealth of Blacks. In the 2006 update to their study (using 2002 data), they found that home equity still comprised 63 percent of Black wealth; in contrast, home equity comprised only 38.5 percent of White wealth (Oliver and Shapiro 2006, 111,

216). As I further explain, these disparities are also important to understand because they indicate the greater vulnerability Black family wealth assets had during the Great Recession's housing crisis.

Homeownership and Foreclosure Patterns by Race

Given the fact that home equity comprises a majority of Black wealth, it is important to ask two questions. How many Blacks (relative to members of other racial and ethnic groups) own homes? And how did the foreclosure crisis that precipitated the Great Recession of 2008–2009 impact Black communities? Figure 11.1 charts home ownership rates by race and ethnicity for Blacks, Whites, Latinos, Asian Americans, and Native Americans from 1994 to 2014. As the graph shows, White homeownership rates have consistently exceeded non-White homeownership rates by large margins. In 1992, the gap between Black and White homeownership was more than 27 percentage points (42.3 percent for Blacks compared to 70 percent for Whites). Put another way, the rate of White homeownership was more than 65 percent higher than the Black homeownership rate in 1994. Black homeownership rates peaked in 2004, when 49.1 percent of Blacks owned their own homes. That increase in Black homeownership did little to narrow the gap between Black and White homeownership. White homeownership rates also peaked in 2004, with 76 percent of Whites owning homes. Thus, the racial gap in homeownership rates only narrowed by half a percentage point, and Whites were still nearly 55 percent more likely than Blacks to own a home.

Economists note that the housing market started to soften in 2006. With the failure of major mortgage lenders like Countrywide in 2007, it was clear that the housing market was in free fall in advance of the stock market crash of 2008 (O'Flaherty 2015, 324). How did homeownership rates fare during and after the recession? Figure 11.1 clearly shows that homeownership rates fell after 2007 for all of the racial groups studied. White homeownership rates declined from their peak of 76 percent in 2004 to 72.6 percent in 2014. However, declines in homeownership were more acute among Blacks and Latinos. After peaking at 49.1 percent in 2004, Black homeownership rates fell to 43 percent by 2014. That year, White homeownership rates were nearly 69 percent higher than Black homeownership rates. Among Latinos, homeownership rates fell from

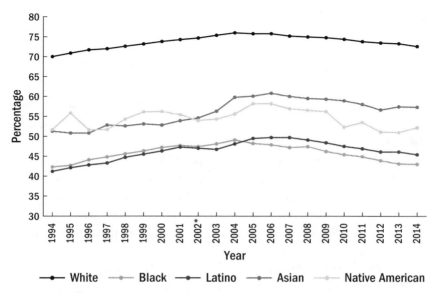

Figure 11.1. Home ownership rates by race and ethnicity, 1994–2014. *Source*: US Census Bureau n.d.b., Table 22.

* 2002 data is revised Census data.

Note: There are slight variations in how the Census Bureau records the race of house-holders. Between 1996 and 2002, respondents who marked "other" for race were reclassified into a category. Persons who marked "other" are not included in this graph. Census tabulations here show rates for people who identify as one race.

their 2007 peak of 49.7 percent to a low of 46.1 percent in 2012. While the Latino homeownership rate remained the same in 2013, it fell further in 2014, to 45.4 percent. By 2014, White homeownership rates were almost 60 percent higher than Latino homeownership rates. Thus, while most minorities did benefit in absolute terms from the housing boom, their increased homeownership rates did little to reduce the gap in White-minority homeownership rates. And any gains in reducing inequality between Whites and minorities, particularly Blacks and Latinos, were wiped away by the contraction of the housing market and subsequent recession.

Given the crash of the housing market, it is also important to consider the impact of the housing crisis on differential foreclosure rates by race. Foreclosures represent a devastating loss of assets for those who are forced to relinquish ownership of their homes. Given the fact

that Blacks' assets are mostly tied to their homes, if Blacks disproportionately lose their homes to foreclosure, then that will have a negative
effect on overall Black net worth. There is abundant evidence to suggest that Blacks were particularly susceptible to foreclosure. Brendan
O'Flaherty notes that the deregulation of the mortgage industry in the
1980s and 1990s made homeownership possible for a broader segment
of the population. He cites several factors that lent to the increase in
minority homeownership rates: the expansion of credit to more individuals, the rise of monoline mortgage lenders (or "banks" that only
issued mortgages but did not accept deposits, like traditional banks), the
introduction of subprime mortgages, and the introduction of adjustable
rate mortgages. However, this expansion of credit came with great risk.
Deregulation allowed investors to speculate on mortgages on a national
scale. Thus, increased foreclosures in one part of the country could lead
to financial losses nationally (O'Flaherty 2015, 315–318).

In addition, the speculative market in foreclosures disproportionately penalized Blacks seeking to own homes. O'Flaherty first noted
that the rise of mortgage speculators and monoline mortgage lenders
also coincided with the rise of mortgage brokers, who had an incentive to push customers to accept loan terms at any cost. O'Flaherty
contends that mortgage brokerages were inherently unethical because
they were paid by mortgage lenders, who would have had an incentive to encourage the processing of as many mortgages as possible
(O'Flaherty 2015, 316).

O'Flaherty notes that Blacks and Latinos were disproportionately offered subprime mortgages. Subprime mortgages are mortgages that were
designed for risky borrowers (i.e., those who had lower credit scores,
who had small down payments, or who had low incomes). Most Blacks
who received mortgages in 2005, for instance, received subprime loans.
O'Flaherty cites studies which found that Black borrowers were more
likely to receive subprime loans even after controlling for income. He
notes that part of the difference might be attributed to the fact that
Blacks and Latinos were more likely to get their mortgages from businesses that offered subprime mortgage products (O'Flaherty 2015, 319).

Figure 11.2 charts high-priced mortgage lending rates across the four
largest racial and ethnic groups in the United States from 2004 to 2013, as
reported by the Federal Reserve. By definition, high-priced mortgages in-

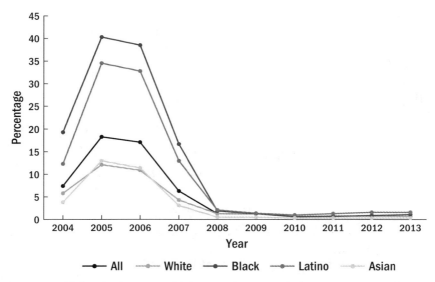

Figure 11.2. High-priced mortgage lending rates by race and ethnicity, 2004–2013. *Source*: Bhutta and Ringo 2014, 17.
Note: Figures for Native Americans include Alaska Natives, and the figures for Latinos are for White Latinos.

clude subprime mortgage products and are defined here as all mortgage lending (conventional and unconventional) in which banks offered borrowers interest rates that were at least 1.5 percentage points higher than the average prime offer rate (APOR) (Bhutta and Ringo 2014, 14–17). The data in this chart may not be perfectly comparable with O'Flaherty's data, but the findings are consistent with his assertion[1] that Blacks and Latinos were disproportionately offered mortgages that were less desirable.

In general, well-qualified minorities—or those who, based on income and good credit, were eligible for traditional mortgage products—were also steered into unattractive mortgage packages. But Blacks were more likely to have challenges in their credit profiles. The Federal Reserve notes that, on average, Black mortgage applicants had lower credit scores, higher debt, and more negative loan outcomes. Looking at data from those who received mortgages in 2006, the Federal Reserve found that Black borrowers had an average credit score of 640, compared to 673 for Latinos, 712 for Whites, and 723 for Asian Americans. More than

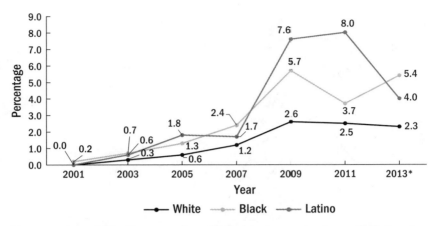

Figure 11.3. Annual foreclosure rates by race/ethnicity, 2001–2013. *Source*: Hall, Crowder, and Spring 2015, 233.
* Hall, Crowder, and Spring note that the 2013 data was preliminary data.

40 percent of Black borrowers had credit scores below 620; no more than a quarter of the borrowers in other racial or ethnic groups had credit scores that low. Blacks also carried more consumer debt on average than their Asian and Latino counterparts. The Federal Reserve calculated that more than a fifth of all Blacks and Latinos (23.3 percent and 21.4 percent respectively) who had acquired mortgages in 2006 had been at least 60 days delinquent at least once in the first two years of receiving that mortgage. By comparison, only 5.8 percent of Asian Americans and 6.7 percent of White borrowers in that cohort found themselves in the same position (Bhutta and Canner 2013, 34).

Hall, Crowder, and Spring (2015, 233) studied foreclosure rates over time using Panel Study of Income Dynamics (PSID) data.[2] It asks the same respondents biennially to disclose whether a bank had initiated a foreclosure on their current home that year. The PSID also asked a cumulative question about foreclosure, asking respondents to indicate if a bank had ever initiated a foreclosure against them since 2001. Figure 11.3 charts the PSID foreclosure responses by race and ethnicity for Blacks, Whites, and Latinos (Hall, Crowder, and Spring 2015, 233). Foreclosure was a rare occurrence among the respondents in 2001. The estimated White and Latino foreclosure rate was zero in 2001, while only 0.2 percent of Black respondents reported a foreclosure that year. Foreclosure rates rose among all racial and ethnic groups studied after 2001, though the rates of foreclosure vary by racial or ethnic group. For example, with the exception of the 2011 wave, foreclosure rates among White respondents were approximately half the rate of foreclosure among Black respondents. The Latino foreclosure rate fluctuated over time but is also consistently higher than the White foreclosure rate after 2001. Latinos were about 42 percent more likely to report a foreclosure in 2007 and more than three times as likely to report a foreclosure in 2011 (Hall, Crowder, and Spring 2015, 233).

Hall, Crowder and Spring also report the cumulative rate of foreclosure since 2001, which is depicted in figure 11.4. This captures the extent to which foreclosure affected respondents at some point since 2001. As would be expected from the annual foreclosure data, increasing numbers of respondents reported having been in foreclosure at least once since 2001 over the course of the time series. And, similar to the biennial data, the cumulative rate of White foreclosure is substantially lower

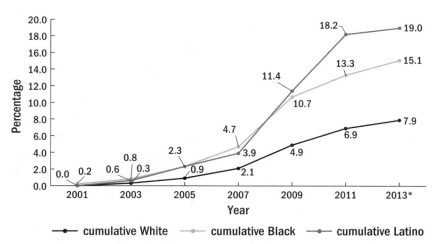

Figure 11.4. Cumulative foreclosure rates by race/ethnicity, 2001–2013. *Source*: Hall, Crowder, and Spring 2015, 233.

* Hall, Crowder, and Spring note that the 2013 data was preliminary data.

than the cumulative rate of Black or Latino foreclosure. From 2001 to 2009, the cumulative Black foreclosure rate is more than double the cumulative White foreclosure rate. While the gap improves in 2011 and 2013, there are still nearly twice as many Black foreclosures as there are White foreclosures. The pattern is similar for Latinos. Their cumulative foreclosure rate in 2007 was nearly double the White cumulative foreclosure rate and at least twice the White foreclosure rate in every other year, excluding 2001 (Hall, Crowder, and Spring 2015, 233).

The Making Home Affordable Initiative

In response to the housing crisis, the Obama administration quickly introduced assistance programs to help homeowners who were adversely affected by the housing crisis. Under the auspices of the 2009 Making Home Affordable (MHA) initiative, the Obama administration sought to provide relief to homeowners. There were two primary programs in the MHA initiative—the Home Affordable Refinance Program (HARP) and the Home Affordable Modification Program (HAMP). HARP was intended to help homeowners who had a track record of paying their mortgage bills on time. HARP would allow homeowners to refinance their mortgages into a lower rate mortgage. This could be particularly attractive to homeowners who had subprime or exotic mortgages. For instance, a homeowner who had an adjustable rate mortgage (ARM) or a mortgage that started out with a low introductory rate that would adjust at a later date to a much higher rate (substantially increasing the mortgage payment) could refinance into a lower interest, fixed-rate mortgage. This would give the borrower a much more predictable, consistent, and cheaper mortgage bill. HARP initially minimized its risk by not refinancing mortgages that were seriously underwater (where the loan amount was substantially greater than the house's value), but the program later relaxed its loan-to-value restrictions and appraisal requirements to accommodate more homeowners (Greene 2012).

HAMP targets homeowners who have fallen behind on their loan payments. HAMP helps homeowners in hardship (i.e., those who are unemployed, who are underwater in their mortgages, or who are already delinquent in payments and facing foreclosure) to modify their mort-

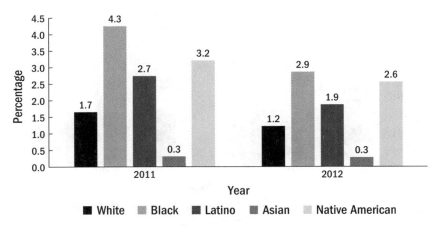

Figure 11.5. High-interest refinancing rates by race and ethnicity, 2011 and 2012. *Source*: Bhutta and Canner 2013, 29.
Note: Figures for Native Americans include Alaska Natives, and the Latino figures are for Hispanic Whites only.

gages or quickly sell their houses without the credit blemish of an actual foreclosure (US Department of the Treasury n.d.).

Both HAMP and HARP run through private lenders. While private lenders are required to report on the number of mortgage and refinance applications they accept and reject monthly, I will not be using aggregate data in this chapter to report if Black or Latino HAMP/HARP applicants fared differently than others. There are important considerations. First, there is evidence to suggest that many people who are eligible for refinancing have not taken advantage of these programs. Looking at a sample of cross-sectional data from 2010, Keys, Pope and Pope (2014) find that about 20 percent of the sample of eligible refinance candidates that they studied had not refinanced their mortgages. More specifically, the Urban Institute contends that White and Asian borrowers were more likely than Latino and Black borrowers to refinance and to refinance early, when interest rates were lower (Prevost 2014; George and Bai 2014).

However, the Federal Reserve provides some contextual data. In 2013, they released data on loan and refinance originations and rejections by race for 2011 and 2012. This data is not HARP or HAMP specific and is

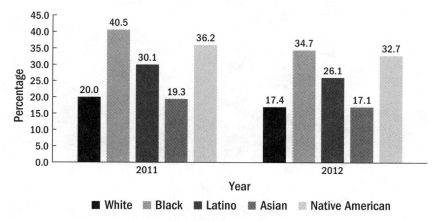

Figure 11.6. Rates at which applicants were denied the opportunity to refinance by race, 2011 and 2012. *Source*: Bhutta and Canner 2013, 29.
Note: Figures for Native Americans include Alaska Natives, and the Latino figures are for Hispanic Whites only.

depicted visually in figure 11.5 and figure 11.6. Figure 11.5 shows the percentage of refinance applicants who received high interest loans by race. Overall, the proportion of refinance applicants receiving high interest loans was small; fewer than 5 percent of any group refinanced under such terms. However, there was variation across racial and ethnic lines. Overall, Asian Americans were the least likely to refinance into high interest loans in 2011 and 2012 (at a rate of less than half of 1 percent). Nearly 2 percent of Whites who refinanced changed to high interest loans in 2011. In 2012, the rate among Whites was just over 1 percent. In contrast, Blacks, Latinos, and Native Americans were still more likely to refinance into high interest loans. In 2011, 4.3 percent of Blacks who refinanced paid high interest rates. That rate falls to 2.9 percent in 2012, but that is still more than double the White rate of high interest refinancing and nearly ten times the rate of Asian American high interest refinancing. Nearly 3 percent of Latinos who refinanced in 2011 refinanced into high interest loans. This number falls to 1.9 percent in 2012. Among Native American refinance applicants, 3.2 percent of applicants paid higher interest rates in 2011, compared to 2.6 percent in 2012 (Bhutta and Canner 2013, 29).

Figure 11.6 shows the rates at which applicants were denied the opportunity to refinance by race. It is important to note that many applicants of all racial and ethnic backgrounds were denied. However, there are racial differences in the refinancing rejection rates. While approximately 20 percent of White and Asian American applicants were denied the opportunity to refinance in 2011 (and approximately 17 percent in 2012), twice as many Black applicants were denied the opportunity to refinance in both years. The rejection rate for Blacks was 40.5 percent in 2011 and 34.7 percent in 2012. Native American applicants were denied at rates of 36.2 percent (in 2011) and 32.7 percent (in 2012), followed by Latino applicants, who were rejected at a rate of 30.1 percent in 2011 and 26.1 percent in 2012 (Bhutta and Canner 2013, 29). Given some of the challenges that faced minority borrowers in 2006 that ultimately were correlated with negative outcomes by 2012, future work should continue to control for indebtedness as it relates to mortgage outcomes and explore the possibility of both structural and personal factors to explain racial gaps in credit scores and indebtedness.

Residential Segregation and Home Values

Finally, it is important to gain a sense of the state of housing segregation by race in the United States. Residential segregation has important social and economic consequences. The presence of persistent spatial segregation by race evinces the extent to which racial divides have not been ameliorated. Moreover, residential segregation has consequences for Black life chances. In their classic study of residential segregation, Massey and Denton argue that residential segregation is "responsible for the perpetuation of Black poverty in the United States" (1993, 9) and relegates Blacks of all economic classes into politically marginalized communities that are beset with "economic disinvestment" (1993, 213).

Residential segregation has historically contributed to the Black-White wealth gap, even among Black homeowners. Massey and Denton note how New Deal era housing policies and practices served to make it harder for Blacks to buy homes and to realize the same level of appreciation on the homes they owned. Similar to the Obama administration's HARP, the Roosevelt administration created the Home Owners' Loan Corporation (HOLC) to help Depression-era homeowners keep their houses. As part of their efforts to determine eligibility for the program, HOLC classified residential areas into four categories, the lowest category being marked in red (hence the term "redlining"). The two most desirable categories (the ones most likely to get loan support) were middle-class, majority White areas whose properties had demonstrated elastic demand (which made them desirable even when the market was soft). Areas within the red lines (i.e., areas with large minority and poorer populations) were often denied federal support. They also pointed out that Federal Housing Administration loans, which provide subsidies to help homebuyers with small down payments to be able to purchase a home, were prioritized for new, single family housing in racially homogenous, suburban communities. Denton and Massey noted that FHA rules discouraged lending for older, urban housing stock, particularly for renovations. Their appraisal requirements also tended to devalue properties that lacked yard space. All of these factors disadvantaged urban communities, particularly those with large minority populations, not only because of their racial composition but because of the fact that urban housing stock was often older, contiguous, multifamily, and not offset from the street (Massey and Denton 1993, 51–54).

While overtly discriminatory housing practices were outlawed in the Fair Housing Act of 1968 (See Massey and Denton 1993, 195–200, for a discussion of the enforcement weaknesses of the act), the legacy of these practices is their contribution to long-term disparities in the value of homes in Black and White communities. Oliver and Shapiro (2006) note that the median appreciation of homes owned by Blacks is lower than the median appreciation in homes owned by Whites. At the time of the initial publication of the book *Black Wealth, White Wealth*, Whites who purchased their homes between 1967 and 1977 realized approximately twice the appreciation as their Black counterparts, with a net appreciation advantage of $31,300. When they updated the book in 2006, they noted Shapiro's 2004 finding that "the typical home owned by White families increased in value by $28,000 more than homes owned by Blacks" (Oliver and Shapiro 2006, 152, 211).

There are still observable racial differences in median home values. Valerie Wilson of the Economic Policy Institute estimates that between 2004 and 2007, the median value of homes owned by Blacks and Latinos appreciated at a faster rate than homes owned by Whites (30.1

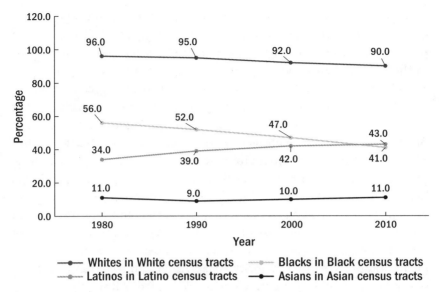

Figure 11.7. Changes in residential segregation patterns by race, 1980–2010. *Source*: Pew Research Center 2013, 34.

percent and 29 percent versus 10.4 percent, respectively). In the immediate aftermath of the housing crash, however, the median value of homes owned by Blacks and Latinos depreciated 23.6 percent and 28.4 percent, respectively, compared to 16.5 percent for Whites. Between 2010 and 2013, Latinos saw their median home values increase 3.7 percent, while White median home values decreased 4.6 percent and Black median home values decreased 18.4 percent. Wilson attributes the disparity to region. At the time of her writing, housing prices had stabilized in the West, where Latinos were more likely to live, while they continued to be soft in places with large Black populations, like the South and Midwest (Wilson 2014). This likely had serious implications for one's ability to refinance. To the extent that loan-to-value ratios factor into refinancing decisions, minority homeowners may have less or negative equity in their homes, making it more difficult for them to refinance.

Next, I examine the persistence of residential segregation. The US Census Bureau reports residential segregation with each decennial census.[3] Using this data, the Pew Research Center reported on segregation trends for the last four censuses. Their findings are recorded in figure 11.7. As figure 11.7 shows, changes in racial segregation patterns have been uneven for the four largest racial and ethnic groups in the United States. On a positive note, residential segregation patterns have improved the most for Blacks. In 1980, 56 percent of Blacks lived in census tracts where a majority of the residents were Black. That number decreased to 41 percent in 2010. According to Pew, the average Black person lived in a census tract that was 45 percent Black in 2010. Whites also saw improvement in their residential segregation patterns, though not to the same extent as Blacks. In 1980, 96 percent of Whites lived in majority White census tracts. That number decreased to 90 percent in 2010. This shows that Whites overwhelmingly still tend to live in majority White census tracts. Asian Americans were the least likely to live in majority Asian American census tracts, though their likelihood of living in a majority Asian American tract remained virtually unchanged over the time period examined. Although there was slight variation in 1990 and 2000, 11 percent of Asian Americans lived in majority Asian American census tracts in 1980 and in 2010 (Pew Research Center 2013, 34).

Latinos were the one group for whom residential segregation seemed to be increasing. In 1980, 34 percent of Latinos lived in majority Latino census tracts. By 2010, 43 percent of Latinos lived in majority Latino census tracts. Pew speculates that the rapidly growing Latino population increases the likelihood of majority Latino census tracts (Pew Research Center 2013, 34).

It is also helpful to consider residential segregation in terms of dissimilarity scores. Sociologists often use dissimilarity scores to depict the level of residential segregation. Dissimilarity scores are a score based on a scale of 0 to 1 (in this case, the scores have been multiplied by 100 to reflect whole integers) that charts the rate of segregation between two groups of people. A dissimilarity score of 50 would suggest that half of the members of each group would have to relocate from their present residences in order to proportionally distribute members of each group across a geographic area.

In table 11.1, I present national dissimilarity scores for Blacks, Latinos, and Asians, with Whites as the comparison category. This data was compiled by the American Communities Project at Brown Univer-

TABLE 11.1. National Dissimilarity Scores by Race

	1980	1990	2000	2010
Black-White Dissimilarity	73	67	64	59
Latino-White Dissimilarity	50	50	51	48
Asian-White Dissimilarity	41	41	42	41

Dissimilarity Indices for Whites and Non-Whites in the United States, 1980–2010
Source: Logan and Stults (2011): 5, 11, 17

sity in conjunction with the US Census Bureau's American Communities Project. Their findings corroborate the Pew findings for Blacks and Asian Americans. While Blacks remain the most segregated from Whites, fewer of them would have to move in order to more evenly distribute their population geographically in 2010 than in 1980. By 2010, only 59 percent of Blacks and Whites would have to be redistributed throughout the population nationally in order to achieve proportionality. That is much lower than the 73 percent of both groups which would have had to move in 1980 and the 79 percent that would have had to move in 1960 and 1970 (Logan and Stults 2011, 4).

Similar to the Pew findings, the dissimilarity indices have changed little for Asian Americans and Whites since 1980. In 1980, 41 percent of Whites and Asians would have to move to achieve proportionality throughout the population. That number was the same in 2010. However, the dissimilarity indices do place Latino-White segregation into a different context. While Pew reports that Latinos are increasingly more likely to live in majority Latino census tracts, the national dissimilarity scores between Whites and Latinos have improved slightly over time. In 1980, half of all Latinos and Whites would have had to move in order to achieve proportional representation throughout the population. By 2010, that number was 48 percent. The small but positive change in the dissimilarity score likely reflects the fact that, on average, Latinos live in neighborhoods where Latinos only outnumber Whites by a small margin. Logan and Stults estimate that the average Latino lives in a neighborhood that is "46% Latino, 35% white, 11% black and 7% Asian," a figure that is partially corroborated by Pew (Logan and Stults 2011, 3; Pew Research Center 2013, 34).

Attempts to Strengthen Enforcement of the Fair Housing Act

Earlier in this chapter, I noted the contention the Fair Housing Act, which sought to prevent discrimination in the housing market, had not had its intended effect due to lack of enforcement capability. Massey and Denton concluded the Fair Housing Act had several limitations, in that it provided a short statute of limitations whereby victims had six months from the time of an alleged incident of discrimination to file suit, limited the enforcement capability of the Department of Housing and Urban Development (their primary recourse was to seek mediation), instructed the Justice Department to pursue legal action on housing discrimination in serious cases only, and limited the punitive damages that could be awarded in cases of housing discrimination (Massey and Denton 1993, 195–198).

The Obama administration took affirmative steps to try to promote greater housing equity. In 2013, the Department of Housing and Urban Development (HUD) started drafting new federal rules to try to strengthen its enforcement capacity with respect to the Fair Housing Act. The Obama administration used the carrot of federal housing funding to encourage public housing authorities to try to reduce residential segregation. It was guided by language in the Fair Housing Act (Sections 3608 d and e) that calls for the federal government to "affirmatively further fair housing" initiatives (See Menendian 2017, 24). It was also aided by a 2015 Supreme Court decision (*Texas Department of Housing and Community Affairs et al. v. Inclusive Communities Project, Inc. et al.*). In this case, the court by a 5–4 decision affirmed a Fifth Circuit Court of Appeals case, which decided that the Texas Department of Housing and Community Affairs had violated the Fair Housing Act by disproportionately issuing affordable tax credits for housing in urban majority-Black neighborhoods versus White suburban neighborhoods. So local governments seeking federal assistance were required to use a HUD-provided statistical portal to vet their proposed housing projects before funding. The information in the portal was intended to help governments identify in advance if their proposed housing projects would have the unintended consequence of exacerbating residential segregation for racial minorities, the elderly, people with disabilities and HIV/AIDS infected residents throughout their jurisdictions. If the local authorities did not comply with federal guidelines in promoting equity, they risked losing their federal funding. These new guidelines went into effect in August 2015, and local housing authorities had to demonstrate compliance with the new guidelines in their regular reports to HUD (Department of Housing and Urban Development 2015; see also Davis and Applebaum 2015; Jones 2015; Menendian 2017, 24–25).

The Trump administration has an entirely different interpretation of the Affirmatively Furthering Fair Housing (AFFH) rule. Under the leadership of HUD secretary Ben Carson, the Trump administration has started to relax and rescind Obama-era rules intended to reduce residential segregation. As of January 2018, for instance, HUD stopped requiring localities to submit reports in which they would have to reflect on how their proposed housing plans would mitigate or exacerbate residential segregation. In late spring of 2018, HUD dismantled the online assessment tool that local governments used to compile those reports. In August of 2018, HUD announced an open comment period to start the process of dismantling the Obama-era interpretation of the Affirmatively Furthering Fair Housing rule. In a press release announcing the open comment period, HUD justified this move by claiming that the Obama-era rules were unwieldy and actually impeded the construction of affordable housing (Burke 2018; HUD 2018).

Because the changes to HUD fair housing policies are still in the process of being formulated, it is too early to know the impact of these changes. That these changes are underway is consistent with the Trump administration's larger deregulation project and with President Trump's apparent desire to dismantle Obama-era policies in particular (see Gillespie 2018, 202–203). And given the racial insensitivities that have manifested themselves in the first eighteen months of the Trump administration, it is not far-fetched to question whether the proposed changes to fair housing policy in the Trump administration will actually lead to reduced residential housing discrimination.

The transition from the Obama to the Trump administrations also highlights classic divisions in American public opinion regarding equality of opportunity versus equality of results (see Kinder and Sanders 1996; Torrance 1990, 75). Secretary Carson's justification for his proposed regulatory changes very much echo his endorsement of equality of opportunity. In the HUD press release announcing the proposed rule changes, Carson is quoted using the word "choice" three times. He affirmed that "HUD believes very deeply in the purposes of the *Fair Housing Act* and that states, local governments, and public housing authorities further fair housing *choice*," that "the AFFH rule, which as designed to expand affordable housing *choices*, is actually suffocating investment," and that "we can craft a new, fairer rule that creates *choices* for quality housing across all communities" (HUD 2018; author's emphasis). These comments—and the overall tenor of the press release—suggest that Carson professes a goal of expanding affordable housing options but that he is less focused on whether some communities disproportionately bear the share of affordable housing or whether these housing policy plans do a lot or a little to promote residential integration.

Conclusion

The preceding review reveals that racial disparities in housing remain a persistent problem in the United States and only further fuel what the co-editors of this volume have cited as the American racial order. These disparities have their origin in systemic practices that, while outlawed years ago, continue to have negative impacts on where people live and how much wealth they accumulate through their housing. Blacks and Latinos who already suffered discrimination in the mortgage market, were devastated by the housing crash of the late 2000s. The evidence suggests that they had not yet recovered as the Obama administration approached its twilight. On the bright side, during Obama's first term, the forty-year trend of increased residential integration for Blacks abated. Without vigorous federal enforcement of fair housing policy under the Trump administration, however, it is an open question as whether such trends will continue.

As President Obama's term drew to a close, his administration took affirmative steps to try to further racially integrate America's cities. By tying federal funding to a requirement that local housing authorities take positive steps toward addressing residential segregation with respect to the placement of affordable housing, the Obama administration sought to make a long-term impact on integrating marginalized groups into mainstream society. My analysis suggests that such policies would benefit Black but also other people of color, such as Latinos and Native

Americans. Those policies were in place for a couple of years but are in the process of being dismantled by the Trump administration. The trajectory of housing policy from the Obama to the Trump administration has important implications for our understanding of policy formation and policy impact. President Obama's marquee housing policy came to fruition in the seventh year of his administration and was in the process of being dismantled by the second year of the next administration. Because the policy took so long to implement and was changed so quickly thereafter, its potential impact will likely be small and difficult to measure. In this regard, the Obama administration did not overcome the inclusionary dilemma discussed in this volume. Obama's responses to Black group interests and needs in the area of housing may be more of a flash in the pan than a sustained set of statutory requirements that have instituted a policy legacy. Stated differently, race and continued racial discrimination may matter more—not less. While the Trump administration's policy takes shape under Secretary Carson, future studies should measure both the outcomes (as well as the intent) of its housing policy reversals.

NOTES

1 The one difference between the O'Flaherty and Federal Reserve data used here is that the Federal Reserve changed its definition of high-price mortgages in 2009. The data in this chart define high-price mortgages according to the broader Federal Reserve definition, which attempts to set a standard metric for defining a subprime mortgage as one with rates that are at least 300 basis points above the treasury rate. That basis point difference translates into percentage point differences between prime and subprime mortgage rates depending on whether interest rates are rising or falling, as reflected in ratio of the value between short to long-term treasury rates (i.e., the treasury yield curve) (Bhutta and Ringo 2014, 19–20).

2 The PSID is a highly respected, longitudinal study from the University of Michigan that started in 1968. It began with about five thousand families and currently tracks the original subjects, their descendants and new respondents. (The PSID has since incorporated immigrant respondents into the study). While the study was originally conceived as a project to track socioeconomically disadvantaged households, the sample does include a cross section of middle- and upper-class households too. As of 2009, nearly 8,700 households were included in the sample. Because of the longitudinal nature of the study, the sample size of the survey has grown over time (as the children and grandchildren of the original respondents form their own households). The PSID investigators have

also maintained a high response rate throughout the study. Their reinterview response rates are consistently above 90 percent for each wave (McGonagle et al. 2012).

3 The Census Bureau has plans to start reporting residential housing data annually using the American Community Survey. In the absence of that data, decennial data will be used here (US Census Bureau, n.d.a)

BIBLIOGRAPHY

Bhutta, Neil and Glenn B. Canner. 2013. "Mortgage Market Conditions and Borrower Outcomes: Evidence from 2012 HMDA and Match HMDA-Credit Record Data." *Federal Reserve Bulletin*. 99(4): November 2013.

Bhutta, Neil and Daniel R. Ringo. 2014. "The 2013 Home Mortgage Disclosure Act Data." *Federal Reserve Bulletin*. 100(6): November 2014

Burke, Neil. 2018. "Ben Carson Takes Steps to Revamp Obama Fair Housing Rule." *The Hill*. August 13, 2018. https://thehill.com.

Caliendo, Stephen M. 2015. *Inequality in America: Race, Poverty and Fulfilling Democracy's Promise*. Boulder, CO: Westview Press.

Davis, Julie Hirschfeld and Binyamin Appelbaum. 2015. "Obama Unveils Stricter Rules against Segregated Housing." *New York Times*. July 8, 2015.

Department of Housing and Urban Development. 2015. "24 CFR Parts 5, 91, 92 et al: Affirmatively Furthering Fair Housing; Final Rule." *Federal Register*. 80(136) (July 16, 2015): 42272–42371.

George, Taz and Bing Bai. 2014. "A Surprising Disparity in the Newest Mortgage Data." *Urban Wire* (blog). Urban Institute. September 25, 2014. www.urban.org.

Gillespie, Andra. 2018. *Race and the Obama Administration: Substance, Symbols and Hope*. Manchester, UK: University of Manchester Press.

Greene, Mark. 2012. "Why HARP Isn't Working." *Forbes*. October 17, 2012. www.forbes .com.

Hall, Matthew, Kyle Crowder and Amy Spring. 2015. "Variations in Housing Foreclosures by Race and Place, 2005–2012." *Annals of the American Association of Political and Social Science* 660 (July 2015): 217–237.

Harris, Fredrick. 2012. *The Price of the Ticket*. Oxford and New York: Oxford University Press.

HUD. 2018. "HUD Seeks to Streamline and Enhance 'Affirmatively Furthering Fair Housing' Rule." Press Release (HUD No. 18–079). August 13, 2018. www.hud .gov.

Jones, Athena. 2015. "Obama Administration Announces New Fair Housing Rules." CNN. July 8, 2015. www.cnn.com.

Keys, Benjamin J., Devin G. Pope and Jaren C. Pope. 2014. "Failure to Refinance." National Bureau of Economic Research Working Paper 20401. Cambridge: National Bureau of Economics Research.

Kinder Donald and Lynn Sanders. 1996. *Divided by Color*. Chicago: University of Chicago Press.

Logan, John R. and Brian J. Stults. 2011. *The Persistence of Segregation in the Metropolis: New Findings from the 2010 Census*. Census report prepared for Project US2010. https://s4.ad.brown.edu.

Massey, Douglas S. and Nancy A. Denton. 1993. *American Apartheid: Segregation and the Making of the Underclass*. Cambridge: Harvard University Press.

Menendian, Stephen. 2017. "Affirmatively Furthering Fair Housing: A Reckoning with Government-Sponsored Segregation in the 21st Century." *National Civic Review* 106: 20–27.

McGonagle, Katherine A., Robert F. Schoeni, Narayan Sastry and Vicki A. Freeman. 2012. "The Panel Study of Income Dynamics: Overview, Recent Innovations and Potential for Life Course Research." *Longitudinal and Life Course Studies* 3(2): 268–284.

O'Flaherty, Brendan. 2015. *The Economics of Race in the United States*. Cambridge: Harvard University Press.

Oliver, Melvin L. and Thomas M. Shapiro. 2006. *Black Wealth/White Wealth: A New Perspective on Racial Inequality*. 10th anniversary edition. New York: Routledge.

Pew Research Center. 2013. *The Rise of Asian Americans*. Updated edition. Washington: Pew Research Center.

Prevost, Lisa. 2014. "Racial Disparity in Mortgage Refinancing Data." *New York Times*. October 4, 2014.

Price, Melanye. 2016. *The Race Whisperer*. New York: New York University Press.

Texas Department of Housing and Community Affairs et al. v. Inclusive Communities Project, Inc. et al. 576 US 2015.

Torrance, Caroline. 1990. "Blacks and the American Ethos: A Reevaluation of Existing Theories." *Journal of Black Studies* 21(1): 72–86.

US Census Bureau. n.d.a. "Housing Patterns: Main." www.census.gov. Retrieved November 16, 2015.

US Census Bureau. n.d.b. "Table 22: Homeownership Rates by Race and Ethnicity of Householder: 1994 to 2014." www.census.gov. Retrieved November 18, 2015.

US Department of the Treasury. n.d. "Making Home Affordable: Home Affordable Modification Program." Updated January 30, 2017. www.treasury.gov.

Wilson, Valerie. 2014. "Home Values Have Seen Starkly Disparate Recoveries by Race." *Economic Policy Institute Snapshot*. October 15, 2014. www.epi.org.

12

The Obama Era and Black Attitudes toward Undocumented Immigration Policies

LORRIE FRASURE AND STACEY GREENE

Pitting African Americans against immigrants is a false dichotomy. African Americans are uniquely positioned, as leaders of the most successful progressive movement in this country's history, to bring about significant change across social issues and should rightly hold President Obama and others in power accountable.
—Opal Tometi, Executive Director of Black Alliance for Just Immigration (BAJI) and a Cofounder of Black Lives Matter

My son was murdered by an illegal alien. . . . If you're going to push illegal immigration in our faces with executive orders and things we can't stop, you owe us at least to make sure nobody is dying. Get the border enforced. How many deaths are enough?
—Jamiel Shaw Sr., father of son killed by an undocumented immigrant in 2008

In this chapter, we examine African American attitudes toward immigration given the policy context of the Obama administration. What the editors of this volume call an "inverted Black linked fate" with Obama and his administration may or may not have affected Black attitudes on immigration. We begin by providing the background for our central questions. The reelection campaign of President Barack Obama in 2012 made promises to the immigrant community, but in particular the Latino immigrant community, to deliver comprehensive immigration reform. An estimated 3.5 million undocumented immigrants lived in the United States in 1990, peaking at around 12 million by 2005. By 2014, this estimate fell to 11.3 million and has remained stable for the years

2009–2014, leveling off after nearly two decades of rapid increase (Kandel et al. 2014; Passel and Cohn 2015; Krogstad and Passel 2015). The four states with the highest shares of undocumented immigrants in their labor forces include Nevada (10 percent), California (9 percent), Texas (9 percent) and New Jersey (8 percent) (Krogstad and Passel 2015).

Immigrants from Mexico make up about half of all undocumented immigrants (49 percent) in the US. Their numbers have declined in recent years due to increased southwestern border enforcement and a controversial spike in deportations under the Obama administration. In early 2014, the National Council of La Raza (NCLR) and other Latino civil rights and advocacy organizations increased pressure on the administration to take unilateral action to address immigration reform and ease deportations, labeling Obama as "the deporter-in-chief." Obama countered that his efforts were stalled in an obstructionist Congress. Then, on November 20, 2014, President Obama announced a series of immigration executive actions to address undocumented immigration at the border called Deferred Action for Parents of Americans and Lawful Permanent Residents, or DAPA. The program would have provided three-year work permits and deportation deferrals for an estimated five million undocumented immigrants who were either brought to the US as children without authorization or who are parents of a child who is a US citizen or legal permanent resident. Such immigrants would be required to pass a criminal background check and to pay taxes in order to temporarily stay in the United States.

President Obama expected his executive actions would spur momentum on immigration reform and provide relief for roughly five million undocumented immigrants. However, Texas led a group of twenty-six states against DAPA. They argued that states would have to pay for driver's licenses if the parents dodge deportation proceedings. On June 23, 2016, the Supreme Court deadlocked in a 4–4 ruling regarding *United States v. Texas*, leaving in place a lower court's decision that the president exceeded his powers in issuing the directive and placed DAPA on hold indefinitely. The court's ruling continued the injunction that started sixteen months prior against the implementation of DAPA and an expanded version of the 2012 DACA program.

On June 15, 2017, six months following the inauguration of Donald Trump, his administration unequivocally revoked DAPA even before the executive order began. Then, on September 5, 2017, the Trump administration repealed DACA, leaving the lives of millions of undocumented childhood arrivals uncertain about whether they could remain in the US and what would be the fate of their parents/guardians, whose documentation status they also revealed to US government officials.

As activists on both sides lobby for their preferred action, political coalitions on the issue of immigration reform become more important. However, immigration has not proven a straightforward issue toward coalition building across race, ethnicity, class, and other identities. Immigration is often considered a racialized policy because many Americans associate undocumented immigration with Latinos—particularly national origin groups from Mexico and Central and South America—rendering these policies racialized (Frasure-Yokley and Greene 2013). African Americans have been relatively positive toward immigration when compared to other racial groups (Citrin et al. 1997). Scholars have long examined the role of Black-Latino intergroup contact and the impact of political and economic competition between these two groups (McClain and Karnig 1990; McClain 1993; Meier et al. 2004; McClain et al. 2006; McClain et al. 2007; McClain et al. 2009; Jackson et al. 1994; Gay 2006; Barreto et al. 2009; Wilson 2001; Thornton and Mizuno 1999). Yet African American views specifically regarding undocumented immigration reform remain understudied (but see Carter and King-Meadows 2019; Frasure-Yokley and Greene 2013; Morris 2000; Nteta 2013, 2014; Smith 2017; Smith and Greer 2018). This is despite both mainstream media and research studies on the purported negative effects of immigrants on the employment opportunities of working-class Blacks (Borjas 1999, 2000; Waldinger 1996; Burns and Gimpel 2000; Marrow 2011).

In 2014, following the announcement of DAPA, Gallup polling found that a majority (51 percent) disproved of Obama's executive actions on immigration. However, both non-Hispanic Blacks and Latinos supported the actions two to one. In fact, a slightly higher percentage of non-Hispanic Blacks supported Obama's executive actions on immigration at 68 percent, followed by Latinos at 64 percent and non-Hispanic Whites at 30 percent. Sixty-nine percent of all immigrants supported Obama's executive actions on immigration (Jones 2014).

Black support for the Obama administration's executive actions is important to examine because while immigration is a racialized issue, it is not often considered a "Black issue" or one relevant to groups interests and Black politics. This is despite how framing immigration as exclusively a "Latino issue" undermines the needs and concerns of 3.8 million Black immigrants in the United States from countries in the Caribbean, Africa, Europe, and Latin America. This limitation also fails to account for the intersectionalities of race, ethnicity, class, religion, and sexuality that Black immigrants, who make up 10 percent of America's foreign-born population face in the US. Adding further complexities, nearly six hundred thousand Black immigrants are undocumented (Zong and Batalova 2016, also see Smith 2017).

Opal Tometi, president of the Black Alliance for Just Immigration (BAJI) stated that the "much-needed executive action taken by the president that will benefit African, Caribbean, Afro-Latino immigrants and African Americans. For me as an immigrant-rights activist and the daughter of Nigerian parents, the president's decision is both politically and personally significant, as it is for my family and the communities that my organization . . . fights for every day."[1] Tometi further argues, "When we take into account the realities of anti-immigrant policy, including voter-ID laws and legalized racial profiling, in measures such as Arizona's S.B. 1070, it is clear that immigrant rights are a racial-justice issue, tied closely to the social and political priorities of African Americans." Recent data suggests that

> the deportation rate of undocumented Black immigrants is five times their numbers in the undocumented population, which is similar to the overrepresentation of African Americans in the criminal justice system. Furthermore, Black immigrants are twice as likely to be detained due to a criminal conviction. Even though Black immigrants make up only 7% of the total immigrant population, 20% of all immigrants in deportation proceedings due to criminal convictions are Black. (Tometi 2014)

The most recent immigration battle leading up the Supreme Court's 2016 decision was marked by activism, organizing, rallies, and acts of civil disobedience largely led by Latino groups but also a broader range of undocumented activists, many of which were Black undocumented college-aged youth. Such groups continue to come out of the shadows under the protections of executive actions under Deferred Action for

Childhood Arrivals (DACA) in 2012. Social media sites on Facebook and Twitter, as well as websites such as the UndocuBlack Network, have emerged to embrace and provide support for the undocumented Black community. In January 2016, the UndocuBlack Network organized the "Undocumented and Black Convening," the first national gathering of Black undocumented persons in Miami. Notably, this network largely made up of Black college-aged youth emerged out of the Black Lives Matter movement, which also serves as an outspoken ally to the undocumented population.

Notwithstanding these recent acts of solidarity across race and ethnicity, immigration is often used as a highly politicized tool to divide along race, ethnicity, and class. During the 2016 presidential election, the Republican Party, in particular GOP presidential nominee Donald Trump used race and immigration as a dividing line. The case of Jamiel Shaw Jr. and other victims of crimes by undocumented immigrants took center stage during the 2016 presidential primaries. An undocumented immigrant named Pedro Espinoza, who mistook him for a rival gang member, killed Shaw, an African American high school football star from Los Angeles, near his home in 2008. Espinoza was convicted and sentenced to the death penalty in 2012. In 2015, parents of the slain youth, Jamiel Shaw Sr. and Althea Shaw, former Democrats, were invited to a private meeting with Trump in Los Angeles. The Shaws hit the campaign trail as surrogates, speaking at rallies, to various media outlets, and were featured in a February 2016 Donald J. Trump for president campaign television advertisement. Shaw Sr. reportedly said he felt relief for the first time after hearing Trump's controversial comments regarding undocumented immigration.[2] He stated, "I knew with him talking like that, it was going to resonate if you are a Democratic, Republican, Black or white. . . . I want to get involved and show my support" (Vernado 2016).

In this chapter, we examine what factors shape Black views toward often racialized and politicized policy issues, such as immigration, in order to provide insight on the prospects for coalition formation and sustainability beyond the Obama administration. Because the goal of this chapter is to examine policy views during the Obama administration, we use data from the 2012 Collaborative Multiracial Post-Election Survey (CMPS) merged with aggregate level data from the 2010 Census. We examine the extent to which factors such as economic attitudes, linked fate, neighborhood context, and sociodemographic factors influence Blacks' views toward undocumented immigrants already living and working in the US. In this sense, we examine the standard conception of group linked fate but consider, to a limited degree, what it says about this volume's notion of "inverted linked fate."

In the next section, we briefly examine the role of these aforementioned factors on public opinion toward immigration, including undocumented immigration in the existing literature. Then we explain the research design and methods used in this study, followed by a discussion of our preliminary findings, which suggest that views toward undocumented immigrants currently living and working in the US are conditioned by factors related to Black economic attitudes as well as contextual measures. Unlike some recent research, our findings do not find support for the linked fate hypothesis on Black views toward undocumented immigration. In short, perceived common interests with their own group do not necessarily drive Black attitudes toward immigration.

The Impact of Economic Attitudes, Linked Fate, Neighborhood Context and Sociodemographics on Immigration Attitudes

Several individual-level factors have been shown to influence policy attitudes toward immigration, including demographic characteristics such as age (Citrin et al. 1997; Espenshade and Calhoun 1993), gender (Hood and Morris 1997; Amuedo-Dorantes and Puttitanun 2011), income and education (Federico 2004; Glaser 2001), as well as local context (Ha 2010). Educational attainment is among the most consistently used predictors of both racial and policy attitudes—though the influence of education is not always intuitive. A labor competition model predicts that those with higher education and income will be more receptive to immigrants because they do not foresee competing with them. Espenshade and Calhoun (1993) find that respondents with higher levels of educational attainment have more favorable attitudes toward undocumented immigrants. Therefore, we expect increased levels of education might lead to more progressive policy views toward undocumented immigration (Frasure-Yokley and Wilcox-Archuleta 2019).

On the other hand, those with less education and lower incomes might be more opposed to immigration because immigrants are seen as taking away jobs from native workers, purportedly depressing wages. The idea of a 'zero-sum' game is especially prevalent in the discussion of low-wage and public sector jobs. Bobo and Hutchings (1996) find that minority groups who have lower incomes tend to see themselves in competition with other minority groups.

Demographic shifts taking place in multiethnic metropolitan areas and the extent to which "place matters," give rise to the need to examine the role of living in proximity to immigrant groups. Some scholars find that closer contact with out-groups fosters greater understanding and empathy. The intergroup contact literature suggests that under the right conditions, increased exposure and contact to out-groups will result in more positive racial attitudes. Ha (2010) finds that "non-Hispanic whites are more likely to hold positive attitudes toward immigrants by having Asian neighbors, whereas those living with Hispanics are more likely to harbor anti-immigrant sentiments. Conversely, African Americans tend to be more prejudiced against immigrants when they are exposed to a sizable proportion of Asians in their communities" (p. 39).

Existing literature also shows support for the role of political orientations on shaping attitudes toward undocumented immigration. Barkan (2003) finds that women, Republicans, and older persons are groups most concerned about undocumented immigration. Scholars have expanded our understanding of the role of group identity or, specifically, Dawson's original conceptualization and extension of linked fate (Dawson 1995; Stokes 2003; Hackshaw 2005; Watts 2009; Sanchez and Masuoka 2010; Brown-Guinyard 2013; Wilkinson and Earle 2013). Linked fate is an increasingly important explanatory measure relative to views toward immigrants. Recent research by Masuoka and Junn (2013) suggests that minorities with a stronger linked fate translate to greater support for progressive immigration policies. According to Masuoka and Junn (2013), "Whites with stronger perceived linked fate with other whites are more likely to support decreasing immigration, while Blacks, Asians, and Latinos with a high degree of perceived linked fate are less likely to support restrictionist immigration policy" (p. 138). Examining data from the "Faces of Immigration Survey," they find that there are racial differences in how people apply racial stereotypes to both Latino and Asian immigrants. For example, 62 percent of Whites believe that most Latino immigrants are in the United States illegally; 46 percent of Blacks, 38 percent of Asians and 32 percent of Latinos. Data from the 2006 Pew Immigration Survey suggest that Black attitudes toward undocumented immigrants generally fall in between White and Latino attitudes. Whites are most likely to support the most restrictive policies, Latinos the least, and Blacks seem to take an in-between view. On a scale from 1 to 5, with 5 being the most restrictive—Whites, on average, score a 3.2, Blacks 2.81, and Latinos 1.95. Again, Whites are more likely to support restrictive and punitive measures against undocumented immigrants than either Blacks or Latinos, with Latinos being the least supportive. Moreover, the illegal-legal distinction is more likely to matter among White respondents, while Blacks often see no difference between legal and illegal when evaluating immigration.

Research Design and Methods

Data

This study uses data from the 2012 Collaborative Multiracial Post-Election Study (CMPS) merged with aggregate level measures from the 2010 Census to examine the extent to which factors such as economic attitudes, linked fate, neighborhood context, and sociodemographic factors influence Blacks' views toward undocumented immigrants already living and working in the US. The CMPS is an online panel survey examining political attitudes and behaviors during the 2012 presidential election.[3] The survey was conducted between November 16, 2012, and November 26, 2012, in both English and Spanish.[4] The data set is comprised of 2,616 registered voters who self-identified as Black (n = 804), Latino (n = 934), or White (n = 878). Unlike most studies, these data provide a national rather than state-specific view of African American opinion toward immigration reform.[5]

Dependent Variable

We examine the influence of economic and contextual factors on Black attitudes toward undocumented immigrants. We are specifically interested in the role that economic views might play in how Black people think about prospective policy prescriptions regarding undocumented immigration. In this analysis, we examine one dependent measure having three possible options using the following survey question:

> [ALL] Which comes closest to your view about [TEXT BASED ON CONDITION A/B: undocumented/illegal] immigrants who are already living and working in the US?
>
> 1 = They should be allowed to stay in their jobs and apply for US citizenship.
> 2 = They should be allowed to stay in their jobs TEMPORARILY and NOT apply for US citizenship.
> 3 = They should be required to leave their jobs IMMEDIATELY and leave the US.

Our outcome measure focuses on immigrants who are not only living but also working in the country. The vast majority of Black respondents in the CMPS 2012 favor undocumented immigrants being able to stay in the country and apply for citizenship (70 percent). The rest of the respondents were almost evenly divided between those who favor allowing immigrants to stay temporarily with no opportunity to apply for citizenship (12 percent) versus requiring the undocumented to leave immediately (12 percent). This question is part of an embedded experiment, with 50 percent of respondents receiving the word "illegal" and 50 percent receiving "undocumented." With regard to this analysis, note there is no statistical difference between the respondents who received the treatment and the control group.[6] Thus, we proceed to analyze the data with this mind.[7]

Independent Measures

Our predictors can be categorized into individual and aggregate (i.e., neighborhood) level variables. To examine economic views concerning immigration policy, we include a measure of respondent's views concerning whether immigration has an overall positive impact on the economy in their state (coded on a scale of strongly disagree to strongly agree) and if respondents believed that federal government spending to tighten border security to prevent undocumented/illegal immigration should be increased, decreased, or stay the same. We also included a measure to examine the extent to which the issue of undocumented/ illegal immigration influenced vote choice for their presidential candidate (coded on a scale of "a lot more likely" to "a lot less likely to vote for your presidential candidate"). For 20 percent of Blacks, the issue of undocumented immigration influenced their vote choice, as compared to 38 percent of Latinos and 30 percent of Whites.[8]

We include two measures of neighborhood social context: residential proximity to immigrants is measured by the percent of immigrants living in a respondent's census tract as reported by the 2010 census, which is a continuous measure that is scaled from 0 to 1, where 1 represents a tract in which 100 percent of the residents are foreign born, and 0 is where none of the residents in a respondent's neighborhood are foreign born, and a measure of the percent of the census tract living in poverty.[9] Given recent research regarding the impact of group identity on views toward immigration, we include a measure of linked fate which examines if Blacks think what happens generally to their racial group in this country will have something to do with what happens in your life (1 = yes). In addition, we control for a set of SES/Demographic measures comprised of the following: *education level* from 1 to 14, where 1 = no formal education, and 14 = Professional or Doctorate Degree; *household income* from 1–19, where 1 = less than $5,000 and 19 = 175,000 or more; *gender* (1 = woman); *age* (measured in years 18–89); *housing tenure* (1 = homeowner); *married* (1 = married); and *ideology* (very liberal = 1 to very conservative = 7).

Findings

In this section we present an overview of the CMPS 2012 sample. Table 12.1 in the Appendix reports select summary statistics regarding views toward policies targeting the undocumented, economic views toward undocumented immigration, group identity, racial/ethnic and economic context, and SES/demographic factors for CMPS 2012 sample. First, we examine the average responses to views about undocumented immigrants who are already living and working in the US by racial and ethnic group. The most favored response was allowing undocumented immigrants to remain in the United States, with over 50 percent of each racial/ethnic group selecting this option. Of the three possible policy options, 71 percent of Blacks and 72 percent of Latinos favored allowing undocumented immigrants to stay in their jobs and apply for US citizenship, followed by Whites at 55 percent. Whites in the sample, on average, were the most likely to choose a more punitive policy option (leave the US immediately) at 28 percent as compared to Blacks at 13 percent, and Latinos at 11 percent.

In our sample, Whites, on average, live in overwhelmingly White neighborhoods at 84 percent. Black and Latino neighborhoods are more diverse. Blacks live in areas that are, on average, 46 percent White and 12 percent Latino, while Latinos live in areas which are, on average, 71 percent White and 10 percent Black. Latino neighborhoods hold a larger percent of the foreign-born population at 18 percent, as compared to Black areas at 10 percent and White areas at 8 percent. On the other hand, Blacks live in neighborhoods with poverty levels (at 17 percent) more than double those in White (7 percent) neighborhoods. Regarding the SES and demographic measures Blacks, on average, were slightly more likely to hold a high school degree or less, at 32 percent; to report incomes below $25,000, at 27 percent; and were the least likely to own their own homes, at 59 percent. On the other hand, 37 percent of White voters reportedly obtaining a bachelor's degree or greater; over a third, or 34 percent, reported incomes exceeding $100,000; and 83 percent reported owning their own homes.

Finally, these descriptive statistics underscore persistent differences and disparities between racial/ethnic groups in the United States. However, they tell us little about how a combination of these factors might influence one's views toward contentious, often racialized and politicized issues such as undocumented immigration. Moving beyond the summary statistics for the CMPS 2012 sample discussed above, the next section examines the extent to which economic attitudes, linked fate, neighborhood context, and sociodemographic factors influence Blacks views toward undocumented groups already living and working in the US.

Black Views toward Undocumented Immigrants

Although a large majority of Black voters prefer for undocumented workers to stay in the United States, they are uncertain about whether illegal immigration has a positive effect on the state economy. In fact, 50 percent of Blacks did not have an opinion about whether immigration has an overall positive effect on their state's economy or not. Latinos and Whites were more likely to take a definitive position on the question. On average, Latinos were twice as likely to agree that immigration has an overall positive effect on their state's economy, at 59 percent, as compared to only 33 percent of Blacks and 32 percent of Whites. It is clear that economic considerations are only a part of what drives Black attitudes on immigration.

The uncertainty Blacks report about immigration's impact on the economy is especially important because these beliefs are associated with beliefs about what should happen to undocumented immigrants. According to table 13.2 in the Appendix, Blacks who believe that immigration has a positive effect on their state's economy are 11 percent more likely to support undocumented immigrants having the opportunity to stay permanently in their jobs and apply for citizenship, as compared to Blacks who do not share this view.

Blacks for whom immigration was important to their presidential vote choice are 15 percent more likely to support a permanent stay over both a temporary stay and leaving the country, as compared to Blacks who did not factor immigration into their vote choice. On the other hand, Blacks who favored increased federal spending to tighten border security were 6 percent less likely to support undocumented immigrants having the opportunity to stay permanently in their jobs and apply for citizenship and were 6 percent more likely to support the idea that immigrants should be required to leave the US.

Given the persistence of racial and economic segregation, Blacks are more likely than Whites to live among Latinos, immigrants, and in high-poverty areas. We hypothesized that increased proximity to Latinos, immigrants, or both would lead to more liberal preferences. Based on contact theories, we expected that increased contact with people who would be directly affected by immigration policies would produce more support for undocumented immigrants to stay in the United States. However, we find that the percent of immigrants living in Black areas posed no statistically significant influence on Black views toward undocumented immigrants. Instead, unlike the economic competition literature would suggest, as the percent of people living in poverty increases in their neighborhood, Blacks prefer allowing undocumented immigrants to stay in the US, over both temporary stay and leaving the country. This finding speaks directly to the role of poverty and shared class-based identities for people of color across race and immigration status. Homeownership is often viewed as both a contextual and sociodemographic measure. Blacks who own a home are 11 percent more likely to support a permanent stay for undocumented immigrants and 11 less likely to support them leaving the country immediately. Homeownership may represent financial security and potentially more progressive attitudes toward immigrants. Blacks with higher levels of educational attainment are more likely to support permanently staying and less likely to support the temporary stay option.

From the economic variables we examined, there does not seem to be a clear link between policy preferences and Blacks' economic position. Income is not statistically related to any of the policy outcomes. As poverty increases, Blacks are more supportive of undocumented immigrants staying in the United States. More economic stability in the form of homeownership is also associated with preferring the stay option. These findings strongly suggest that while economic considerations may be a factor, there are others which are equally or more important.

As we discussed previously, immigration is a racialized issue, particularly as it involves undocumented immigrants. We expected that as Blacks felt more linked fate with their group, they would also be more supportive of liberal immigration outcomes. However, unlike recent research, linked fate posed no influence on Black views toward undocumented immigrants. While these findings are preliminary, it is possible that other measures, such as economic views or educational attainment, may suppress the salience of linked fate, resulting in the lack of support for the linked fate hypothesis in this model.

Controlling for all other factors, women are more likely than men to select the permanent stay option. However, gender does not predict support for the other outcomes. Our findings regarding ideology suggest that more conservative Blacks are less likely to favor a temporary stay for undocumented immigrants and are more likely to favor deportation than Blacks who identify as more liberal. In short, we find that views toward undocumented immigrants currently living and working in the US are conditioned by factors related to Black economic attitudes, particularly those related to whether immigrants have a positive impact on the state economy, contextual measures such as increasing poverty in Black neighborhoods, and individual-level factors such as Black educational attainment. Unlike recent research, our findings do not find support for the linked fate hypothesis on Black views toward undocumented immigration.

Conclusion

One of the reasons that President Obama moved to executive actions was to counteract the intractable gridlock in Congress. Coalitions, including those between Blacks, Latinos, and other allies, will need to continue to put pressure on congress to act on immigration reform. In the most recent immigration debate, African American groups, including Black Lives Matter have joined with the many Latino and Black immigrant advocacy organizations for more progressive reforms. However, some previous research and media reports suggest that economic fears directly impact Blacks' attitudes toward immigration. One argument for the anti-immigrant, xenophobic, and nativist attitudes of many Trump supporters is rooted in rationales of economic competition between non-Hispanic Whites and these immigrants. In this chapter, we investigated some of the factors driving Black public opinion toward undocumented immigration. We find that Blacks do not engage in a single economic calculation. Instead, a series of contextual and demographic factors influence attitudes toward undocumented immigration and immigrants. In this regard, our chapter finds no empirical evidence not only for Black group linked fate being part of a calculus of immigration attitudes, but in this iteration of the work, it is difficult to even speculate if Black support for the Obama administration (inverted linked fate) might have been an intervening variable in Black immigration attitudes. This is worthy of further investigation.

Much of the debate in the US often focuses on Mexican immigrants and the Latino experience, leaving out the experiences of Black immigrants, including a broader understanding of Black views toward and support (of lack thereof) for Black immigrants, in particular Blacks who are undocumented. Activists such as Opal Tometi contend, "Not only is immigration a Black issue, but African Americans and immigrants of color are also facing common threats, which we can defeat if we stand united" (Tometi 2014). For those interested in the formation and maintenance of coalitions across race, ethnicity, and class in the post-Obama era, they should continue to examine these factors in light of the role of intersectionality, as it is clear that immigration status is just a part of one's identity. Many immigrants also identify as women, youth, people of color, Muslim, Christian, LGBTQ, etc. An increasing number of community-based advocacy organizations and college-aged youth groups seek to forge alliances for immigration reform through this broader intersectional lens, and continue the fight, after Obama.

Appendixes

TABLE 12.1. Policy Views by Race. Collaborative Multiracial Post-Election Survey (CMPS 2012)

	Black	Latino	White
Views about Undocumented Immigrants in US			
Apply Citizenship	0.71	0.71	0.55
Temporary Stay	0.12	0.13	0.15
Leave	0.13	0.11	0.28
Immigration Positive on Economy			
Disagree	0.17	0.14	0.34
Indifferent	0.50	0.27	0.33
Agree	0.33	0.59	0.32
Undocumented Immigration Influenced Vote Choice 2012			
Less Likely to Vote for Cand.	0.08	0.04	0.06
No Difference	0.72	0.59	0.64
More Likely to Vote for Cand.	0.20	0.38	0.30
Spending on Border Security			

TABLE 12.1. (*cont.*)

	Black	Latino	White
Undocumented Immigration Influenced Vote Choice 2012			
Decrease	0.11	0.13	0.11
Same	0.37	0.46	0.35
Increase	0.50	0.39	0.54
Group Identity			
Linked Fate	0.64	0.41	0.54
Context (tract-level)			
% Black	46.34	9.856	7.52
% Latino	12.43	40.10	9.86
% White	45.71	71.05	84.13
% Foreign Born	9.74	18.28	8.40
% Poverty	16.86	12.32	7.21
Demographics			
Age	47.72	45.81	51.57
Less than HS	0.11	0.18	0.05
High School Diploma	0.32	0.27	0.27
Some College	0.34	0.34	0.31
BA More	0.23	0.21	0.37
Income > 25K	0.27	0.14	0.12
Income < 25K and > 50K	0.25	0.22	0.21
Income < 50K and > 100K	0.32	0.44	0.34
Income < 100K	0.16	0.19	0.33
Own Home	0.60	0.71	0.83
Female	0.57	0.52	0.52
Party ID			
Democrat	0.80	0.52	0.28
Independent	0.10	0.19	0.26
Republican	0.02	0.18	0.36
No PID Preference	0.07	0.10	0.09
Observations	804	934	878

Select Summary Statistics for Respondents in CMPS 2012 Sample, by Racial/Ethnic Group
Source: Collaborative Multi-Racial Post-Election Survey (CMPS 2012)
Note: Table entries represent the means of a given variable and should be interpreted as percentages. The data used in this study are weighted by race and national origin.

TABLE 12.2. Economic Variables. Source: Collaborative Multiracial Post-Election Survey (CMPS 2012) / 2010 Census

	Apply Citizenship	Temporary Stay	Leave US
Economic Views			
Immigration positive for economy	0.11***	−0.04***	−0.07***
Immigration influenced vote choice	0.15***	−0.10***	−0.05*
Increase border spend	−0.06**	−0.00	0.06**
Group Identity			
Linked Fate	0.05	−0.01	−0.04
Context			
% Foreign Born	−0.00	0.00	−0.00
% Poverty	0.004**	−0.002*	−0.00*
Political Predisposition			
Ideology	0.01	−0.03***	0.02*
Demographics			
Education	0.02*	−0.01	−0.01
Income	−0.04	0.02	0.01
Woman	0.08**	−0.04	−0.04
Homeowner	0.11***	−0.01	−0.11***
Age	−0.00	−0.00	0.00
Married	0.03	−0.01	−0.02
Observations	750	750	750

Blacks' Views toward Undocumented Immigrants Currently Living and Working in US (Marginal Effects)
Source: Collaborative Multi-Racial Post-Election Survey (CMPS 2012) / 2010 Census
Notes: Each column represents the results of the marginal effects after the multinomial logistic regression analysis. Unlike logistic regression, the marginal effects are easier to interpret and help us to understand the impact of each independent variable on the dependent measure from its minimum to maximum value, holding all other variables at their means. For chapter presentation, we include only the marginal effects here, and the asterisk indicates that the variable is statistically significant in the regressions coefficients (*** $p < 0.01$, ** $p < 0.05$, * $p < 0.10$). We provide all of the variables for comparison here. However, several of the corresponding logistic regression coefficients are not statistically significant, and the marginal effects would not typically be calculated. The multinomial logistic regression table with coefficients and standard errors are available from the authors upon request.

NOTES

1 Founded in 2006, BAJI educates and engages African American and Black immigrant communities to organize and advocate for racial, social, and economic justice. It holds Organizing Committees in New York, Georgia, California, and Arizona. Its goals are to build coalitions and initiate campaigns among communities to push for racial justice (http://Blackalliance.org).

2 During the press conference to announce his candidacy for president in June 2015, Trump said of Mexican immigrants, "They're bringing drugs. They're bringing crime. They're rapists. And some, I assume, are good people." (Haberman 2016). Despite calls to apologize, he doubled down on these comments and continued to rally his supporters with calls to build a wall between Mexico and the US, for which, he claimed, Mexico would pay for.

3 The CMPS 2012 uses probability-based web panels designed to be representative of the United States instead of "opt-in" panels that include only individuals with internet access who volunteer themselves for research. As a result, panel members come from listed and unlisted telephone numbers, telephone and nontelephone households, and cell phone–only households, as well as households with and without internet access, which creates a representative sample. Panel members were recruited through national random samples (both by telephone and mail). Households are provided with access to the internet and a netbook computer, if needed. Otherwise, participants are rewarded with incentive points that are redeemable for cash. The median completion time of the survey was twenty minutes, and the completion rate was 56.3 percent.

4 Pretests of the survey were conducted between November 8, 2012, and November 19, 2012, in both English and Spanish.

5 The CMPS 2012 includes thirty-seven items dealing with sociopolitical attitudes, mobilization, political activity, advertising exposure, and neighborhood context, as well as three embedded survey experiments. Additionally, there are fifteen items that capture demographic information, including: age, ancestry, birthplace, education, ethnicity, Latin American racial descriptors, skin color, marital status, number in the household, religiosity, gender, sexual orientation, internet usage, and residential context.

6 We conducted an independent samples t-test, and comparisons revealed no significant difference in opinion between those who were asked about "illegal" immigrants versus those asked about "undocumented" immigrants: $t(2558) = 0.32$ $p > 0.744$.

7 When selecting the most appropriate regression methodology, we decided not to treat the outcome variable as ordinal because to do so assumes a natural ordering within the variable. Instead we use multinomial logistic regression. Interpreting the results of multinomial logistic regression analyses can be a difficult, and thus, we use the postestimation command MARGINS in STATA to generate the marginal effects for each of the three possible outcomes in order to make the interpretations of our analysis clearer. The marginal effect is the change in the dependent variable as a function of a change in a certain dependent variable while keeping all the other covariates constant. In this case, they represent the probability of selecting one of the three policy choices when holding all other variables in the model at their means.

8 Ninety-five percent of Blacks in the sample reported casting a ballot for Obama in 2012, as compared to 70 percent of Latinos and 42 percent of Whites.

9 We decided not to include percent Black in the model because it presented multi-collinearity with percent living in poverty. We also decided not to include percent Latino because it presented multicollinearity with percent immigrant.

REFERENCES

Amuedo-Dorantes, Catalina, and Thitima Puttitanun. 2011. "Gender Differences in Native Preferences toward Undocumented and Legal Immigration: Evidence from San Diego." *Contemporary Economic Policy* 29 (1): 31–45.

Barkan, Elliott R. 2003. "Return of the Nativists? California Public Opinion and Immigration in the 1980s and 1990s." *Social Science History* 27 (2): 229–83.

Barretto, Matt A, Gabriel Sanchez, and Jason Morin. 2011. "Perceptions of Competition between Latinos and Blacks: The Development of a Relative Measure of Inter-Group Competition." In *Just Neighbors? Research on African American and Latino Relations in the United States*, eds. Edward Telles, Mark Sawyer, and Gaspar Rivera-Salgado. New York: Russell Sage Foundation.

Bobo, Lawrence, and Vincent L Hutchings. 1996. "Perceptions of Racial Group Competition: Extending Blumer's Theory of Group Position to a Multiracial Social Context." *American Sociological Review* 61(6): 951–72.

Borjas, George J. 1999. "Economic Research on the Determinants of Immigration: Lessons for the European Union." Washington, DC: World Bank.

———. 2000. *Issues in the Economics of Immigration*. Chicago: University of Chicago Press.

Brown-Guinyard, Sherral Y. 2013. "Race, Class, Gender, and Linked Fate: A Cross-Sectional Analysis of African American Political Partisanship, 1996 and 2004." PhD dissertation, University of South Carolina, Ann Arbor.

Burns, Peter, and James G. Gimpel. 2000. "Economic Insecurity, Prejudicial Stereotypes, and Public Opinion on Immigration Policy." *Political Science Quarterly* 115 (2): 201–25.

Carter, Niambi, and Tyson D. King-Meadows. 2019. "Perceptual Knots and Black Identity Politics: Linked Fate, American Heritage, and Support for Trump Era Immigration Policy." *Societies* 9:1–11.

Citrin, Jack, Donald P. Green, Christopher Muste, and Cara Wong. 1997. "Public Opinion toward Immigration Reform: The Role of Economic Motivations." *Journal of Politics* 59 (3): 858–81.

Change.gov, Office of the President-Elect. United States, 2008. Archived Web Site. www.loc.gov.

Dawson, Michael C. 1995. *Behind the Mule: Race and Class in African-American Politics*: Princeton, NJ: Princeton University Press.

Diaz, Priscila, Delia S. Saenz, and Virginia S. Y. Kwan. 2011. "Economic Dynamics and Changes in Attitudes toward Undocumented Mexican Immigrants in Arizona." *Analyses of Social Issues and Public Policy* 11 (1): 300–13.

Espenshade, Thomas J., and Charles A. Calhoun. 1993. "An Analysis of Public Opinion toward Undocumented Immigration." *Population Research and Policy Review* 12 (3): 189–224.

Federico, Christopher M. 2004. "When Do Welfare Attitudes Become Racialized? The Paradoxical Effects of Education." *American Journal of Political Science* 48 (2): 374–91.

Frasure-Yokley, Lorrie, and Stacey Greene. 2013. "Black Views toward Proposed Undocumented Immigration Policies: The Role of Racial Stereotypes and Economic Competition." In Laura Pulido and Josh Kun (eds.) *Black and Brown Los Angeles: Beyond Conflict and Coalition.* Berkeley and Los Angeles, CA: University of California Press. 90–111.

Frasure-Yokley, Lorrie, and Bryan Wilcox-Archuleta. 2019. "Geographic Identity and Attitudes toward Undocumented Immigrants." *Political Research Quarterly* 72: 944–59.

Fortner, Michael. 2015. *Black Silent Majority: The Rockefeller Drug Laws and the Politics of Punishment.* Cambridge, MA: Harvard University Press.

Gay, Claudine. 2006. "Seeing Difference: The Effect of Economic Disparity on Black Attitudes toward Latinos." *American Journal of Political Science* 50 (4): 982–97.

Glaser, James M. 2001. "The Preference Puzzle: Educational Differences in Racial-Political Attitudes." *Political Behavior* 23: 313–34.

Ha, Shange E. 2010. "The Consequences of Multiracial Contexts on Public Attitudes toward Immigration." *Political Research Quarterly* 63 (29): 29–42.

Haberman, Maggie. 2016. "New Donald Trump Ad Highlights Father of Teenager Killed by Illegal Immigrant" *New York Times*, February 13, 2016.

Hackshaw, Alana Christine. 2005. "Ethnic Diversity and Pan-Black Racial Solidarity: Locating the Bonds of Political Unity among Black Americans and Black Caribbean Immigrants in the U.S." (Doctoral Dissertation.) http://hdl.handle.net.

Hood, M. V., and Irwin L. Morris. 1997. "¿Amigo o Enemigo? Context, Attitudes, and Anglo Public Opinion toward Immigration." *Social Science Quarterly* 78(2): 309–323.

Jackson, Byran O., Elisabeth R. Gerber, and Bruce E. Cain. 1994. "Coalitional Prospects in a Multi-Racial Society: African-American Attitudes toward Other Minority Groups." *Political Research Quarterly* 47 (2): 277–94.

Jones, Jeffery M. 2014. "U.S. Hispanics Back Obama Immigration Actions." Gallup, December 10, 2014, www.news.gallup.com.

Kandel, William, Jerome P. Bjelopera, Andorra Bruno, and Alison Siskin. 2014. "President's Immigration Accountability Executive Action of November 20, 2014: Overview and Issues." In *CRS Report for Congress.* Washington, DC: Library of Congress Congressional Research Service.

Krogstad, Jens Manuel, and Jeffery S. Passel. 2015. "5 Facts about Illegal Immigration in the U.S." Pew Research Center, www.pewresearch.org.

Marrow, Helen B. 2011. *New Destination Dreaming: Immigration, Race, and Legal Status in the Rural American South.* Palo Alto, CA: Stanford University Press.

Masuoka, Natalie, and Jane Junn. 2013. *The Politics of Belonging: Race, Public Opinion, and Immigration.* Chicago: University of Chicago Press.

McClain, Paula D. 1993. "The Changing Dynamics of Urban Politics: Black and Hispanic Municipal Employment—Is There Competition?" *Journal of Politics* 55 (2): 399–414.

McClain, Paula D., and Albert K. Karnig. 1990. "Black and Hispanic Socioeconomic and Political Competition." *American Political Science Review* 84 (2): 535–45.

McClain, Paula D., Niambi M. Carter, Victoria M. DeFrancesco Soto, Monique L. Lyle, Jeffrey D. Grynaviski, Shayla C. Nunnally, Thomas J. Scotto, J. Alan Kendrick, Gerald F. Lackey, and Kendra Davenport Cotton. 2006. "Racial Distancing in a Southern City: Latino Immigrants' Views of Black Americans." *Journal of Politics* 68 (3): 571–84.

McClain, Paula D., Monique L. Lyle, Niambi M. Carter, Victoria M. DeFrancesco Soto, Gerald F. Lackey, Kendra Davenport Cotton, Shayla C. Nunnally, Thomas J. Scotto, Jeffrey D. Grynaviski, and J. Alan Kendrick. 2007. "Black Americans and Latino Immigrants in a Southern City." *Du Bois Review: Social Science and Research on Race* 4 (01):97–117.

McClain, Paula D, Monique L. Lyle, Efren O. Peréz, Jessica Johnson Carew, Jr. Eugene Walton, Candis S. Watts, Gerald F. Lackey, Danielle Clealand, and Shayla C. Nunnally. 2009. "Black and White Americans and Latino Immigrants: A Preliminary Look at Attitudes in Three Southern Cities." Paper presented at the annual meeting of the American Political Science Association. Toronto, Canada, September 3–6.

Meier, Kenneth J., Paula D. McClain, J. L. Polinard, and Robert D. Wrinkle. 2004. "Divided or Together? Conflict and Cooperation between African Americans and Latinos." *Political Research Quarterly* 57 (3): 399–409.

Morris, Irwin L. 2000. "African American Voting on Proposition 187: Rethinking the Prevalence of Interminority Conflict." *Political Research Quarterly* 53 (1): 77–98.

Nteta, Tatishe. 2013. "United We Stand? African Americans, Self-Interest, and Immigration Reform." *American Politics Research* 41 (1): 147–72.

Nteta, Tatishe. 2014. "The Past Is Prologue: African American Opinion toward Undocumented Immigration." *Social Science History* 38 (3–4): 389–410.

Passel, Jeffery S., and D'Vera Cohn. 2015. "Unauthorized Immigrant Population Stable for Half a Decade." Pew Research Center, September 21, 2015, www.pewresearch.org.

Sanchez, Gabriel R., and Natalie Masuoka. 2010. "Brown-Utility Heuristic? The Presence and Contributing Factors of Latino Linked Fate." *Hispanic Journal of Behavioral Sciences* 32 (4): 519–31.

Smith, Candis Watts. 2017. "Monkey Cage: Black Immigrants in the U.S. Face Big Challenges. Will African Americans Rally to Their Side?" *Washington Post*, September 18, 2017. www.washingtonpost.com.

Smith, Candis Watts, and Christina Greer, eds. 2018. *Black Politics in Transition: Immigration, Suburbanization, and Gentrification.* New York: Routledge.

Stokes, Atiya Kai. 2003. "Latino Group Consciousness and Political Participation." *American Politics Research* 31 (4): 361–78.

Thornton, Michael C., and Yuko Mizuno. 1999. "Economic Well-Being and Black Adult Feelings toward Immigrants and Whites, 1984." *Journal of Black Studies* 30 (1): 15–44.

Tometi, Opal. 2014. "Immigration Reform Is a Black Thing, Too." In *The Root.*

———. 2016. "Black Lives Matter Co-Founder: The Immigration Challenge No One Is Talking About." *Time*, April 29, 2016.

Vernado, Debra. 2016. "Still-Grieving Father of Slain Youth Finds an Ally in Donald Trump" *Los Angeles Wave Newspapers*, July 16, 2016, http://wavepublication.com.

Waldinger, Roger David. 1996. *Still the Promised City? African-Americans and New Immigrants in Postindustrial New York*. Cambridge, MA: Harvard University Press.

Watts, Candis. 2009. "Expanding Contours of Black Politics? Understanding Linked fate Among Afro-Caribbeans." Paper presented at annual meeting of the Midwest Political Science Association, Chicago, IL, April 2–5, 2009.

Wilkinson, Betina Cutaia, and Emily Earle. 2013. "Taking a New Perspective to Latino Racial Attitudes: Examining the Impact of Skin Tone on Latino Perceptions of Commonality with Whites and Blacks." *American Politics Research* 41 (5): 783–818.

Wilson, Thomas C. 2001. "Americans' Views on Immigration Policy: Testing the Role of Threatened Group Interests." *Sociological Perspectives* 44 (4): 485–501.

Zong, Jie, and Jeanne Batalova. 2016. "Frequently Requested Statistics on Immigrants and Immigration to the United States in 2014." www.migrationpolicy.org.

13

Foreign Policy during and after Barack Obama

ROBERT B. PACKER

A doctrine is how a president is forced to operate foreign policy
in the reality in which he finds himself. Sometimes, presidents
proclaim their own foreign policy doctrines. Other times, observers see a coherent pattern in a president's foreign policy and
outline the doctrine for him. In both cases, doctrines ought to
be seen not as strokes of genius or decisions made at the will of
the president but as actions imposed on him and dictated by
reality.
—George Friedman, Global Futures (2018)

This chapter differs from the other contributions of this volume. I do not
explicitly foreground questions of race and the Obama administration's
Black politics legacy in the realm of foreign affairs. Instead, I apply the
literature on the broad left-right ideological content of presidential foreign policy to Obama. Then in my conclusion I discuss the significance
of Obama's foreign policy legacy as the first African American to serve
as president. I examine the major constraints and opportunities Obama
and his foreign policy team navigated as he led as a racially transcendent, so-called "commander in chief of the American empire" (Harris
2012); though his African heritage from his father and experience as a
Black American fostered some identification with Black/African peoples
and vice versa (BBC News 2017).

Barack Obama came into office in the midst of a domestic economic
crisis. But the foreign policy arena was just as fraught with turmoil. His
predecessor's term had been transformed by the September 11, 2001, terror attack in New York, which led to new focus in American foreign
policy. George W. Bush gave an ultimatum to the Taliban government
in Afghanistan that it turn over al-Qaeda members living in sanctuary

in that central Asian country. When the Taliban refused, Bush launched Operation Enduring Freedom, marking the beginning of a global "war on terror." In January 2002 Bush expanded the parameters of that war by pointing out state sponsors of terrorism, the "Axis of Evil." He claimed that foremost among them was Iraq, under Saddam Hussein. Using the pretext of clandestine weapons of mass destruction (WMD) program as justification, Bush launched Operation Iraqi Freedom with the expressed goal of toppling the Iraqi dictator. In his second inaugural, Bush laid out a doctrine of regime change and democratization, which was the culmination of decades of neoconservative policy advocacy. Afghanistan and Iraq were the twin pillars of American foreign policy that Obama faced when he entered the Oval Office.

While the Afghanistan operation had the broad support of both NATO and the UN, the latter setting up the International Security Assistance Force (ISAF) providing broad international authorization, Iraq proved to be internationally divisive and a departure from multilateralism. The Iraq War divided American allies, most of whom, France and Germany included, opposed it. The Iraq War brought the first major open split between the United States and Putin's Russia. And the Iraq War fanned the flames of anti-Americanism in the Islamic world, as many there viewed the conflict as neocolonialism. By 2008, favorable opinions of the United States internationally (including in Europe) had fallen, and animosity toward the United States in the Middle East had grown (Pew Research Center, 2009).

Against this backdrop, Obama, the first African American to serve as commander-in-chief, came into office promising to end the Iraq War and restore favorable image of America internationally. The latter would involve a very public break and repudiation of neoconservative strategy, an embrace of multilateralism, and a focus on nonideological foreign policy and addressing overlooked global issues. In this chapter, I will review what I see as the essential characteristics of the Obama foreign policy style and whether we can discern a clear "Obama doctrine" from his foreign policy actions and rhetoric. In order to do so, I will lay out the four major approaches to American foreign policy-making, and then assess how Obama's policies fit within these approaches. While domestic economic recovery was paramount early in the administration, Obama's early foreign policy moves emphasized reconciliation and a more focused approach on counterterrorism as opposed to regime change. However, domestic political and international geopolitical constraints came to limit his ambitions. What began with soaring rhetoric of change was replaced with cautionary tales of avoiding mistakes. After laying out the four schools of American foreign policy (nationalist, realist, liberal institutionalist, neoconservative), I move to discuss Obama's policy style—the "nonideological doctrine"—that was purposively deliberative and cautious, in contrast to the ideological Bush regime-change crusade. Obama was careful to weigh the costs and benefits of policy options, keeping an eye on his predilection that foreign affairs must not interfere with domestic agenda. This caution, which avoided major commitments to overseas conflicts, came under criticism from both the left and right of the political spectrum, including some African American leaders. Among some of his critics on the left where progressive members of the Congressional Black Caucus (Hudson 2013).

However, it would be unfair to conclude that Obama had no overarching vision of America's place in a changing world. Obama saw his administration in terms of preparing for long-term change and dealing with global issues, like climate, proliferation, and Western-Islamic relations. He viewed the short-termism of the "war on terror" as diverting precious time and energy away from these emerging issues. Indeed, Obama was constantly balancing the need to end long land wars in the Middle East with a desire to get on with dealing with longer-term challenges. Change, as he reminded audiences during his presidential run, was a long-term project that would be fraught with setbacks and stalemates along the way. Nowhere was this truer than in the greater Middle East, where the tempered optimism of the 2009 Cairo speech had diminished into the sobering realities of Benghazi and the Syrian civil war.

If divining an Obama Doctrine and matching it to a policy style is the first requirement of assessment, the second must be pointing out the disconnect between rhetoric and action. To be certain, every president comes into office faced with both domestic constraints and international obstacles that limit the ability of the president to implement a change agenda. Domestically, following the catastrophic defeat in the 2010 congressional midterms, Obama faced the most confrontational Congress since the 1970s. The effect of this is found mostly in domestic policy, especially civil rights, but it came to influence foreign policy as well. The latter was amplified following Republican takeover of the Senate in 2014. Obama's attempt at reconciliation was much derided by Republicans as "an apology tour," with well-publicized pictures of Obama seemingly bowing to the Saudi King making the rounds of conservative media. This worsened the post–Vietnam War tendency to view Democrats as "soft" on national security. Despite his promise to close the Guantanamo Bay prison and end American participation in the Iraq War, Obama did not deviate significantly from the post-9/11 national security focus on terrorism. His innovation was not to end the war on terror as much as it was to fight it smarter. Even during the 2008 campaign, as he derided Bush administration for having "taken the eye off the ball" of fighting al-Qaeda in order to shift resources to fight Saddam Hussein, he nonetheless called the Afghanistan War against al-Qaeda and allies as the war that needed to be won. In his determination to pursue Osama bin-Laden, Obama perhaps reasoned that he would receive some measure of acceptance among Republicans as he tried to build political consensus. While the eventual killing of bin-Laden burnished Obama's reputation as a serious wartime president among Democrats and Independents, it did not among Republicans, who continued their opposition. Meanwhile, Obama's pursuit of fighting the war on terror smarter came to alienate many of his initial supporters on the Left. The vast expansion of both drone strikes and Special Forces engagements throughout the Obama presidency left a sour taste among Democratic progressives.

Obama was further hindered internationally. While he did successfully extricate American ground troops from Iraq in 2011, the event coincided with the region-wide breakout of antiregime popular revolutions, known collectively as the Arab Spring. These popular revolutions put the administration in an uncomfortable position between supporting long-standing regimes whose regional policy preferences, if not their domestic politics, coincided with America's, and dumping those same regimes in favor of a full-throated embrace of change. Obama the cost-benefit pragmatist versus Obama the idealist came into play. Obama equivocated, eventually calling for the resignation of Egypt's Hosni Mubarak, but not reacting to the Saudi crackdown in Bahrain. When the popular revolution in Libya mutated into full-blown civil war, Obama was pressed by liberal internationalists in his administration to act—a decision that would lead to the disastrous Benghazi incident that would further stain his relations with Republicans in Congress.

While the Arab Spring and its aftermath captured immediate attention in 2011, it was the rise of the Islamic State of Iraq and Syria (ISIS) in the aftermath of the American withdrawal from Iraq that had the most damaging effect on Obama's plan to extricate from the Middle East. Obama efforts to withdraw from the Middle East were not an isolationist impulse but a calculated effort to shift the focus of American foreign policy to managing relations with an increasingly recalcitrant Russia and assertive China.

The third area of review of the Obama administration consists of the policies themselves, from fighting the war on terror "smarter" to the disengagement efforts from the Middle East to managing Russian and Chinese relations to dealing with emerging global issues like climate change and nuclear proliferation.

Finally, the fourth area of review is a critique and retrospective based on what has occurred since the end of the Obama presidency.

American Foreign Policy Positions

The schools of American foreign policy differ over whether and when to intervene in overseas conflict zones. Noninterventionist nationalists from both the political Left (i.e., progressive) and Right (i.e., conservative) have long argued that foreign intervention is unwise (i.e., based on Washington's Farewell Address, foreign intervention creates more enemies for the US, or "blowback") and/or unconstitutional (e.g., invoking the notion of limited government, both at home and abroad). Nationalists argued that bad foreign state behavior is not the business of the United States unless such a state directly threatens the US. To that end, America is not the world's police, nor is it an empire. America should set its own example domestically (constitutional government) and just engage in trade with the rest of the world.

Realists, who became the dominant group in setting American foreign policy after World War II, argued that the United States did have a global role. Realists argued that the country is a major power, and with that comes major power interests and a responsibility to uphold international order. To that end, realists argue that the US should intervene abroad when there are compelling American national security interests at stake. They argued that deterrence policy, such as a strong military posture and forward bases overseas, could stop bad state behavior. Thus, America is the reluctant sheriff, the leader of the world whose responsibility it is to maintain a sense of global order. This global order is not the result of charity but a necessary condition for American business interests to thrive. International institutions, such as the United Nations (UN) and the International Monetary Fund (IMF), were collective organizations forged to promote American interests in a liberal international economic order. As long as other states abided by the principle of an open stable order, their internal affairs were not America's concern.

Liberal institutionalists shared the realist view of an America engaged with the world but differed over its "exceptional" role. While realists viewed international institutions as vehicles to promote American interests, liberal institutionalists viewed them as vehicles to promote "global community." Liberal institutionalists are much more willing to subsume American interests to a global order based on transnational liberal values of democracy and open commerce. To that end, while Realists were hesitant to intervene in the internal affairs of other states, as long as their foreign policies were in concert with the United States, liberal institutionalists viewed inconsistent values as the basis of bad state behavior that would undermine global order. With the US acting not as a regular "great power" but as a part of a liberal "global community," intervention, especially humanitarian intervention, was viewed as important. Furthermore, the US should balance American business interests with the need to address global needs, such as climate change. Whereas realists emphasize the hard power of military capabilities, liberal institutionalists placed near equal weight on the soft power of diplomacy and cooperative ventures.

Neoconservatives (neocons) represent the newest American foreign policy orientation. Born out of frustration with nonideological Realism, neocons argued, ironically similar to liberal institutionalists, that values matter in foreign policy. But where liberal institutionalists placed emphasis on global consensus through an array of cooperative agreements and institutions, neocons argued that these very institutions were fetters on the advance of American values and power. Neocons, similar to many nationalists on the political Right, came to view international agreements as compromises with corrupt governments. Neocons took the realist view of American exceptionalism and infused it with the crusading zeal to "make the world safe for democracy"; thus, America was a not-so-reluctant sheriff on the world stage. But whereas liberal internationalists saw such crusades as collective struggles, neocons viewed them as a unitary one, or one that required converting would-be allies to American values, lest the very principles being fought for be diluted in the name of consensus.

On the spectrum of intervention, neocons tend to be most interventionist, based on promoting American values and interests. Liberal institutionalists are next, leading a global community to promote transnational liberal values. Realists are third, intervening to promote strategic great-power and commercial interests. Nationalists, of both progressive and conservative persuasions, are the least interventionist. While both neocons and conservative nationalists emphasize American exceptionalism, neocons wish to recast the world in the country's image while conservatives (echoing the isolationists of the past) do not. While realists and liberal institutionalists both argue for an American international role, realists limit intervention to promotion of American interests while liberal institutionalists expand it to the promotion of global values. Progressive nationalists, like their counterparts on the Right, call for nonintervention. But while conservatives speak of near perfection of American institutions, progressives speak of an imperfect union in constant internal struggle over reform. For progressives, overseas intervention takes the eye off the most important goal of domestic reform. Occasionally, in more recent decades, progressives may side with liberal institutionalists in order to lever the influence of more progressively inclined governments overseas in promoting international agreements that may impart those ideas here at home.

A Post-Post-9/11 Foreign Policy

While domestic policies were his primary focus upon taking office, Obama also attempted to reverse the decline in America's favorability ratings abroad. His visit to Berlin during the campaign and contrasts with Bush administration policies elicited positive responses from European governments. The heart of the European angst over Bush was also the source of public discord over foreign policy at home—the Iraq War. Obama made his opposition to the war his foreign policy calling card and won over progressives within the Democratic Party by decrying regime-change interventionism. Unlike his rivals within the party who played the conventional Washington playbook of supporting the Iraq War as part of an overarching war on terrorism, Obama chastised American involvement and called for an open break with post-9/11 view of the permanent war state. Just as progressives throughout the Cold War decried the influence of the military-industrial complex in straitjacketing American foreign policy choices, Obama spoke for a new generation who took just as jaundiced a view of the post-9/11 national security state. The idea of the national security state is rooted in the notion that, similar to the Cold War, America would fight a long twilight struggle with a virulent strain of fundamentalist Islamism and its affiliate organizations. These organizations use terror as their principal weapon to weaken the resolve of Western governments. Similar to its proponents in Israel, advocates of the national security state argue that terrorists are irrational and guided by transcendent ideas; thus, deterrence policies would not work. What are needed to defeat the threat are constant vigilance, the erection and strengthening of security measures, and a proactive counterterrorism strategy to take the fight directly to terrorists rather than responding to their initiatives.

To that end, the Bush administration had an aggressive policy of taking the fight to them before they bring it to us, which included the use of American military personnel to defeat not only foreign terrorist cells but also the governments that may give sanctuary to them. This morphed into a larger regime-change policy with a core rationale that bad behavior comes from bad actors. Rather than trying to reform bad actor behavior through carrots and sticks, regime-change advocates posit that the nature of actors (regimes) predispose them to bad behavior and that only their removal can bring about regional and international stability and peace. Regime change and the related "democracy agenda" imparted a crusading zeal among its advocates in the Bush administration. Critics would later argue that hubris led them to believe that the ouster of the Saddam Hussein regime in Iraq would reorient the Middle East toward a more democratic and peaceful path. Regional specialists, steeped in local cultural and political understanding, warned against the application of such universalist conventions as regime change and a democracy agenda. In many ways, the debate that was to rage following the initial failure of securing Iraq that followed the March 2003 invasion mirrored the Cold War debate over the sources of turmoil in third-world societies (Packer 1991). Eventually, the Bush administration was forced to course correct in Iraq with a long-term counterinsurgency campaign. Although packaged as a temporary "surge," counterinsurgency involves long-term commitment to a besieged country's citizens in order to defeat an entrenched adversary. Counterinsurgency involves the provision of public goods of security, electrical and other power production, health care, and education services to the local population in order to earn their trust and support. Counterinsurgency involves "draining the swamp" of insurgent support over time. But time is the biggest enemy of any outside power attempting such policies, as home publics tire of the loss of life and stress on existing armed forces of long and repeated deployments.

Obama's post-post-9/11 foreign policy had four major features. The first was to leave the obsession with terrorism behind. This required a new relationship with the Islamic world in general and the greater Middle East in particular. Neocon ideology would be replaced with careful rational pragmatism. The second was to focus on other transnational challenges, such as nuclear proliferation (e.g., North Korea having exploded a nuclear device and Iran having an active nuclear acquisition program), climate change, global pandemics, and cybersecurity. The third—related to the first and burdens of the counterinsurgency—was to end "stupid wars" and practices that exacerbate anti-Americanism (i.e., ending the Iraq War and closing the Guantanamo Bay prison). And fourth, shift away from the "hard power" of military deployments and toward greater emphasis on the "soft power" of diplomacy and greater use of norm-generating international institutions to deal with global issues.

Extrication from the Middle East

The major foreign policy challenge for the incoming Obama administration was to bring the wars in the greater Middle East to an end. But the administration's approach to the two big wars in Iraq and Afghanistan were quite different. Obama campaigned on Iraq being the wrong war at the wrong time. He argued the Saddam Hussein regime was not an existential threat to the American homeland, that Saddam was not working with the al-Qaeda terrorists that attacked the United States, and that continuing the war had substantially damaged America's reputation not only in the Middle East but among allies as well. (France and Germany voted against the United Nations' authorization of the use of force against Iraq, leading the Bush administration to create a "coalition of the willing" to invade the country.) Likewise, the war on terror fueled anti-Americanism in the Middle East. The Abu Ghraib scandal and the indefinite internment of detainees at Guantanamo Bay added to increased distrust of the United States in the Middle East. Obama made moves on both of these fronts but ultimately was frustrated by events both in the region and at home.

A major change from the Bush administration came in the form in *how* the war on terror was fought. Rather than end the war, as progressives hoped, Obama emphasized how to fight smarter. In a way, Obama returned to the conundrum posed by former Secretary of Defense Donald Rumsfeld: How do you fight a war using a "light footprint" so as not to overtax the military or arouse public opposition. The "light footprint" strategy proved a failure by 2006, but counterinsurgency, as mentioned earlier, was not sustainable. Furthermore, the government of Iraq was not cooperating, as the Shia-led al-Maliki regime discriminated against Sunnis, squandering the limited gains won by the surge of American forces in 2006–2009. Obama attempted to sign a new Status of Forces Agreement (SOFA) that would leave a small contingent of American trainers in Iraq; however, negotiations bogged down as al-Maliki increasingly saw Tehran, not Washington, as his chief ally. Iraqi foreign policy became a sideshow to the sectarian divide that was slowly ripping the country apart. As al-Maliki cracked down on Sunni dissent, he inadvertently stoked the fires that were to burst out in the ISIS insurgency in 2013. As SOFA negotiations reached a standoff, the Obama administration began its withdrawal from Iraq in 2009, concluding in 2011.

The year 2011 would prove to be decisive as minor street protests erupted into popular revolutions in a number of Arab countries. While Washington, under both Bush and Obama, had championed the cause of democratic change rhetorically in the region, neither was comfortable with the prospect of abandoning long-lasting alignments with autocratic regions. This came to a head when the Arab Spring wave crashed on the shores of Egypt. President Hosni Mubarak had been in power since the assassination of his predecessor, Anwar el-Sadat, in 1981. Mubarak placed Egypt, the most populous Arab country and historically the regional leader, firmly in the American camp during the Cold War. By being the first Arab government to sign a peace treaty with the Israelis in 1979, the Camp David Accords, Egypt was the largest recipient of American foreign assistance. The US military also maintained close ties with their Egyptian counterparts. As long as Egypt remained aligned with Washington, it was unlikely that any other Arab state would take on the Israelis in sustained armed conflict. Thus, the Mubarak regime was central to an American realpolitik strategy of regional stability. While Mubarak was good for American interests, his regime was highly corrupt, with the Mubarak family, members of the ruling party, and their cronies, making millions of dollars off of state contracts in one of the poorest societies in the Middle East. Although Mubarak was not brutal like a Saddam Hussein or even the Assad family in Syria, the military-backed regime held firm control. Elections were regularly held, but the ruling party dominated with only token state-approved opposition. Egypt in 2011 became a powder keg, and Obama had to decide how to react.

In what would become a familiar theme, Obama faced a split among his foreign policy advisors, with the secretaries of state and defense—Hillary Clinton and Robert Gates—arguing for caution, while junior advisors, such as Deputy National Security Adviser Ben Rhodes, pushing for a more assertive approach to support the pro-democracy movement (Philips 2016). Obama's cautious decision style was evidenced as he reviewed the unfolding situation in Cairo, a city where he gave his first major presidential speech beyond American shores. Obama came down on the side of his junior advisors when he phoned the Egyptian president and advised him to announce he was stepping down and begin an orderly transition (Philips 2016). After Mubarak refused, the administration opened a line of communication to the Egyptian military to take control in order to prevent chaos. Obama would later claim that his goal was to prevent "tanks shooting into the crowds in Tahrir Square similar to what happened in Tiananmen Square" in Beijing in 1989 (Philips

2016). While initially hailing the downfall of Mubarak as ushering in a new day for the long-suffering Egyptians, the subsequent election of an Islamist Muslim Brotherhood government, its antidemocratic crackdown on its critics, and its eventual ouster by another military regime have left many dubious as whether much was gained at all. For Obama, the election of the Muslim Brotherhood became fodder for his critics on the Right that he had "lost Egypt" and was another manifestation of a "weak foreign policy."

If Egypt was a case of discomfort, Libya was to become disastrous. As in Egypt, a popular revolution arose in 2011 to oust Muammar Gaddafi, who had ruled the oil-rich North African country since 1969. Unlike Egypt, Libya did not have close ties to the US government or military. Indeed, Libya was a target of American ire during the Reagan administration, when Gaddafi unsuccessfully challenged the Sixth Fleet in the Gulf of Sidra showdown in 1981 and supported a variety of terrorist groups operating in the Middle East and Europe throughout the 1970s, 1980s, and 1990s. When Gaddafi was implicated in the Berlin discotheque bombing in 1986, the Reagan administration again struck the country, this time killing close members of the Gaddafi family. In 1988, Libyan intelligence officers were found complicit in the Lockerbie bombing over the skies of Scotland. The Republican-led US Congress would pass the Iran and Libya Sanctions Act that not only forbade American companies from doing business with Gaddafi but punished European subsidiaries of those American companies as well. During the lead-up to the Iraq War, Libya could be called an unindicted member of the Axis of Evil. But then a major change occurred. Following the invasion of Iraq, Gaddafi reached agreement with the United States on Lockerbie damages. Gaddafi was being readmitted into the community of nations. Obama even briefly met and shook hands with the Libyan leaders during their mutual visit to the United Nations in New York in 2009.

When Gaddafi's security personnel fired on protesters in Benghazi in February 2011, Obama faced in Libya what he avoided in Egypt. Following the precepts of liberal institutionalism, the United Nations Security Council passed a resolution to freeze Libyan assets in an attempt to pressure the regime. As an opposition government was established and rebellion spread, Gaddafi was on the defensive. However, unlike Mubarak,

Gaddafi was prepared to fight, and the country descended into civil war. As the Gaddafi regime used harsh measures, including aerial attacks on civilian areas, Western governments, fearing the mass exodus of Libyan refugees coming across the Mediterranean, pushed for more punitive sanctions. France, in particular, called for Gaddafi's removal. The African Union attempted to mediate between Gaddafi and the rebels, but the rebels rebuffed the initiative in favor of Gaddafi's immediate removal. As the UN passed a resolution to enforce a no-fly zone, France and Britain pushed for NATO enforcement of the resolution. Obama demurred, as divisions emerged in the White House. Secretary of State Hillary Clinton made the liberal institutionalist case for intervention along with UN Ambassador Samantha Power, a long-time advocate of the "responsibility to protect" view (Welsh 2012), which holds that state sovereignty may be violated when regimes commit human rights violations against their own people. Many neocons likewise joined the chorus to bomb Gaddafi as part of their regime-change agenda. Despite the array of pro-interventionist forces, Obama was loath to commit American pilots to once again bomb an Arab country. He found the "easy regime change" case suspect. However, he was persuaded by arguments made by the French and British that they had made plans for the postwar political transition. Lack of such planning was a charge that Obama and other critics had lobbed at the Bush administration regarding Iraq. Following seven months of sustained NATO bombing and offshore cruise missile strikes (Operation Unified Protector), combined with a Libyan rebel ground offensive, Gaddafi was ousted from power. The interim National Transitional Council was recognized as the new Libyan government, with elections to a new parliament held the following July.

Despite the optimistic beginning, the aftermath of the Libyan civil war turned out disastrously, as even Obama lamented that the postwar planning by allies fell far short of what was promised (Somin 2016). Like Iraq, internal divisions in the country would produce irreconcilable fissures, igniting more political violence barely a year later. Armed militia clashed with each other as the official government held only tenuous sway in the eastern part of the country. Lack of internal security was brought painfully to attention following the September 11, 2012, attack on the American diplomatic compound in Benghazi, leading to the deaths of four Americans—including US ambassador Christopher Stevens. The Benghazi attack would become a major event that critics of Obama's (and Hillary Clinton's) stewardship of foreign policy pointed to as a failure of humanitarian intervention and planning for the postwar political vacuum.

Rather than extricating himself from the Middle East, the Arab Spring and its fallout would not let Obama go. The year after reelection, Obama faced a new challenge in the region, from the dead-end Sunni resistance to the al-Maliki regime in Iraq and the Assad regime in Syria: ISIS.

From Stupid to Smart Wars–Counterinsurgency to Counterterrorism

Nowhere did candidate Obama say that he would change the course of American foreign policy more than in the prosecution of the war on terror. In evaluating the Obama policy, I look at two fronts—the land war in Afghanistan and the drone war against transnational terror networks. Despite enunciating lofty goals of stabilizing the country and preparing the Afghans to govern themselves peacefully, the war in Afghanistan would frustrate Obama as much as it frustrated his predecessor. The reason lies in the nature of all indigenous insurgencies. Outsiders cannot provide what the domestic regime is unable to. Back in 2006, then Afghan president Hamid Karzai was privately derided as the "mayor of Kabul," given that his NATO-supported regime firmly controlled only the capital city and some key roads around the mountainous country. Beyond those roads, especially in the Pashtun-populated areas of the south and southeast, the Taliban or the Haqqani network held sway. Obama said during 2008 that Afghanistan was the "good war" that should be waged to defeat al-Qaeda and their Taliban defenders. Obama said that Bush had "taken the eye off the ball in Afghanistan" in order to wage the "stupid war" in Iraq. Obama was not Pollyannaish in his assessment of turning things around in Afghanistan, but he believed that a combination of smart strategy from Washington and competent noncorrupt leadership in Kabul could turn the tide in what became a stagnant, dead-end war.

Within months of taking office, Obama learned the full extent of the disastrous situation. In mid-2009, after a thorough review, the generals and policy professionals offered the president a sobering picture (Baker 2009). According to a *New York Times* report just months after the president opted for a surge of American military forces, Obama received the recommendation of his generals—a massive increase in both expenditures (nearly $1 trillion over ten years, equal to the cost of health care reform) and personnel (doubling the total US military to nearly one hundred thousand). Rather than modest midcourse correction, Afghanistan would be a generation-spanning war. Not wishing the fate of Lyndon Johnson, whose domestic ambitions were thwarted by the war in Vietnam, Obama pushed back on his generals, hoping for a smaller commitment of forces. Thus, the start of a three-month review. Obama was careful and deliberative, traits that he would display throughout his administration. In the words of the *Times*, the review was an

> intense, methodical, rigorous, earnest and at times deeply frustrating for nearly all involved. It was a virtual seminar in Afghanistan and Pakistan, led by a president described by one participant as something "between a college professor and a gentle cross-examiner." Obama peppered advisers with questions and showed an insatiable demand for information, taxing analysts who prepared three dozen intelligence reports for him and Pentagon staff members who churned out thousands of pages of documents. (Baker 2009)

But while careful deliberation is usually laudatory, in a situation teetering on disintegration without immediate action, Obama's caution was derided as "dithering" by critics (Cheney 2009). His generals, some of the leading military minds of the post–Vietnam War era, became uneasy. Rather than quickly accepting their recommendation, Obama held ten meetings with his national security team. He invited competing voices to debate in front of him, while guarding his own thoughts. General Stanley McChrystal, architect of the Afghan surge, warned of failure in summer 2009 and called an immediate commitment of forty thousand new troops. This on top of the twenty-one thousand Obama had ordered earlier in the year. McChrystal and his advisers would go public in their criticism of the administration's civilian advisers, including Vice President Biden, in *Rolling Stone* later in the summer.

In the end, the President approved thirty thousand additional troops, topping the combined NATO commitment in Afghanistan to one hundred thousand. But the surge would be temporary, with a drawdown to commence a year later. While the Pentagon, and to a lesser extent the State Department pushed for a more robust footprint, Vice President Biden, as alluded to earlier, was skeptical of a big troop influx. What Biden proposed—rather than focus on nation building and population protection, do more to disrupt the Taliban, improve the quality of the training of Afghan forces, and expand reconciliation efforts to peel off some Taliban fighters—became the basis of shift from counterinsurgency to counterterrorism. Obama came to the conclusion that successful counterinsurgency was not possible as long as corruption inundated the Afghan government. Karzai, similar to Maliki in Iraq, was a weak thread to build strong institutions upon. Karzai was too compromised in terms of public credibility to effectively lead the country to a democratic future, and Obama would not mortgage his administration to that of the mercurial "mayor of Kabul." While much hope was placed on the outcome of the 2014 elections to replace Karzai, the result did not meaningfully change the situation on the ground. By 2015, the administration began contemplating some sort of accommodation with the Taliban. With NATO allies pulling troops out, the US was increasingly alone. The previous long-term goal of modern progressive democratic Afghanistan was replaced with the shorter-term goal of stabilization. Negotiations began with elements of the Taliban, hoping to find some more moderate factions with which to bring into legitimacy while isolating the extremists. But just as the US found in Vietnam, strategic withdrawal—the phased withdrawal of military presence as local authorities take on the burden ("as we stand down, they stand up") is not easy. Issues of reputation and the possible long-term costs of a complete collapse make immediate military withdrawal unlikely. But strategic withdrawal requires a local government strong enough and elements of the opposition moderate enough that some long-term coalitional arrangement can be created. The problem that faced Obama was that despite some military successes, they were never definitive. The Afghan War is a seasonal one, with gains in one season reversed in the next. As a result, costly pressure was never so great that it forced the entire or large parts of the Taliban into compromise. With the war entering its decade-and-a-half watershed by the end of the Obama term, time was working more on the Taliban's time. Furthermore, the Afghan National Army has yet to prove itself as an autonomous fighting unit capable of defeating the Taliban on its own.

While the war to stabilize Afghanistan was indeterminate at the end of the Obama term, the overall war on terror had taken a few dramatic turns. First, related to the Afghan War, was the continued shadow war against al-Qaeda in northwestern Pakistan. Second, the rise of the al-Qaeda offshoot, ISIS (the Islamic State of Iraq and Syria), out of the ruins of Iraqi and Syrian civil wars. And third was the deepening of the global war on terror, with Sahelian and East Africa becoming more prominent battlefields.

Perhaps the greatest foreign policy success of the Obama administration was the raid that led to the assassination of the Osama bin Laden. That raid resonated domestically as proper closure to one of the more horrific attacks in American history. Obama had said that by going into Iraq, the Bush administration had taken their eye off the ball the real war against al-Qaeda. Obama had said, during the 2008 campaign that the administration was willing to violate Pakistani sovereignty in pursuit of al-Qaeda suspects. Unlike Bush, who viewed alliance with a mercurial Pakistani military as key to fighting al-Qaeda, Obama came to see Pakistan as an obstacle. Due to its internal politics, Pakistan could never fully abandon the Taliban and, by extension, al-Qaeda. The Pashtuns who live astride the Afghanistan-Pakistan border view the region as Pashtunistan more than part of either of the sovereign states. For Pakistan, whose core regions sit barely outside artillery range of rival India to the east, Afghanistan provides strategic depth. For the Pakistani military and intelligence services, support for (or acquiescence of) the Taliban offered a hedge that kept border regions of the northwest from open rebellion. Furthermore, by 2008, opinion surveys showed much greater support in Pakistan for al-Qaeda than for the United States. Challenging Pakistan was a fork in the road that members of the Obama team believed was necessary if either Afghan stability (forcing Taliban to negotiate) or finally defeating al-Qaeda would ever be possible. For years, American intelligence agencies had surmised with high certainty that Osama bin Laden and compatriots were holed up in the Pashtun-populated region of northwest Pakistan. However, as long as the Pakistani military denied such intelligence, there was little America could do. Obama's decision to violate Pakistan's sovereignty was not a snap decision but rather an expansion of American extraterritoriality that started with the increased use of drones. According to data from the New America Foundation, Obama authorized 355 drone strikes in Pakistan alone from 2009 to November 2016, killing between 1,904 and 3,114 people (Boyle 2017).

Drone warfare is perhaps the ultimate use of rational "smart warfare" for advanced democracies. It has been demonstrated that democracies tend to be "casualty averse" in war-fighting. Since democratic leaders stay in power by providing public goods to their large winning coalitions, avoiding high casualties in long wars are essential to staying in power, especially in wars of choice. Furthermore, advanced economies have incentive to substitute technology for manpower in fighting war. Since the late nineteenth century, with the advent of mass industrialization, advanced economies became more efficient in killing their enemies while keeping their own losses relatively low, as numerous imperial and colonial expeditions proved. The increased use of drones in the early twenty-first century is simply the latest manifestation of the "revolution in military affairs" that has slowly been taking place since the end of the Vietnam War, the last war that was to claim more than ten thousand American lives (i.e., the Vietnam War claimed nearly sixty thousand American lives, arguably leading to the downfall of two US presidencies). While drones were around, and were used periodically by the Clinton and Bush administration, the Obama administration greatly expanded their usage. In keeping with his pledge to reduce the costliness of the war on terror, drone strikes had the twin benefits of avoiding casualties, thus making the eternal struggle against transnational terror networks more palatable, and permanently removing enemy combatants off the battlefield. Furthermore, drone usage also had some of the benefits attributed to "gray zones" conflict, given that they were not viewed as flagrant a violation of state sovereignty as would troop incursion.

By expanding the use of drones across the Afghan-Pakistani border, the Obama team set up the conditions that eventually led to the Osama bin Laden raid. While the Pakistani government and various opposition groups in the country became increasingly critical of the drone strikes, they did not lead to a full break with Washington. The relative success of the drone war early on led to further use in other theatres of operations, such as Yemen. The drone strikes in Yemen were notable in that the administration targeted an American citizen who had joined al-Qaeda. The drone strike that killed Anwar al-Awlaki in 2011 sparked a debate over due process rights and whether even American citizens could be killed without having them afforded.

While the willingness to engage in extraterritorial acts against transnational terror networks and the increased use of drones were the predicates behind the bin Laden raid of May 2011, the final element that would prove critical to the "smart war" was the expanded use of Special Forces. Like drones, Special Forces have a certain "gray zones" feel to them. While part of the regular armed forces, Special Forces are designed to do quick hit-and-run operations, like targeting infrastructure and command centers, and capturing or assassinating targeted individuals before the government of the territory that actions were being taken against would even know what happened. Like drone usage, these "not quite regular" military actions are more palatable to home and foreign publics—and their use has expanded. In many ways, the frustrations of the counterinsurgency for stabilization in Afghanistan and the success of the bin Laden raid in Pakistan offer contrasting outcomes of past and future war doctrines. If counterinsurgency offered the possibility of *fixing* failing states, the cost in time and casualties (recall the democratic leader need to fight short, low-casualty wars) have rendered them impractical without a stable local regime in place to take up reins quickly. Sadly, that is rarely the case. Counterterrorism, the trinity of extraterritoriality, drone strikes, and Special Forces operations offer the possibility of perhaps *managing* those failing states so that their maladies (e.g., lack of stable government allowing them to become havens for transnational terror networks) do not metastasize into surrounding areas and become more of a problem for the West.

The emerging Obama counterterrorism doctrine was to be put most extensively to use in Sahelian and East Africa, that band of states straddling the Sahara and the savanna of West Africa (Mauritania, Mali, Niger, Burkina Faso, Nigeria, and Chad) to the Horn (Ethiopia, Eritrea, Djibouti, Somalia, and Kenya) in the east. There is no evidence that Obama's Kenyan (thus African) heritage had the most direct bearing on his counterterrorism policy. But admittedly there was the powerful symbolism of him, a son of Africa, visiting the continent as president of the United States to speak to African heads of state and their many constituencies (Kieh 2014). The aforementioned Sahelian and East Africa region is where Islam, Christianity, and traditional religions meet, where Arab culture abuts those of sub-Saharan Africa, and where a number of governments command only tenuous holds over much of their territory. This is the region where many of the world's failing states reside. I had mentioned earlier how the Libyan civil war created space for al-Qaeda and ISIS affiliates to set up camp there. Neighboring Algeria, which had its own civil war in the 1990s, saw a mild upsurge in extremist activity, including an attack on an oil installation in 2013 by a group formerly linked to al-Qaeda in the Islamic Maghreb (AQIM) (Dorell, McPhedran, and Osborne 2013). In Mali, in 2012, following a disintegrating political situation in the capital of Bamako, Islamist groups declared an Islamic state of Azawad in the northern two thirds of the country that included the legendary city of Timbuktu. While Mali had long been plagued by the on-off rebellions of Tuareg groups in the north, the ability of new Islamist groups tied to transnational terror networks to push back older nationalist movements were yet another wakeup call as to the importance of Africa as a battleground in the war on terror. Boko Haram, the local Islamist extremist group in Nigeria that had started in insurgency in 2009, declared allegiance to ISIS in 2012. It is estimated that thousands have been killed in the insurgency, which gained international exposure following the abduction of 276 schoolgirls in Bornu state. Boko Haram threatened to destabilize what had been a promising economic resurgence of Nigeria, Africa, as the largest economy and leader of the Economic Community of West African States (ECOWAS). In East Africa, the al-Shabaab movement, taking advantage of the collapse of the Somali state, engaged in systemic acts of terror against societies in the region, including a devastating shopping mall attack in Nairobi, Kenya, killing at over seventy, and numerous terror bombings in Mogadishu, Somalia. Al-Shabaab has been linked to al-Qaeda.

With the Sahel and the Horn becoming recognized as the soft underbelly in the war on terror, new resources were devoted to the region. The US Africa Command had been created in 2007 to "strengthen our security cooperation with Africa and create new opportunities to bolster the capabilities of our partners in Africa [and] . . . enhance our efforts to bring peace and security [to the continent]" (White House 2007). In 2012, General Carter Ham, commander of the Africa Command, outlined its goals as to: (1) neutralize al-Shabaab and transition the security responsibilities of the African Union's Mission in Somalia (AMISOM) to the internationally recognized Somali government; (2) degrade violent extremist organizations in the Sahel Magreb region and contain instability in Libya; (3) contain and degrade Boko Haram; (4) interdict illicit activity in the Gulf of Guinea and Central Africa with willing and capable African partners; and (5) build peacekeeping, humanitarian assistance and disaster response capacity of African partners (Waldhauser 2017).

The scale of military intervention in Africa made a decisive jump during Obama's tenure, with a 200 percent increase in military missions, as well as a widening presence of Defense Department staff into State Department realms. For example, Camp Lemonnier in Djibouti became host to two thousand military personnel, while US Department of Defense staff were assigned to US embassies across Africa, reflecting the enlarged scope of antiterror activities (Wengraf 2016).

The New Cold War and Emerging Threats

Obama's desire to reduce the American footprint in the Middle East was partially based on the idea that the greatest security challenges lay outside that region. For Obama's presidency, the Middle East was a region embroiled in a cocktail of demographic youth bulge, the revolution of rising expectations among that young population, economic challenges that brought on a decline in oil prices, and socioreligious battles between modernists and fundamentalists. Obama believed the US cannot solve the maelstrom that the region is confronting. That is left to the people of the region. The US should be on the side of progressive modernist forces, but it is their fight, which may be a long one. In the meantime, a more immediate security challenge for the US is the rise of China. With these ideas in mind, Obama and his team began to speak of "the pivot to Asia." This idea had its genesis in the increasing unease over Chinese assertiveness in the South China Sea, and the need to reassure allies in the region over America's commitment to their security.

To understand the China challenge, I must briefly review the power transition theory (Organski 1968), which has been rechristened in recent years as the "Thucydides Trap" (Allison 2017). According to this argument, contrary to a balance of power, which holds that uncertainty imparts caution on the part of would-be geopolitical revisionists, power transition theory holds that it is the clear dominance of a hegemon as "geopolitical sheriff" that maintains order and stability. When that hegemon, due to costs of system maintenance, is unwilling or unable to play the role of sheriff, would-be revisionists are more likely to challenge. Furthermore, hegemon-provided system stability allows for the international public good of higher economic growth to take place, allowing formerly weak and poorer minor and lesser major powers to rapidly advance. As lesser major powers rise in capabilities to approach those of the hegemon, a power transition takes place. Power transitions are not inherently violent. Declining hegemons, such as turn-of-century Britain, were able to come to a mutual understanding with a rising America over leadership in the Western Hemisphere. However, while satisfied rising powers may join the hegemon to become stakeholders in guaranteeing continued regional and international stability, dissatisfied rising powers may become revisionists, seeking to undermine and overthrow a system that they feel undervalues their position in an emerging power dynamic. Think Wilhelmine Germany during the same turn of the twentieth-century period vis-à-vis Britain. Thus, the question today is whether China is the twenty-first-century version of satisfied America or dissatisfied Germany. American foreign policy since the Deng Xiaoping reforms of the 1980s (and especially since 1992, following the three-year hiatus after the Tiananmen Square crackdown) has been one of accommodating an emerging China. China should be welcomed as a full partner in the international community. As China grows and witnesses the benefits that integration into the global economy can bring, Chinese leaders will become satisfied stakeholders who can help maintain the regional and international order alongside the US. Global economic integration would strengthen the hand of Chinese progressives against recalcitrant nationalists. However, the relatively benign Jiang Zemin was replaced by Hu Jintao, who took a more nationalistic stance, in 2003. He was later replaced by Xi

Jingping, who further heightened China's role in creating new international institutions that served Chinese interests to rival rather than buttress the American-led international system.

Nowhere was the American concern over Chinese assertiveness more apparent than in the South China Sea. For decades, China had laid claim to the entirety of the sea, up to the three-mile coastal waters of the countries that border the sea (Vietnam, the Philippines, Malaysia, Indonesia, and Brunei). China has made similar claims on the East China Sea as well, challenging Japan over a number of islands. Back in the South China Sea, the Chinese government began construction of new artificial islands in the middle of the sea (i.e., the "Great Wall of Sand"). These artificial islands, complete with landing strips for fixed winged aircraft and docking facilities for large ships, give China the ability to project power into the region, upsetting the security of the surrounding smaller states. This created a problem for the US, bogged down as it was in the Middle East. Smaller states like Vietnam and the Philippines face a hard choice when confronted with a rising aggressive regional power. They may either balance against that rising threat or bandwagon with it (Walt 1990). Both policies are attempts to preserve some sovereignty by either (1) finding a protector and joining it in an alliance against the threatening state or (2) appeasing the threatening state in the hopes that the threatening state will not attack. The United States has, since the Second World War, been the natural protector of smaller states in the Asia-Pacific region. However, with American military overtaxed in the Middle East and a military budget shrinking under the weight of budgetary sequestration, doubts over the American commitment to the region crept in. The "pivot to Asia" was a strategic move to address this concern. For Obama, the pivot was economic as well as military. The Trans-Pacific Partnership, a transoceanic trade pact embracing many of the Southeast Asian states, along with the United States, Canada, Mexico, Australia, New Zealand, Japan, and South Korea, forged new economic ties that were to cement an American commitment to the region. The fact that the TPP did not include China was telling. The TPP was a commitment device used to enhance the credibility of American determination to stay engaged in the region. This determination would lead the smaller states of the region to balance alongside the United States rather than bandwagon into a Chinese sphere of influence. The Obama team did not want to isolate China but rather create a series of institutions that could hedge against a China that became revisionist.

While Obama maintained cordial relations with China, the same could not be said of Russia. US-Russian relations had already deteriorated since the 1990s when talk of Russia possibly joining NATO was voiced. Indeed, NATO expansion, first to include the former Warsaw Pact states of Poland, the Czech Republic, and Hungary in 1996, and later the rest of the Warsaw Pact and Baltic States had fed Russian paranoia of isolation. The NATO attack on long-time Russian friend Serbia, despite Russian protests, proved to many that the once superpower was nothing more than weak paper tiger on the world stage. Following the collapse of the Soviet Union, Russia itself was under threat of collapse as nationalist movements arose in the Caucasus, calling for more breakaway republics. Enter Vladimir Putin, who, in 2000, quickly restarted a military campaign to combat and defeat Islamist rebels in Chechnya at a horrific cost in lives. This stanching of the disintegration of the country came just in time, as oil prices were rebounding, which brought new revenue into the country. Moscow experienced a renaissance of sorts, as it became a second-tier global city on par with Chicago, Frankfurt, and Toronto. Putin took a more assertive stance on the global stage by breaking with the US over the war in Iraq and defying the US by invading Georgia in support of Abkhazian and South Ossetian separatists in 2008 (the 1999 NATO attack on Serbia was in support of Kosovo separatists). As Obama entered the White House, he and his foreign policy team hoped to reset relations with Russia.

However, as time would prove, Putin was not interested in being America's junior partner on the world stage. Unlike China, a country clearly rising in military and especially economic capabilities, Russia is a shadow of the former Soviet Union. While the oil boom provided robust economic growth and Putin used the revenues to build his small winning coalition of oligarchs while having plenty left to win over the masses, the oil boom was short-lived. Furthermore, Russia's weakness was constantly revealed with political instability in neighboring Ukraine, a country long regarded as its historic frontier. Ukrainian politics vacillated between more autocratic pro-Russian elements, who wanted close ties to Moscow, and more democratic pro-Western parties, who argued for Ukraine to join NATO. As the old Russian adage says, "Russia without Ukraine is a mere country, but Russia with Ukraine is an empire." To lose Ukraine to NATO would be a dire national security setback to Moscow. The protests at the Maidan in 2013 were viewed with alarm in Moscow. With oil prices in free fall, Putin faced unexpected resistance in his return to the presidency following the Medvedev interregnum. As the pro-Moscow leader lost power, Moscow faced the prospect of deeper isolation from Europe. Putin then moved to secure the Russian naval base in Sevastopol, Crimea, by using Special Forces to seize key area of the peninsula. Then he used a combination of Special Forces and pro-Russia militia on the ground to foment an insurrection in the Danesk and Luhansk regions of eastern Ukraine.

For Obama, the moves in Ukraine shattered any glimmer of hope for a US-Russia rapprochement. Obama faced a firestorm from opposition Republicans, calling his response to Putin as tepid and weak. Rather than ratchet up the rhetoric, Obama used economic instruments to squeeze the Kremlin, opting for a series of sanctions that could be slowly increased over time. Furthermore, the Obama State Department began deploying new "smart sanctions" designed to specially target members of the Russian oligarchy. In the past, "dumb sanctions" were applied in a way that hurt regular citizens of the targeted state. The rationale behind this was that once citizens were hurt, they would put pressure on their government to change policies in the direction of the sanctioning state. Unfortunately, autocratic regimes do not need regular citizen support to stay in power. Furthermore, autocratic regimes in control of local media can use agitation and propaganda techniques to (at least temporarily) turn public attention in its favor (e.g., "They are attacking us. We must stick together"). The sanctions, combined with the more important decline in oil revenues, weakened the Russian economy. Putin began to employ new techniques to break the solidarity of the West on sanctions. Russia, however, is not China. It does not have the geopolitical heft to shift regional alliances, but it could attempt to disrupt them. Disinformation campaigns have a long history, dating back to Soviet times. Now armed with the tools of modern communications—the internet and social media—Russian intelligence began a series of efforts to disrupt Western political institutions, perhaps even that of the United States.

Finally, let me say a few words about Obama's approach to emerging threats, in particular, proliferation and climate change. His responses on these two issues would prove to be those that most endeared Obama to his base of progressive followers and yet revealed most starkly the transitory nature of policy innovations since aspects of these initiatives have been reversed by the Trump administration (Brânda 2018). In both cases, Obama challenged the conventional wisdom. He helped to broker the Joint Comprehensive Plan of Action (JCPOA), which was a compromise agreement to freeze the Iranian nuclear program in place. Obama faced opposition from the Netanyahu government in Israel and the Republican Party at home for being too permissive of the Iranian mullahs' actions, which was viewed as condoning financial support to perceived Hizb'allah terrorists. However, Obama was in a bad situation. Sanctions cannot work unless they are fairly comprehensive. Russia and China would not go along with the type of sanctions that many wanted at the start. However, the Israelis were threatening unitary military action if Obama could not stop the Iranian program. Given past Israeli strikes in Iraq and Syria in the 1980s and 2000s, the Israeli threat was credible. While Israel was not in position to stop the Iranian program (Iran learned from Iraq and Syria to have deep underground and mountainside facilities), any attack would inflame an already combustible Middle East. Obama had to walk a fine line in keeping the Russians and Chinese on board to get the Iranians to agree to inspections, while being tough enough to placate the Israelis. No doubt Netanyahu's unyielding pressure on the Iran issue made for frosty relations between the two leaders. In the end, Obama could not get a treaty passed and instead opted for an executive agreement to implement the JCPOA. Likewise, climate change, which has become a partisan issue, could not pass a Republican-controlled Senate. As a result, again, an executive agreement was substituted for a formal treaty. These decisions, though implementing the agreements, weakened their legitimacy and made them susceptible to reversal by the current president.

Conclusion

As the first African American president of the United States, Barack Obama broke the ultimate glass ceiling, and for many, his presidency raised hopes for an amelioration of racial divisions at home and more progressive, if not liberal institutionalist, foreign policy abroad. But stubborn societal and political obstacles thwarted many of those hopes. Obama's reliance on congressional Democrats, including of course the Congressional Black Caucus, during the health care debate weakened what little opportunity existed for bipartisan domestic legislation. Obama's attempts at resetting American foreign policy were rebuffed and criticized by Republicans as weakness, throwing allies (principally Israel) under the bus, coddling the Iranian mullahs, and "the apology tour" (Rove 2009). For all the rhetorical flourishes that inspired his progressive base and won over many moderates, Obama was cautious by temperament. In this volume, he has been referred to as a politician who had a personal linked fate with Black people (in the US and around the globe) but was somewhat restrained in using or framing racial or ethnic justice as policy rationales, including foreign policy. Thus, I conclude that Obama was a mix of wanting bold change but acting politically cautious for fear of backlash. He relied heavily on advisers to debate policy choice in classic "team of rivals" fashion and then carefully (critics would say overcautiously) analyzed pros and cons before making a decision. While Obama was most comfortable addressing long-range goals (the JCPOA, the TPP, the Paris Climate Change Accord) and his rhetoric spoke of great change, he did not want to veer too far away from the Washington playbook on security due to persistent domestic opposition. Because he was the first African American president, like Jackie Robinson, he felt he needed to get things right—moving boldly only when the facts were clear-cut, and proving that—counter to his critics—he was no wild-eyed idealist and could keep the country safe. He needed to hold the center of American politics, and this reined in his ambition. His commitment to reduce lengthy overseas military deployments led to the increased use of drones and Special Forces (Obama's version of Rumsfeld's "light footprint") that ironically has meant a dramatic increase in American military operations abroad (Africa has moved from a marginal to a major scene of American military operations). By fighting the war on terror "smarter," Obama may have unwittingly made it more politically palatable, much to the chagrin of the Left, but without any support from the Right. Ultimately, he managed the country's foreign policy well, smoothing some edges but not eliminating them. We will see what the legacy of the Obama foreign policy is, given the different and sometimes diametrically opposite directions the Trump administration has taken after Obama (Brânda 2018).

BIBLIOGRAPHY

Allison, Graham (2017). *Destined for War: Can America and China Escape the Thucydides Trap?* New York: Houghton Mifflin Harcourt.

BBC News (2017). "Barack Obama: How Will Africa Remember Him?" BBC News, January 18, 2017 (www.bbc.com).

Baker, Peter (2009). "How Obama Came to Plan the 'Surge' in Afghanistan," *New York Times*, December 6, 2009 (www.nytimes.com).

Boyle, Michael (2017). "The Tragedy of Obama's Foreign Policy," *Current History* (January): 10–16.

Brânda, Oana-Elena. 2018. "Changes in the American Foreign Policy: From Obama to Trump." Paper presented at the International Conference Knowledge-Based Organization.

Brands, Hal (2016). "Paradoxes of the Gray Zones," *E-Notes* (blog), *Foreign Policy Research Institute*, February 5, 2016 (www.fpri.org).

Cheney, Dick. (2009). Speech before the Center for Security Policy, October 21, 2009.

Clinton, Hilary R. (2011). "America's Pacific Century," *Foreign Policy*, October 11, 2011 (https://foreignpolicy.com).

Dorell, Oren, Charles McPhedran, and Louise Osborne. 2013. "Algeria Hostage Crisis Ends; Death Toll Unclear." *USA Today*, January 17 (www.usatoday.com).

Friedman, George (2018). "The Trump Doctrine," *Global Futures*, July 11, 2018 (https://geopoliticalfutures.com).

Gallagher, Adam (2016). "Obama's Dangerous Drone Policy," *American Prospect*, September 29, 2016 (http://prospect.org).

Hudson, John (2013). "Congressional Black Caucus Instructed to Hold Tongue on Syria." *FP Insider Access*, September 5, 2013 (https://foreignpolicy.com).

Kieh, George Klay, Jr (2014). "The Obama Administration's Policy toward Africa." In *Obama and the World: New Directions in Us Foreign Policy*, eds. Inderjeet Parmar, Linda B. Miller, and Mark Ledwidge, Abingdon, UK: Routledge. 165–84.

Organski, A. F. K. (1968). *World Politics*. New York: Alfred A Knopf.

Packer, Robert B. (1991). "Formulating American Security Policy in Peripheral Regions: Cognitive and Bureaucratic Dynamics," unpublished manuscript.

Pew Research Center (2009). "Confidence in Obama Lifts U.S. Image Around the World," Pew Research Center, July 23, 2009 (www.pewglobal.org).

Philips, Alan (2016). "How Mubarak Decision Divided the White House," *National*, March 31, 2016 (www.thenational.ae).

Rove, Karl (2009). "The President's Apology Tour." *Wall Street Journal*, April 23 (www.wsj.com).

Somin, Ilya (2016). "Obama Admits That His Handling of the Libya War Was His Worst Mistake—But Not That It Was Unconstitutional," *Washington Post*, April 13, 2016 (www.washingtonpost.com).

Waldhauser, Thomas D. (2017). "United States Africa Command 2017 Posture Statement," United States Senate, One Hundred Fifteenth Congress. Committee on Armed Services, First Session, March 9, 2017 (www.hlsd.org).

Walt, Stephen M. (1990). *The Origin of Alliances*. Ithaca: Cornell University Press.

Welsh, Jennifer (2012). "The Responsibility to Protect: Dilemmas of New Norm," *Current History* (November): 291–298.

Wengraf, Lee (2016). "Obama in Africa: Secret Bases and Drone Warfare," *African Political Economy* (http://roape.net).

Conclusion

The Next "Black President" and the Next Black Politics

JOSEPH P. MCCORMICK II, TODD C. SHAW, AND
ROBERT A. BROWN

Obama is deeply, perhaps excessively, cautious when it comes
to propounding public policy. His avoidance of race [racial is-
sues] is also due in part to the constraints that would impinge
upon any person serving as the nation's first black chief executive. Any black president speaking with informed candor about
the continued subordination of black America would widely be
seen as a whiner perpetrating racial favoritism and thus would
invite electoral retribution. In other words, it is, I think, virtually impossible for a black president today to lead a productive
conversation on race without committing himself to political
martyrdom.
—Randall Kennedy, "Race Talk in the Obama Era."[1]

Now, I'm not calling Mr. DeSantis a racist, I'm simply saying the
racists believe he's a racist.
—Andrew Gillum, Democratic nominee for Florida governor, October 25, 2018, debate against Republican challenger,
US Rep. Ron DeSantis.[2]

What have we learned about how race relations in the United States
and our constitutional order have imposed limits on what is possible
in addressing issues of racial inequality in American society? We have
chosen to open our conclusion with an observation from Randall Kennedy, who has been one of the more astute students of the Obama
presidency. Along with certain features of our constitutional form of

government, e.g., separation of powers and the electoral possibility of a divided government, the cautious temperament of President Obama and the persistency of racial animus found in sections of the American electorate serve as constraints on any president who would attempt to ameliorate the enduring vestiges of American slavery and Jim Crow segregation. In our conclusion, we will discuss why Kennedy's quote suggests we must be sanguine about the ability of the next "Black president" to fully ameliorate racial inequality. It is true that at the time of our writing, the Black Lives Matter Movement had gained widespread public support. Historians caution us, however, that there is always the lingering prospect of a White supremacist backlash that reinforces systemic racism. Gillum's quote, which we also address in the conclusion, speaks to the logic of White candidates like Donald Trump stoking White racial fears as a campaign strategy.[3]

Revisiting Our Framework

For at least a year after he and his family departed the White House, President Barack Obama maintained a fairly low public profile.[4] But in the spring and summer of 2018, he slowly reemerged into the public view several months ahead of the US Congressional midterm elections. On July 17, 2018, in Johannesburg, South Africa, he delivered the annual Nelson Mandela lecture to a crowd of about fifteen thousand. In this speech that lasted nearly ninety minutes, and was frequently interrupted by cheers and laughter, he praised Nelson Mandela as a transformative political figure and humanitarian. While Obama lionized Mandela as a figure who brought a world of racial and democratic progress, he cautioned that "a politics of fear and resentment and retrenchment . . . is now on the move. It's on the move at a pace that would have seemed unimaginable just a few years ago." The latter was likely a veiled reference to Donald Trump winning the US presidency after Obama's historic presidency. Obama went on to say, "Look around. (Applause.) Strongman politics are ascendant suddenly, whereby elections and some pretense of democracy are maintained—the form of it—but those in power seek to undermine every institution or norm that gives democracy meaning."[5] While Obama philosophically characterized the current politics of "resentment and retrenchment" as a 'sudden' aberration in an otherwise fitful but linear American (and Western) progress toward racial justice and equality, we reiterate our agreement with King and Smith.[6] These politics are only the latest configuration of governing coalitions to maintain a specific American racial order. It is an order that over time has led to the racial and economic subjugation of African Americans and other racial/ethnic minorities (ascriptivism) at one pole or has unevenly incorporated these groups into the American political system (egalitarianism) at the other. Author Ta-Nehisi Coates goes so far to refer to Trump as "the first white president" because he so blatantly reaffirms the White nationalist tendencies of the present exclusionary American racial order.[7]

In this volume, we have presented a conceptual framework that argues the American constitutional order has been utilized by various racial orders to advance either right-center (more racially exclusive) or left-center (more racially inclusive) policy agendas, and the American presidency has been a central actor in these processes. One key conclusion we reach based on this backdrop and the analyses of our contributors is that the historic presidency of Barack Obama attempted to advance the policy interests of various African American communities across several dimensions—e.g., voting rights, criminal justice reform, health care, and housing. And while African American communities may have had what we call an "inverted linked fate" with Obama (or linked their sense of well-being with Obama's perceived political well-being), Obama's personal linked fate and identity with African American communities—i.e., Black women, Black LGBTQ persons, faith-based communities, etc.—did not overcome what we call the "inclusionary dilemma." In summary, this dilemma is that despite African American voters being critical to Obama's electoral victories, the aforementioned racial and constitutional order imposed constraints upon the Obama Policy Agenda and fueled the president's willingness or reluctance to press more left-of-center policy prescriptions that would be of greater benefit to Black communities. Thus, we agree with the conclusions of Andra Gillespie's excellent examination of race and the Obama presidency.[8]

In a discussion of President Obama's 2008 presidential campaign, Thomas Sugrue discussed Obama's use of what Sugrue calls "colorblind"[9] rhetoric that Obama employed as a pre-presidential politician.

This leadership trait carried over into the governing style of his presidency. Sugrue tells us, "To expand his base of support among whites and to dodge his opponents' criticisms, Obama had every political incentive to avoid racially charged issues [during his 2008 campaign]."[10] President Obama's practice of color blindness was a political, strategic choice that guided his initial election in 2008 and reelection in 2012. What made this particular variant of color blindness politically strategic is that the issue of racial inequality was artfully finessed by a person who many considered this nation's first Black president. President Obama's pre-presidential political behavior suggests that he held a strategic color-blind point of view, one that acknowledged the persistence of racial inequality in American society as an inescapable reality and also recognized that a political strategy that "focused on race-specific grievances [would generate] political liabilities that outweigh[ed] any benefits."[11] As evidenced by Franklin and his co-authors in chapter 10 of this volume, Sugrue further explains the character of the Obama policy agenda: "Those who call for strategic color blindness often push for 'universal' policies that provide benefits for disadvantaged people regardless of their race or ethnicity, in lieu of 'targeted' programs that specify racial or ethnic beneficiaries."[12] The election and reelection of Barack Obama as president of the United States did not mean the end of African American politics as Bai asked and as we have defined in this volume.[13] It instead indicates an unprecedented point in American politics when a politician who happens to be Black has hesitated to use the authority of his office to ameliorate the legacy conditions of historic racism, partly out of a concern of preserving the idea that he equally values the policy concerns of all of this nation's citizens. This has indeed been President Obama's inclusionary dilemma. Recall our somewhat incendiary contention at the beginning of this volume—there is no such thing as a Black president. History has indicated that pressure from Black constituents (at times joined by their non-Black allies) is essential for those who believe that civil rights, on the basis of race, can be advanced. In the next section we review the scholarly insights each of this volume's contributors have provided as to how various constituencies and policies of the Obama era shaped African American politics during his presidency and will affect them from hereon.

Reviewing the Contributions

Using both qualitative and quantitative evidence, the contributors to this volume have presented a complex, composite picture of the Obama presidency's relevance to African American communities and Black politics. While employing, critiquing, and/or expanding upon our framework's central concepts of inverted linked fate and/or the inclusionary dilemma, contributors have considered how various Black constituencies (part 1) or various public policies (part 2) were impacted by the Obama presidency. They have done so in three ways: (1) employed our framework; (2) critiqued/challenged our framework; or (3) expanded upon or discussed questions beyond our framework.

At least six chapters employed or responded to aspects of our framework by examining what were the ideological or institutional constraints the Obama administration confronted or imposed upon itself in responding to Black America. In chapter 1, Nunnally demonstrated how Black political trust in the Obama presidency led to a trust in other national institutions and prompted higher levels of Black political participation. In this respect, Obama's presidency was the conduit through which African Americans hoped the federal government would be responsive to Black group interests; they invested a form of linked fate in his administration's capacity to respond to the Black community. In chapter 2, King-Meadows examines the rhetorical responsiveness of Obama to the demands of Black elected and civic or interest groups leaders. His analysis of Obama's speeches and statements—rhetorical cues—is very useful to understanding the symbolism of a presidency for which African American leaders had high expectations. During the Obama administration, King-Meadows suggests how presidentialism—a governmental framework where the executive and legislative branches must cooperate to achieve policy ends—may have imposed genuine constraints on Obama's ability to address articulated Black interests. Block and Lewis-Maddox in chapter 3 analyze how political party polarization was fueled in part by racial divisions during Obama's presidency. While racial divides by party and African Americans leaning toward the Democratic Party long preceded the Obama administration, Block and Lewis-Maddox suggest the challenges the Obama coalition confronts as an electoral majority that, at times, can be demobilized. Their findings are particularly useful in this current political moment. In chapter 7, Brazelton and Pinderhughes give clear evidence of how the Obama administration's appointments diversified the federal judiciary, especially through the appointment of African American jurists. Of equal importance is Brazelton and Pinderhughes's examination of the impact the Obama-appointed judiciary could have in upholding African American voting rights. They detailed the clear barriers imposed by the 2013 *Shelby v. Holder* Supreme Court case that weakened the proactive ability to challenge state and local government efforts at voter disenfranchisement as well as the Trump Justice Department's complete reversal on voting and civil rights, while the latter administration installed very conservative jurists. Gillespie, in chapter 11, delineates how the housing and home mortgage crisis of the 2008–2009 Great Recession further exacerbated the homeownership and lending inequities African Americans and Latinos confronted prior to the period. Gillespie notes that residential segregation actually declined for African Americans during the Obama presidency. But the open question she concluded with is precisely what the Trump administration would do to reverse the Obama housing policies and signs of progress. In the final chapter of this volume, Packer examines a domain of public policy not often associated with African American group interests— foreign and military policy. Packer suggests that for all the ways the Obama administration in its two terms sought to press a liberal internationalist and multilateral American foreign policy, with Obama as the first Black person to serve as US head of state, his regime was still relatively cautious in its temperament. Packer's analysis suggests there is no domain of presidential policy-making more constrained by the norms, policy precedents, and structural impediments (such as a major superpower's economic and political interests) than the domain of foreign and military policy. We contend his chapter further makes the case—there is no such thing as a Black president.

Another four chapters provided implicit critiques of our framework by noting the need for the African American politics literature to increasingly treat questions of Black group interests and political incorporation as more than unitary considerations because of the intersecting identities and cross-cutting cleavages within Black constituencies. In chapter 5, Smooth critiques how Barack Obama failed to craft a policy agenda that addressed the substantive interests and needs of his and the Democratic Party's most loyal constituency—African American women. Instead, by way of the popularity and authenticity of the First Lady, Michelle Obama, President Obama and his administration engaged in a form of symbolic, linked fate politics—a "politics of recognition"—that in Smooth's view served as a distraction for the ways in which the administration privileged gendered initiatives aimed at Black men—such as My Brother's Keeper. True for many other elections, no doubt Black women will be a voting bloc critical to any Democratic victories in 2020.[14] Perry, in chapter 6, analyzes how African American LGBTQ communities fared under the Obama administration and its liberalization of both its interpretation and policy and legal inclusion of LGBTQ civil rights, including same-sex marriage. Somewhat akin to Smooth, Perry demonstrates that the Obama administration's use of policy universalism—all LGBTQ individuals and families are relatively the same—led to policies not targeted at the specific barriers of race, gender, and/or sexuality that Black LGBTQ communities confronted and confront even further under a Trump administration. As another complement to Smooth's contribution, in chapter 9, Jordan-Zachery conducts a policy analysis of the Obama administration's employment and anti-poverty policies, most especially their urban policy initiatives. The latter coincides with Gillespie's chapter 11. Jordan-Zachery posits the administration used policy language and advanced race-gender tropes that privileged Black patriarchal conceptions of economic solutions to poverty at the expense of rendering Black women invisible. In line with a Black feminist analysis, Jordan-Zachery identifies a larger problem in Black politics of failing to consistently envision the intersections of race, gender, and class in conceptualizing Black interests so as to devise policy responses. A fourth chapter that challenges our framework is chapter thirteen as co-authored by Frasure and Greene. Through an analysis of Black attitudes about the Obama administration immigration reform proposals, these authors discovered African American respondents support efforts of immigration liberalization, especially immigrants having wider pathways to apply for citizenship. But this is more positively associated with socioeconomic factors than ethnic or racial linked fate. In effect, Frasure and Greene note that Black politics infrequently conceive of the intersections between the identifies of "Black" and "immigrant"—as would be true for persons who self-identify as Black and have African, Caribbean, or Latin American ancestry or nativity.

The third of set of chapters have in some way expanded upon or spoken beyond our framework. They argue the Obama administration had greater political and policy agency than it publicly claimed or accomplished more for Black communities than some critics have concluded. McKenzie explicates in chapter 4 how Obama in his leadership style had a "complicated relationship" as he connected with Black faith-based organizations or churches. McKenzie explains that there were clearly moments when Obama experienced subtle or not so subtle strains with either the theological radicalism or conservatism of various Black churches—from the Reverend Jeremiah Wright incident that began his 2008 campaign to mainline Black Christian denominations disagreeing with his administration's eventual support of same-sex marriage. Still McKenzie concluded that given the unique racial linked fate that Black churches and church leaders had with Obama, his presidency likely enjoyed deeper ties to these core Black civil society institutions than any other presidency—Democratic or Republican. In this limited respect of connecting with Black Protestants, the Obama administration (as led by a self-identified Black Christian) may have been exceptional in its ability to overcome some of the aforementioned constraints of the US presidency. In chapter 8, Brown-Dean provides a fascinating analysis of how the Obama administration, especially as led by US attorney general Eric Holder, made or attempted various reforms in the federal criminal justice system. These Obama second-term reforms were, in part, aimed at the mass incarceration crisis and its racial disparities. Measures ranged from reducing the crack cocaine versus powder cocaine disparity to efforts to reform sentencing guidelines. As fueled by the activist demands of the Black Lives Matter movement and their allies, Brown-Dean suggests the Obama administration was compelled to make at least modest gains in helping to shift the public dialogue around criminal justice reform, and this shift redounded to the benefit of African American and other racially policed communities. Her chapter is quite relevant to current Black Lives Matter debates. Lastly, in chapter eleven, Franklin, Ford Dowe, and Lewis-Maddox examine the initial inroads that the signature Obama administration policy—the Affordable Care Act (ACA), or "Obamacare"—made in reducing the number of African Americans and other groups who are uninsured. Despite this law's limitations as a subsidized private insurance model, as well as deep and persistent opposition from a Republican-led Congress and state legislators (particularly in the South), these authors provide evidence that this law has the potential to improve the health care outcomes of Black communities and, thus, at least modestly reduce health disparities. While our framework would suggest that the universalist approach of the Obama policy agenda constrains its ability to address the specific concerns and needs of Black communities, the Franklin et. al. analysis also indicates the scope of health care is so large and the racial disparities in health and well-being are so large that this is a law that still benefits African American consumers. To conclude this chapter and this volume, we turn to an assessment of Obama's legacy relative to the new Black politics it might have inspired.

Rethinking the Obama Legacy—the Next Black Politics

We believe this edited volume is among the first scholarly works written long enough after President Obama's second term to more fully understand the impact of his leadership and policy legacy upon Black America, most especially in the light of the presidency of Donald Trump. Much like the Obama presidency, the available evidence of how well the Obama era benefited Black America is mixed and nuanced, though the rhetorical genius and personal charisma of Barack and Michelle Obama will continue to have an indelible appeal for African American and other audiences.[15] We chose to open this final chapter using two contrasting observations to illustrate the complexity of the Obama legacy. The first is from Harvard University law professor Randall Kennedy, who has been an astute student of the Obama presidency. As his opening quote implies, along with certain features of our constitutional form of government—e.g., the separation of powers and the electoral possibility of a divided government—the persistency of racial animus found in segments of the American electorate[16] meant Obama would (and did) confront political and electoral constraints in attempting to ameliorate the enduring vestiges of American slavery and Jim Crow segregation. This was particularly true given the initially cautious, political temperament of President Obama and his articulated belief that there is certainly racism but there is no racial order per se—the present American constitutional order is fully capable of creating an inclusive, socially just society.[17] Along with the findings of some of our colleagues in this volume, Kennedy's above observation leads us to this somber conclusion: at present, Americans should not expect a self-identified African American who is elected president of the United States to be an overt and forceful advocate for public policies meant to address the vestiges of racial inequality. The various responsibilities of the American presidency go far beyond the amelioration of racism and racial inequality as this issue applies to African Americans. Again, we and other contributors to this volume have varying agreement with the conclusions of Harris or Price[18] in asserting that Obama's left-of-center policy pragmatism meant he limited the scope of the policies he would present to address racial and economic inequalities even while partisan elements of the American racial order pushed back. As a former president, Obama conceded his regret and even expressed doubt that he had not more fully realized the strength of White racial opposition to his presidency, his policy agenda, and thus the rise of Trump. In an interview with a *New York Times* reporter, President Obama expressed several misgivings, "What if we were wrong? [About America's readiness for his agenda] . . . Maybe we pushed too far . . . Maybe people just want to fall back into their tribe." He even conjectured, "Sometimes I wonder whether I was 10 or 20 years too early [in becoming president]."[19] Throughout this volume, we and our contributors have discussed the tensions of the inclusionary dilemma. But we have gone beyond political values, attitudes, and identities—the politics of "tribe"—to bring in the institutional and juridical arrangements that frame all presidencies. We argue the challenges facing Obama's presidency were due to both the racial politics as well as the institutional dynamics of the American political system.

The second quote we use to introduce this concluding chapter is from Andrew Gillum. He was the mayor of Tallahassee, Florida, who narrowly lost his 2018 bid to become the first African American to serve as governor of the state of Florida by about thirty-four thousand votes.[20] Along with the historic, Democratic, gubernatorial candidacies of state legislator Stacey Abrams of Georgia and NAACP president Ben Jealous of Maryland, the 2018 midterm elections witnessed the emergence of an interesting post-Obama Black politics.[21] This Black politics differed in that on the campaign trail, its proponents not only openly espoused progressive policy prescriptions—i.e., criminal justice reform/restorative justice, Medicare for all, environmental justice, etc.—but used stronger rhetoric even in majority-White southern states to challenge racism and other inequalities when compared to the rhetoric and policy proposals of candidate Obama. Price concluded, "This new class of candidates is pushing the Democratic Party farther left. They also represent the new political power of black progressives who defy stereotypes of black politicians as wedded to respectability politics and unwilling to take on issues of people who live on the margins of the black community. While Black establishment politicians may still command considerable influence within Black politics, the time of Black progressives is in ascent."[22] Taylor, in an astute *New York Times* opinion piece, argued that younger Black voters fueled by the Black Lives Matter mass movement are demanding a progressive politics much further to the left of older Black voters and former Vice President Joe Biden, the presumptive 2020 Democratic presidential nominee.[23] In today's shifting political environment, the challenge that confronts researchers is how to characterize and unpack the influence of the various "competing camps" of Black politics.[24]

Albeit, the outlines of the Obama legacy are still taking shape. Due to the 2018 midterm elections, when a number of women and candidates of color ran as Democrats with progressive agendas and won election to Congress and state offices,[25] there may be at least two conclusions this new progressive Black politics draws from the Obama years. First, Obama's electoral and policy successes have apparently inspired this new cohort of progressive Black leaders to run for office and to demand policy and political changes further to the left of Obama's ideological and policy stances. This new progressive Black politics respects the political genius of Obama—many asked Obama to endorse them—while it learns from the example of how his presidency grappled with the inclusionary dilemma. Second, precisely because of Obama's left-of-center, deracialized policy agenda—from the Affordable Care Act to immigration reform—he confronted an unrelenting, partisan opposition within the American racial order, including from the White working class. Thus, the Democratic Party should abandon the project of attempting to win back the White working class, or "Reagan Democrats." It should instead expand its electoral coalition by continuing to mobilize the Obama coalition—e.g., young people, educated women, and minorities—while recruiting new, unregistered voters in a nation that in twenty years will have no majority racial or ethnic group.[26]

This debate is far from settled and will only intensify during subsequent elections. A post-2018 Democratic majority in the US House prompted African American Congresswoman Marcia Fudge (D-OH) to contemplate a bid for Speaker of the House as a direct challenge to former speaker Nancy Pelosi. Fudge argued that relative to the Democrats 2018 victories, "If we run on change, then we need change." In light of representational politics, Fudge's possible challenge (which was not realized due to Pelosi concessions) is not surprising given how African American women voters remain the most loyal constituency of the Democratic Party and are in part responsible for the party's recent victories. For example, Joe Biden must thank Black women in South Carolina and many other state primaries for the votes they cast to help make him the presumptive Democratic presidential nominee. In return, Biden overtly considered several Black women as his vice-presidential running mates and finally selected US Senator Kamala Harris of California. Harris self-identifies as a Black woman of Afro-Jamaican and Indian (Tamil) heritage. And if elected president, Biden has publicly pledged to fill the next Supreme Court vacancy with a Black woman.[27]

A constant feature of African American politics—old and new—is the question raised famously by Martin Luther King Jr. more than fifty years ago. The question is, "Where Do We Go from Here?"[28] Like Gillum in Florida, Abrams of Georgia and Jealous of Maryland lost their 2018 gubernatorial bids. But Abrams did not give a concession speech to her Republican opponent Brian Kemp. She accused him of not winning fairly because as Georgia Secretary of State (an office he held while running for governor) he deliberately practiced vote suppression through his agency, eliminating thousands of minority and other voters from the rolls. "So let's be clear," Abrams said, "this is not a speech of concession, because concession means to acknowledge an action is right, true or proper. . . . As a woman of conscience and faith, I cannot concede that." Instead she acknowledged there were no further legal remedies available for challenging the fourteen thousand–vote margin of Kemp while defiantly asserting, "I don't want to hold public office if I need to scheme my way into the post. . . . We [will] fight on."[29] This call to "fight on" is a historic feature of African American politics or what Hanes Walton and his co-authors have called the "African American quest for universal freedom." It rests upon a "democratic faith"—a belief that grassroots mobilization eventually will matter and will revive American democracy.[30] To this end, Obama concluded his 2017 presidential farewell address by expressing such a faith in and optimism about the younger generation's ideals and engagement:

> This generation coming up—unselfish, altruistic, creative, patriotic—I've seen you in every corner of the country. You believe in a fair, just, inclusive America; you know that constant change has been America's hallmark, something not to fear but to embrace, and you are willing to carry this hard work of democracy forward. You'll soon outnumber any of us, and I believe as a result that the future is in good hands.[31]

No matter what is next for Black politics, the genius and contradictions of the Obama presidency—whether it was a so-called Black presidency or not—have provided a fascinating point of departure for emergent African American elected leaders, activists, and communities.

NOTES

1 Randall Kennedy. "Race Talk in the Obama Era." *American Prospect* 22, no. 3 (April 1, 2011): A22.

2 Eugene Scott. "'Racist Thinks He's a Racist': Gillum on White Supremacists' Support for DeSantis." *Washington Post*, October 25, 2018, www.washingtonpost.com.

3 Kim Parker, Juliana Menasce Horowitz, and Monica Anderson. "Amid Protests, Majorities across Racial and Ethnic Groups Express Support for the Black Lives Matter Movement: Deep Partisan Divides over Factors Underlying George Floyd Demonstrations." Pew Research Center, www.pewsocialtrends.org; Glickman, Lawrence. "How Backlash Controls American Progress: Backlash Dynamics Are One of the Defining Patterns of the Country's Progress." *Atlantic*, May 21, 2020. www.thealantic.com.

4 Adam Edelman, "Life after the White House: How Obama Spent His First Year out of Office," NBC News, January 20, 2018, www.nbcnews.com.

5 "Transcript: Obama's Speech at the 2018 Nelson Mandela Annual Lecture," NPR, July 17, 2018, www.npr.org.

6 Desmond S. King and Rogers M. Smith, "Racial Orders in American Political Development," *American Political Science Review* 99, no. 1 (2005). See also Rogers

M. Smith, "Beyond Tocqueville, Myrdal, and Hartz: The Multiple Traditions in America," *American Political Science Review* 87, no. 3 (1993).

7 Ta-Nehisi Coates, "The First White President," *Atlantic* 320, no. 3 (2017).

8 Manning Marable, "Racializing Obama: The Enigma of Post-Black Politics and Leadership," *Souls* 11, no. 1 (2009). Andra Gillespie, *Race and the Obama Administration: Substance, Symbols, and Hope* (Manchester University Press, 2019).

9 Thomas J Sugrue, *Not Even Past: Barack Obama and the Burden of Race*, vol. 2 (Princeton University Press, 2010), 116. Sugrue's concept, "strategic color-blindness," is akin to no less than three other, similar concepts that have been used by political scientists to describe efforts by African American candidates for public office to maintain White support by *deemphasizing* any attention to potentially divisive racial issues. For "electoral deracialization," see Joseph McCormick and Charles E Jones. "The Conceptualization of Deracialization: Thinking through the Dilemma." *Dilemmas of Black politics: Issues of leadership and strategy* (1993): 66-84. For a discussion of "racial transcendence," see Dewey M. Clayton. *The Presidential Campaign of Barack Obama: A Critical Analysis of a Racially Transcendent Strategy* (Routledge Press, 2010). And for discussion of "ethnic avoidance," see Robert C. Smith. *John F. Kennedy, Barack Obama, and the Politics of Ethnic Incorporation and Avoidance: Mysticism and Myth in the Hekhalot and Merkavah Literature* (SUNY Press, 2013).

10 Sugrue, *Not Even Past*, vol. 2, 116. What Sugrue calls "strategic color blindness," applies to Barack Obama's *campaign style* in both his 2008 and 2012 presidential campaigns. Proponents of "strategic color blindness," Sugrue tells us, "might acknowledge the persistence of racial inequality [which Obama rarely did], but who contend that attention focused on race-specific grievances generates political liabilities that outweigh any benefits." Sugrue further goes on to say, "An emphasis on racial disparities stokes a backlash politics, inhabiting the formation of an interracial coalition necessary for the revitalization of social democratic policies," which Obama advocated via the Affordable Care Act (see chapter 10 by Franklin et al.) "that [would] mitigate inequality."

11 The clearest example of this point of view can be found in President Obama's "race speech"—"A More Perfect Union"—which he delivered in Philadelphia in March 2008. See Barack Obama, "A More Perfect Union," March 18, 2018, speech transcript and audio, American Rhetoric: Online Speech Bank, updated September 29, 2018, www.americanrhetoric.com.

12 Sugrue, *Not Even Past*, vol. 2, 116.

13 Matt Bai, "Is Obama the End of Black Politics?" *New York Times*, August 10, 2008.

14 Haines, Errin. "Black Female Voters Say They Want What They're Owed: Power." *Washington Post*, July 6, 2020. www.washingtonpost.com.

15 Ron Charles, "Michelle Obama's 'Becoming' Is the Best-Selling Hardcover Book of the Year," *Washington Post*, November 30, 2018.

16 See Michael Tesler and David O. Sears, *Obama's Race: The 2008 Election and the Dream of a Post-Racial America* (University of Chicago Press, 2010); and Michael

Tesler, *Post-Racial or Most-Racial? Race and Politics in the Obama Era* (University of Chicago Press, 2016).

17 Rogers M. Smith, "The Constitutional Philosophy of Barack Obama: Democratic Pragmatism and Religious Commitment," *Social Science Quarterly* 93, no. 5 (2012).

18 Fredrick C. Harris, *The Price of the Ticket: Barack Obama and the Rise and Decline of Black Politics* (Oxford: Oxford University Press, 2012); Melayne Price, *The Race Whisperer: Barack Obama and the Political Uses of Race* (New York: New York University Press, 2016).

19 Peter Baker, "How Trump's Election Shook Obama," *New York Times*. May 31, 2018.

20 Glenn Thrush and Liam Stack, "Andrew Gillum Concedes to Ron Desantis in Florida Governor's Race," *New York Times* November 17, 2018.

21 Michael Dresser, "Jealous, Abrams, Gillum Call for New Playbook in Majority-White States," *Baltimore Sun*, September 13, 2018.

22 Melayne Price, "Ayana Pressley and the Might of the Black Political Left," *New York Times*, Setember 5, 2018.

23 Keeanga-Yamahtta Taylor. "The End of Black Politics." *New York Times*, June 13, 2020.

24 For interesting typologies, see Perry Bacon Jr. 2020. "Charles Booker, Jamaal Bowman and the 7 Competing Camps in Black Politics." FiveThirtyEight: July 1. https://fivethirtyeight.com. We also refer the reader to Andra Gillespie. 2010. "Meet the New Class: Theorizing Young Black Leadership in a 'Postracial' Era." In *Whose Black Politics? Cases in Post-Racial Black Leadership*, ed. Andra Gillespie. New York and London: Routledge. 1–44.

25 Samantha Cooney, "Here Are Some of the Women Who Made History in the Midterm Elections," *Time*, November 19, 2018.

26 Susan Milligan, "The Civic Report: Destiny in the Demographics," *US News & World Report*, November 16, 2018.

27 Clare Foran, "Who Is Marcia Fudge, the Democrat Considering Challenging Nancy Pelosi for House Speaker?" CNN, November 17, 2018, www.cnn.com. Eugene Robinson, "If There Is a 'Blue Wave,' Democrats Would Have Black Women to Thank," *Washington Post*, October 22, 2018. Sean Sullivan. "Biden Running Mate Search Zeroes in on a Group That Includes at Least Four Black Women." *Washington Post*, June 13 2020. Sahil Kapur. "Biden Pledged to Put a Black Woman on the Supreme Court. Here's What He Might Have to Do." NBC News, May 6, 2020, www.nbcnews.com. Matt Viser and Sean Sullivan. "Sen. Kamala D. Harris Named as Joe Biden's Running Mate." *Washington Post*, August 11, 2020.

28 Martin Luther King Jr., *Where Do We Go from Here: Chaos or Community?* vol. 2 (Boston, MA: Beacon Press, 2010).

29 Gregory Kreig, "Stacey Abrams Says 'Democracy Failed' Georgia as She Ends Bid for Governor," CNN, November 16, 2018, www.cnn.com.

30 Hanes Walton and Robert Charles Smith, *American Politics and the African American Quest for Universal Freedom*, 6th ed. (New York: Pearson Longman,

2011). The concept of "democratic faith" is articulated in the last chapter of Todd Shaw, *Now Is the Time: Detroit Black Politics and Grassroots Activism* (Durham, NC: Duke University Press, 2009).

31 "President Obama's Farewell Address: Full Video and Text." *New York Times*, January 10, 2017.

Todd C. Shaw is the College of Arts and Sciences Distinguished Associate Professor of Political Science and African American Studies at the University of South Carolina, Columbia. He researches and teaches in the areas of African American politics, US racial and ethnic politics, urban politics, grassroots/citizen activism, and public policy. He is the author of *Now Is the Time! Detroit Black Politics and Grassroots Activism*. He has served as the interim chair and then chair of the Department of Political Science at U of SC (2016–2019) and as the interim director of the African American Studies Program at U of SC (2015–2016). He graduated from Howard University in 1987 with a BA in Political Science and from the University of Michigan, Ann Abor, in 1996 with a Political Science MA and then PhD. He is a past president of the National Conference of Black Political Scientists.

Robert A. Brown is Associate Professor of Political Science at Spelman College, Atlanta, Georgia. He researches and teaches in the areas of African American politics, US racial politics, public health and racial health disparities, and urban politics. His research has appeared in the *DuBois Review*, the *International Journal of Disability and Human Development*, the *Journal of Politics*, and the *Urban Affairs Review*. He has previously taught at Emory University. He graduated from Brown University in 1985 with a BA in History and from the University of Michigan, Ann Arbor, with a PhD in Political Science in 1996. He graduated from the Rollins School of Public Health at Emory University with an MSPH in Epidemiology in 2011.

Joseph P. McCormick II is Associate Professor Emeritus of Political Science at Howard University and Emeritus Director of Academic Affairs from the Pennsylvania State University (York Campus). He earned BA, MA, and PhD degrees from the University of Pittsburgh. His research areas were African American political behavior and public opinion research. His publications include a book chapter (with Charles E. Jones) on the concept deracialization, a set of magazine essays on the 1984 Jesse Jackson campaign (with Robert C. Smith), a book chapter on the treatment of racial issues in two key political science journals (with Hanes Walton Jr. and Cheryl Miller), and a book chapter (with Ravi Perry) on Barack Obama's evolutionary stance on same-sex marriage. Dr. McCormick is a past president of the National Conference of Black Political Scientists, and he was a member of the Council of the American Political Science Association.

ABOUT THE CONTRIBUTORS

Shenita Brazelton is a licensed attorney and Associate Professor of Political Science at Tuskegee University, located in Tuskegee, Alabama. She currently serves as book review editor for the *National Review of Black Politics* (University of California Press), a publication of the National Conference of Black Political Scientists. Her research interests include examining decision making in federal appellate courts, with an emphasis on issues pertaining to race and diversity within the judiciary. She authored "A Hollow Hope? Social Change, the U.S. Supreme Court and Affirmative Action" and co-authored "Diversity Abound: Will Federal Judicial Appointees Mirror a Changing Citizenry?" in *Race, Gender, Sexuality, and the Politics of the American Judiciary*. She earned a BA from Tuskegee University in political science, a JD from Vanderbilt University Law School, and a PhD in political science from Georgia State University.

Khalilah L. Brown-Dean is Associate Professor of Political Science at Quinnipiac University, the Senior Director for Inclusive Excellence, and former Faculty Co-Coordinator of the Health Policy and Advocacy concentration in the Frank H. Netter School of Medicine. Her scholarship and teaching center on the politics of punishment, voting rights, race, election administration, and public policy. Her book *Identity Politics in the United States* traces how conflicts over group identity are an inescapable feature of American political development. She has authored numerous pieces, including "Felon Disenfranchisement after *Bush v. Gore*: Changes and Trends," in *Election Administration in the United States: The State of Reform After Bush v. Gore*, edited by Michael Alvarez and Bernard Grofman. She is co-author of a Joint Center for Political & Economic Studies report, "50 Years of the Voting Rights Act: The State of Race in Politics." Brown-Dean received her PhD in Political Science from Ohio State University in 2003 and a BA in Government from the University of Virginia in 1998.

Ray Block Jr. is Associate Professor of Political Science and African American Studies at Penn State University. Ray received his undergraduate degree from Howard University and his PhD from Ohio State University. He studies racial and ethnic group politics, voter mobilization, campaigns and elections, and public opinion. Ray has published dozens of book chapters, peer-reviewed journal articles, and other manuscripts, and is co-author of *Losing Power: Americans and Racial Polarization in Tennessee Politics*. Beyond his day job as a college professor, Ray Block serves as an analyst for both the African American Research Collaborative and Latino Decisions, and as a faculty coach for the National Center for Faculty Development & Diversity.

Pearl K. Ford Dowe is Asa Griggs Candler Professor of Political Science and African American Studies at Oxford College, Emory University. Dowe's most recent research focuses on African American women's political ambitions and public leadership. Her published writing includes co-authorship of *Remaking the Democratic Party: Lyndon B. Johnson as Native-Son Presidential Candidate* and editorship of *African Americans in Georgia: A Reflection of Politics and Policy Reflection in the New South*. She has published numerous articles and book chapters that have appeared in the *Journal of African American Studies, Political Psychology, Presidential Studies Quarterly, Journal of Black Studies*, and *Social Science Quarterly*. During her time at the University of Arkansas, she served as department chair (2017–2019). She graduated from Savannah State University in 1994 with a BS in Political Science and earned the PhD in Political Science from Howard University in 2003.

Sekou Franklin is Associate Professor in the Department of Political Science and International Relations at Middle Tennessee State University (MTSU). He is the author of *After the Rebellion: Black Youth, Social Movement Activism, and the Post-Civil Rights Generation* and edited the *State of Blacks in Middle Tennessee*. He also has a forthcoming book (co-authored with Ray Block Jr.) called *Losing Power: African Americans and Racial Polarization in Tennessee Politics*. He is currently President-Elect of the National Conference of Black Political Scientists.

Lorrie Frasure is Associate Professor of Political Science and African American Studies at the University of California—Los Angeles. Her research interests include racial/ethnic political behavior, immigrant political incorporation, African American politics, women and politics, and state and local politics. Her book *Racial and Ethnic Politics in American Suburbs* is the 2016 winner of two national book awards by the American Political Science Association (APSA). She is the co-principal investigator of the Collaborative Multiracial Post-Election Survey (CMPS), a national post-presidential election survey of registered and nonregistered adults in the United States. She received her PhD and MA in Political Science from the University of Maryland—College Park, a Master's in Public Policy (MPP) from the University of Chicago, and a BA in Political Science from the University of Illinois, Urbana-Champaign.

Andra Gillespie is Associate Professor of Political Science and Director of the James Weldon Johnson Institute at Emory University. She earned her BA in Government and Foreign Affairs and African American Studies from the University of Virginia and her PhD in Political Science from Yale University. Her research focuses on the effectiveness of deracialized campaign strategies—how African American voters respond to Black politicians who use deracialization and whether these politicians are more effective in reducing inequalities in Black communities. She is the author of *The New Black Politician: Cory Booker, Newark and Postracial America*. More recently, she wrote *Race and the Obama Administration: Substance, Symbols and Hope*. She is also the editor of *Whose Black Politics? Cases in Postracial Black Leadership*.

Stacey Greene is Assistant Professor of Political Science at Rutgers University—New Brunswick. She researches and teaches in the areas of race and ethnic politics, political psychology, and public opinion in the United States. Her research focuses on when marginalized members of society see themselves as similar to or different from other groups and when they create coalitions or have conflict. She received her PhD in Political Science from the University of California Los Angeles in 2016.

Julia S. Jordan-Zachery is Professor and Chair of the Africana Studies Department at University of North Carolina Charlotte. Her interdisciplinary teaching and research focuses on African American women and public policy. She is also the author of the award winning books *Black Women, Cultural Images and Social Policy* and *Shadow Bodies: Black Women, Ideology, Representation, and Politics*, and a number of articles and edited volumes, including *Black Girl Magic Beyond the Hashtag*. Jordan-Zachery was awarded the Accinno Teaching Award, Providence College (2015–2016). Jordan-Zachery serves as the President of the Association for Ethnic Studies.

Tyson D. King-Meadows is Professor in the Department of Political Science at the University of Maryland Baltimore County (UMBC). He researches and teaches in the areas of African American politics, voting rights, public opinion, electoral behavior, and American institutions. His books include *Devolution and Black State Legislators: Challenges and Choices in the Twenty-First Century* (with co-author Thomas F. Schaller) and *When the Letter Betrays the Spirit: Voting Rights Enforcement and African American Participation from Lyndon Johnson to Barack Obama*. His research has been funded by the American Political Science Association, the Ford Foundation, and the Fulbright US Scholar Program. He served as the Associate Dean for Research and College Affairs in the College of Arts, Humanities, and Social Sciences at UMBC (2016–2019). He received his undergraduate degree from North Carolina Central University and his PhD from the University of North Carolina at Chapel Hill.

Angela K. Lewis-Maddox is a professor of political science and public administration. She researches and teaches in the areas of African American politics, state government, and women and politics. Her research appears in the *National Political Science Review*, *Journal of African American Studies*, *Polity*, the *International Journal of African Studies*, *Whose Black Politics*, and the *Constitutionalism of American States*. Most notably, she is the author of "Conservatism in the Black Community: To the Right and Misunderstood." She is a member of Delta Sigma Theta Sorority, Incorporated; Jack and Jill of America; and is involved in various professional associations. She is currently a member of the executive council of the Southern Political Science Association. She graduated with a BA in Political Science and Regional and Urban Planning from the University of Alabama, and an MPA and PhD from the University of Tennessee at Knoxville.

Brian D. McKenzie has previously served as a political science faculty member at the University of Maryland and Texas A&M University. His research interests include American political behavior, public opinion, and race, ethnicity, and politics. He has published multiple journal articles and edited volume chapters. The articles appear in leading scholarly journals, including the *American Journal of Political Science*; *Journal of Politics*; *Political Research Quarterly*; *Political Behavior*; *Political Psychology*; *Politics, Groups, and Identities*; *Journal for the Scientific Study of Religion*; *Review of Faith and International Affairs*; and *African-American Research Perspectives*. In addition, his co-authored book *Countervailing Forces in African-American Civic Activism, 1973–1994* received the Ralph J. Bunche Book Award and the W. E. B. Du Bois Outstanding Book Award.

Shayla C. Nunnally is a professor of political science and chair of the Africana Studies Program at the University of Tennessee, where she teaches undergraduate and graduate courses in American politics and African American politics, public opinion, and political behavior. Formerly she was an Associate Professor of Political Science and the Africana Studies Institute at the University of Connecticut, Storrs. She researches and teaches in the areas of American politics, African American politics, US racial and ethnic politics, and American public opinion, political behavior, and public policy. She is the author of *Trust in Black America: Race, Discrimination, and Politics*. She is a summa cum laude B.A. graduate in Political Science from North Carolina Central University, and received an MA and PhD in Political Science from Duke University.

Robert B. Packer is College of Liberal Arts Associate Teaching Professor of Political Science at Pennsylvania State University, University Park. He researches and teaches in the areas of international politics, American foreign policy, political economy, and conflict processes.

He is a contributor to the *Oxford Encyclopedia of International Peace* and author of *Financial Liberalization and the Reconstruction of State-Market Relations*, volume 4 of the *Routledge Library Editions: International Finance*. He graduated from Wayne State University with a BA in Business Administration and from the University of Michigan, Ann Arbor, by 1996, with a MA in Applied Economics and an MA and PhD in Political Science.

Ravi K. Perry is Chair and Professor of Political Science at Howard University. Perry is Immediate Past President of the Association for Ethnic Studies. He is the author/editor of three books: *Black Mayors, White Majorities: The Balancing Act of Racial Politics, 21st Century Urban Race Politics: Representing Minorities as Universal Interests*; and *The Little Rock Crisis: What Desegregation Politics Says About Us*. Perry is currently writing *Black Queer Electoral Politics: Introducing America's Openly LGBTQ Black Politicians*.

Dianne M. Pinderhughes is Notre Dame Presidential Faculty Fellow at the University of Notre Dame, where she chairs the Department of Africana Studies and is a member of the Department of Political Science. She teaches courses on civil rights and racial and ethnic politics. Her research addresses inequality with a focus on racial, ethnic, and gender politics and public policy in the Americas; explores the creation of American civil society institutions in the twentieth century; and analyzes their influence on the formation of voting rights policy. Her most recent work includes *Uneven Roads, An Introduction to US Racial and Ethnic Politics* and *Contested Transformation: Race, Gender, and Political Leadership in 21st Century America*, both co-authored. She has been President of the National Conference of Black Political Scientists, President of the American Political Science Association, and Vice President of the International Political Science Association. She earned her BA from Albertus Magnus College in 1969 and her MA and PhD from the University of Chicago, 1973 and 1977. She was elected to the American Academy of Arts and Sciences in 2019.

Wendy G. Smooth is Associate Dean for Diversity, Equity and Inclusion and Chief Diversity Officer for the College of Arts and Sciences at

Ohio State University. She holds a faculty appointment as an Associate Professor of Women's Gender and Sexuality Studies, and courtesy appointments with Political Science and the John Glenn School of Public Policy. Smooth's research and writing reflect significant expertise in legislative studies, institutions, state and local politics, and public policy. Her writings appear in numerous journals, including *Politics and Gender, Journal of Women Politics and Policy,* and the *National Political Science Review*. Her work appears in edited volumes such as *Situating Intersectionality: Politics, Policy and Power; Gender and Elections: Shaping the Future of American Politics; Legislative Women: Getting Elected, Getting Ahead;* and *Still Lifting, Still Climbing: Black Women's Contemporary Activism.*

INDEX

Page numbers in *italics* indicate figures and tables.